Canon EOS 7D Mark II: From Snapshots to Great Shots

Jeff Revell

Peachpit Press

Canon EOS 7D Mark II: From Snapshots to Great Shots
Jeff Revell

Peachpit Press
www.peachpit.com

To report errors, please send a note to errata@peachpit.com
Peachpit Press is a division of Pearson Education.

Project Editor: Valerie Witte
Production Editor: Danielle Foster
Copyeditor: Patricia Pane
Proofreader: Liz Welch
Composition: Danielle Foster
Indexer: Valerie Haynes Perry
Cover Image: Jeff Revell
Cover Design: Aren Straiger
Interior Design: Mimi Heft

ISBN-13: 978-0-13-400945-2
ISBN-10: 0-13-400945-2

9 8 7 6 5 4 3 2 1
Printed and bound in the United States of America

Dedication

For my good friend Ted

Acknowledgments

Back in 2007, I was sitting in an airport lounge with my buddy Scott Kelby waiting for our connecting. I was checking my emails when I came across an interesting message from an agent who was asking if I would be interested in writing a book about iPhoto for a popular how-to series of books. I'd never given book writing any consideration, but had read an article that I had written on my blog about using iPhoto and thought I might like to expand it into a book. I showed the email to Scott, and he said that if I was interested in writing books, he'd have his editor get in touch with me.

A few weeks later I received a call from Ted Waitt, acquisitions editor at Peachpit. Ted said Scott had mentioned that I might be interested in writing a book and that he should give me a call. He asked a lot of questions and said he had already read a lot of my articles on my blog. We talked for a couple of hours and, at the end of our conversation, we had developed the framework of what would become the Snapshots to Great Shots series of books.

Ted held my hand on the project and we successfully got my first book, Canon 50D: From Snapshots to Great Shots, on the store shelves. It was a new experience for me, but Ted was patient and offered advice and suggestions when needed. We went on to publish many more books in the series and expanded beyond just camera books into all corners of photography. More important, though, was the friendship that Ted and I developed over the six years and 14 books that I have since that initial phone call.

Ted recently moved on to another career adventure in publishing and I will miss our bull sessions, speculations over the next big camera, or just whatever was going on in our lives. Even though I feel a loss on some levels, I know that he has moved on to challenges that will bring him happiness and success for years to come.

I would also like to acknowledge the good folks at B&H Photo. They worked with me to ensure that I had a brand-new camera in hand as soon as they started arriving on our shores. Of course, this doesn't surprise me at all, because I have been purchasing photography equipment from B&H for years. I can say without a doubt that they are fantastic at what they do. They are always courteous and helpful, their knowledge is second to none, and they always give me a great deal. B&H is my number one go-to resource for anything photographic, so check them out on the Web when you get the chance: www.bhphotovideo.com.

Contents

Introduction

Walk into any bookseller, go to the photography section, and you will see countless books on the subject of photography. Look a little further and you will locate the camera-specific books. It is this divide between the camera-specific and instructional photography books that inspired me to write this book. I was seeing a lot of books that were just sort of missing the mark—especially when it came to using a specific brand and model of camera along with actual photographic instruction. So with that, I set about to write the Snapshots to Great Shots books, not as a rehash of the owner's manual but as a resource to teach photography with the wonderful technology present in the 7D Mark II. I have put together a short Q&A to help you get a better understanding of exactly what you can expect from this book.

Q: Is every camera feature going to be covered?

A: Nope, just the ones I felt you need to know about in order to start taking great photos. Believe it or not, you already own a great resource that covers every feature of your camera: the owner's manual. Writing a book that just repeats this information would have been a waste of my time and your money. I did, however, want to write about how to harness certain camera features to the benefit of your photography. As you read through the book, you will also see callouts which point you to specific pages in your owner's manual that are related to the topic being discussed. For example, in Chapter 1, I discuss the quality settings, but more information on this feature is available in the manual. I cover the function that applies to our specific needs but also give you the page numbers in the manual to explore this function even further.

Q: So if I already own the manual, why do I need this book?

A: The manual does a pretty good job of telling you how to use a feature or turn it on in the menus, but it doesn't necessarily tell you *why* and *when* you should use it. If you really want to improve your photography, you need to know the whys and whens to put all of those great camera features to use at the right time. To that extent, the manual just isn't going to cut it. It is, however, a great resource on the camera's features, and that is why I treat the manual like a companion to this book. You already own it, so why not get something of value from it?

Q: What can I expect to learn from this book?

A: Hopefully, you will learn how to take great photographs. My goal, and the reason the book is laid out the way it is, is to guide you through the basics of photography as they relate to different situations and scenarios. By using the features of your 7D Mark II and this book, you will learn about aperture, shutter speed, ISO, lens selection, depth of field, and many other photographic concepts. You will also find plenty of large, full-page photos that include captions, shooting data, and callouts so you can see how all of the photography fundamentals come together to make great images. All the while, you will be learning how your camera works and how to apply its functions and features to your photography.

Q: What are the assignments all about?

A: At the end of most of the chapters, you will find shooting assignments, where I give you some suggestions as to how you can apply the lessons of the chapter to help reinforce everything you just learned. Let's face it—using the camera is much more fun than reading about it, so the assignments are a way of taking a little break after each chapter and having some fun.

Q: Should I read the book straight through, or can I skip around from chapter to chapter?

A: Here's the easy answer: yes and no. No, because the first three chapters give you the basic information that you need to know about your camera. These are the building blocks for using the camera. After that, yes, you can move around the book as you see fit because the later chapters are written to stand on their own as guides to specific types of photography or shooting situations. You can bounce from portraits to shooting landscapes and then maybe to a little action photography. It's all about your needs and how you want to address them. Or, you can read it straight through. The choice is up to you.

Q: What do I do with all the photos that I am taking?

I'm glad you asked. What fun is taking photos if you never get to share them? That's why we have created a Flickr Group dedicated to you. It's a great place to upload your best shots and share them with other 7D Mark II users. Don't worry, there's no judging here, just a bunch of folks who enjoy photography as much as you do. So go ahead, gather up your great shots and load them up for everyone to enjoy. You will need to join Flickr and join the group, but don't worry, it's free to join. Just head to www.flickr.com/groups/7dmarkii_fromsnapshotstogreatshots and join in the fun.

Q: Is that it?

A: One last thought before you dive into the first chapter. My goal in writing this book has been to give you a resource that you can turn to for creating great photographs with your Canon 7D Mark II. Take some time to learn the basics, and then put them to use. Photography, like most things, takes time to master and requires practice. I've been a photographer for 30 years and I'm still learning. Always remember, it's not the camera but the person using it who makes beautiful photographs. Have fun, make mistakes, and then learn from them. In no time, I'm sure you will transition from a person who takes snapshots to a photographer who makes great shots.

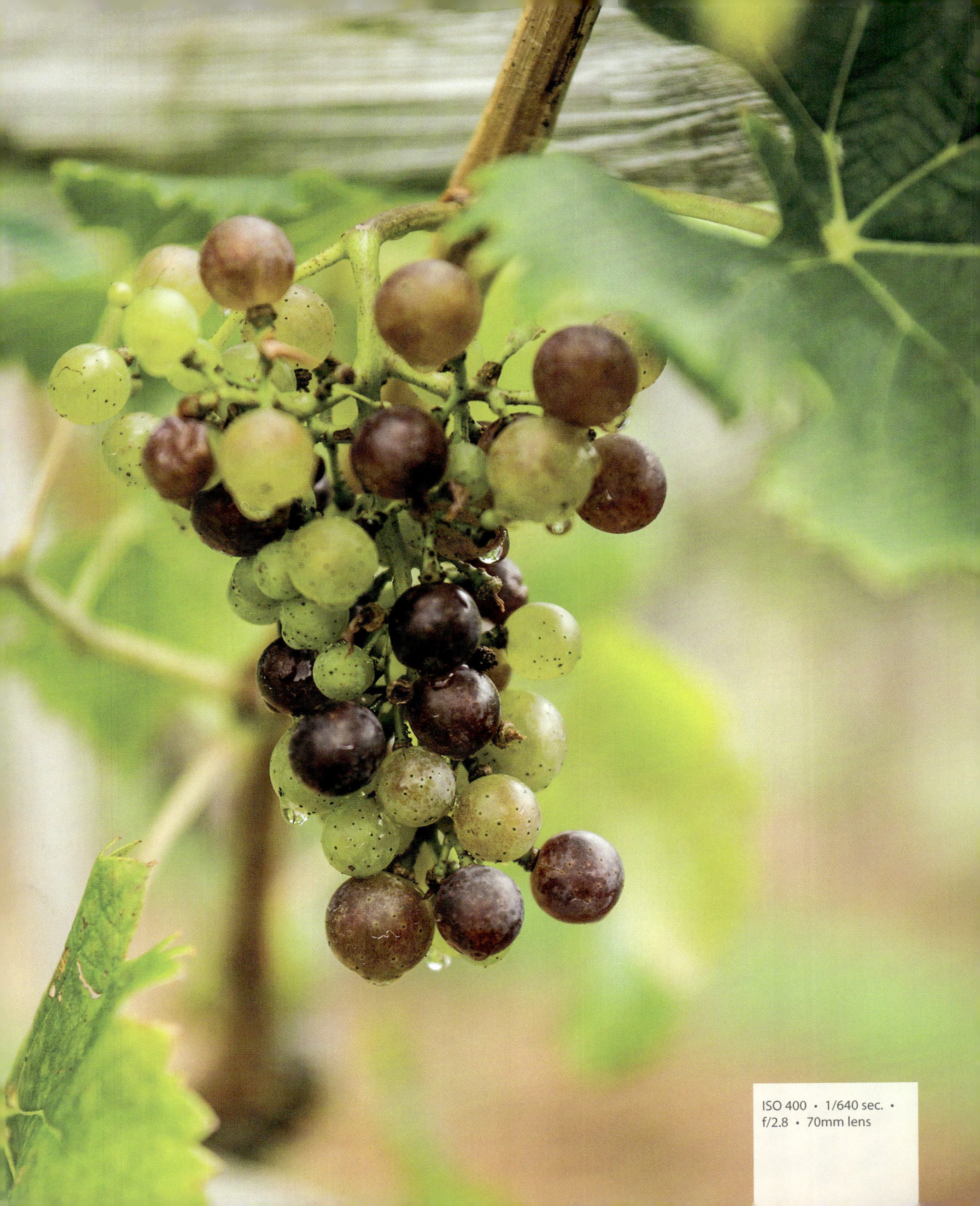

ISO 400 • 1/640 sec. • f/2.8 • 70mm lens

1

The 7D Mark II Top Ten List

Ten Tips to Make Your Shooting More Productive Right Out of the Box

To a photographer, nothing is quite as exciting as unboxing a new camera. Underneath all the manuals and bags of cords and warranty slips lies the potential for your next great image. The excitement can be overwhelming, and it can lead to an urgent need to unwrap and assemble the camera as quickly as possible so that you can start the picture making right away. It's okay, we've all been there. Unfortunately, all of the excitement of shooting with a new camera can cause you to bypass some pretty important housekeeping chores related to your new camera, such as reading your owner's manual. But what am I thinking? No one reads those things anyway. So how about this: Instead of telling you to sit down and read your manual from cover to cover, how about I give you a list of ten things you should do and know to start being productive with your camera?

Poring Over the Camera

Camera Front

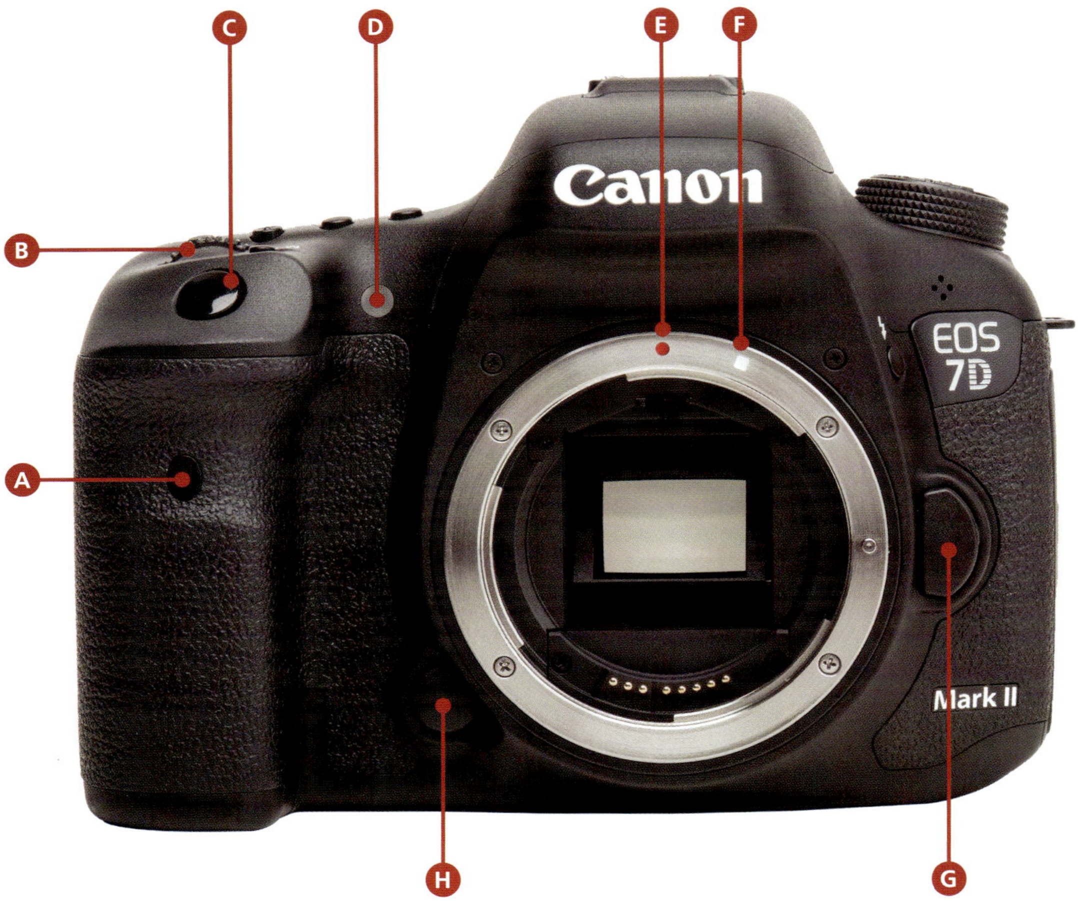

A Remote Control Sensor
B Main Dial
C Shutter Release Button
D Self-Timer Lamp
E EF Lens Align Mark
F EF-S Lens Align Mark
G Lens Release Button
H Depth-of-Field Preview Button

Camera Back

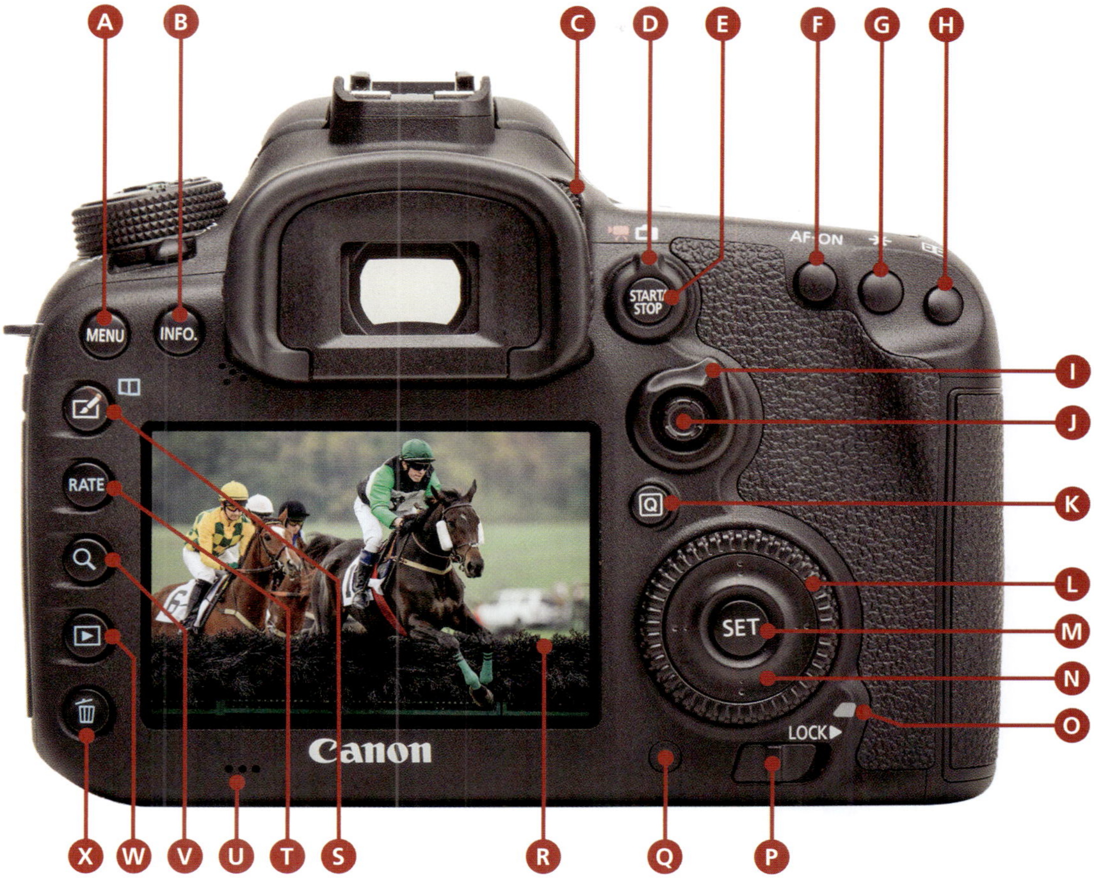

A Menu Button
B INFO Button
C Dioptric Adjustment
D Live View/Movie Shooting
E Start/Stop Button
F AF-ON AF Start Button
G AE Lock Button
H AF Point Selection Button
I AF Area Selection Lever
J Multi-controller
K Quick Control Button
L Quick Control Dial
M Set Button
N Touch Pad
O Access Lamp
P Multi-function Lock Switch
Q Light Sensor
R Display Screen
S Creative Photo Button
T Rating Button
U Speaker
V Magnify Button
W Playback Button
X Erase Button

Camera Top

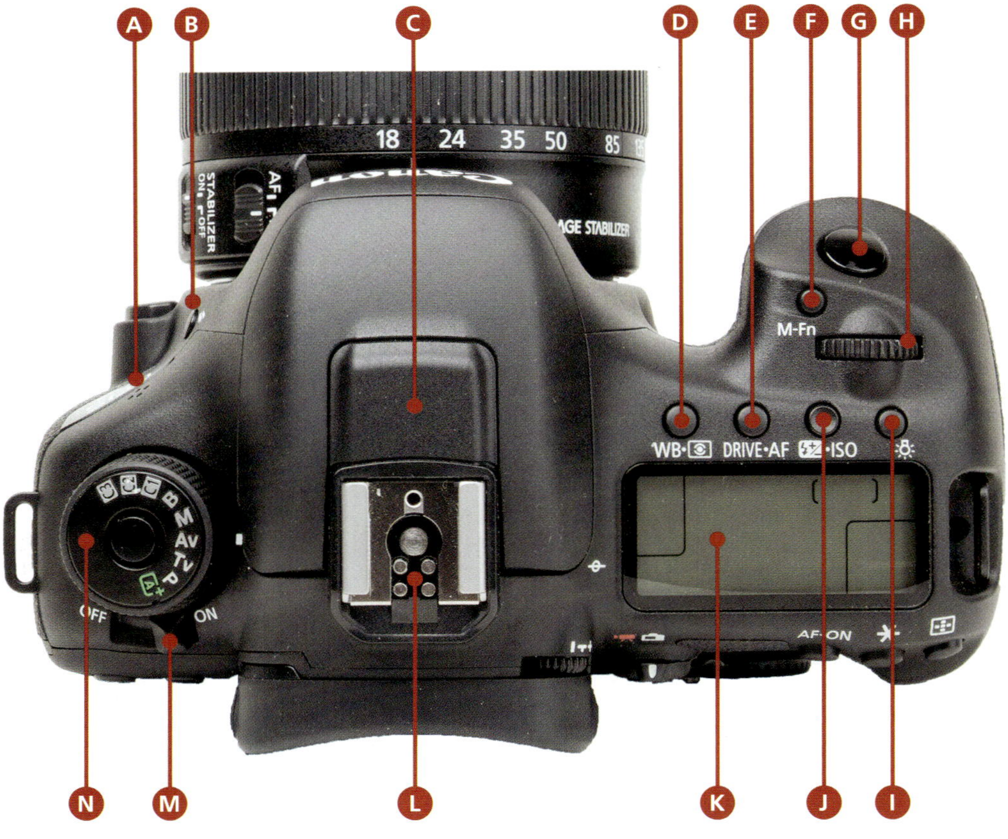

- **A** Microphone
- **B** Pop-Up Flash
- **C** GPS Antenna
- **D** White Balance/Meter Mode
- **E** Drive Mode/AF Method
- **F** Multi-function Button
- **G** Shutter Release Button
- **H** Main Dial
- **I** LCD Illumination Button
- **J** Flash Compensation/ISO Button
- **K** LCD Panel
- **L** Speedlite Hot Shoe
- **M** On/Off Switch
- **N** Mode Dial

The following list will get you up and running without suffering many of the gotchas that come from not being at least somewhat familiar with your new camera. So let's take a look at the top ten things you should know before you start taking pictures with your Canon 7D Mark II. But before you get started with the list, check out the illustrations of the camera on the following pages and get familiar with all of the knobs, switches, and buttons that you will be using to adjust your camera.

1. Charge Your Battery

When you first unboxed your camera and slid the battery into the battery slot, you were probably pleased to find that there was already juice in the battery and you could start shooting right away. The best thing to do, though, is to get out the battery charger and give that power cell a full charge. Not only will this give you more time to shoot later on, but it will also start the battery off on the right foot. No matter what claims the manufacturers make about battery life and battery memory, I always find I get better life and performance when I charge my batteries fully, and then use them right down to the point where they have nothing left to give. To check your battery level, insert the battery into the camera, turn on the camera, and look for the battery indicator on the rear LCD. You might have to press the shutter release button to wake up the camera. Doing so will activate the rear LCD display and allow you to see the battery-level indicator located in the bottom-left portion of the display panel (**Figure 1.1**).

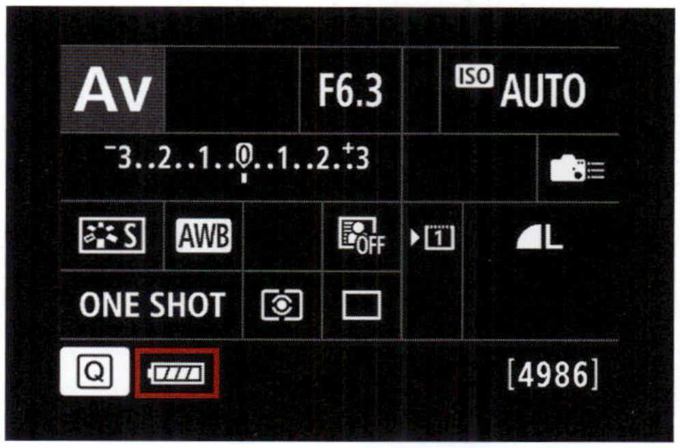

Figure 1.1
The LCD shows how much charge is left on your battery.

One more piece of advice about your battery: Don't overcharge it. I'm not talking about leaving it on the charger for too long. Your charger knows when the battery is full and will stop charging it automatically. I am referring to charging too often, before the battery is drained. If you go out and shoot 20 or 30 pictures and then charge your almost-full battery you should be fine, but if you do this over and over again, your battery could develop a memory where it will look fully charged but contain only a partial charge. Instead, try running the battery down fairly low, and then give it a full charge. You will find that it lasts much longer this way.

Keeping a backup battery

If I were to suggest just one accessory that you should buy for your camera, it would probably be a second battery. It really stinks being out in the field and having your camera die with no way to recharge it. Keeping a fully charged battery in your bag will always give you the confidence that you can keep on shooting without fail. Not only is this a great strategy to extend your shooting time, but it also helps to lengthen the life of your batteries by alternating between them. No matter what the manufacturers say, batteries do have a life, and using them half as much will only lengthen their usefulness.

2. Turn Off the Release Shutter Without Card Setting

If you want to ruin your day, try shooting for a couple of hours only to find that you didn't put a memory card in your camera and therefore didn't save any of the pictures that you've taken. This was always a concern with film shooters, and it hasn't gone away with digital SLRs. You see, camera manufacturers want to give prospective buyers a way to test out the camera without having to keep a memory card in it, so they came up with a setting called Release Shutter Without Card. This is usually a default mode for the camera, and it will act and shoot just as it would when you have a memory card inserted. The camera will even go so far as to display your shot on the rear LCD display. Unfortunately, this is where most photographers get fooled into thinking they are saving their images. If they were to look closely at the LCD, they would see that Canon was nice enough to overlay a message on the display that clearly reads No Card. This is nice, but if you are shooting without looking at the display, you could be easily fooled.

Unfortunately, there is no visual clue within the viewfinder to alert you to this No Card status. So here is the simple solution.

Turning off the Release Shutter Without Card setting

1. Turn the camera on.
2. Press the Menu button on the back of the camera to bring up the menu list.
3. Use the Main dial to select the far-left menu tab.
4. Scroll down to the Release Shutter Without Card option using the Cross keys, and press the Set button (**A**).
5. Use the Cross keys to select the Disable option, and then press the Set button once again (**B**).

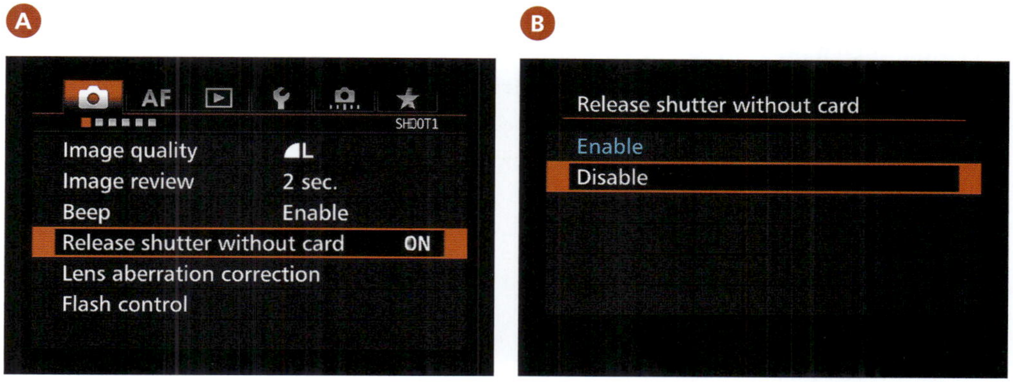

6. Press the Menu button again to return to shooting mode.

Now when you try to take a photo without a memory card inserted in the camera, you will see a message in the bottom left of your viewfinder that flashes the word Card. This is your clue that you need to insert your memory card before the camera will fire. The rear display will also display a large No Card In Camera message if you activate the shutter button (**Figure 1.2**).

We will have an in-depth discussion on memory cards and proper formatting in Chapter 2, "First Things First."

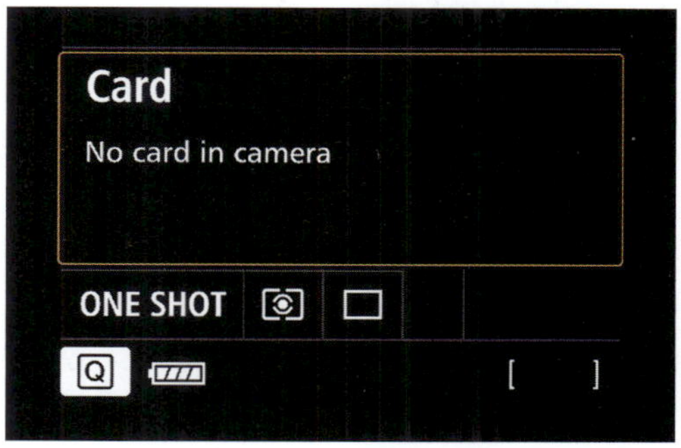

Figure 1.2
This screen is a reminder that you need to put a memory card in your camera.

3. Set Your JPEG Image Quality

Your new 7D Mark II has a number of image-quality settings to choose from, and depending on your needs, you can adjust them accordingly. Most people shoot with the JPEG option because it allows for a large number of photos on their memory cards. The problem is that unless you understand how JPEG works, you might be degrading the quality of your images without realizing it.

The JPEG format has been around for over 20 years and stands for Joint Photographic Experts Group. JPEG was developed by this group as a method of shrinking the size of digital images down to a smaller size for the purpose of reducing large file sizes while retaining the original image information. (Technically, JPEG isn't even a file format—it's a mathematical equation for reducing image file sizes—but to keep things simple, we'll just refer to it as a file format.) The problem with JPEG is that, in order to reduce a file size, it has to throw away some of the information. This is referred to as "lossy compression." This is important to understand because, although you can fit more images on your memory card by choosing a lower-quality JPEG setting, you will also be reducing the quality of your image. This effect becomes more apparent as you enlarge your pictures.

The JPEG file format also has one other characteristic: To apply the compression to the image before final storage on your memory card, the camera has to apply all the image processing first. Image processing involves such factors as sharpening, color adjustment, contrast adjustment, and noise reduction. Many photographers now prefer to use the RAW file format to get total control over the image processing. We will take a closer look at this in Chapter 2, but for now let's just make sure that we are using the best-quality JPEG possible.

The 7D Mark II has eight quality settings for the JPEG format. There are two settings each for the Large, Medium, and Small settings. The two settings represent more or less image compression based on your choice. The Large, Medium, and Small settings determine the actual physical size of your image in pixels. There are also an additional two settings for small (S2 and S3), which are even smaller in physical size than Small 1 but do not have compression options. Let's work with the highest-quality setting possible. After all, our goal is to make big, beautiful photographs, so why start the process with a lower-quality image?

Manual Callout

For a complete chart that shows the image-quality settings with the number of possible shots for each setting, turn to page 151 in the EOS 7D Mark II Instruction Manual.

Setting the image quality

1. Press the Menu button on the back of the camera to bring up the menu list.
2. Use the Main dial to select the far-left menu tab.
3. At the top of this Menu tab, locate the Image Quality option (**A**).
4. Press the Set button to bring up the options screen.

A

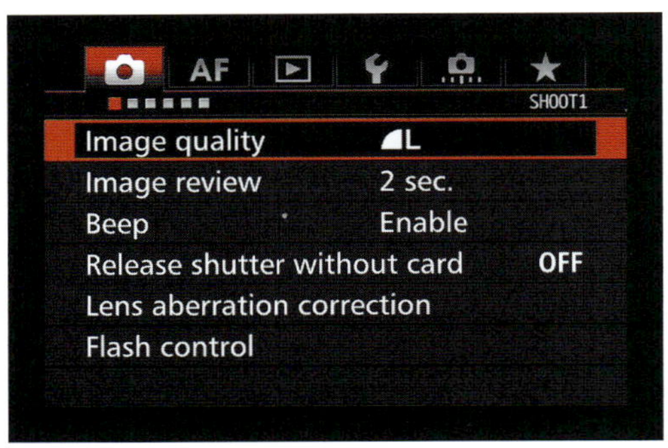

5. Use the Quick Control dial to select the first L (this will render a 20-megapixel image with a dimension of 5472 by 3648 pixels) (**B**).
6. Press the Set button to lock in this change.
7. Later on, when you want to use the RAW file formats, you can use the Main dial to move through the different RAW file format options.

B

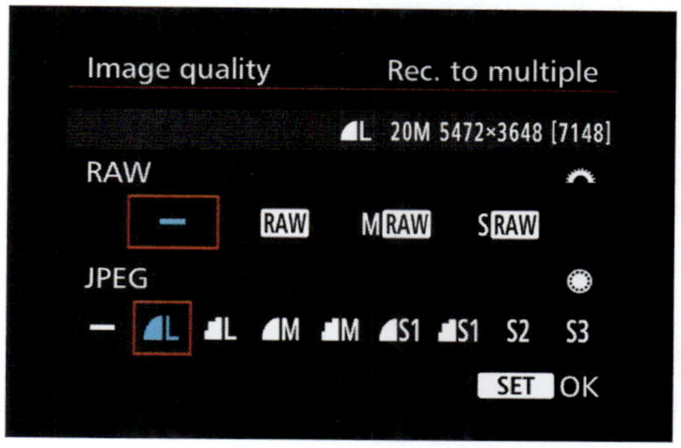

4. Turn Off the Auto ISO Setting

The ISO setting in your camera allows you to choose the level of sensitivity of the camera sensor to light. The ability to change this sensitivity is one of the biggest advantages to using a digital camera. In the days of film cameras you *had* to choose the ISO by film type. This meant that if you wanted to shoot in lower light, you had to replace the film in the camera with one that had a higher ISO. Not only did you have to carry different types of film, but you also had to remove one roll from the camera to replace it with another, even if you hadn't used up the current roll. Now all you have to do is go to the menu and select the appropriate ISO for your current lighting situation.

Having this flexibility is a powerful option but, just as with the Quality setting, the ISO setting has a direct bearing on the quality of the final image. The higher the ISO, the more digital noise the image will contain. Since your goal should be to produce the highest-quality photographs possible, it is important that you get control over all the camera controls and bend them to your will. When you turn your camera on for the first time, the ISO will be set to Auto. This means that the camera is determining how much light is available and will choose what it believes is the correct ISO setting. Because you want to use the lowest ISO possible, you will need to turn this setting off and manually select the appropriate ISO.

Noise

Noise is the enemy of digital photography, but it has nothing to do with the loudness of your camera operation. It is a term that refers to the electronic artifacts that appear as speckles in your image. They generally appear in darker shadow areas and are a result of the camera trying to amplify the signal to produce visible information. The more the image needs to be amplified—for example, raising the sensitivity through higher ISOs—the greater the amount of noise there will be.

Which ISO you choose depends on your level of available or ambient light. For sunny days or very bright scenes, use a low ISO such as 100 or 200. As the level of light is reduced, raise the ISO level. Cloudy days or indoor scenes might require you to use ISO 400.

Low-light scenes, such as when you are shooting at night, will mean you need to bump up that ISO up to 1600 or higher. The thing to remember is to shoot with the lowest setting possible for maximum quality. Later, we will cover some other specifics of exposure so that you know just how and why to raise your ISO.

Setting the ISO

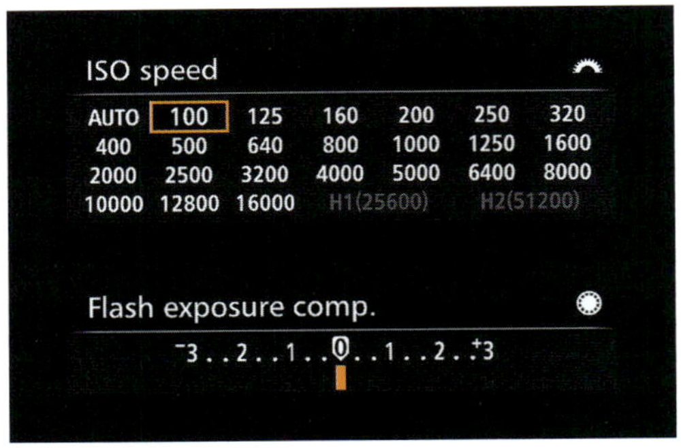

1. Activate the camera by lightly pressing the shutter release button.
2. Press the ISO button on the top of the camera.
3. Use the Main dial to select an ISO between 100 and 16000.
4. Lightly press the shutter release button, or press the ISO button again to lock in your change.
5. Just to be clear, the Auto ISO will use the meter to determine what the camera believes to be a proper setting for your current conditions. While I usually advise against using it, there are some situations where the Auto ISO will be an effective tool to use. We will cover this option in more depth in Chapter 4, "Moving Target."

Set your ISO on the fly

You can also change the ISO without taking your eye from the viewfinder by following the same steps given here. When you press the ISO button, you will see all of the camera settings in the viewfinder disappear, leaving just the ISO information viewable. Once you press the ISO button again, your new ISO setting will be displayed along with the regular shooting data. This will get easier to do as you become more familiar with the camera buttons.

5. Set Your Focus Point and Mode

The Canon focusing system is legendary for its speed and accuracy. The Artificial Intelligence (AI) focus modes will give you a ton of flexibility in your shooting. There is, however, one small problem that is inherent with any focusing system. No matter how intelligent it is, the camera is looking at all the subjects in the scene and determining which is closest to the camera. It then uses this information to determine where the proper focus point should be. It has no way of knowing what your main emphasis is unless you tell it first, so it is using a best-guess system. To eliminate this factor, you should make sure the camera is set to single-point focusing to ensure that you are focusing on the most important feature in the scene.

The camera has 65 separate focus points to choose from. They are arranged in three groups, with 25 points in the middle and groups of 20 on either side. To start things off, you should select the focus point in the middle. Once you have become more familiar with the focusing system, you can experiment with the other points, as well as the automatic point selection.

You should also change the focus mode to One Shot so that you can focus on your subject, and then recompose your shot while holding that point of focus. This method will allow you to recompose your shot for a better composition.

Setting the focus point and focus mode

1. To choose a single point of focus, wake the camera (if necessary) by lightly pressing the shutter release button.
2. Press the focus point selection button located in the upper-right area of your camera back.
3. Select the Manual Selection: 1 pt AF option by using the AF area selection lever or by pressing the M-Fn button on top of the camera until your choice is highlighted.
4. Now use the Cross keys or the Main dial and Quick Selection dial to move the focus point around the different points until it is in the center spot location, as seen on the rear LCD display (you can also do this in the viewfinder by moving the red dot to the desired position) (**A**). You can also use the Multi-controller to move the point selection around.
5. Lightly press the shutter release button once more to set your new focus point.
6. To set the focus mode, press the Drive/AF button to open the options.
7. Using the Main dial, select the One Shot mode, and then press the Set button (**B**).

A

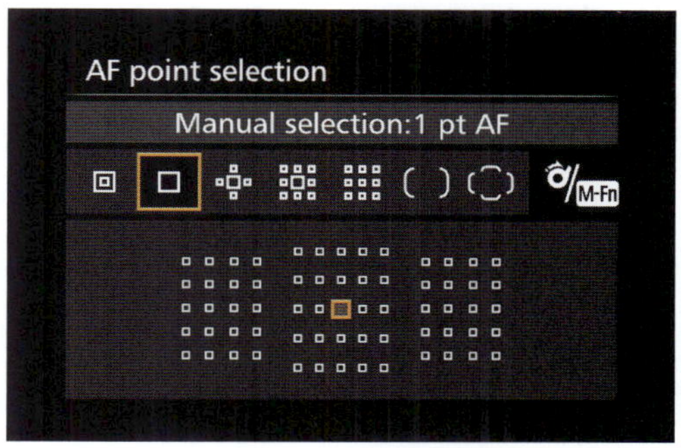

B

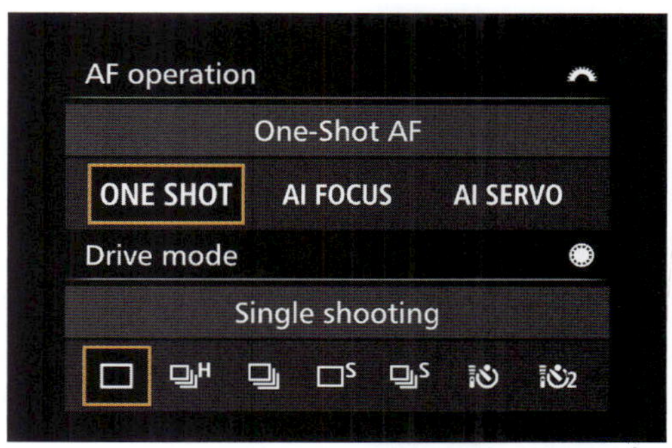

The camera is now ready for single focusing. You will hear a chirp when the camera has locked in and focused on the subject. To focus on your subject and then recompose your shot, just place the focus point in the viewfinder on your subject, depress the shutter release button halfway until the camera chirps, and without letting up on the shutter button, recompose your shot and then press the shutter button all the way down to make your exposure (**Figure 1.3**).

Figure 1.3
Using the center single-focus point in One Shot mode allows you to focus on your subject in the center (top), and then recompose your photograph for a better composition (bottom).

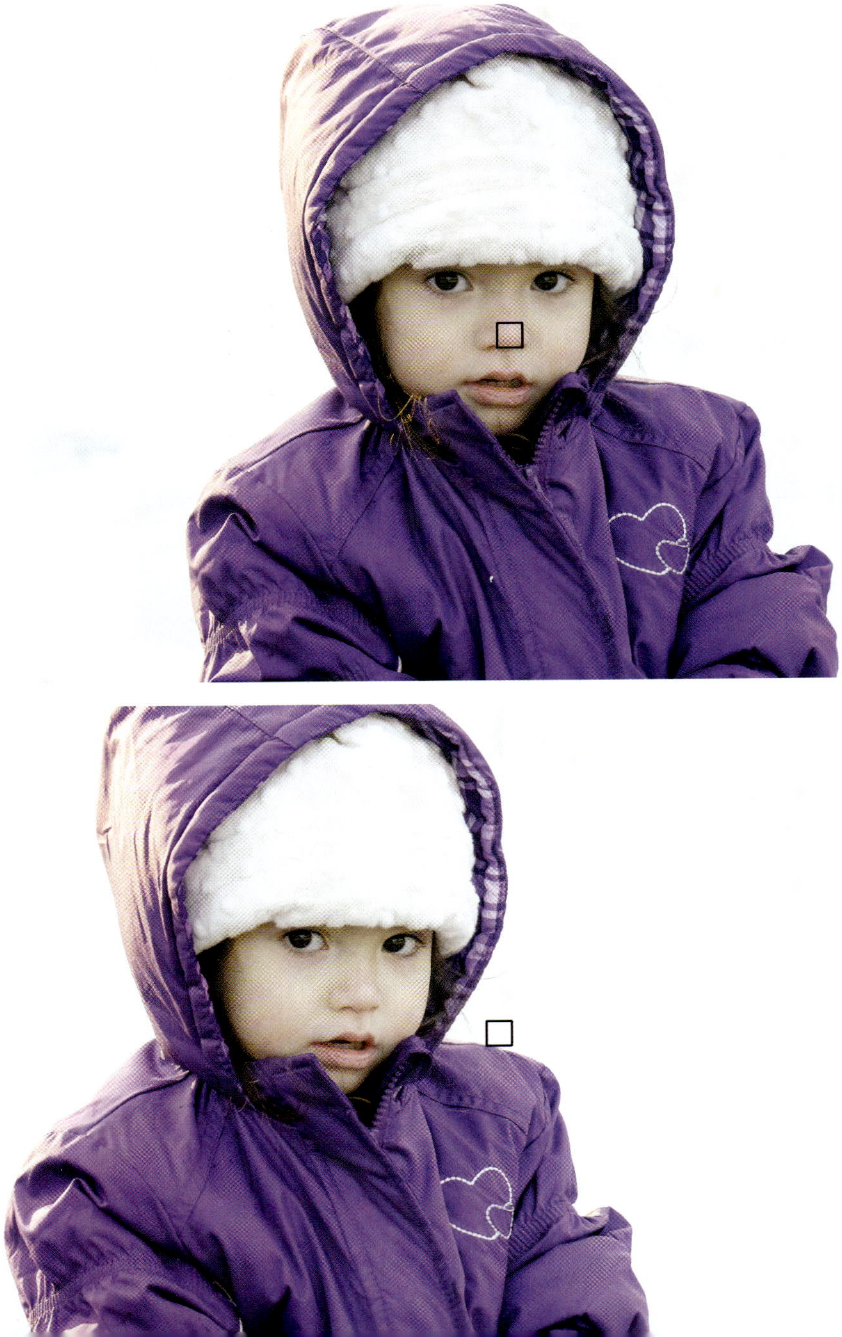

6. Set the Correct White Balance

White balance correction is the process of rendering accurate colors in your final image. Most people don't even notice that light has different color characteristics because the human eye automatically adjusts to different color temperatures—so quickly, in fact, that everything looks correct in a matter of milliseconds.

When color film ruled the world, photographers would select which film to use depending on what their light source was going to be. The most common film was balanced for daylight, but you could also buy film that was color balanced for tungsten light sources. Most other lighting situations had to be handled by using color filters over the lens. This process was necessary for the photographer's final image to show the correct color balance of a scene.

Your camera has the ability to perform this same process automatically, but you can also choose to override it and set it manually. Guess which method we are going to use? You're catching on fast! Once again, your photography should be all about maintaining control over everything that influences your final image.

Luckily, you don't need to have a deep understanding of color temperatures to control your camera's white balance. The choices are given to you in terms that are easy to relate to and that will make things pretty simple. Your white balance choices are:

- **Auto:** The default setting for your camera. It is also the only option available when shooting in the Scene Intelligent mode.
- **Daylight:** Most often used for general daylight/sunlit shooting.
- **Shade:** Used when working in shaded areas that are still using sunlight as the dominant light source.
- **Cloudy:** The choice for overcast or very cloudy days. This and the Shade setting will eliminate the blue color cast from your images.
- **Tungsten light:** Used for any occasion where you're using regular household-type bulbs for your light source. Tungsten is a very warm light source and will result in a yellow/orange cast if you don't correct for it.
- **White Fluorescent light:** Used to get rid of the green-blue cast that can result from using regular fluorescent lights as your dominant light source. Some fluorescent lights are actually balanced for daylight, which would allow you to use the Daylight white balance setting.

- **Flash:** Used whenever you're using the built-in flash or using a flash on the hot shoe. You should select this white balance to adjust for the slightly cooler light that comes from using a flash. (The hot shoe is the small bracket located on the top of your camera, which rests just above the eyepiece. This bracket is used for attaching a more powerful flash to the camera [see Chapter 7, "Mood Lighting," and Chapter 11, "Pimp My Ride," on camera accessories].)
- **Custom:** Indicates that you are using a customized white balance that is adjusted for a particular light source. If you know what the color temperature of your light source is, you can manually create a white balance setting specifically for that light source.
- **Color Temp:** This is a setting that might be considered more of an advanced white balance mode since it requires you to know the actual color temperature that you are using. This is very often used in the studio when the color temperature of the lights is supplied by the lighting manufacturer. Check out the "White Balance and the Temperature of Color" sidebar for more information on color temperatures.

White balance and the temperature of color

When you select different white balances in your camera, you will notice that underneath several of the choices is a number, for example, 5200K, 7000K, or 3200K. These numbers refer to the Kelvin temperature of the colors in the visible spectrum. The visible spectrum is the range of light that the human eye can see (think of a rainbow or the color bands that come out of a spectrum). The visible spectrum of light has been placed into a scale called the Kelvin temperature scale, which identifies the thermodynamic temperature of a given color of light. Put simply, reds and yellows are "warm," and greens and blues are "cool."

Even more confusing can be the actual temperature ratings. Warm temperatures are typically lower on the Kelvin scale, ranging from 3000 degrees to 5000 degrees, whereas cool temperatures run from 5500 degrees to around 10,000 degrees. Take a look at this list for an example of Kelvin temperature properties.

The most important thing to remember here is how the color temperature of light will affect the look of your images. If something is "warm," it will look reddish-yellow, and if something is "cool," it will have a bluish cast.

Kelvin temperature properties

FLAMES	DAYLIGHT	INCANDESCENT BULB	CAMERA FLASH	WHITE FLUORESCENT	OVERCAST SKY	MOONLIGHT	OPEN SHADE
1700K–1900K	5000K	2800K–3300K	5500K	4000K	6000K	4000K	7000K

Setting the white balance

1. After turning on or waking the camera, select one of the shooting modes on the mode dial that is not the Intelligent Auto mode.
2. Press the WB/Metering button on the top of the camera to bring up the white balance menu.
3. Use the Quick Control dial to select the proper white balance for your shooting situation.
4. Press the Set button to lock in your selection.
5. Check the camera display to ensure that the proper white balance is selected.

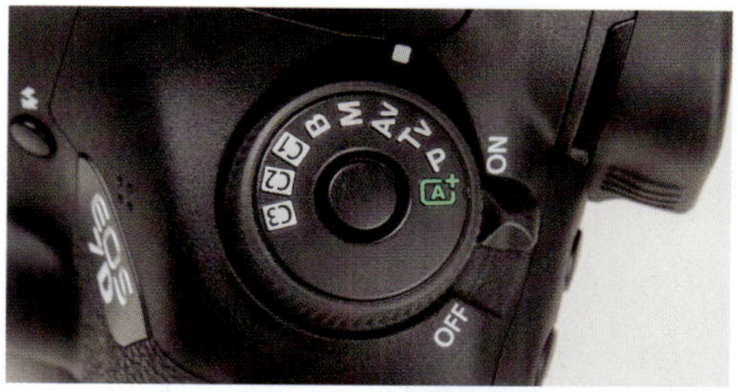

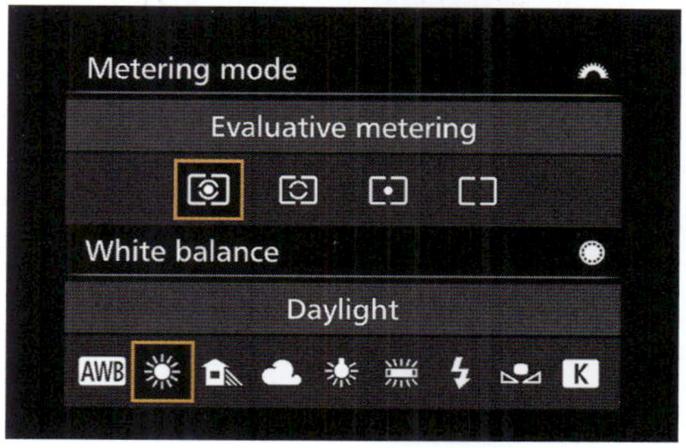

7. Adjust the Viewfinder Diopter

If you wear glasses, or are just like me and your eyes are getting older, you might have trouble looking through the viewfinder. Actually, you will be able to see through the viewfinder, but what you see might not look like it is in crisp focus. This may not be a huge problem when you are using autofocus, but if you are trying to manually focus your lens or read the information in the viewfinder, you might struggle a bit. To remedy this, you should use the dioptric adjustment knob, located to the right of the viewfinder, to adjust the viewfinder focus for your particular vision needs. There is no "correct" setting for this adjustment, so you will have to dial it in yourself. It's easy if you know this little trick.

Adjusting the diopter

1. Remove your lens and point your camera at a light-colored wall or surface.
2. Place your index finger on the dioptric adjustment knob and look through the viewfinder (if you normally wear glasses when you shoot, you should have themon).
3. Rotate the wheel until the focus point and shooting data in the viewfinder look sharp.
4. That's it. Just replace your lens and start shooting with a clearer view.

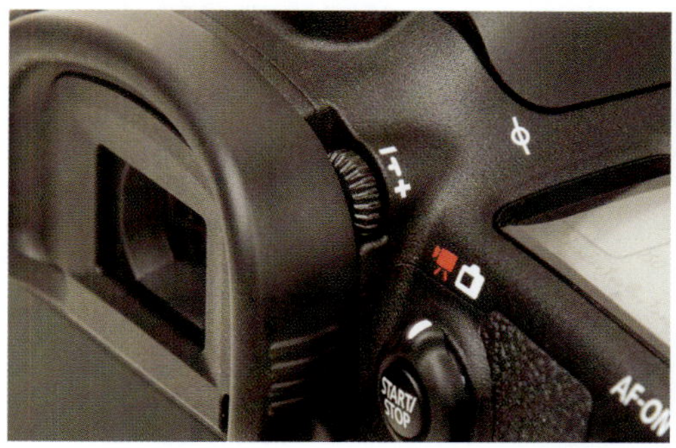

If you have tried adjusting the diopter and still can't seem to get it right, you may want to consider purchasing a dioptric lens to replace the standard viewfinder lens. They can be found on the Canon website under the accessories section for the 7D Mark II.

8. Review Your Shots

One of the greatest features of a digital camera is its ability to give you instant feedback. By reviewing your images on the camera's LCD screen, you can instantly tell if you got your shot. This visual feedback allows you to make adjustments on the fly and make certain that you nailed the shot before moving on.

When you first press the shutter release button, your camera quickly processes your image and then displays it on the rear LCD display. The default duration setting for that display is only 2 seconds. Personally, I don't find this to be nearly enough time to take in all the visual feedback that I might want. Instead of using this quick-glance method, change your display time to the Hold setting. This will keep the image up on the display until you decide that you are ready to move on to your next shot. (Note that this option will drain your batteries a little faster than the default setting.)

Changing your Image Review time setting

1. Press the Menu button, and then use the Main dial to select the leftmost menu item.
2. Using the Cross keys or Quick Control dial, scroll down to Image Review and press the Set button (**A**).
3. Scroll down to Hold, and then press the Set button once again (**B**).

A

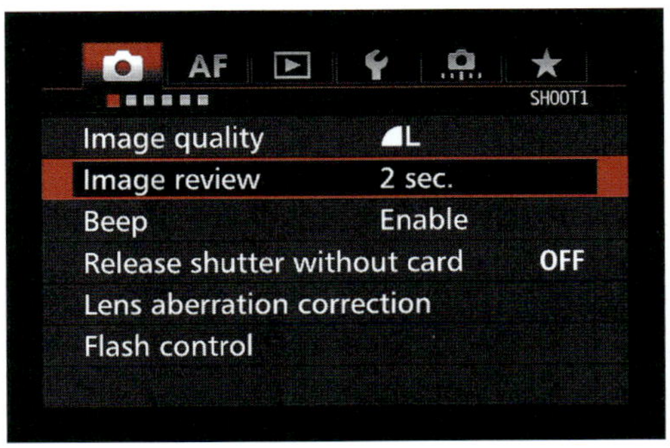

B

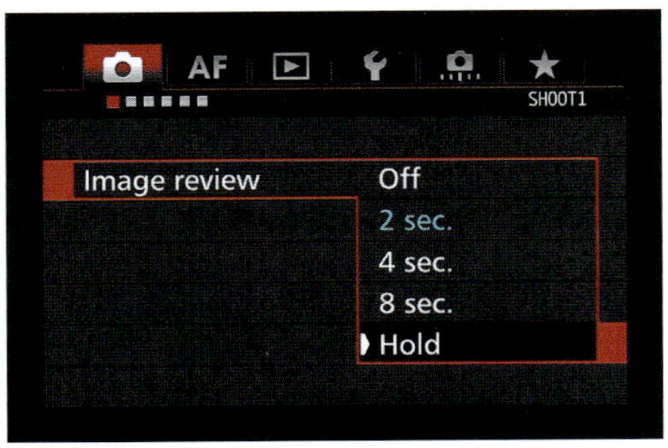

4. Press the Menu button to leave the menus and continue shooting.

Now that the image display is set, let's check out some of the other visual information that will help you when shooting.

There are three display modes that give you different amounts of information while reviewing your photos. The default view (**Figure 1.4**) simply displays your image.

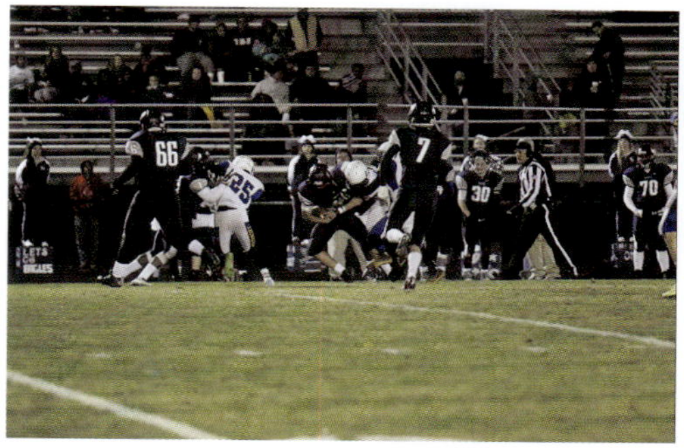

Figure 1.4
The default No Information display mode on the 7D Mark II.

To get more visual feedback, press the INFO button located to the left of the viewfinder. Press it once and you will be in the Basic Information mode, where you will see the shutter speed, aperture, exposure compensation, filename, and image number that you are currently viewing ("8/8" would mean that you're looking at the eighth image of a total of eight images). See **Figure 1.5**.

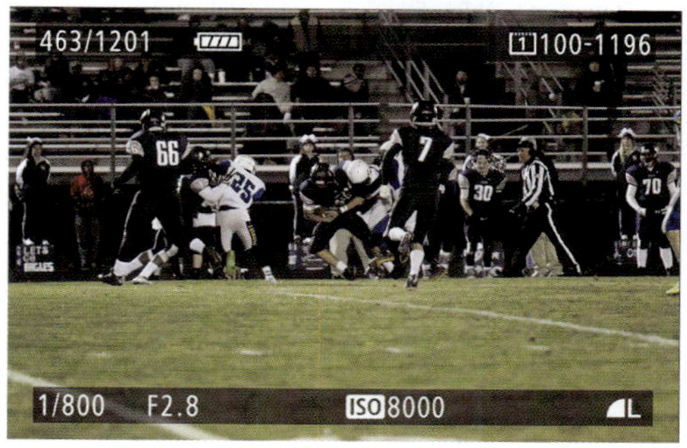

Figure 1.5
Pressing the INFO button puts you in the Basic Information display mode.

Pressing the INFO button again puts you in the Shooting Information display, which results in a huge amount of information being displayed along with the image. You will now be able to see all of the shooting information related to your image (**Figure 1.6** on the next page)

That's a huge amount of information available on a 3-inch screen! You probably won't want to use this display option as your default review setting, but if you are trying to figure out what settings you used, or if you want to review the histogram (see "The Value of the Histogram" sidebar), you now have all this great information available.

Figure 1.6
This display mode offers you a huge amount of information at a glance.

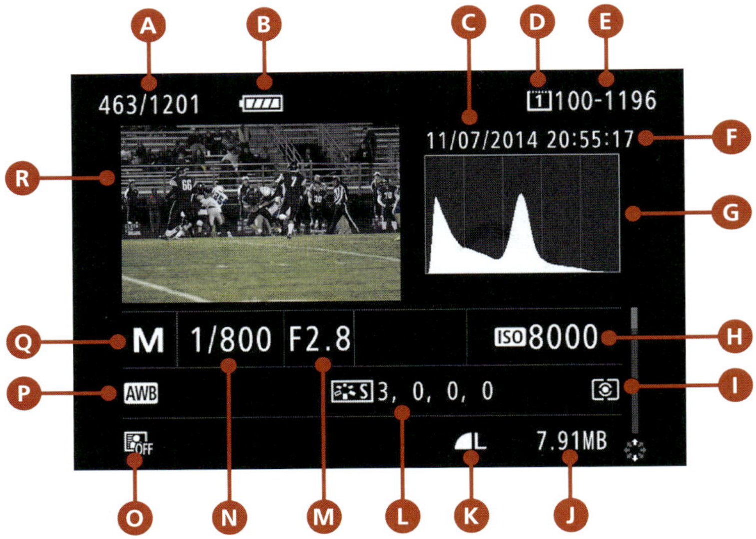

A Playback Number	G Histogram	M Aperture
B Battery Check	H ISO	N Shutter Speed
C Date	I Metering Mode	O Auto Lighting Optimizer
D Card Slot	J Image File Size	P White Balance
E Filename	K Quality Setting	Q Shooting Mode
F Time	L Picture Style	R Image Thumbnail

If you need more information, fear not, because it's just a simple scroll away. If you look at the right side of the viewfinder in the Shooting Information display mode, you will see a scroll bar along the right side of the screen. This is an indicator that there is even more information available to be seen. If you press the Multi-controller down, it will cause the next info screen to scroll into view. Keep pressing down to display the information that you are looking for (**Figure 1.7**).

Even though a lot of information is available on the Shooting Information display, you would probably be best served by selecting one of the first two viewing modes for active shooting. This way you get the largest view of your image.

The different display modes are activated by pressing the INFO button while an image is actively being displayed on your LCD screen. The display mode will remain the same for all future images that are displayed until you press the INFO button again. Also, pressing the shutter release or Menu button will result in closing the image display. To get your image back up on the LCD screen, simply press the blue Image Review playback button on the back of the camera.

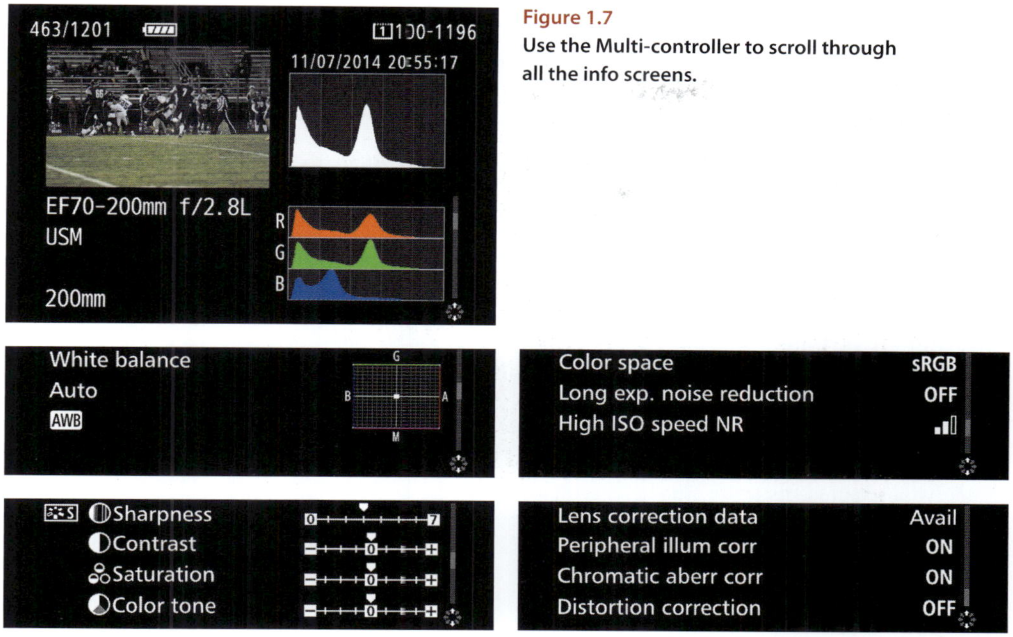

Figure 1.7
Use the Multi-controller to scroll through all the info screens.

Deleting images

Deleting or erasing images is a fairly simple process that is covered on page 392 of your manual. To quickly get you on your way, simply press the Image Review playback button and find the picture that you want to delete. Next, press the Trash button to the lower left of the display screen and use the Multi-controller to select Erase, and then press the Set button (**Figure 1.8**).

Caution: Once you have deleted an image, it is gone for good. Make sure you don't want it before you drop it in the trash.

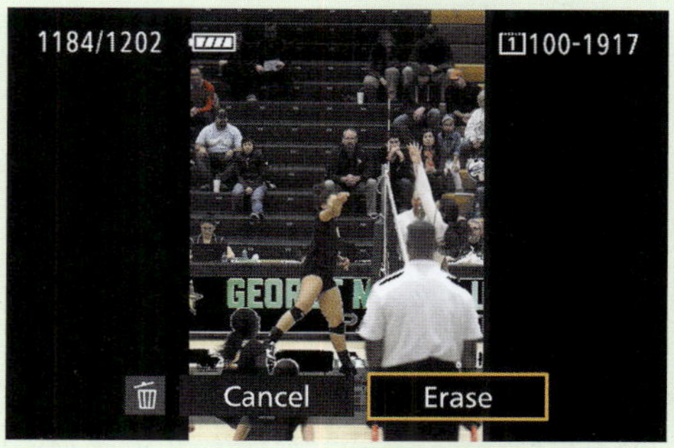

Figure 1.8
Deleting images on the 7D Mark II is very easy.

The value of the histogram

Simply put, histograms are two-dimensional representations of your images in graph form. There are two different histograms that you should be concerned with: the luminance and the color histograms. Luminance is referred to in your manual as "brightness" and is most valuable when evaluating your exposures. In **Figure 1.9**, you see what looks like a mountain range. The graph represents the entire tonal range that your camera can capture, from the whitest whites to the blackest blacks. The left side represents black, all the way to the right side, which represents white. The heights of the peaks represent the number of pixels that contain those luminance levels (a tall peak in the middle means your image contains a large amount of medium-bright pixels). Looking at an image, it can be hard to determine where all of the ranges of light and dark areas are and how much of each I have. If I look at the histogram, I can see that the largest peak of the graph is in the middle and trails off as it reaches the edges. In most cases, you would look for this type of histogram, indicating that you captured the entire range of tones, from dark to light, in your image. Knowing that is fine, but here is where the information really gets useful.

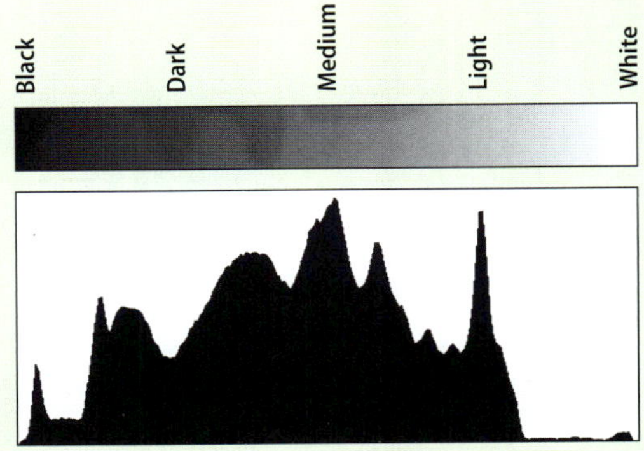

Figure 1.9

This is a typical histogram, where the dark to light tones run from left to right. The black to white gradient above the graph demonstrates where the tones lie on the graph and does not appear above your camera histogram display.

When you evaluate the histogram that has a spike or peak riding up the far left or far right side of the graph, it means that you are clipping detail from your image. In essence, you are trying to record values that are either too dark or too light for your sensor to accurately record. This is usually an indication of over- or underexposure. It also means that you need to correct your exposure so that the important details will not record as solid black or white pixels (which is what happens when clipping occurs). There are times, however, when some clipping is acceptable. If you are photographing a scene where the sun will be in the frame, you can expect to get some clipping because the sun is just too bright to hold any detail. Likewise, if you are shooting something that has true blacks in it—think coal in a mineshaft at midnight—there are most certainly going to be some true blacks with no detail in your shot. The main goal is to ensure that you aren't clipping any "important" visual information, and that is achieved by keeping an eye on your histogram. Take a look at **Figure 1.10**. The histogram displayed on the image shows a heavy skew toward the left with no part of the histogram touching the right side. This is a good example of what an underexposed image histogram looks like. Now look at **Figure 1.11** and compare the histogram for the image that was correctly exposed. Notice that even though there is still a large peak toward the left, there is more of an even distribution across the entire histogram.

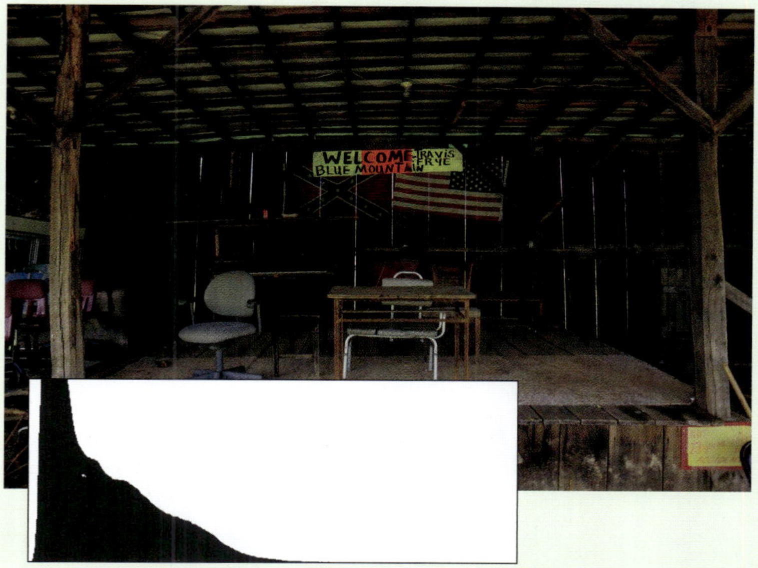

Figure 1.10
This image is about two stops underexposed. Notice the histogram is skewed to the left.

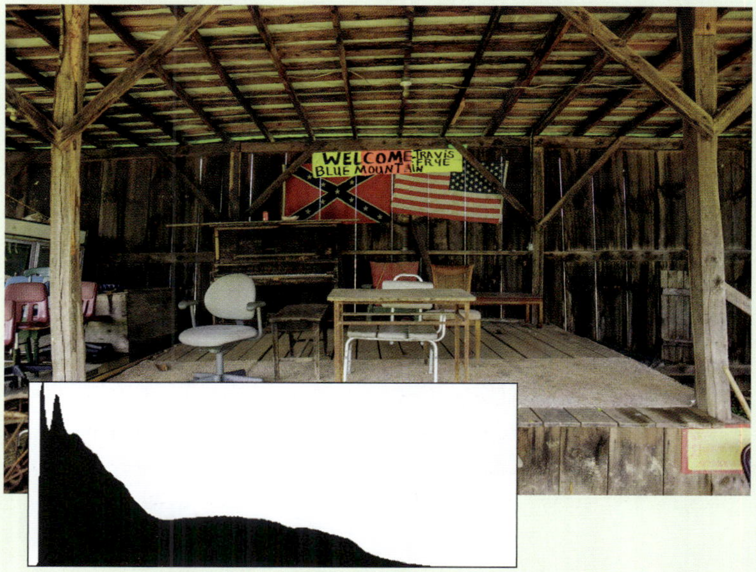

Figure 1.11
This histogram reflects a correctly exposed image.

9. Turn On the Highlight Alert

The previous tip showed how you can use the histogram in the Shooting Information display to see if you are overexposing or clipping your highlights. Although this is good information, there is a quicker way to see if this is happening, and you can use it in all of the display modes, including the default and basic modes. It is called the Highlight warning, and it evaluates your image for clipped highlights and makes those areas blink black and white in the image preview screen. This is a very popular setting that pro photographers have been using for years, and now you can easily set it up and quickly evaluate your image's highlights.

1. Press the Menu button and use the Main dial to get to the third Playback menu.
2. Use the Quick Control dial to highlight the Highlight Alert option, and press the Set button (**A**).
3. Change the option to Enable, and press the Set button to lock in the change (**B**).

A

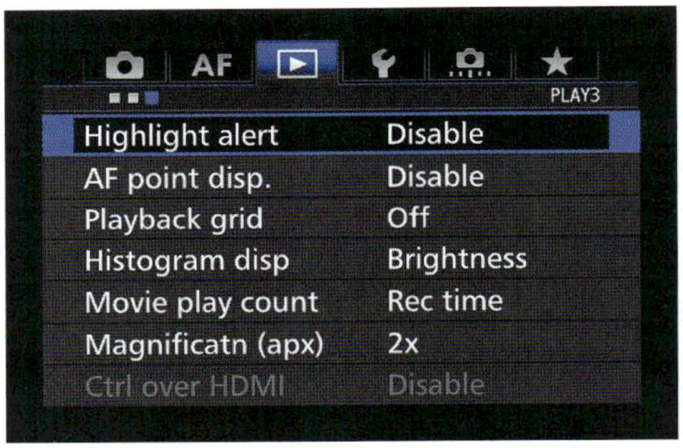

B

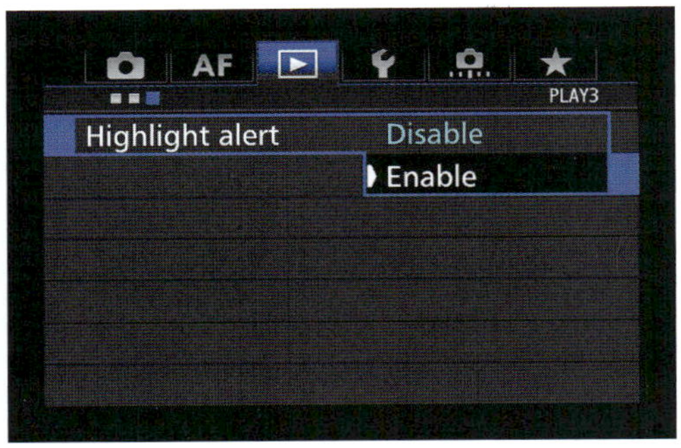

4. Now press your Image Playback button, and use the Quick Control dial to move through your images on your memory card and see if there are any areas that are blinking black and white (**Figure 1.12**).

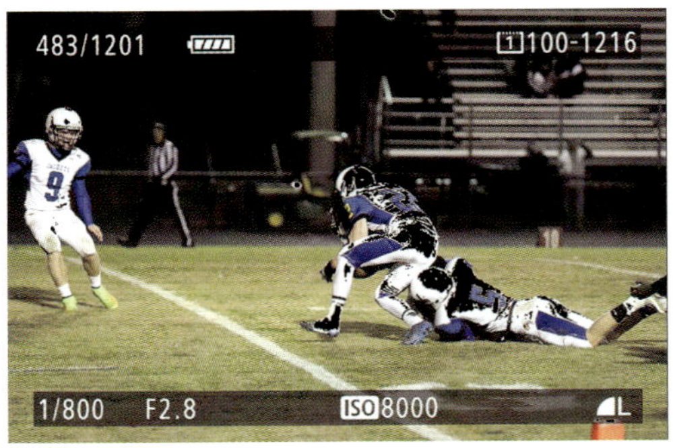

Figure 1.12
The blinking black and white area warns of lost details in the highlights of the image.

Just remember that a blinking highlight doesn't necessarily indicate that you need to adjust your exposure. Sometimes white is white, and there are no details to be saved. Other times you will need to sacrifice some detail in the highlights to get the details that you want in the shadow areas. Use this alert as a simple way of taking notice of your highlights, and then decide whether they are worth saving.

10. Hold Your Camera for Proper Shooting

Digital SLR cameras are made to favor the right-handed individual. The basics of properly holding the camera begin with grasping the camera body with the right hand. You will quickly find that most of the important camera controls are within easy reach of your thumb and forefinger. The next step is to create a stable base for your camera to rest on. This is accomplished by placing the camera body on the up-facing palm of your left hand (**Figure 1.13**). Now you can curl your fingers around the lens barrel to quickly zoom or manually focus the lens.

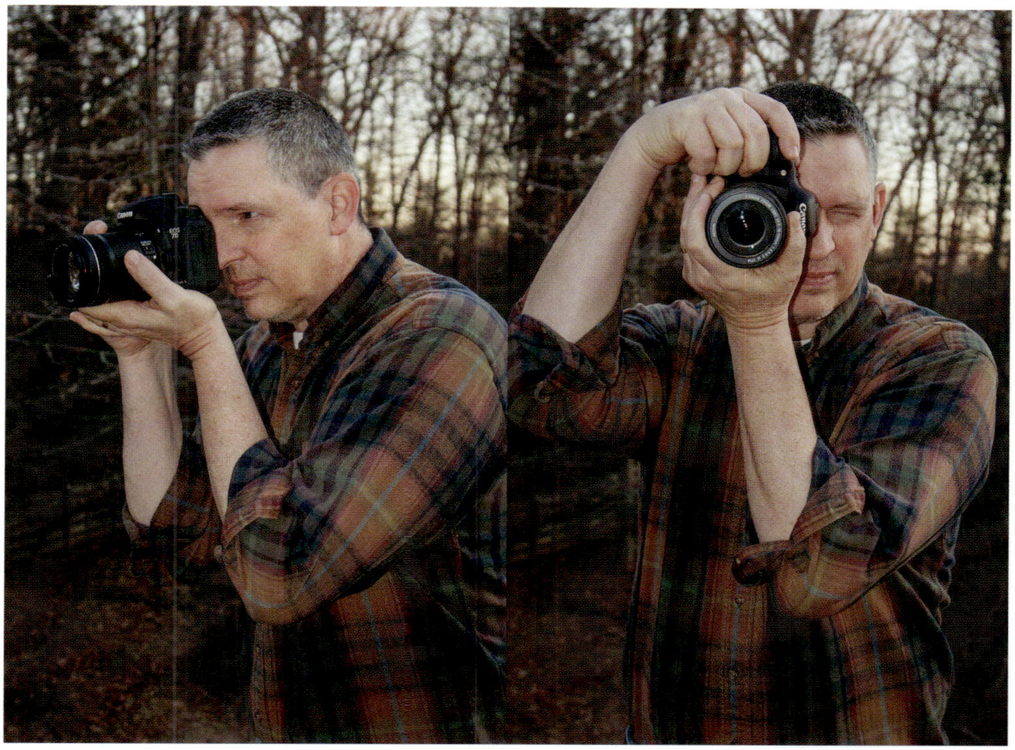

Figure 1.13
The proper way to hold your camera to ensure sharp, blur-free images.

Now that you know where to put your hands, let's talk about what to do with the rest of your body parts. By using the underhand grip, your elbows will be drawn closer to your body. You should concentrate on pulling them in close to your body to stabilize your shooting position. You should also try to maintain proper upright posture. Leaning forward at the waist will begin to fatigue your back, neck, and arms. Nothing ruins a day of shooting like a sore back, so make sure you stand erect, with your elbows in. Finally, place your left foot slightly in front of your right foot and face your subject with a slightly wide stance. By combining all of these aspects into your photography, you will give yourself the best chance of eliminating self-imposed camera shake (or hand shake) in your images, which will result in much sharper photographs.

Chapter 1 Assignments

Let's begin our shooting assignments by setting up and using all of the elements of the Top Ten list. Even though I have yet to cover the shooting modes, you should set your camera to the P (Program) mode. This will allow you to interact with the various settings and menus that have been covered thus far.

Basic camera setup

Charge your battery to 100 percent to get it started on a life of dependable service. Next, using your newfound knowledge, set up your camera to address the following: shooting without a card, image quality, and Auto ISO.

Selecting the proper white balance

Take your camera outside into a daylight environment, and then photograph the same scene using various white balance settings. Pay close attention to how each setting affects the overall color cast of your images. Next, move inside and repeat the exercise while shooting in a tungsten lighting environment. Finally, find a fluorescent light source and repeat once more. Doing this simple exercise will quickly let you identify the ways in which the white balance setting controls the overall color cast of your image.

Focusing with single point and One Shot

Change your camera setting so that you are focusing using the single-point focus mode. Try moving the focus point around to different focus points to see how they work in focusing your scene. Next, set your focus mode to One Shot and practice focusing on a subject and then recomposing before taking the picture. Try doing this with subjects at varying distances.

Evaluating your pictures with the LCD display

Set up your image display properties, and then review some of your previous assignment images using the various display modes. Review your shooting information for each image and take a look at the histograms to see how the content of your photo affects the shape.

Get a grip: proper camera holding

This final assignment is something that you should practice every time you shoot: proper grip and stance for shooting with your camera. Use the described technique, and then shoot a series of images. Try comparing it with improper techniques to compare the stability of the grip and stance.

Share your results with the book's Flickr group!
Join the group here: flickr.com/groups/7dmarkii_fromsnapshotstogreatshots

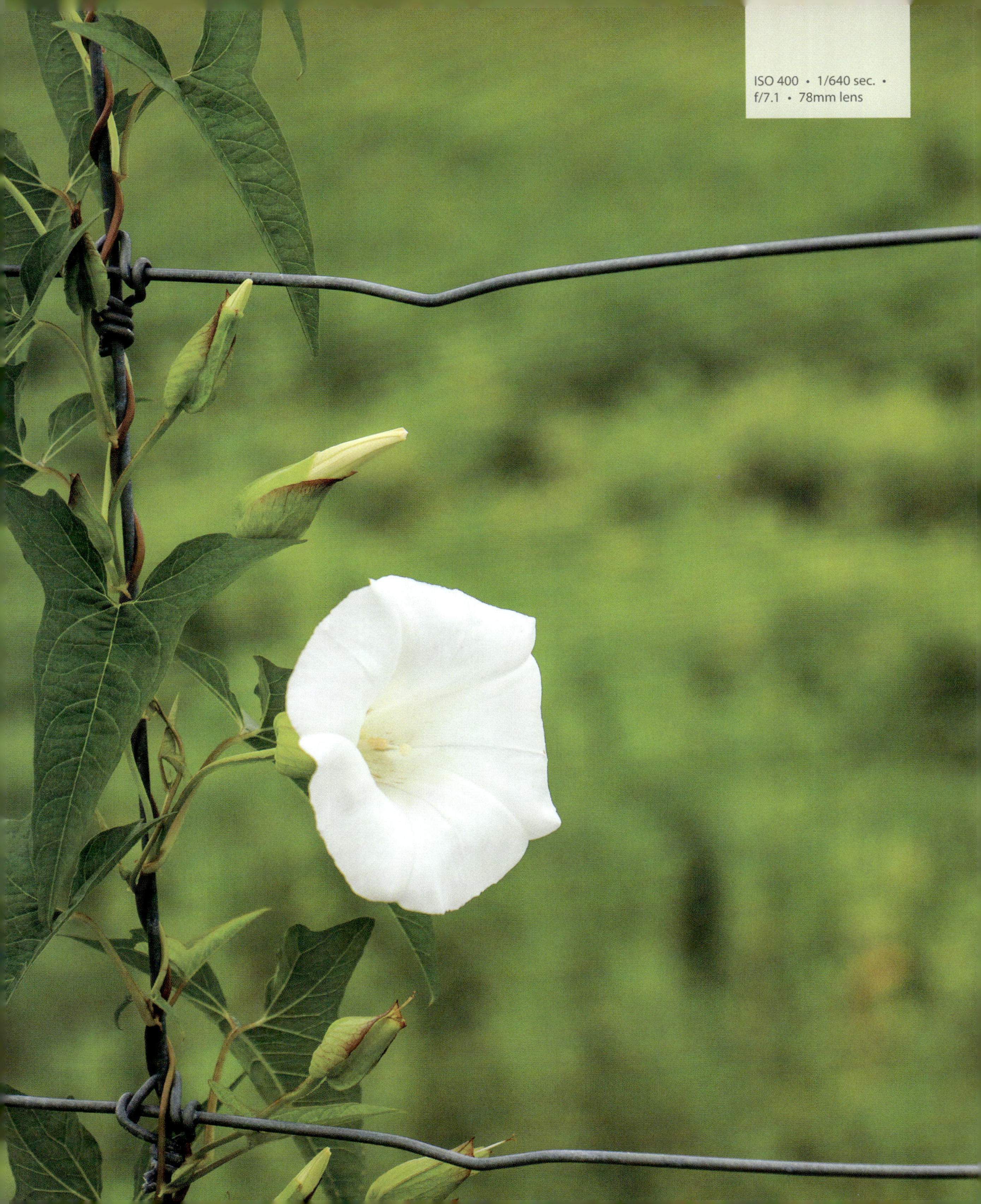

ISO 400 • 1/640 sec. • f/7.1 • 78mm lens

2

First Things First

A Few Things to Know and Do Before You Begin Taking Pictures

Now that we've covered the top ten tasks to get you up and shooting, we should probably take care of some other important details. You need to become familiar with certain features before you can take full advantage of your camera. Additionally, you should take some steps to prepare the camera and memory card for use. So to get things moving, let's start with something that you will definitely need before you can take a single picture: a memory card.

Poring Over the Picture

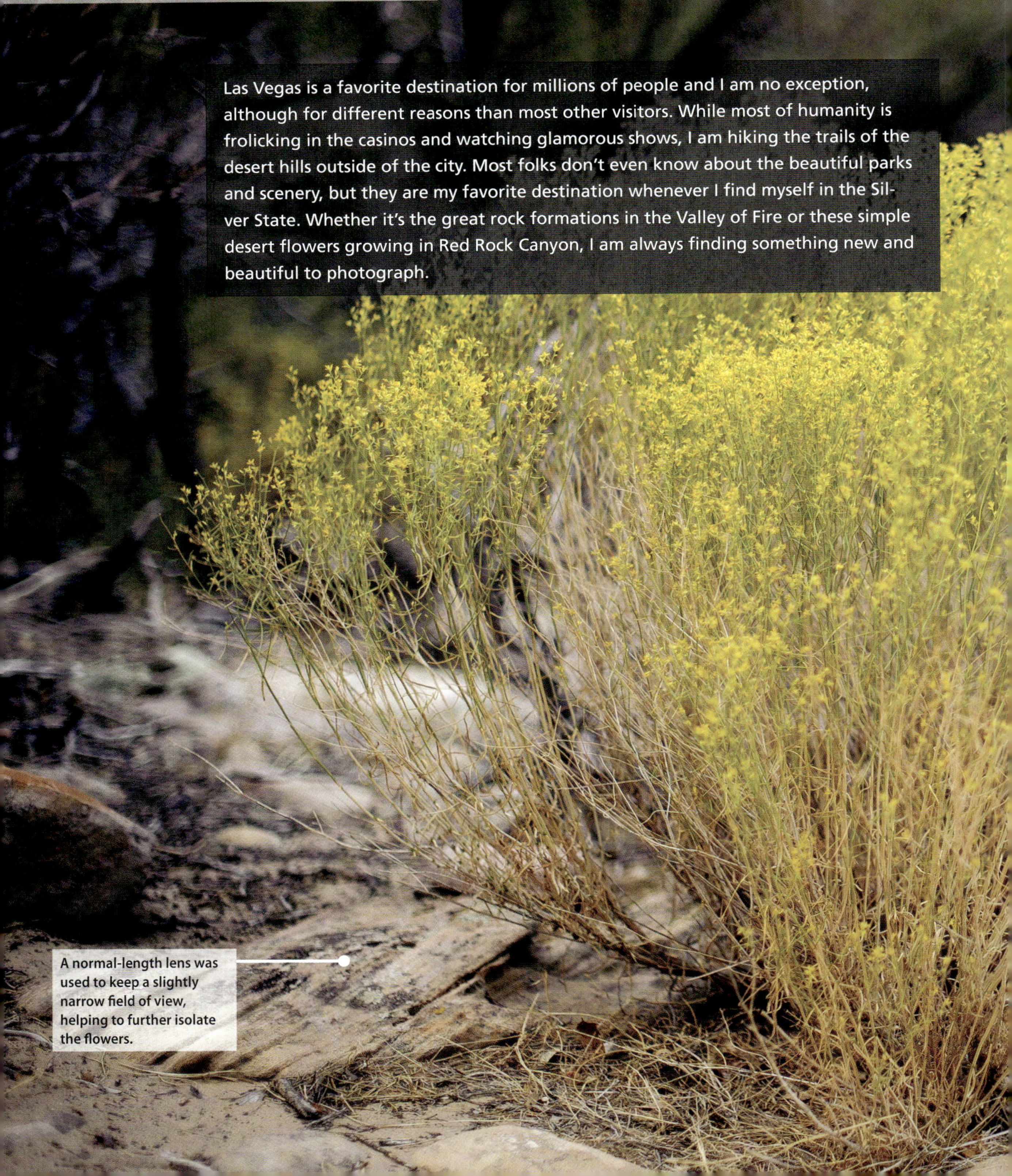

Las Vegas is a favorite destination for millions of people and I am no exception, although for different reasons than most other visitors. While most of humanity is frolicking in the casinos and watching glamorous shows, I am hiking the trails of the desert hills outside of the city. Most folks don't even know about the beautiful parks and scenery, but they are my favorite destination whenever I find myself in the Silver State. Whether it's the great rock formations in the Valley of Fire or these simple desert flowers growing in Red Rock Canyon, I am always finding something new and beautiful to photograph.

A normal-length lens was used to keep a slightly narrow field of view, helping to further isolate the flowers.

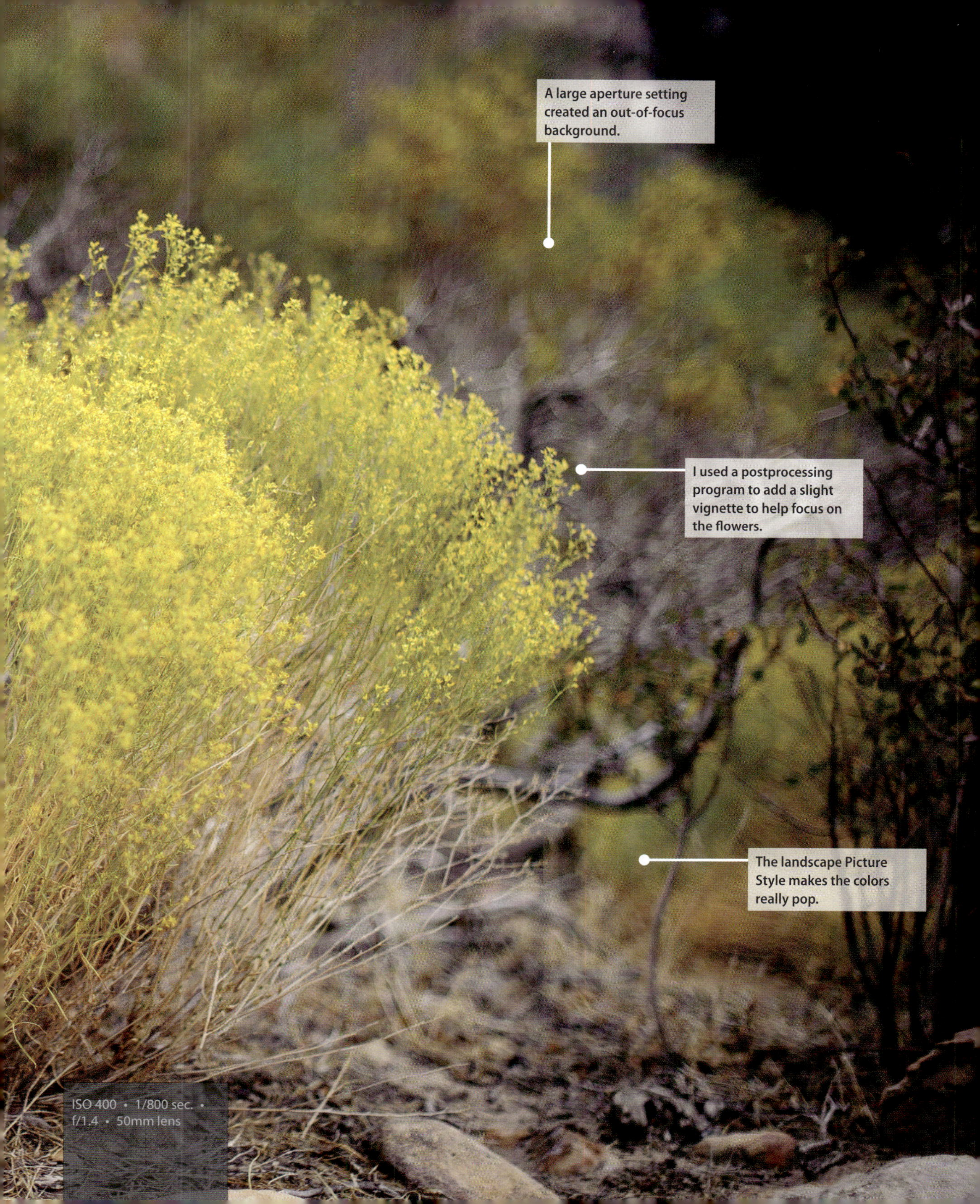
A large aperture setting created an out-of-focus background.
I used a postprocessing program to add a slight vignette to help focus on the flowers.
The landscape Picture Style makes the colors really pop.
ISO 400 • 1/800 sec. • f/1.4 • 50mm lens

Choosing the Right Memory Card

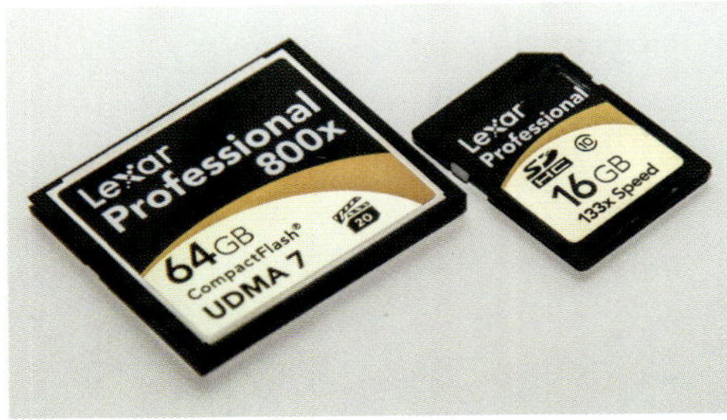

Figure 2.1
Make sure you select a memory card that has enough capacity and speed to handle your photography needs.

Memory cards are the digital film that stores every shot you take until you move them to a computer. They come in all shapes and sizes, and they are an essential accessory for capturing your photos and videos. Most people give very little thought to the memory card, but please take my word for it when I say that you should choose your cards carefully. Choosing the wrong card can result in missing a shot because of slow write speeds to simply losing your images from card failure. Spending a little time on card selection will pay benefits down the road. The 7D Mark II uses both Secure Digital (SD) memory cards as well as Compact Flash cards (**Figure 2.1**).

If you've been using a point-and-shoot camera, chances are you may already own an SD media card, which may or may not be suitable for use in your 7D Mark II. Which brand of card you use is completely up to you, but here's some advice about choosing your memory card:

- Size matters, at least in memory cards. At 20 megapixels, the 7D Mark II will require a lot of storage space, especially if you shoot in the RAW or RAW+JPEG mode (more on this later in the chapter) or shoot HD video. You should definitely consider using a card with a storage capacity of at least 16 GB to 32 GB.
- Consider buying High Capacity (SDHC) cards. These cards are generally much faster, both when writing images to the card as well as when transferring them to your computer. If you are planning on using the Continuous mode (see Chapter 4, "Moving Target") for capturing fast action, you can gain a boost in performance just by using an SDHC card with a class rating of at least 6. The higher the class rating, the faster the write speed. Having a fast card will also benefit your video capture by keeping the flow of video frames moving quickly to your card.
- Buy more than one card. If you have already purchased a memory card, consider getting another. It's a bad day when your card is almost full and you have to either erase shots or choose a lower-quality image format so that you can keep shooting. With the cost of memory cards what it is, keeping a spare just makes good sense. Also, since your camera supports two cards, you can configure them for any number of options, including overflow, where the camera will go to the second card when the first is full. You can also write copies to both cards at the same time as backups. If you are

capturing two different image formats, RAW and JPEG, you can designate each format to a separate card. The choice is completely yours.

- To get the fastest memory possible, you could consider purchasing an SDXC memory card. Although they appear to be the same as SD and SDHC cards, they are made to new specifications that allow memory capacities above 32 GB. Your camera is SDXC compliant, but you should be warned that if you plan on sharing SDXC cards between devices such as your 7D Mark II and a video camera, make sure the other device is SDXC compatible, too. SDXC cards will only work in SDXC devices. Also, you should only format your SDXC card in your camera.
- For Compact Flash cards, look for UDMA Mode 7 cards. They come in many flavors and sizes, but simply put, UDMA will provide the speed you need for quickly saving video and still images.

Canon recommends write speeds of 30 MB/sec for compact flash cards and 20 MB/sec for SD cards. Just know that all cards are not created equally, and if you plan on using your camera to record video or shoot sports at fast frame rates for extended bursts, you will want the fastest card you can get your hands on. I have used minimally acceptable cards and had failures due to the speeds required for HD video recording, so don't slouch when it comes to your memory.

Formatting Your Memory Card

Now that you have your card, let's talk about formatting for a minute. When you purchase any new memory card, you can pop it into your camera and start shooting right away—and probably everything will work as it should. However, what you *should* do first is format the card in the camera. This process allows the camera to set up the card to record images from your camera. Just as a computer hard drive must be formatted, formatting your card ensures that it is properly initialized. The card may work in the camera without first being formatted, but chances of failure down the road are much higher.

As a general practice, I always format new cards or cards that have been used in different cameras. I also reformat cards after I have downloaded my images and want to start a new shooting session. Note that you should always format your card in the camera, not your computer. Using the computer could render the card useless in your camera. You should also pay attention to the manufacturer's recommendations with respect to moisture, humidity, and proper handling procedures. It sounds a little cliché, but when it comes to protecting your images, every little bit helps.

Most people are under the impression that formatting the memory card is equivalent to erasing it, but that is wrong. The truth is that when you format the card, all you are doing is changing the file management information on the card. Think of it as removing the table of contents from a book and replacing it with a blank page. All of the contents are still there, but you wouldn't know it by looking at the empty table of contents. The camera will see the card as completely empty so you won't be losing any space, even if you have previously filled the card with images. Your camera will simply write the new image data over the previous data.

Formatting your memory card

A

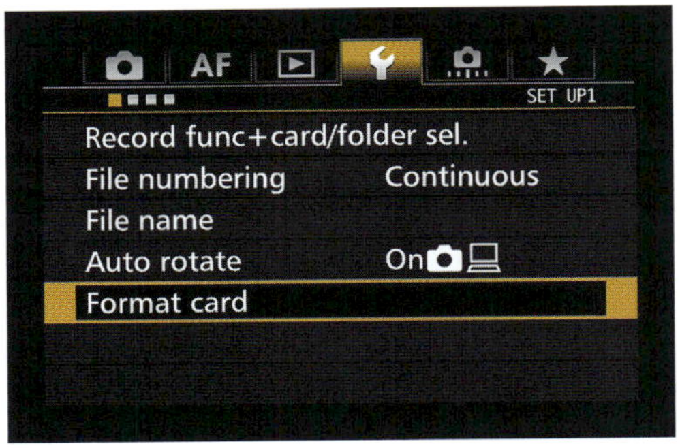

1. Insert your memory card/s into the camera.
2. Press the Menu button and navigate to the first setup menu screen (the one with the wrench icon on top).
3. Use the Quick Control dial on the back of the camera to highlight the Format Card option, and press Set (**A**).
4. Select which of the two card slots you would like to format, and press Set (**B**).
5. The default selection for the Format screen is Cancel, just in case you didn't want to format the card (**C**). Turn the Quick Control dial to highlight OK. The screen will warn you that you will lose any data by formatting your card, so make sure that you have saved any images that you want onto your computer or elsewhere before formatting.

B

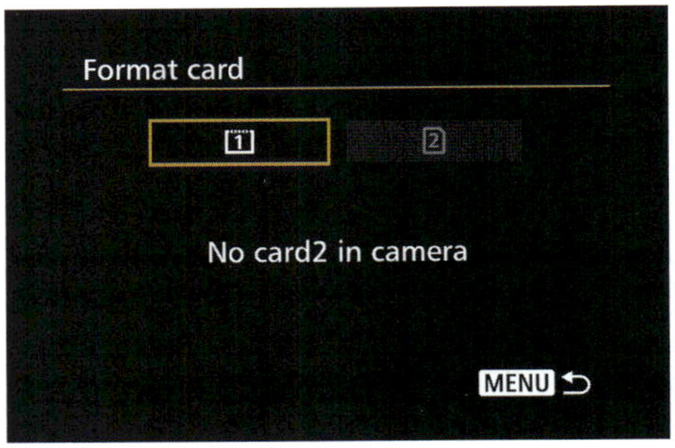

C

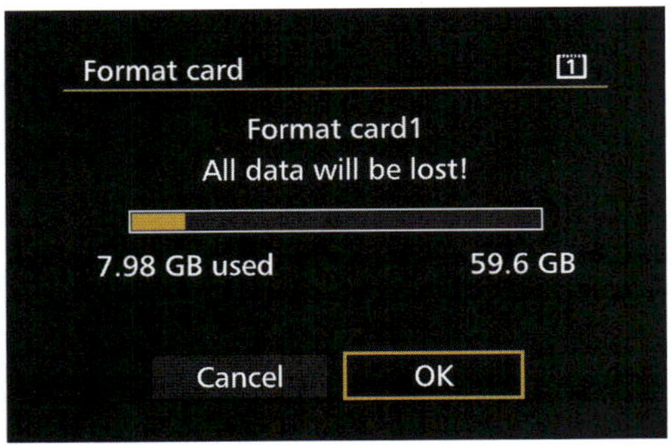

6. Press the Set button to finalize the formatting of the card.

Note that when you only have one card in the camera, you will only be able to choose one slot for formatting. If you do have two cards, you will need to format them independently from each other. Once you finish the format process, just repeat it for the other card slot.

Updating the 7D Mark II's Firmware

I know that you want to get shooting, but having the proper firmware can impact the way the camera operates. It can fix problems as well as improve operation, so you should take care of it sooner rather than later. Updating your camera's firmware is something that the manual completely omits; yet it can change the entire behavior of your camera's operating systems and functions. The firmware of your camera is the set of computer operating instructions that controls how your camera functions. Updating this firmware is a great way to not only fix little bugs but also gain access to new functionality. You will need to check out the information on the Canon Firmware update page (www.usa.canon.com/cusa/professional/standard_display/support_pro/pro_firmware-updates) to review how a firmware update will affect your camera, but it is always a good idea to be working with the most up-to-date firmware version available.

Checking the camera's current firmware version number

1. Rotate the Mode dial to select P (or any of the other modes besides Scene Intelligent Auto mode).
2. Press the Menu button to display the menu.
3. Turn the Main dial to get to the fourth camera setup menu, use the Quick Control dial to highlight the firmware option, and then press Set (**A**).

A

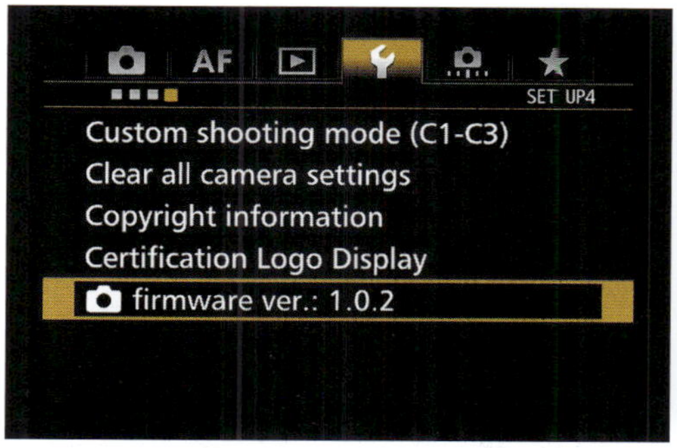

B

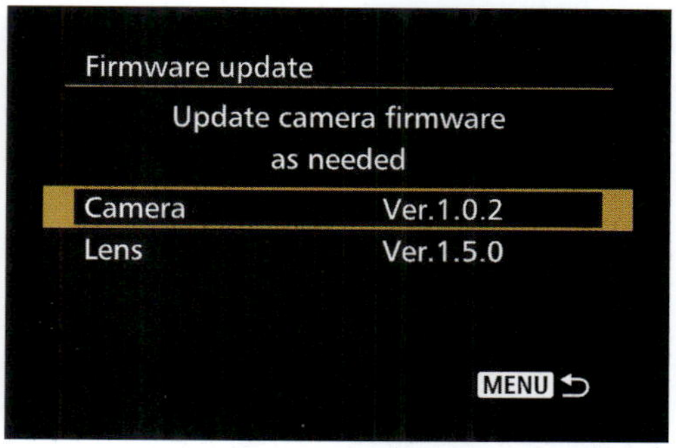

4. Check the version numbers for the camera and lens (**B**). If these versions are not the latest ones listed on the Canon website, follow the steps in the next section to load the latest version.

As of this writing, the current version of the firmware for the 7D Mark II was 1.0.2 for the camera and 1.5.0 for the lens, and no updates were available. Be sure to check the Canon website often for updates, and then follow these directions for updating your camera (**Figure 2.2**).

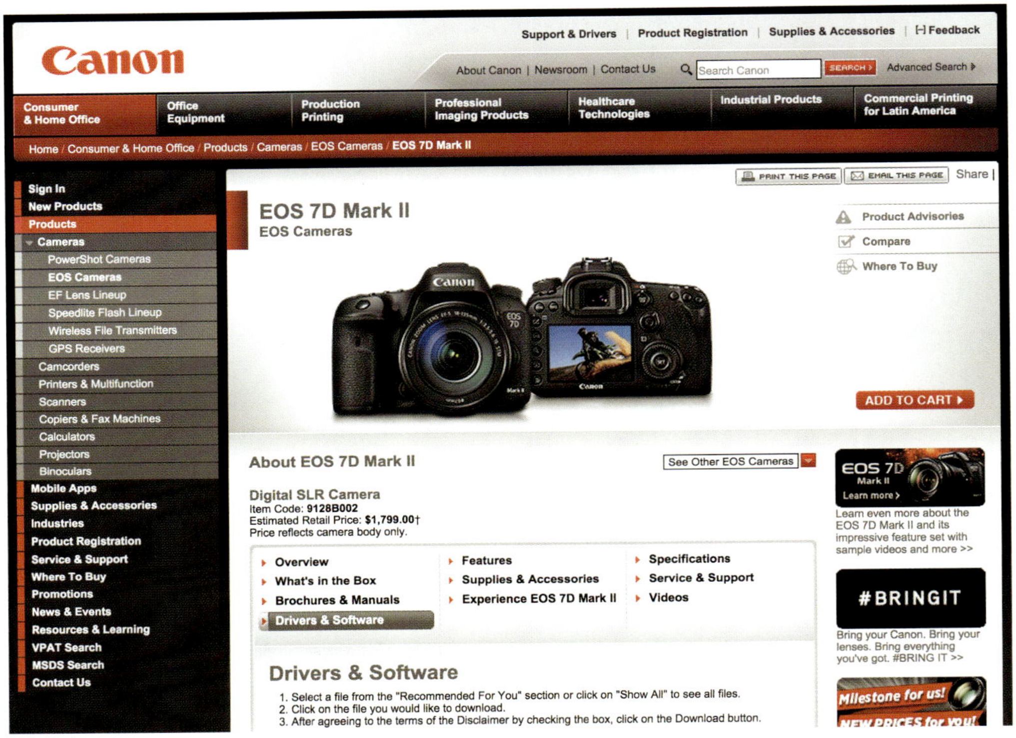

Figure 2.2
Check the Canon website for firmware updates.

Updating the firmware

1. If there is an update for the camera, you will be guided to the proper version to download based on your computer's operating system.
2. Download the file and extract it to your computer hard drive (usually by double-clicking on the downloaded file).
3. The file will expand into a folder that contains the firmware update as well as a PDF file with detailed instructions for updating your camera.
4. Ensure that your camera battery is fully charged and that you have a formatted memory card, and then follow the directions in the camera's PDF file.
5. You will also need a card reader to transfer the firmware file to the memory card.

Cleaning the Sensor

Cleaning camera sensors used to be a nerve-racking process that required leaving the sensor exposed to scratching and even more dust. Now cleaning the sensor is pretty much an automatic function. Every t me you turn the camera on and off, the sensor in the camera vibrates to remove any dust particles that might have landed on it.

There are three choices for cleaning in the camera setup menu: Auto Cleaning, Clean Now, and Clean Manually. By default, the camera is set to automatically clean the sensor every time you power on and off. You can disable this function, but it is best to leave it on.

The one cleaning function that you will need to use via this menu is the Clean Now feature. This should be done every time you remove the lens from the camera body. Removing or changing a lens can leave the camera body open and susceptible to dust sneaking into the body. If you never change lenses, you shouldn't have too many dust problems. The more often you change lenses, the more chances you are giving dust to enter the body. For this reason, I have the Clean Now function added to the custom My Menu list (see Chapter 10, "Advanced Techniques").

Every now and then, there will be a dust spot that is impervious to the shaking of the Auto Cleaning feature. This will require manual cleaning of the sensor. When you activate this feature, it will raise the camera mirror and give you access to the sensor so that you can use a blower or other cleaning device to remove the stubborn dust speck. The camera will need to be turned off after cleaning to allow the mirror to reset.

If you choose to manually clean your sensor, please use a device that has been made to clean sensors (not a cotton swab from your medicine cabinet). There are dozens of commercially available devices such as brushes, swabs, and blowers that will clean the sensor without damaging it. To keep the sensor clean, always store the camera with a body cap or lens attached.

The camera sensor is an electrically charged device. This means that when the camera is turned on, there is a current running through the sensor. This electric current can create static electricity, which will attract small dust particles to the sensor area. For this reason, it is always a good idea to turn off the camera prior to removing a lens. You should also consider having the lens mount facing down during lens removal so that there is less opportunity for dust to fall into the inner workings of the camera.

Using the Clean Now feature

1. Press the Menu button and use the Main dial to get to the third camera setup menu.
2. Use the Quick Control dial to highlight Sensor Cleaning, and then press the Set button (**A**).
3. Use the Quick Control dial to select Clean Now, and press the Set button again (**B**).
4. Press Set one more time to start the cleaning function (**C**).

A

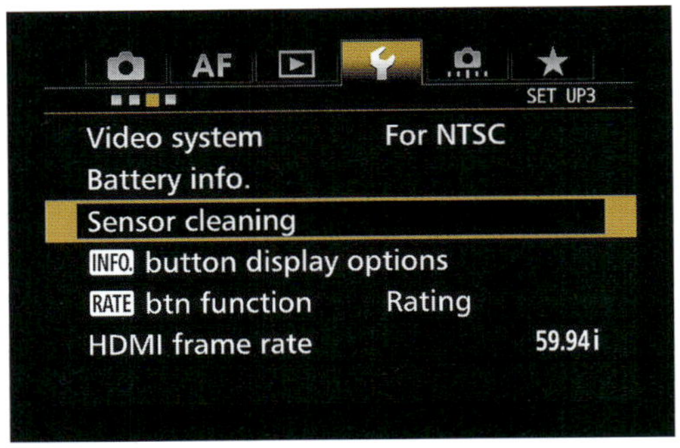

B

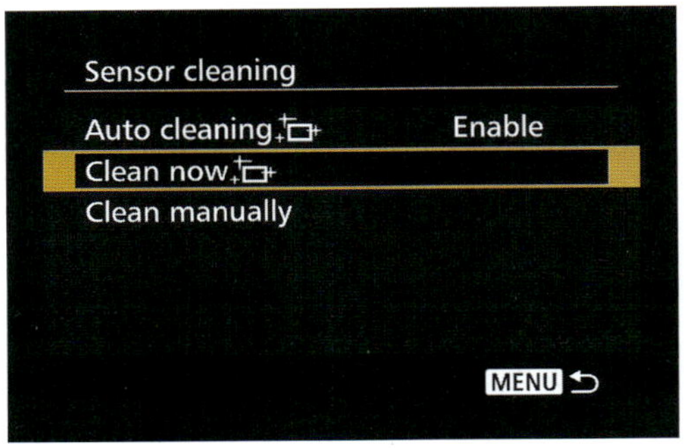

C

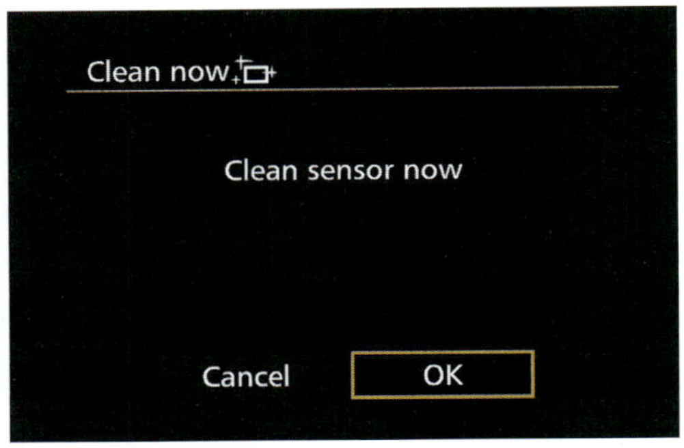

5. To return to shooting mode, lightly press the shutter release button.

Using the manual cleaning feature

1. Follow steps 1 and 2 from the preceding section.
2. Use the Quick Control dial to select Clean Manually, and press the Set button again (**D**).

D

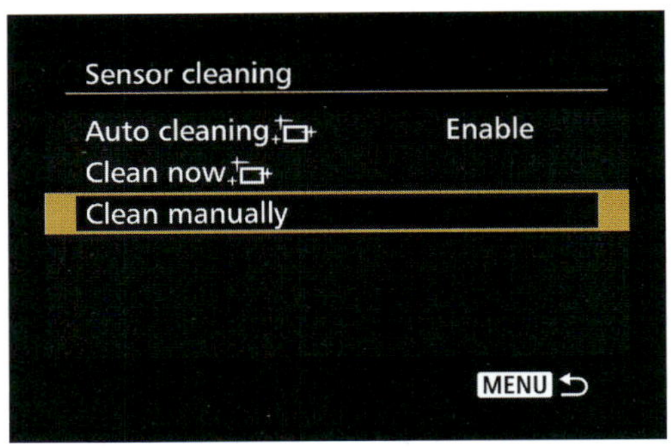

3. Use the Quick Control dial to select OK, and press the Set button again (**E**).
4. Remove your lens, carefully clean the sensor, and then replace the lens or put on the body cap.
5. Turn the camera off to reset.

E

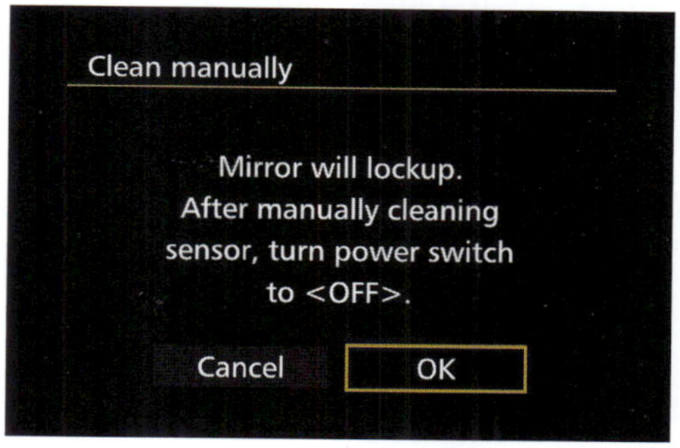

Using the Right Format: RAW vs. JPEG

When shooting with your 7D Mark II, you have a choice of image formats that your camera will use to store the pictures on the memory card. JPEG is probably the most familiar format to anyone who has been using a digital camera. I touched on this topic briefly in Chapter 1, “The 7D Mark II Top Ten List,” so you have a little background on what JPEG and RAW files are.

There is nothing wrong with JPEG if you are taking casual shots. JPEG files are ready to use, right out of the camera. Why go through the process of adjusting RAW images of the kids opening presents when you are just going to email them to Grandma? Also, for journalists and sports photographers who are shooting 10 frames per second and need to transmit images across the wire, again, JPEG is just fine. So what is wrong with JPEG? Absolutely nothing—unless you care about having complete creative control over how your image looks (as opposed to what a compression algorithm thinks is important).

As I mentioned in Chapter 1, JPEG is not actually an image format. It is a compression standard, and compression is where things can go bad. When your camera is set to JPEG—whether it is set to High or Low compression—you are telling the camera to process the image however it sees fit, and then throw away enough image data to make it shrink into a smaller space. In doing so, you give up subtle image details that you will never get back in postprocessing. That is an awfully simplified statement but still fairly accurate.

So what does RAW have to offer?

First and foremost, RAW images are not compressed. (There are some cameras that have a compressed RAW format, but it is lossless compression, which means there is no loss of actual image data.) Note that RAW image files will require you to perform postprocessing on your photographs. This is not only necessary; it is the reason that most photographers use it.

RAW images have a greater dynamic range than JPEG-processed images. This means that you can recover image details in the highlights and shadows that just aren't available in JPEG-processed images.

There is more color information in a RAW image because it is a 14-bit image. That means it contains more color information than a JPEG, which is almost always an 8-bit image. The more color information in the image, the more you have to work with and the smoother the changes will be between tones. It's kind of like the difference between performing surgery with a scalpel as opposed to a butcher's knife. They'll both get the job done, but one will do less damage.

Regarding sharpening, a RAW image offers more control because you are the one who is applying the sharpening according to the look you want to achieve. Once again, JPEG processing applies a standard amount of sharpening that you cannot change after the fact. Once it is done, it's done.

Finally, and most important, a RAW file is your negative. No matter what you do to it, you won't change it unless you save your file in a different format. This means you can come back to that RAW file later and try different processing settings to achieve differing results and never harm the original image. By comparison, if you make a change to your JPEG and accidentally save the file, guess what? You have a new original file, and you will never get back to that first image. That alone should make you sit up and take notice.

Advice for new RAW shooters

Image resolution

When discussing digital cameras, image resolution is often used to describe pixel resolution, or the number of pixels used to make an image. Resolution can be displayed as a dimension such as 5472x3648. It is the physical number of pixels in width and height of the image sensor. Resolution can also be referred to in megapixels (MP) such as 20.2 MP. This number represents the number of total pixels on the sensor and is commonly used to describe the amount of image data that a digital camera can capture.

Don't give up on shooting RAW just because it means more work. Hey, if it takes up more space on your card, buy bigger cards. Will it take more time to download your images? Yes, but good things come to those who wait. Don't worry about needing to purchase expensive software to work with your RAW files, because you already own a program that will allow you to work with your RAW files. Canon's Digital Photo Professional software comes bundled in the box with your camera and gives you the ability to work directly on the RAW files, and then output the enhanced results.

My recommendation is that you shoot in JPEG mode while you are using this book. This will allow you to quickly review your images and study the effects of future lessons. Once you are comfortable with all of the camera features, you should switch to shooting in RAW mode so that you can start gaining more creative control over your image processing. After all, you took the photograph—shouldn't you be the one to decide how it looks in the end?

Selecting RAW + JPEG

Your camera has the added benefit of being able to write two files for each picture you take, one in RAW and one in JPEG. This capability can be useful if you need a quick version to email but want a higher-quality version for more advanced processing.

Keep in mind that using both formats requires more space on the memory card. I recommend that you use only one format or the other unless you have a specific need to shoot both, or have two memory cards where you can use one for the RAW files and the other for JPEGs.

Selecting your image-quality setting

1. Press the Menu button and use the Main dial to select the first shooting menu tab.
2. Use the Quick Control dial to highlight the Image Quality setting, and press the Set button to enter the settings page (**A**).
3. Use the Main dial to change the quality setting of the RAW file and the Quick Control dial to change the JPEG quality setting (**B**).

A

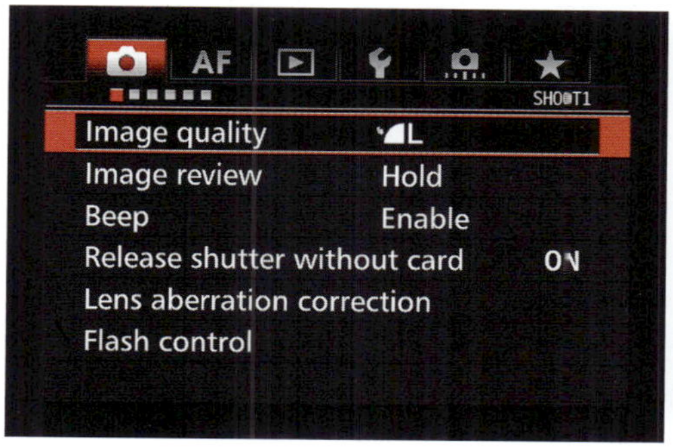

B

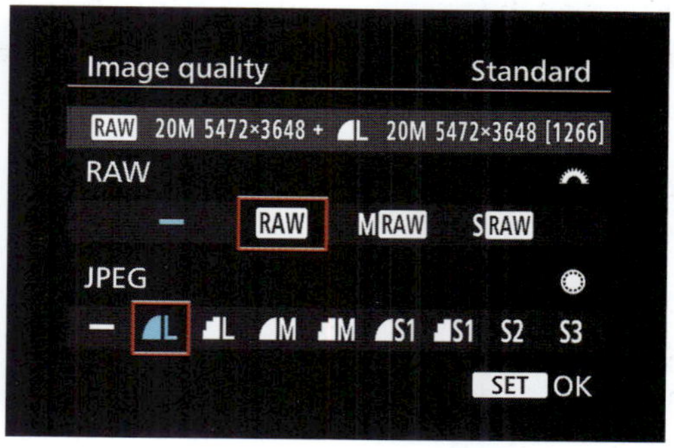

4. Press the Set button to lock in your changes (**C**).

C

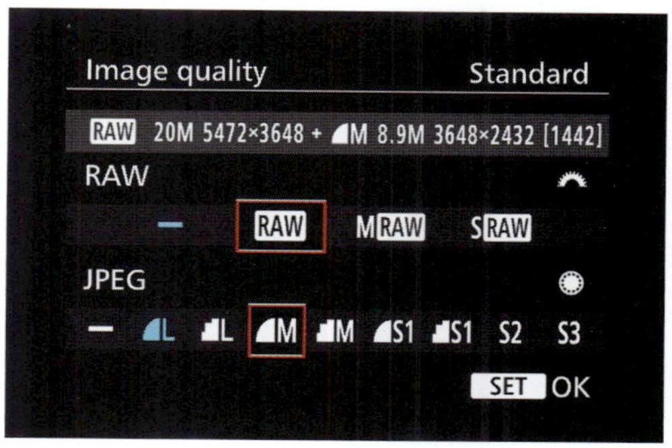

If you only want to capture a RAW file, you should change the JPEG quality to the dash. The same goes for the RAW setting. If the RAW option is set to the dash, you will only record JPEG files. If you have both the JPEG and RAW options set to something other than the dash, you will record both formats on your card. If you happen to set both options to the dash, setting the camera will default to a large JPEG format.

Previously, I mentioned that you could change the options for how your camera uses two memory cards. When I am shooting two formats, I like to split them between the two cards, using one for JPEG and one for RAW. To do this, you will need to make some menu adjustments and tell the camera how you want your files handled. This is a two-step process. The first step tells the camera that you want to record your two formats to different cards, and the second step assigns the formats to the two slots.

Setting up dual-slot recording

1. Press the Menu button and use the Main dial to select the first setup menu tab.
2. Use the Quick Control dial to highlight the Record Func+Card/Folder Sel. option, and press Set (**A**).
3. Using the Quick Control dial, select the Record Func. option, and press the Set button (**B**).

A

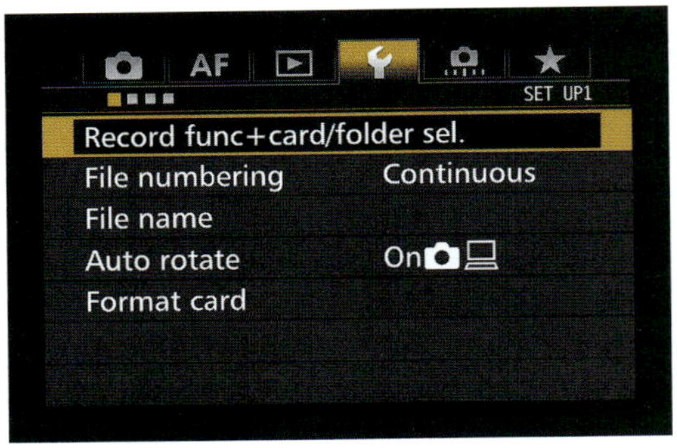

B

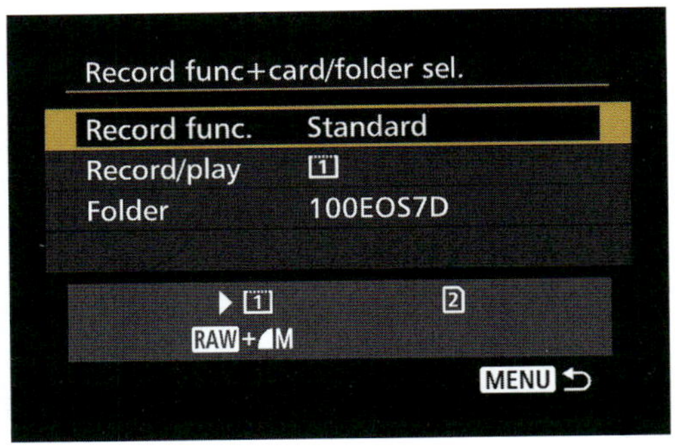

4. Select the Rec. Separately option, and press the Set button (**C**).

C

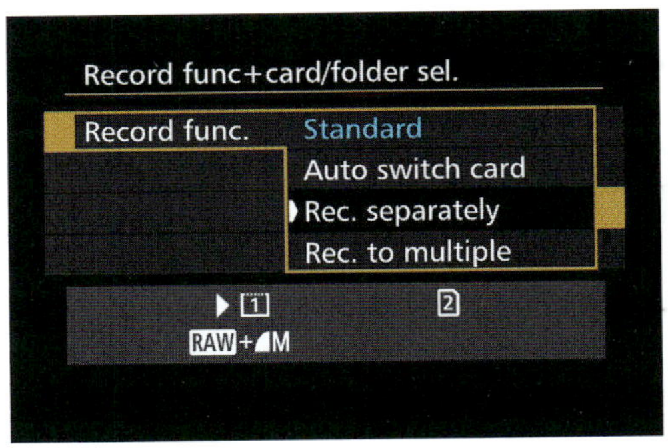

5. Now use the Main dial to go back to the first shooting menu and highlight the Image Quality setting, and then press Set (**D**).
6. In the next window, you will now see two card options. Choose card 1, and press the Set button (**E**).

D

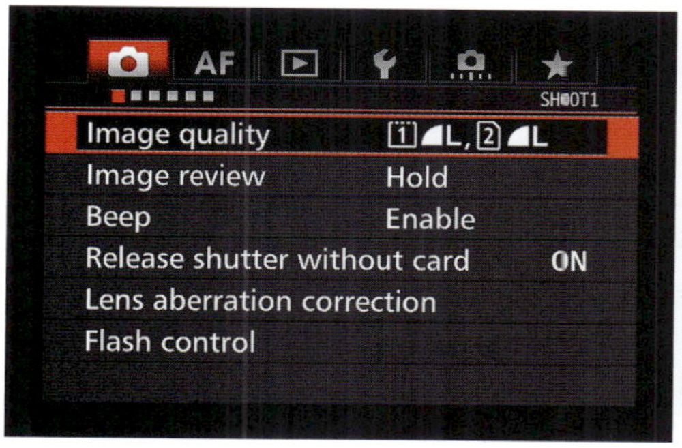

E

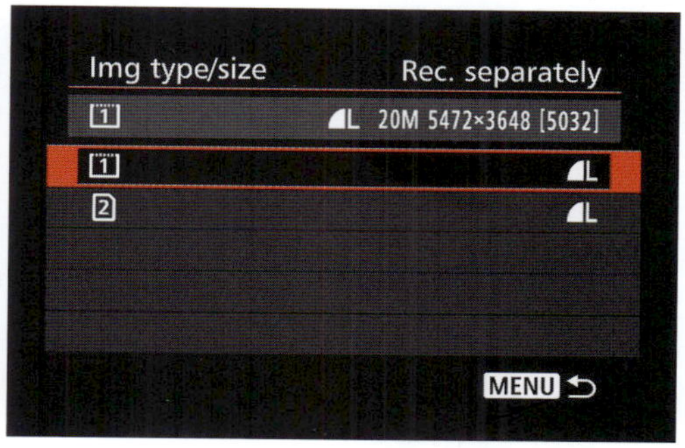

7. Using just the Quick Control dial, scroll through all of the quality options until you have the file format set to your desired choice. The choices will jump from JPEG to RAW as you turn the dial (**F**). Press Set to lock in your choice and go back to the slot selection screen.
8. Select slot 2 and repeat the previous step to choose the quality setting for the second card.
9. Once you are done selecting the quality options for both cards, press the Menu button to go back to the first setup menu screen, where you should now see your two cards with their different quality options displayed in the Image Quality section (**G**).

F

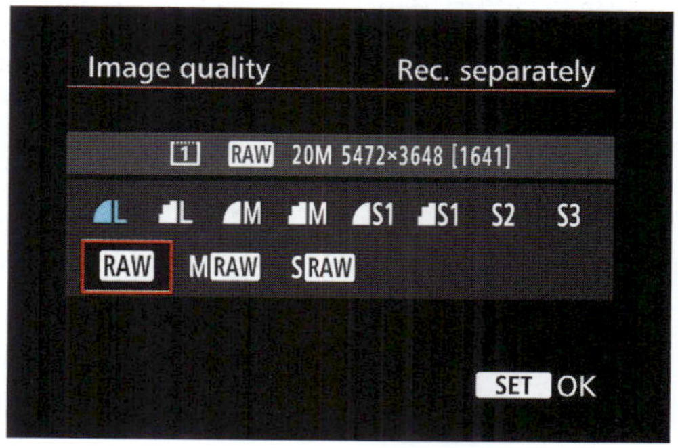

G

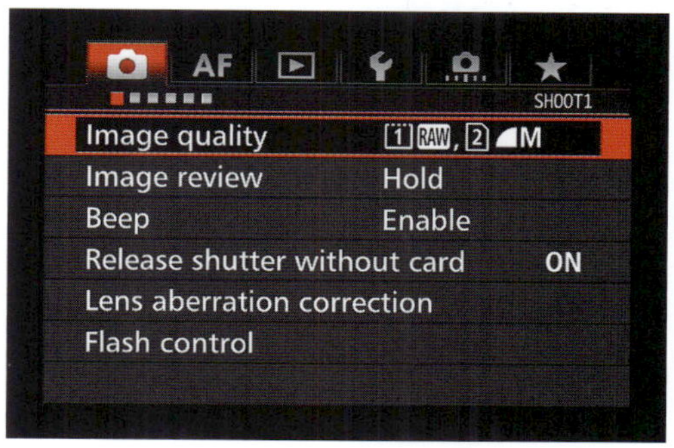

Lenses and Focal Lengths

If you ask most photographers what they believe to be their most critical piece of photographic equipment, they would undoubtedly tell you that it is their lens. The technology and engineering that goes into your camera is a marvel, but it isn't worth a darn if it can't get the light from the outside world onto the sensor. The 7D Mark II, as a digital single lens reflex (DSLR) camera, uses the lens for a multitude of tasks, from focusing on a subject, to metering a scene, to delivering and focusing the light onto the camera sensor. The lens is also responsible for the amount of the scene that will be captured (the frame). With all of this riding on the lens, let's take a more in-depth look at the camera's eye on the world.

Lenses are composed of optical glass that is both concave and convex in shape. The alignment of the glass elements is designed to focus the light coming in from the front of the lens onto the camera sensor. The amount of light that enters the camera is also controlled by the lens, the size of the glass elements, and the aperture mechanism within the lens housing. The quality of the glass used in the lens will also have a direct effect on how well the lens can resolve details and the contrast of the scene (the ability to deliver great highlights and shadows). Most lenses now routinely include things like the autofocus motor and, in some cases, an image-stabilization mechanism.

There is one other aspect of the camera lens that is often the first consideration of the photographer: lens focal length, which determines the angle of view delivered through the lens. Lenses are typically divided into three or four groups depending on the field of view they cover.

Wide-angle lenses cover a field of view from around 110 degrees to about 60 degrees (**Figure 2.3**). There is also a tendency to get some distortion in your image when using extremely wide-angle lenses. This will be apparent toward the outer edges of the frame. As for which lenses would be considered wide angle, anything 30mm or smaller could be considered wide.

Wide-angle lenses can display a large depth of field, which allows you to keep the foreground and background in sharp focus. This feature makes them useful for landscape photography. They also work well in tight spaces, such as indoors, where there isn't much elbow room available (**Figure 2.4**). They can also be handy for large group shots, but due to the amount of distortion, not so great for close-up portrait work.

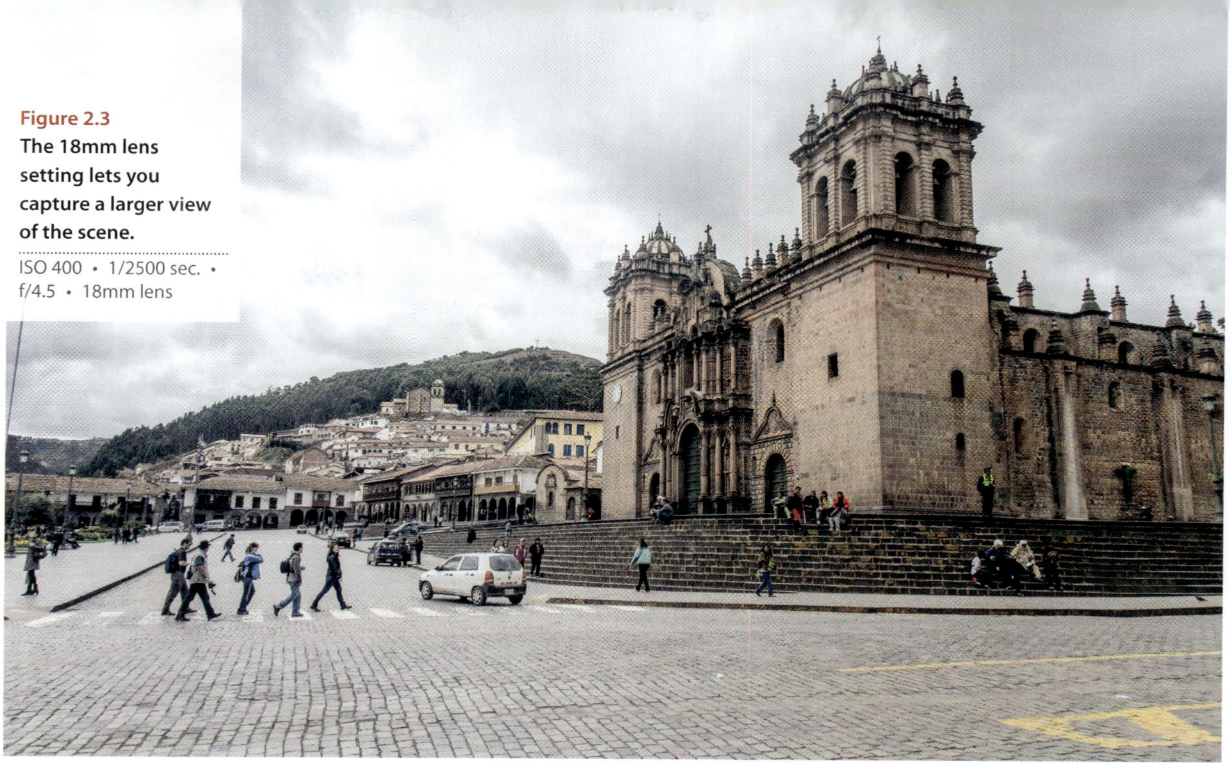

Figure 2.3
The 18mm lens setting lets you capture a larger view of the scene.

ISO 400 • 1/2500 sec. • f/4.5 • 18mm lens

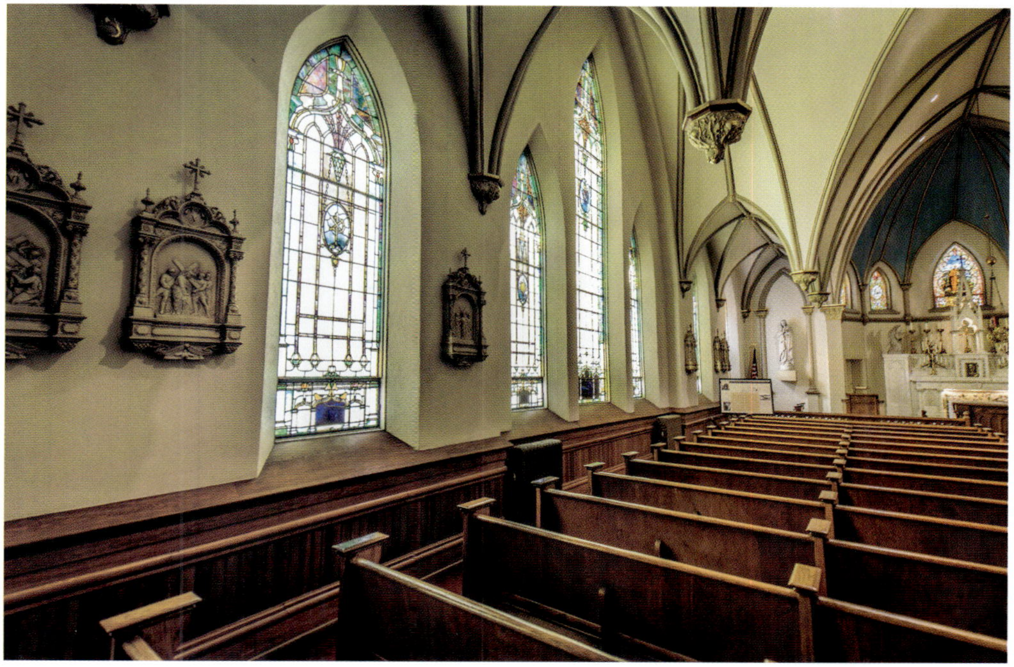

Figure 2.4
When shooting in tight spaces where you want to capture a large subject, a nice wide-angle lens helps capture more of the scene.

ISO 100 • 1/10 sec. • f/3.5 • 18mm lens

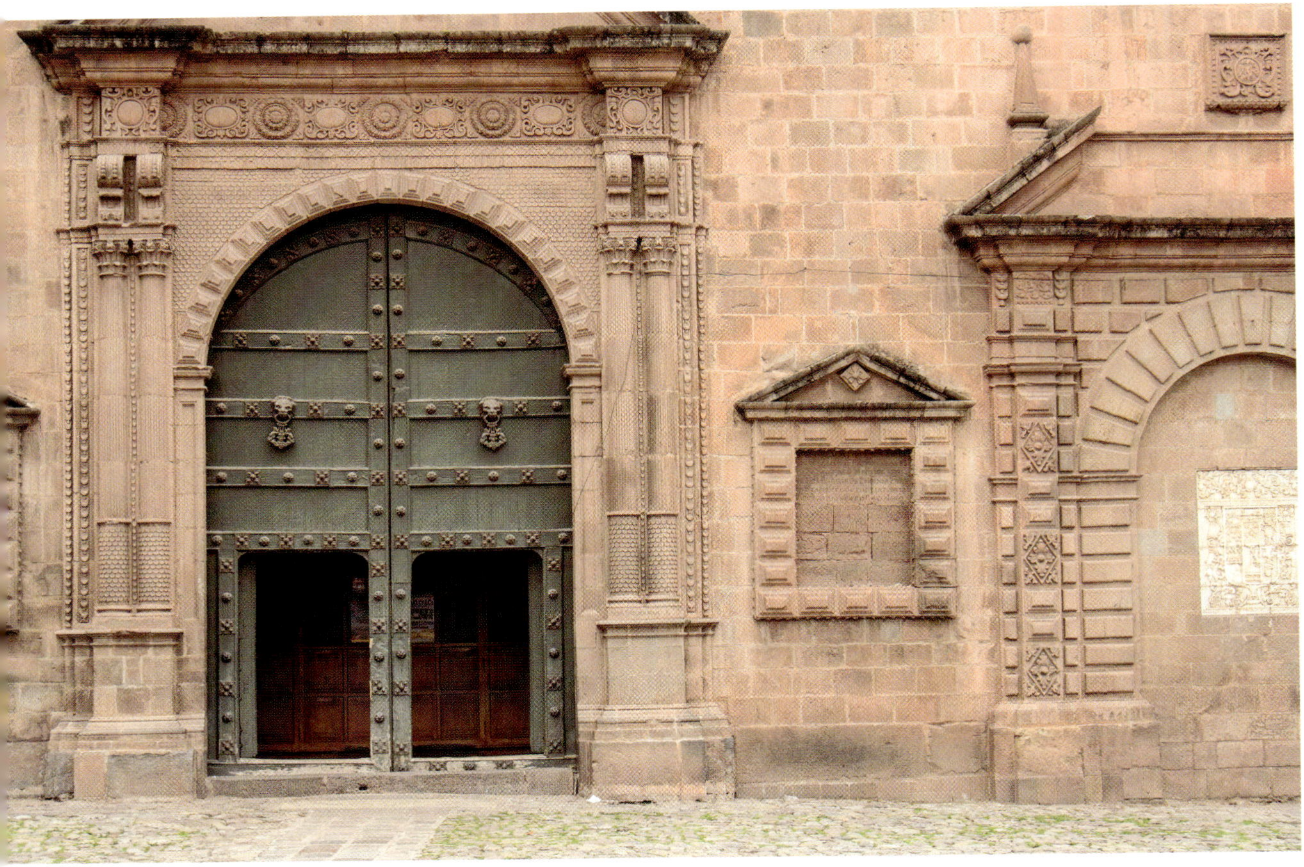

Figure 2.5

Long considered the "normal" lens for 35mm photography, the 50mm focal length can be considered somewhat of a telephoto lens on the 7D Mark II, because it has the same angle of view and magnification as an 80mm lens on a 35mm camera body.

ISO 400 • 1/250 sec. • f/7.1 • 50mm lens

A *normal* lens has a field of view that is about 45 degrees and delivers approximately the same view as the human eye (not in angle of view but in size and perspective of subjects). The perspective is very natural and there is little distortion in objects. The normal lens for full-frame and 35mm cameras is the 50mm lens, but for the 7D Mark II it is more in the neighborhood of a 35mm lens (**Figure 2.5**).

Normal focal-length lenses are useful for photographing people, architecture, and most other general photographic needs. They have very little distortion and offer a moderate range of depth of field (**Figure 2.6**).

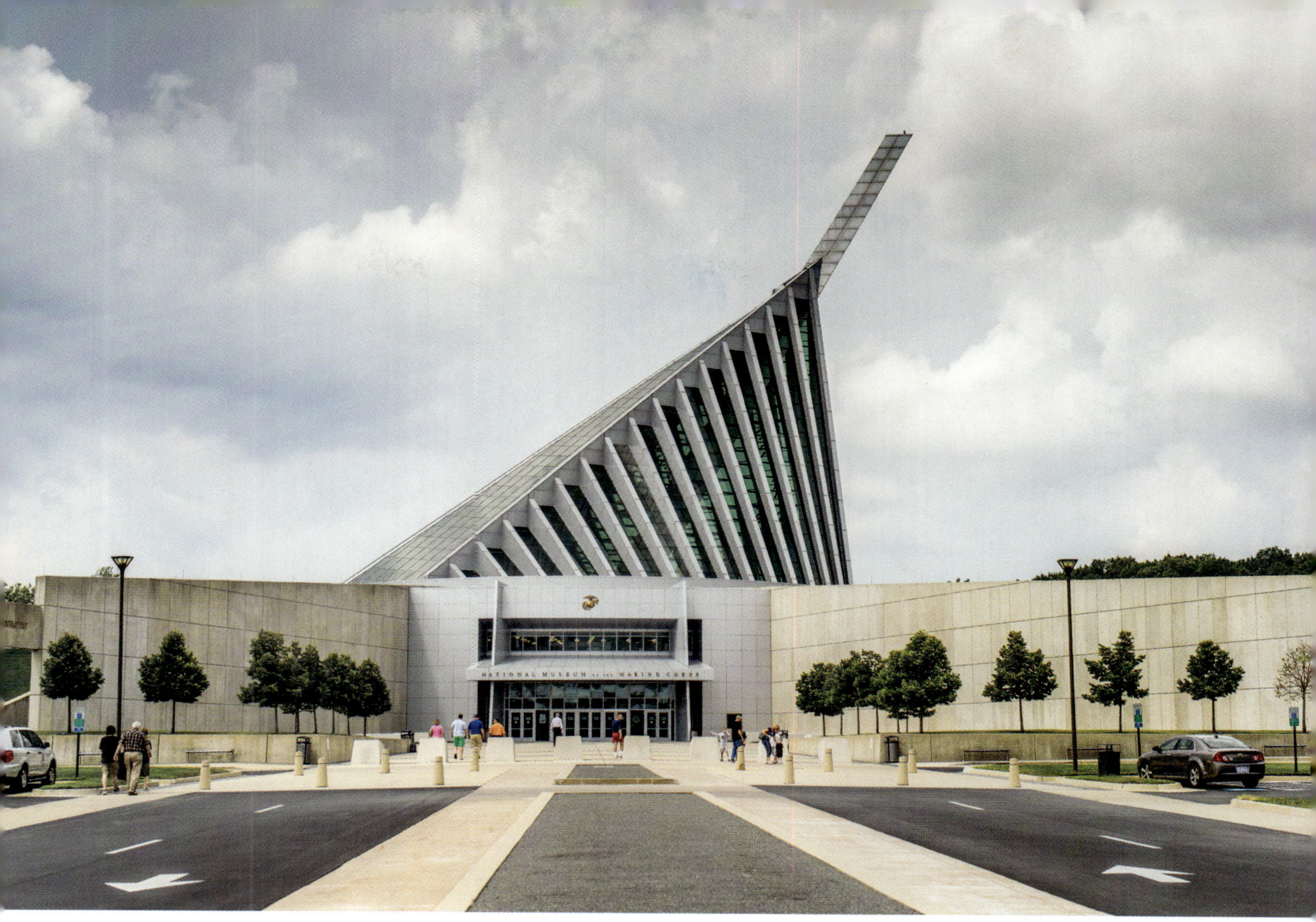

Figure 2.6
The normal lens worked well in this image by providing just the right amount of coverage to capture the architecture of the Marine Corps Museum.

ISO 100 • 1/1600 sec. • f/4 • 55mm lens

Most longer focal-length lenses are referred to as *telephoto* lenses. They can range in length from 100mm up to 800mm or longer, and have a field of view that is about 35 degrees or smaller. These lenses have the ability to greatly magnify the scene, allowing you to capture details of distant objects, but the angle of view is greatly reduced (**Figure 2.7**). You will also find that you can achieve a much narrower depth of field. They also demonstrate something called *distance compression*, which means they make objects at different distances appear to be much closer together than they really are.

Telephoto lenses are most useful for sports photography or any application where you just need to get closer to your subject (**Figure 2.8**). They can have a compressing effect—making objects look closer together than they actually are—and a very narrow depth of field when shot at their widest apertures.

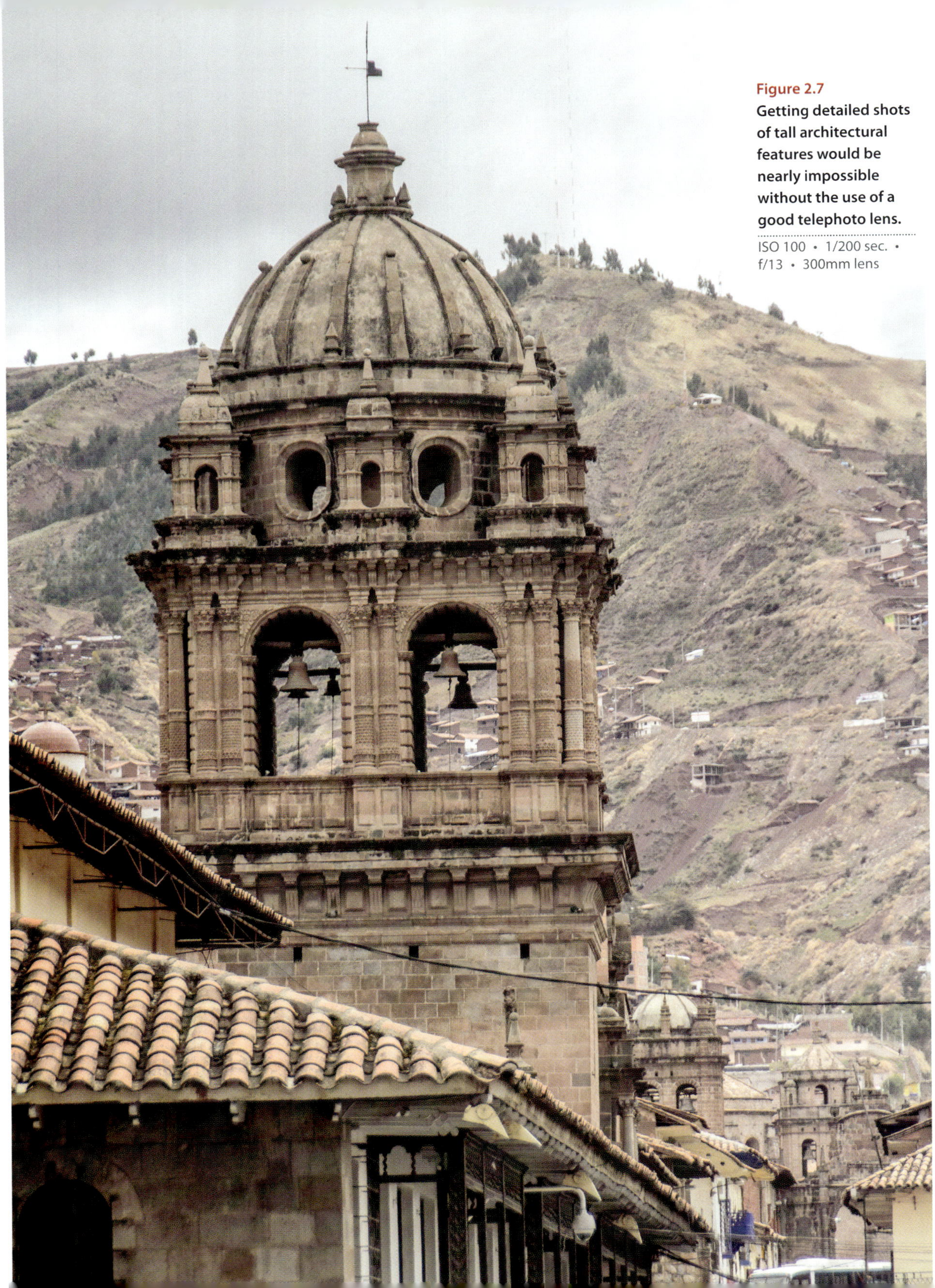

Figure 2.7
Getting detailed shots of tall architectural features would be nearly impossible without the use of a good telephoto lens.

ISO 100 • 1/200 sec. • f/13 • 300mm lens

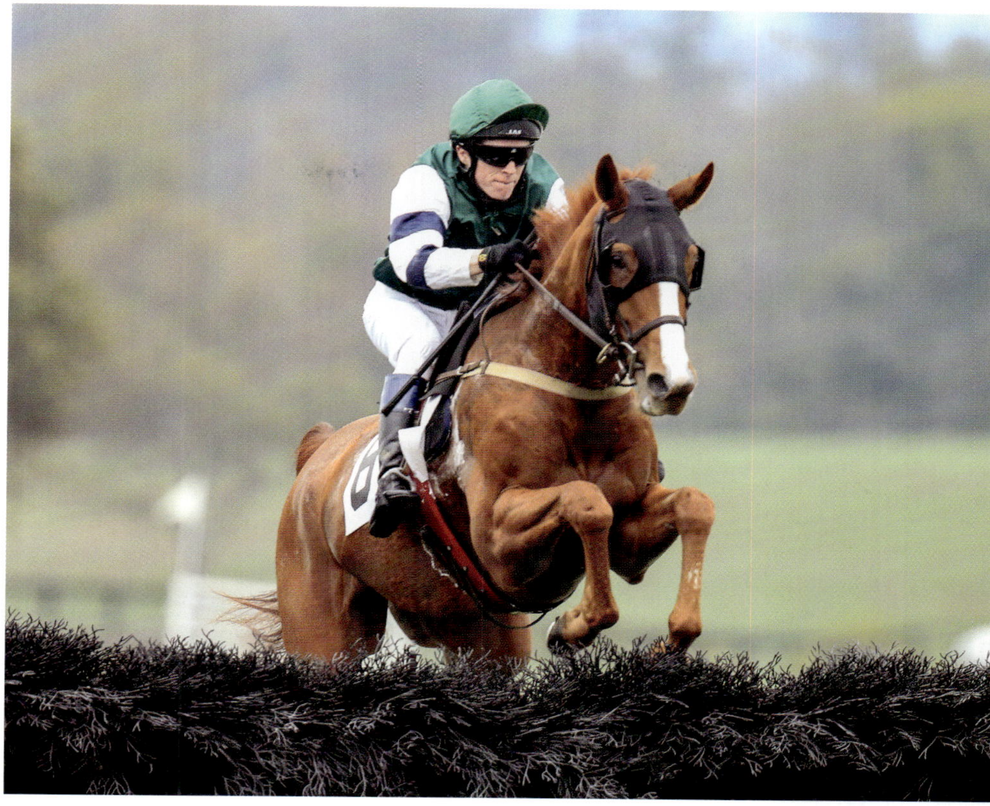

Figure 2.8
The long telephoto lens allowed me to capture the close-up action of the horse and rider going over the jump, while keeping a safe distance from the action.

ISO 1000 • 1/1000 sec. • f/2.8 • 300mm lens

A *zoom* lens is a great compromise to carrying a bunch of single focal-length lenses (also referred to as "prime" lenses). They can cover a wide range of focal lengths because of the configuration of their optics. However, because it takes more optical elements to capture a scene at different focal lengths, the light must pass through more glass on its way to the image sensor. The more glass, the lower the quality of the image sharpness. The other sacrifice that is made is in aperture. Zoom lenses typically have smaller maximum apertures than prime lenses, which means they cannot achieve a very narrow depth of field or work in lower light levels without the assistance of image stabilization, a tripod, or higher ISO settings. (We'll discuss all this in more detail in later chapters.)

The 7D Mark II can be purchased with the body only, but many folks will purchase it with a kit lens. The most common kit lens is the 18–135mm IS STM f/3.5–5.6. Another great lens option for the 7D Mark II is the 18–200mm EF-S IS lens. It is a great all-around lens that provides a range of focal lengths from the very wide to the medium telephoto. Combine that with some great image stabilization, and you have what I like to call the perfect vacation lens. Unfortunately, it is not available as a kit lens at the moment, but it should definitely be considered if you are thinking of adding a new lens to your camera bag.

What Is Exposure?

In order for you to get the most out of this book, I need to briefly discuss the principles of exposure. Without this basic knowledge, it will be difficult for you to move forward in improving your photography. For our purposes, I will just cover some of the basics of exposure. This will give you the essential tools to make educated decisions in determining how best to photograph a subject.

So what is exposure? It is the process whereby the light reflecting off a subject reflects through an opening in the camera lens for a defined period of time onto the camera's sensor. The combination of the lens opening, shutter speed, and sensor sensitivity is used to achieve a proper exposure value (EV) for the scene. The EV is the sum of these components necessary to properly expose a scene. A relationship exists between these factors that is sometimes referred to as the *exposure triangle*.

At each point of the triangle lies one of the factors of exposure:

- **ISO:** Determines the sensitivity of the camera sensor. ISO stands for the International Organization for Standardization, but the acronym is used as a term to describe the sensitivity of the camera sensor to light. The higher the sensitivity setting, the less light is required for a good exposure. These values are a carryover from the days of traditional color and black-and-white films.
- **Aperture:** Also referred to as the f-stop, this determines how much light passes through the lens at once.
- **Shutter Speed:** Controls the length of time that light is allowed to hit the sensor.

So here's how it all comes together. The camera sensor has a level of sensitivity that is determined by the ISO setting. To get a proper exposure—not too much, not too little—the lens needs to adjust the aperture diaphragm (the size of the lens opening) to control the volume of light entering the camera. Then the shutter is opened for a relatively short period of time to allow the light to hit the sensor long enough for it to record on the sensor.

ISO numbers for the 7D Mark II start at 100, and then double in sensitivity as you double the number. So 200 is twice as sensitive as 100. The camera can be set to use half- or third-of-a-stop increments, but for ISO, just remember that the base numbers double: 100, 200, 400, 800, and so on. There is also a wide variety of shutter speeds that you can use in achieving a proper exposure. The speeds on the 7D Mark II range from as long as 30 seconds to as short as 1/8000 of a second. When using the camera, you will not see the 1 over the number while looking through the viewfinder or the top LCD screen, so you will need to remember that anything shorter than a full second will be a fraction. However, the shutter speed is displayed as a fraction when looking at the rear LCD display. Typically, you will be working with a shutter speed range from around 1/30 of a second to about 1/2000, but these numbers will change depending on your circumstances and the effect that you are trying to achieve. The lens apertures will vary slightly depending on which lens you are using. This is due to the differing maximum apertures for each lens. The typical apertures at your disposal are f/4, f/5.6, f/8, f/11, f/16, and f/22.

When it comes to exposure, a change to any one of these factors can require changing one or more of the other two. This is referred to as a reciprocal change. If you let more light in the lens by choosing a larger aperture opening, you will need to shorten the amount of time the shutter is open. If the shutter is allowed to stay open for a longer period of time, the aperture needs to be smaller to restrict the amount of light coming in. If you want to use a faster shutter speed and the lens is already at the largest aperture, you will need to raise the ISO setting to a higher number.

How is exposure calculated?

You now know about the exposure triangle—ISO, shutter speeds, and aperture—so it's time to put all three together to see how they relate to one another and how you can change them as needed.

When you point your camera at a scene, the light reflecting off your subject enters the lens and is allowed to pass through to the sensor for a period of time as dictated by the shutter speed. The amount and duration of the light needed for a proper exposure depends on how much light is being reflected and how sensitive the sensor is. To figure this out, your camera uses a very sophisticated built-in light meter that looks through the lens and measures the amount of light. That level is then calculated against the sensitivity of the ISO setting and an exposure value is rendered. Here's the tricky part: There's more than one way to achieve a perfect exposure, because the f-stop and shutter speed can be combined in various ways to allow the same amount of exposure. See, I told you it was tricky.

Stop

You will hear the term *stop* thrown around all the time in photography. It relates back to the f-stop, which is a term used to describe the aperture opening of your lens. When you need to give some additional exposure, you might say that you are going to "add a stop." This doesn't just equate to the aperture; it could also be used to describe the shutter speed or even the ISO. So when your image is too light or dark, or you have too much movement in your subject, you will probably be changing things by a "stop" or two.

Here is a list of reciprocal settings that would all produce the same exposure result. Let's use the "sunny 16" rule, which states that, when using f/16 on a sunny day, you can use a shutter speed that is roughly equal to the ISO setting to achieve a proper exposure. For simplification purposes, we will use an ISO of 100.

Reciprocal Exposures: ISO 100							
F-STOP	2.8	4	5.6	8	11	16	22
SHUTTER SPEED	1/4000	1/2000	1/1000	1/500	1/250	1/125	1/60

If you were to use any one of these combinations, each would have the same result in terms of the exposure (that is, how much light hits the camera's sensor). Also take note that every time we cut the f-stop in half, we reciprocated by doubling our shutter speed. For those of you wondering why f/8 is half of f/5.6, it's because those numbers are actually fractions based on the opening of the lens in relation to its focal length. This means that a lot of math goes into figuring out just what the total area of a lens opening is, so you just have to take it on faith that f/8 is half of f/5.6 but twice as much as f/11. A good way to remember which opening is larger is to think of your camera lens as a pipe that controls the flow of water. If you have a pipe that is 1/2 inches in diameter (f/2) and one that was 1/8 of an inch (f/8), which would allow more water to flow through? It would be the 1/2-inch pipe. The same idea works here with the camera f-stops: f/2 is a larger opening than f/4 or f/8 or f/16.

Now that you know this, you can start using this information to make intelligent choices in terms of shutter speed and f-stop. Let's bring the third element into this by changing our ISO by one stop, from 100 to 200.

Reciprocal Exposures: ISO 200							
F-STOP	2.8	4	5.6	8	11	16	22
SHUTTER SPEED	1/8000	1/4000	1/2000	1/1000	1/500	1/250	1/125

Notice that, since we doubled the sensitivity of the sensor, we now require half as much exposure as before.

So why not just use the exposure setting of f/16 at 1/250 of a second? Why bother with all of these reciprocal values when this one setting will give us a properly exposed image? The answer is that the f-stop and shutter speed also control two other important aspects of our image: motion and depth of field.

Motion and Depth of Field

There are distinct characteristics that are related to changes in aperture and shutter speed. Shutter speed controls the length of time the light has to strike the sensor; consequently, it also controls the blurriness (or lack of blurriness) of the image. The less time light has to hit the sensor, the less time your subjects have to move around and become blurry. This can let you control things like freezing the motion of a fast-moving subject (**Figure 2.9**) or intentionally blurring subjects to give the feel of energy and motion (**Figure 2.10**).

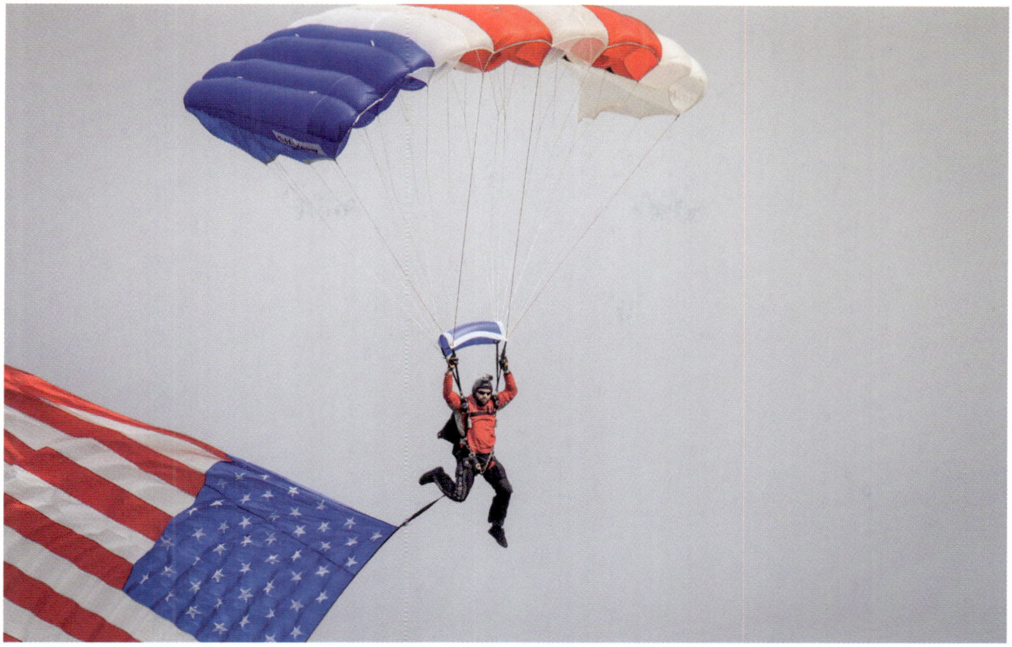

Figure 2.9
A fast shutter speed was used to freeze the action of the parachutist as he prepared to land.

ISO 400 • 1/8000 sec. • f/4 • 420mm lens

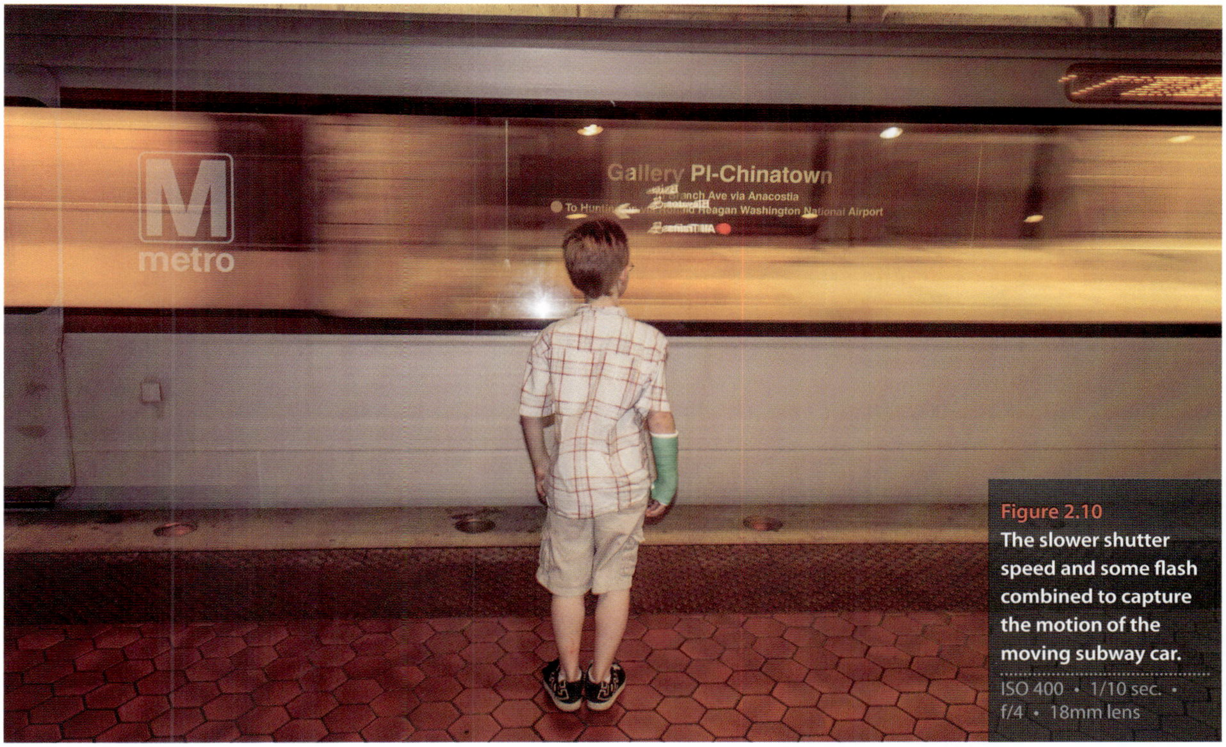

Figure 2.10
The slower shutter speed and some flash combined to capture the motion of the moving subway car.

ISO 400 • 1/10 sec. • f/4 • 18mm lens

Figure 2.11
A small aperture kept the image in focus from the grass to the distant windmill.

ISO 400 • 1/60 sec. • f/22 • 46mm lens

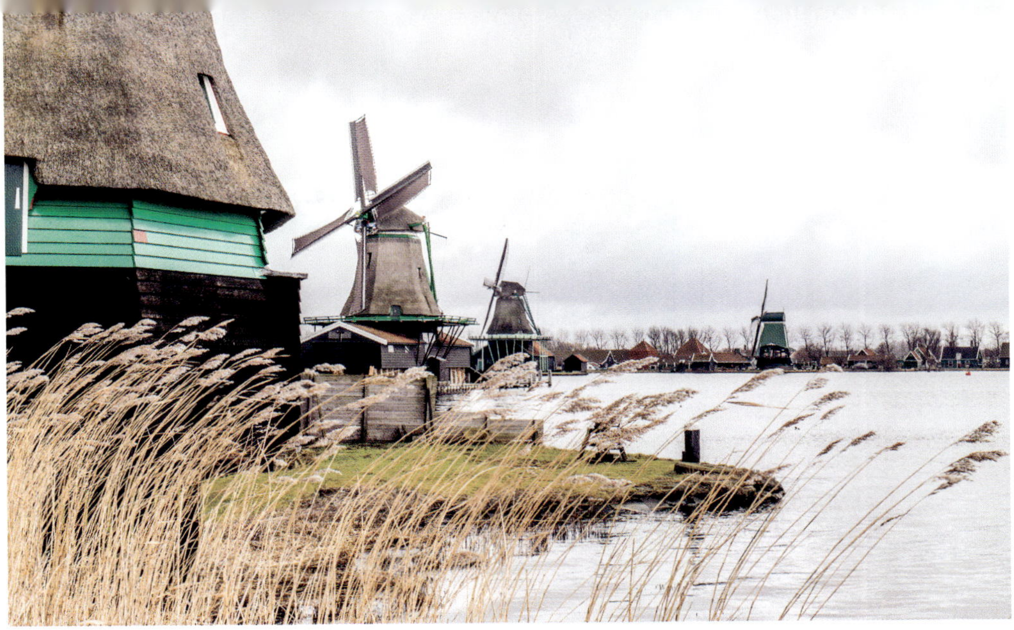

The aperture controls the amount of light that comes through the lens but also determines what areas of the image will be in focus. This is referred to as *depth of field*, and it is an extremely valuable creative tool. The smaller the opening is (the larger the number such as f/22), the greater the sharpness of objects from near to far will be (**Figure 2.11**).

A large opening (or small number, like f/2.8) means more blurring of objects that are not at the same distance from the camera as the subject you are focusing on (**Figure 2.12**).

As we further explore the features of the camera, you will learn not only how to use the elements of exposure to capture properly exposed photographs, but also how you can make adjustments to emphasize your subject. It is the manipulation of these elements—motion and focus—that will take your images to the next level.

Figure 2.12
By using a large aperture setting, I was able to isolate these desert flowers from the background.

ISO 400 • 1/800 sec. • f/1.4 • 50mm lens

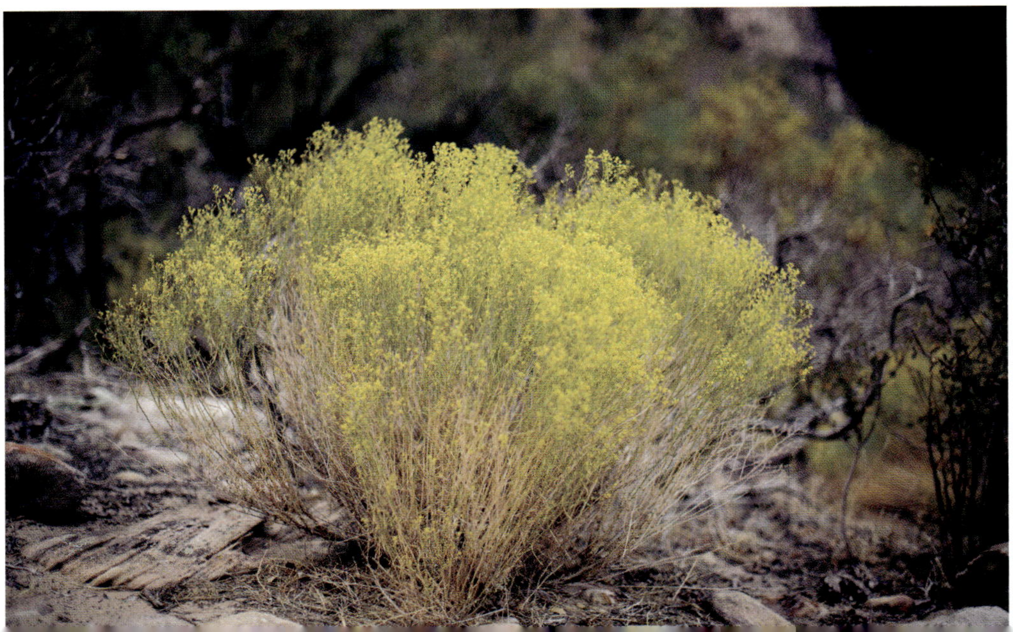

Chapter 2 Assignments

Now it's time for a little pre-shooting housekeeping. Taking care of these little things will keep your camera and your shooting shipshape for years to come.

Formatting your card

Even if you have already begun using your camera, make sure you are familiar with formatting the memory card. If you haven't done so already, follow the directions given earlier in the chapter and format as described (make sure you save any images that you may have already taken). Then perform the Format function every time you have downloaded or saved your images or use a new card.

Checking your firmware version

Using the most up-to-date version of the camera firmware will ensure that your camera is functioning properly. Use the menu to find your current firmware version, and then update as necessary using the steps listed in this chapter.

Cleaning your sensor

You probably noticed the sensor-cleaning message the first time you turned on your camera. Make sure you are familiar with the Clean Now command so you can perform this function every time you change a lens.

Exploring your image formats

I want you to become familiar with all of the camera features before using the RAW format, but take a little time to explore the Format menu so you can see what options are available to you.

Exploring your lens

If you are using a zoom lens, spend a little time shooting with all of the various focal lengths, from the widest to the longest. See just how much of an angle you can cover with your widest lens setting. How much magnification will you be able to get from the telephoto setting? Try shooting the same subject with a variety of focal lengths to note the differences in how the subject looks, and also note the relationship between the subject and the other elements in the photo.

Share your results with the book's Flickr group!
Join the group here: flickr.com/groups/7dmarkii_fromsnapshotstogreatshots

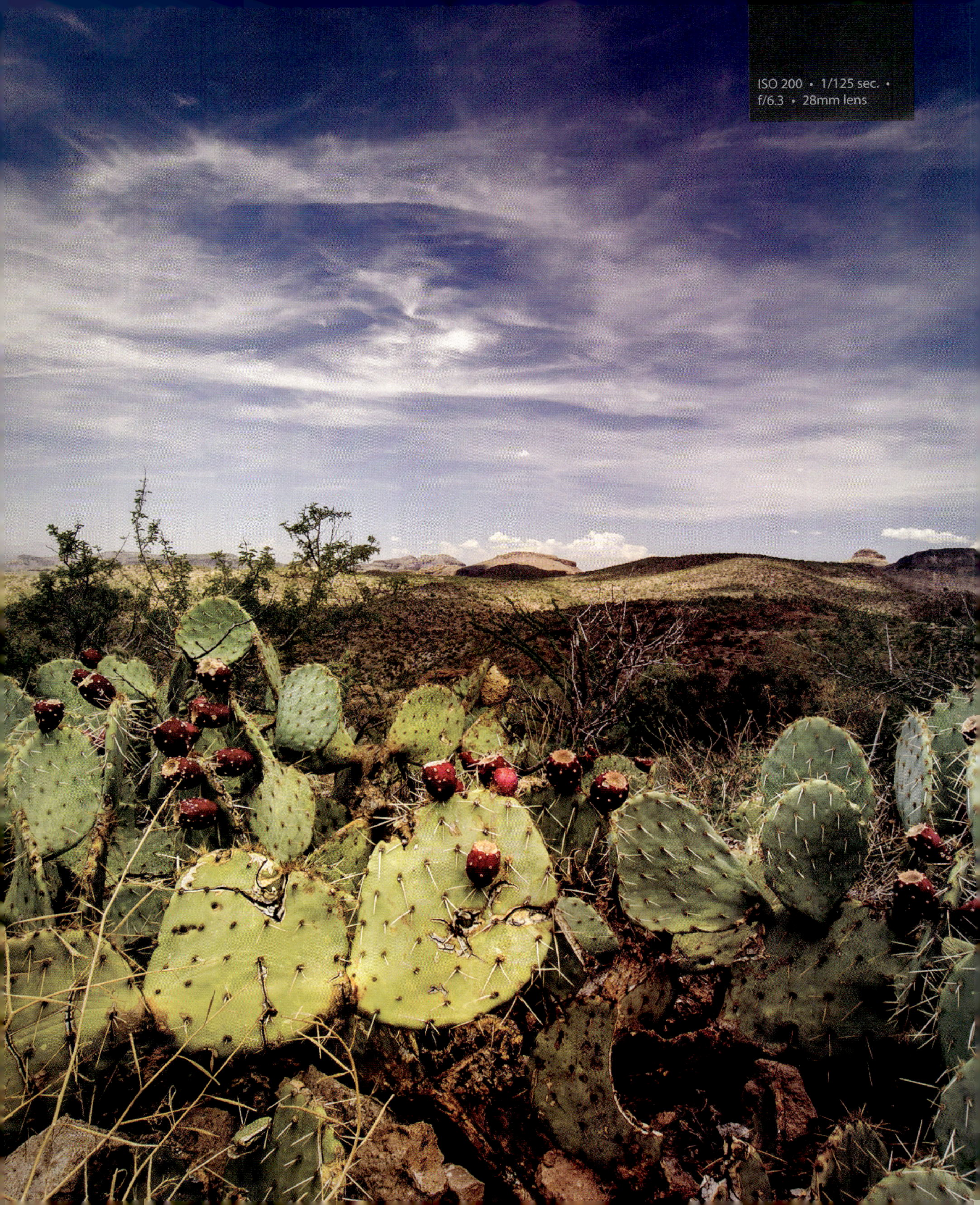

ISO 200 • 1/125 sec. • f/6.3 • 28mm lens

3

Camera Shooting Modes

Taking Your Photography to the Next Level

If you moved up to the 7D Mark II from a more amateur DSLR or even a point-and-shoot camera, you might have noticed a lack of icons on the mode dial. If you are looking for that little portrait, or the running figure, or that cute little flower, you can stop looking, because this is one serious camera. Those little icons were handy, but they can also be a crutch that keeps you from getting total control over your photography. Instead of using a sports mode, you can choose your own shutter speeds and control the action the way you see fit. Instead of using the little mountain mode for landscapes, you can pick the right aperture, ISO, and even color enhancements to create the perfect image. All the tools are there. All you need to do is learn how they work and start making decisions. Canon has always called the nonautomatic modes the Creative Zone because this is where you get to let your creativity soar. Don't feel like you're quite ready to soar on your own? Well, fear not, because Canon left you a little something called Intelligent Auto to fall back on while you are learning. So let's kick those icons to the curb and start getting creative.

Poring Over the Picture

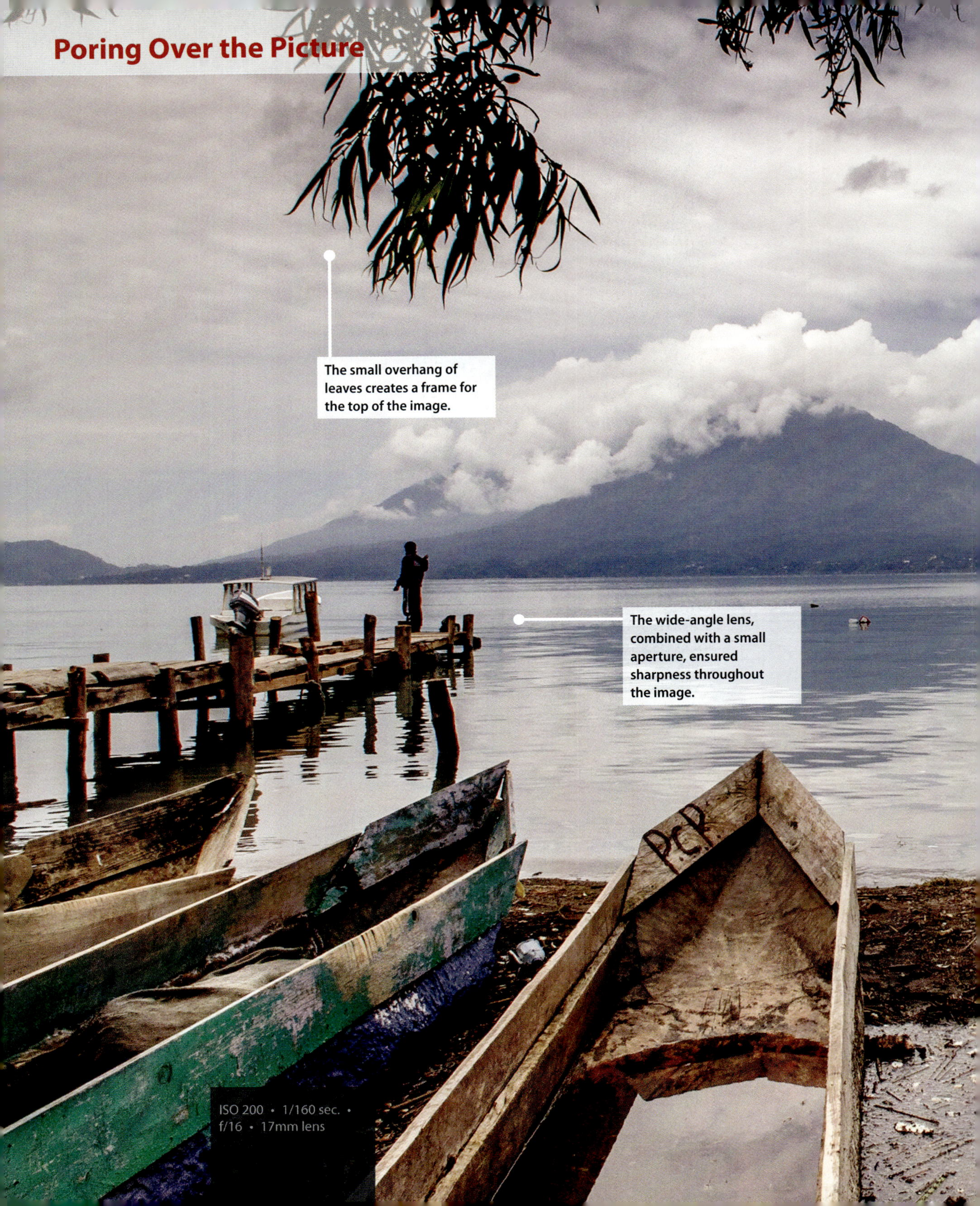

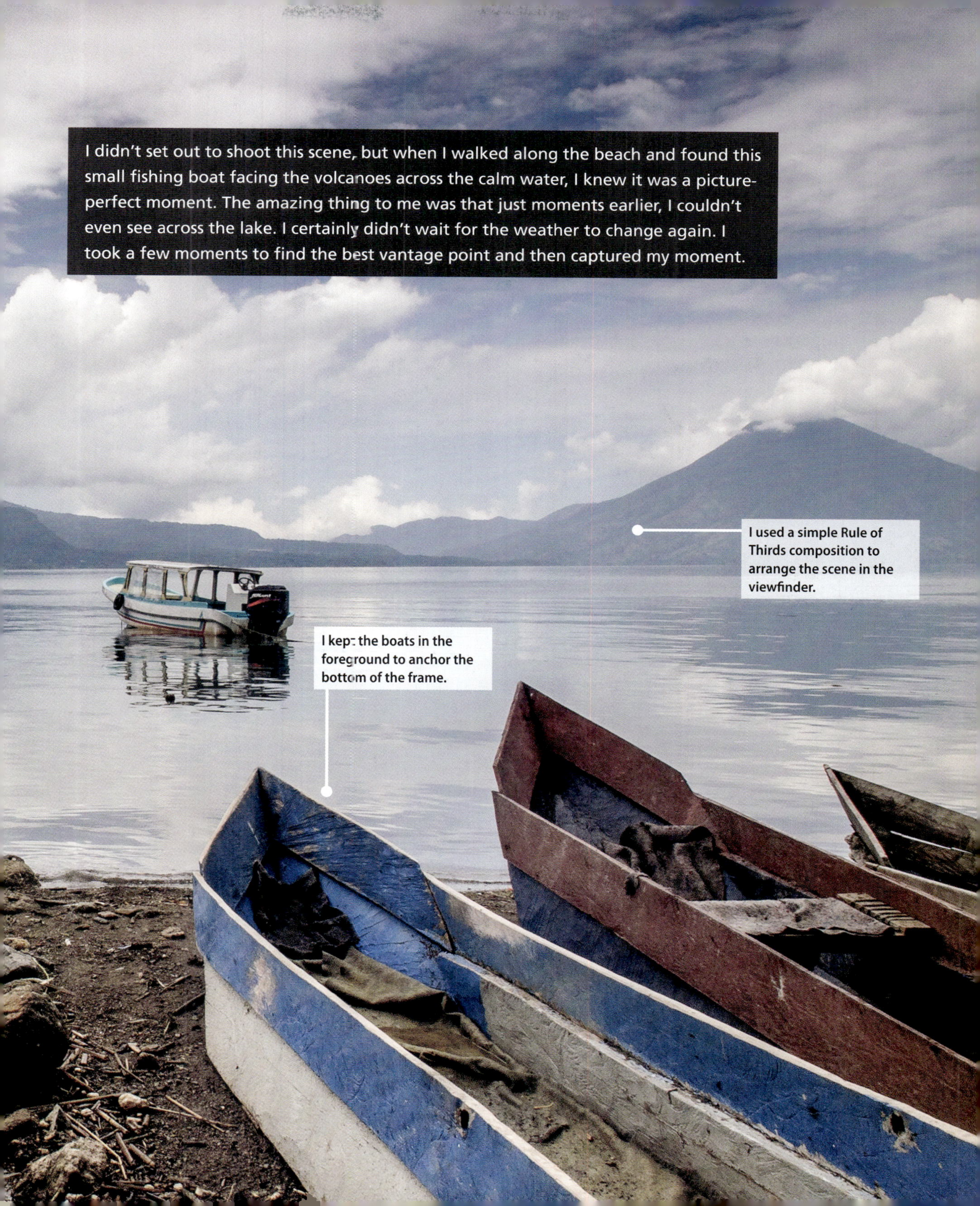

I didn't set out to shoot this scene, but when I walked along the beach and found this small fishing boat facing the volcanoes across the calm water, I knew it was a picture-perfect moment. The amazing thing to me was that just moments earlier, I couldn't even see across the lake. I certainly didn't wait for the weather to change again. I took a few moments to find the best vantage point and then captured my moment.

Scene Intelligent Auto Mode

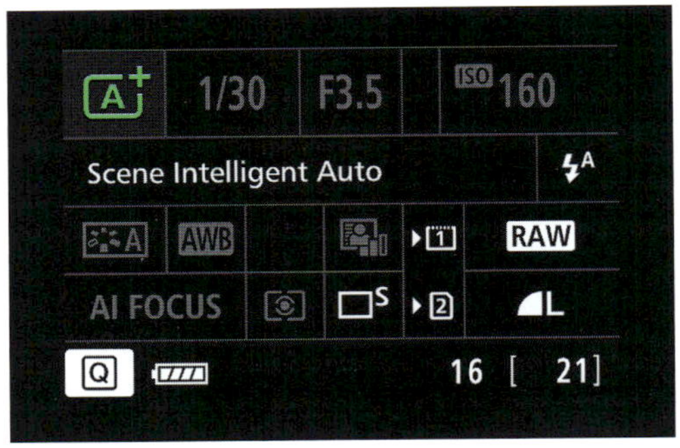

Figure 3.1
Scene Intelligent Auto mode.

Scene Intelligent Auto mode is all about thought-free photography. There is little to nothing for you to do in this mode except point and shoot. Your biggest concern when using Scene Intelligent Auto mode is focusing. The camera will use the automatic focusing modes to achieve the best possible focus for your picture. Naturally, the camera assumes that the object closest to the camera is the one that you want to have the sharpest focus. Simply press the shutter button halfway down while looking through the viewfinder, and you should see one of the focus points light up over the subject. Of course, putting your subject in the middle of the picture is not always the best way to compose your shot. So wait for the chirp to confirm that the focus has been set, and then, while still holding down the button, recompose your shot. Just press the shutter button down the rest of the way to take the photo. It's that easy (**Figure 3.1** and **Figure 3.2**). The camera will take care of all your exposure decisions, including when to use flash.

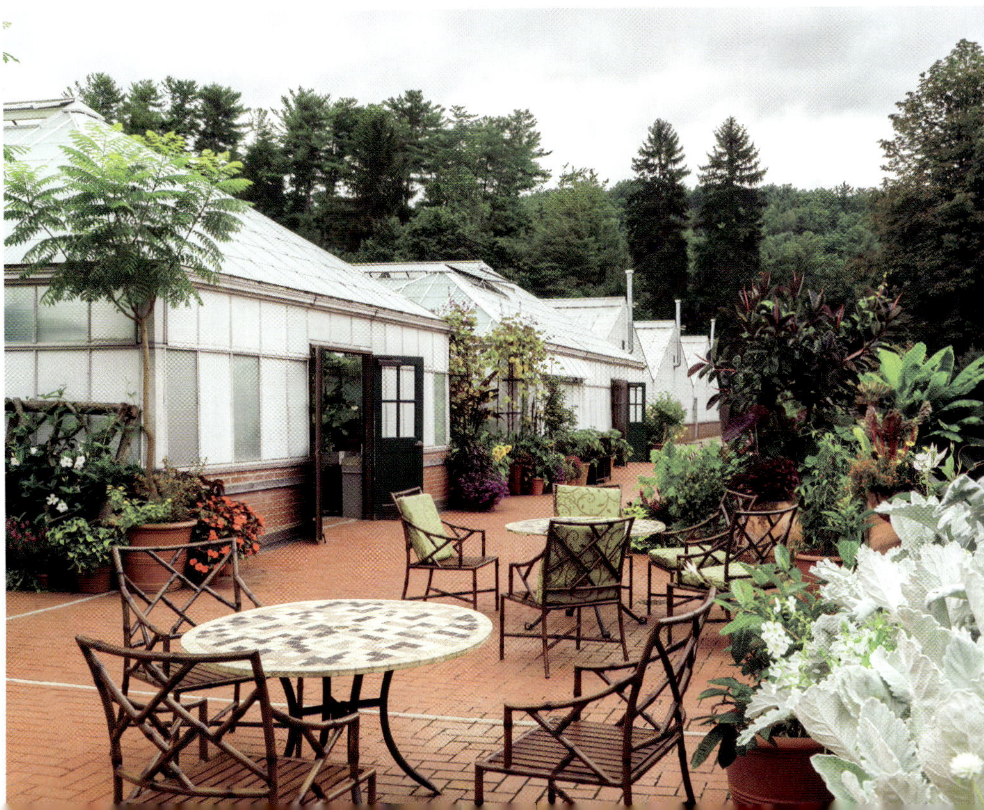

Figure 3.2
Scene Intelligent Auto mode works great when you don't want to think too much and just want to snap some shots, like when I was strolling through this lovely garden area.

ISO 1000 • 1/200 sec. • f/9 • 30mm lens

You do have a couple of options that can be changed while using this mode: whether or not you want to use the single, continuous, or self-timer drive mode; which mode the flash will be set to (Auto, On, or Off); and what file format you want to use. To change the drive mode, press the Drive button on top of the camera, and then use the Quick Control dial to select Single, High Speed Continuous, Low Speed Continuous, or Self-timer mode. The self-timer has two options to choose from depending on your needs. The first is 10 Second/Remote. Using this option will give you a 10-second countdown before the shutter is active, which should be enough time for you to run around and get in the photo. You can also set the camera in this mode if you are going to be using the RC-6 wireless remote (sold separately). If you are looking for a shorter delay, try using the 2-second self-timer option. I like to use this for shooting longer exposures on a tripod because it lets me activate the camera without having my hands on it. This helps to eliminate camera shake. You will also see two additional modes that are basically the same as continuous and single, but they are in the silent mode, as indicated by the small "s" over the icon. These drive modes allow you to shoot the camera with a little less noise. They aren't exactly silent, but they are a bit quieter and would be nice for occasions like plays or weddings.

Let's face it: This is the lazy person's mode. But sometimes it's just nice to be lazy and click away without giving thought to anything but preserving a memory. There are times, though, when you will want to start using your camera's advanced features that are tailored to specific shooting environments. That's where the Creative modes come into play.

P: Program Mode

There is a reason that Program mode is only one click away from the Scene Intelligent Auto mode: With respect to apertures and shutter speeds, the camera is doing most of the thinking for you. So, if that is the case, why bother with Program mode? First, let me say that I will rarely use Program mode because it just doesn't give as much control over the image-making process as the other Creative modes. There are occasions, however, when it comes in handy, like when I'm shooting in widely changing lighting conditions and I don't have time to think through all my options, or when I'm not concerned with having ultimate control of the scene. Think of an outdoor picnic in partial shade/sun. You want great-looking pictures, but you aren't looking for anything to hang in a museum. If that's the scenario, why choose Program over the Scene Intelligent Auto mode? Because it gives you choices and control that the Auto mode just can't deliver.

Manual Callout

To see a comparison of all of the different modes in the Basic and Creative zones, check out the tables on pages 480–481 of your owner's manual.

When to use Program (P) mode

Here's a guide to help you decide when to use Program (P) mode instead of the Basic zone modes:

- When shooting in a casual environment where quick adjustments are needed
- When you want control over the ISO
- If you want to use exposure compensation
- If you want to make corrections to the white balance
- If you want to make adjustments to your flash exposure
- If you want or need to shoot in the Adobe RGB color space

Let's return to our picnic scenario. The light is moving from deep shadow to bright sunlight, which means that the camera is trying to balance your three photo factors (ISO, aperture, and shutter speed) to make a good exposure. From Chapter 1, "The 7D Mark II Top Ten List," you know that Auto ISO is just not a consideration, so you have already turned that feature off (you did change it, didn't you?). Well, in Program mode, you can choose which ISO you would like the camera to base its exposure on. The lower the ISO number, the better the quality of your photographs, but the less light sensitive the camera becomes. It's a balancing act, with the main goal always being to keep the ISO as low as possible—too low an ISO, and you will get camera shake in your images from a long shutter speed; too high an ISO means you will have an unacceptable amount of digital noise. Go ahead and select ISO 400 so that you provide enough sensitivity for those shadows, while allowing the camera to use shutter speeds that are fast enough to stop motion.

Starting points for ISO selection

There is a lot of discussion concerning ISO in this and other chapters, but it might be helpful if you know where your starting points should be for your ISO settings. The first thing you should always try to do is use the lowest-possible ISO setting. That being said, here are some good starting points for your ISO settings:

- 100: Bright sunny day
- 200: Hazy or outdoor shade on a sunny day
- 400: Indoor lighting at night or cloudy conditions outside
- 800: Late night, low-light conditions or sporting arenas at night

These are just suggestions, and your ISO selection will depend on a number of factors that will be discussed later in the book. You might have to push your ISO even higher as needed, but at least now you know where to start.

With the ISO selected, you can now make use of the other controls built into Program mode. By rotating the Main dial, you now have the ability to shift the program settings. Remember, your camera is using the internal light meter to pick what it believes are suitable exposure values, but sometimes it doesn't know what it's looking at and how you want those values applied (**Figure 3.3** and **Figure 3.4**). With the program shift, you can influence what the shot will look like. Do you need faster shutter speeds in order to stop the action? Just turn the Main dial clockwise. Do you want a smaller aperture so that you get a larger depth of field? Then turn the dial counterclockwise until you get the desired aperture. The camera shifts the shutter speed and aperture accordingly in order to get a proper exposure, and you will get the benefit of your choice as a result.

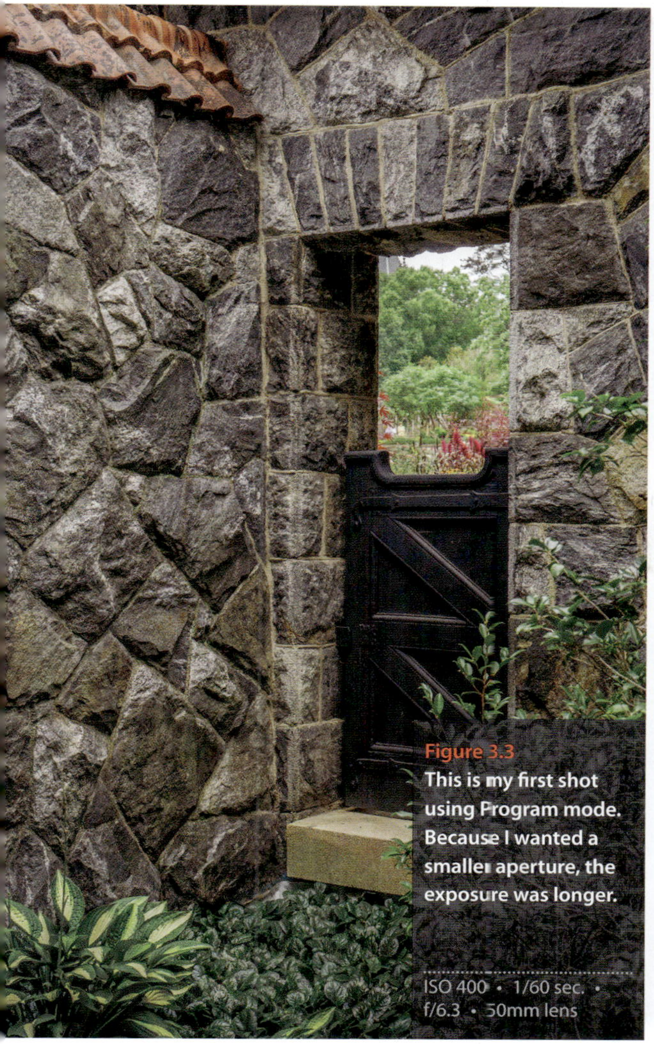

Figure 3.3
This is my first shot using Program mode. Because I wanted a smaller aperture, the exposure was longer.

ISO 400 • 1/60 sec. • f/6.3 • 50mm lens

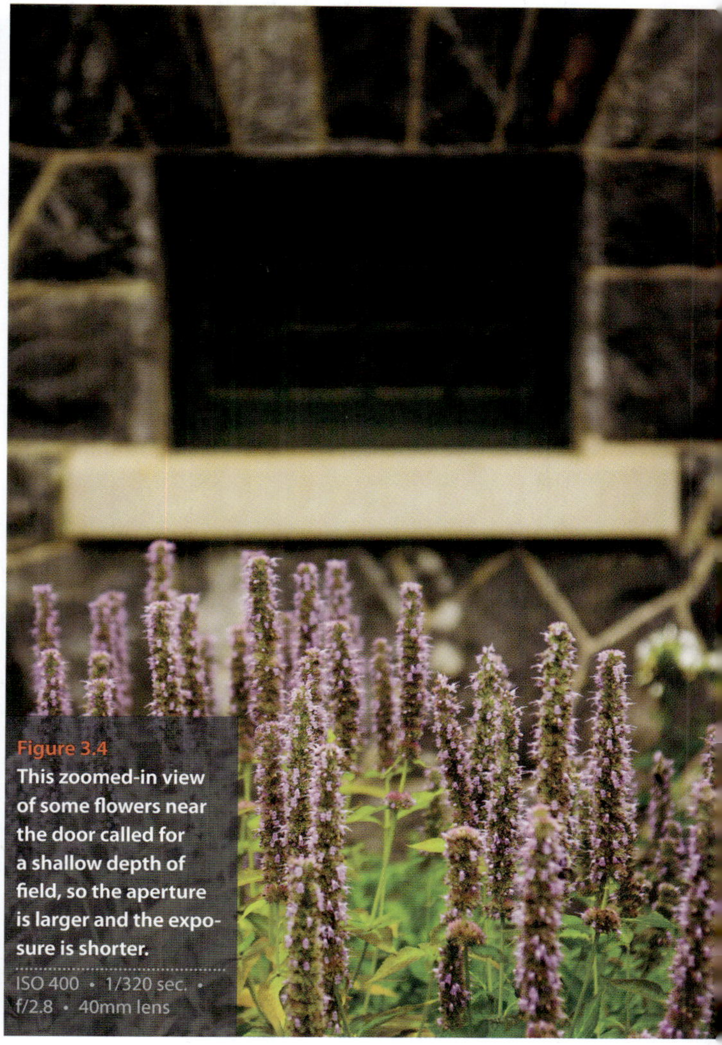

Figure 3.4
This zoomed-in view of some flowers near the door called for a shallow depth of field, so the aperture is larger and the exposure is shorter.

ISO 400 • 1/320 sec. • f/2.8 • 40mm lens

Let's set up the camera for Program mode and see how you can make all of this come together.

Setting up and shooting in Program mode

1. Turn your camera on, and then press the button on top of the mode dial and turn to align the P with the indicator line.
2. Select your ISO by pressing the ISO button on top of the camera and then turning the Main dial to the desired setting. Then press the ISO button again (the ISO selection will appear in the rear LCD panel).
3. Point the camera at your subject, and then activate the camera meter by depressing the shutter button halfway.
4. View the exposure information in the bottom of the viewfinder or by looking at the display panel on the back of the camera.
5. While the meter is activated, use your index finger to roll the Main dial left and right to see the changed exposure values.
6. Select the exposure that is right for you and start shooting. (Don't worry if you aren't sure what the right exposure is. We will start working on making the right choices for those great shots beginning with the next chapter.)

Tv: Shutter Priority Mode

> **Shutter speeds**
>
> A *slow* shutter speed refers to leaving the shutter open for a long period of time—like 1/30 of a second or longer. A *fast* shutter speed means that the shutter is open for a very short period of time—like 1/250 of a second or less.

Tv mode is what most photographers refer to as Shutter Priority mode. If you dig deep in your manual, you will actually see that Tv stands for Time Value. I'm not sure who came up with this term, but I can tell you that it wasn't a photographer. In all my years of shooting, I don't ever recall thinking, "Hey, this would be a great situation to use the Time Value mode." However, you don't need to know why it is called Tv mode; the important thing is to know why and when to use it.

Just as with Program mode, Tv mode gives you more freedom to control certain aspects of your photography. In this case, I'm talking about shutter speed. The selected shutter speed determines just how long you expose your camera's sensor to light. The longer it remains open, the more time your sensor has to gather light. The shutter speed also, to a large degree, determines how sharp your photographs are. This is different from the image being sharply in focus. One of the major influences on the sharpness of an image is camera shake as well as the subject's movement. Because a slower shutter speed means that light from your subject is hitting the sensor for a longer period of time, any movement by you or your subject will show up in your photos as blur.

When to use Shutter Priority (Tv) mode

Here's a guide to help you decide when to use Shutter Priority (Tv) mode:

- When working with fast-moving subjects where you want to freeze the action (**Figure 3.5**); you'll learn more about this in Chapter 4, "Moving Target."
- When you want to emphasize movement in your subject with motion blur (**Figure 3.6**).

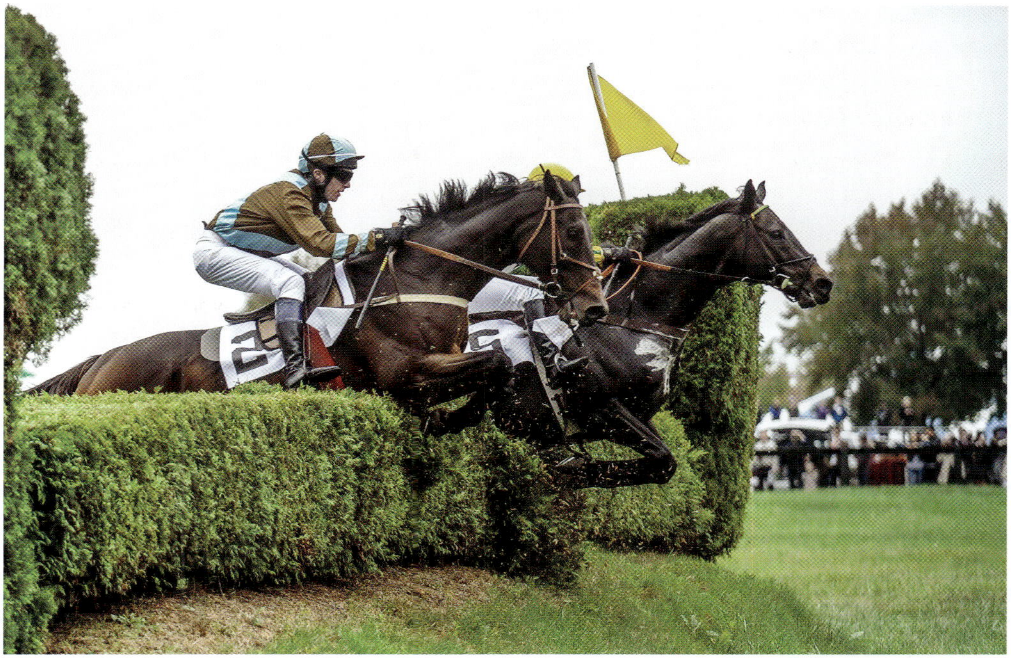

Figure 3.5
The steeplechase riders were frozen at the peak of action with a fast shutter speed.

ISO 640 • 1/2000 sec. • f/2.8 • 120mm lens

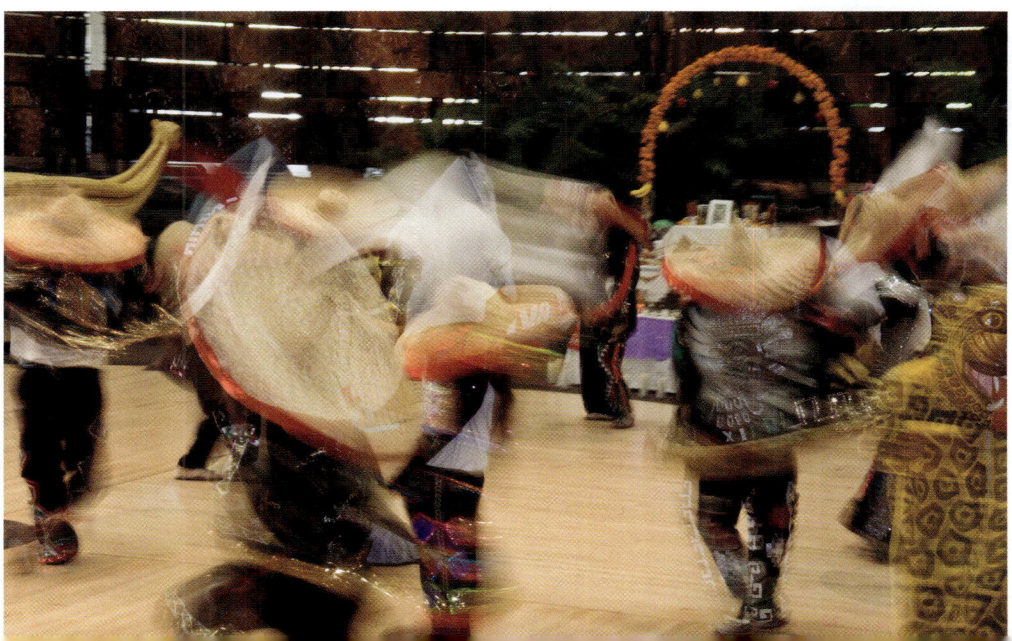

Figure 3.6
Slowing down the shutter speed allows your photographs to convey a sense of movement.

ISO 1600 • 1/8 sec. • f/18 • 52mm lens

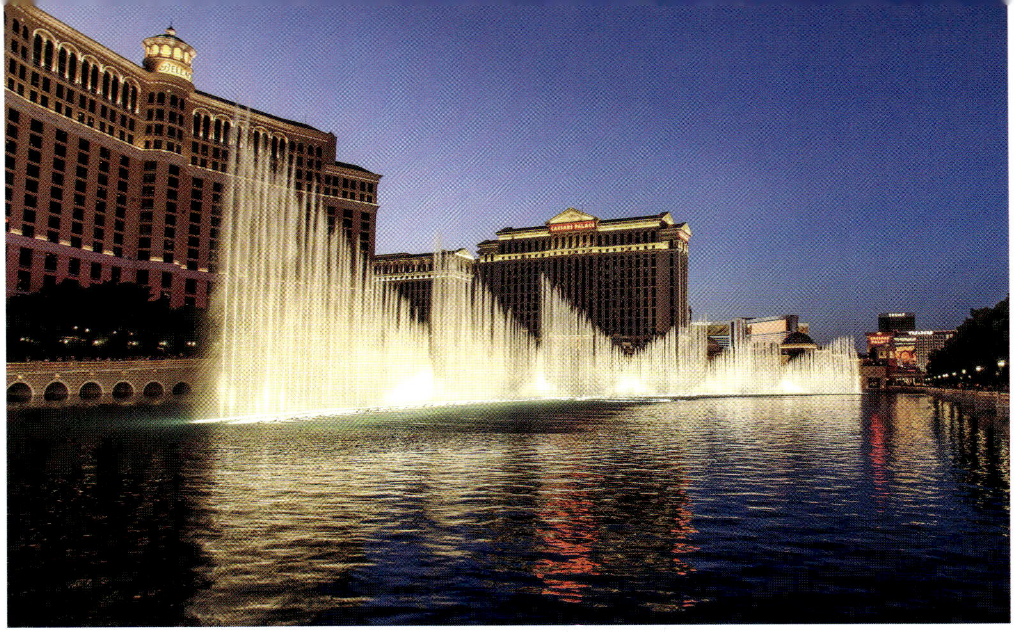

Figure 3.7
A long exposure and a steady tripod helped capture this view of the water show in Las Vegas.

ISO 400 • 1/8 sec. • f/5.6 • 15mm lens

- When you want to use a long exposure to gather light over a long period of time (**Figure 3.7**); you'll learn more about this in Chapter 7, "Mood Lighting."
- When you want to create that silky-looking water in a waterfall or fountain (**Figure 3.8**).

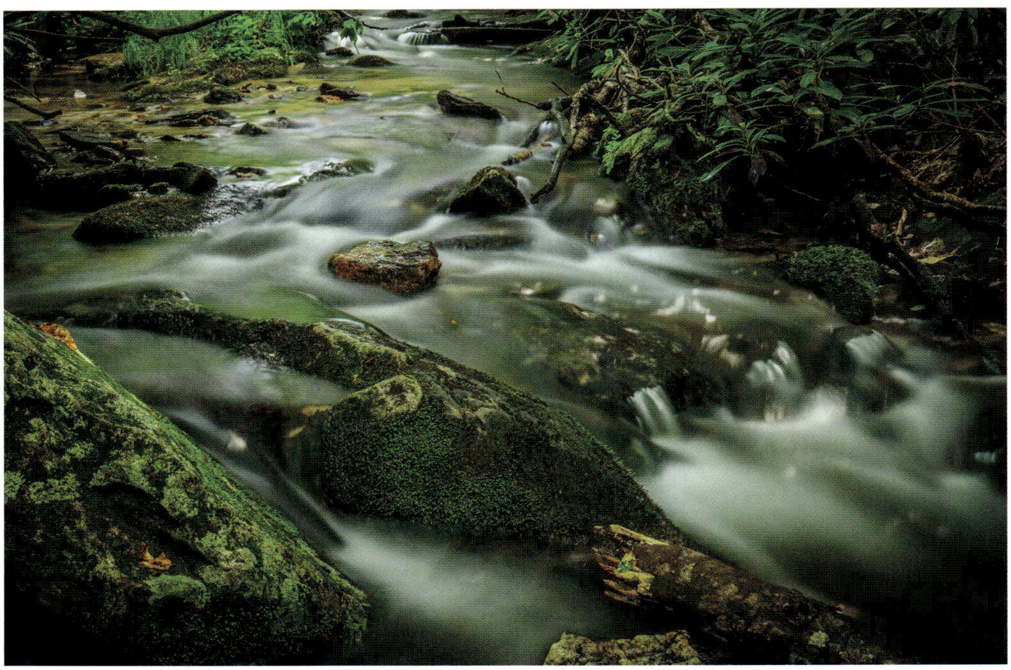

Figure 3.8
Increasing the length of the exposure time gives flowing water a silky look.

ISO 100 • 10 sec. • f/16 • 50mm lens

As you can see, the subject of your photo usually determines whether you will use Tv mode. You must be able to visualize the result of using a particular shutter speed. The great thing about shooting with digital cameras is that you get instant feedback by checking your shot on the LCD screen. But what if your subject won't give you a do-over? Such is often the case when shooting sporting events. It's not like you can go ask the quarterback to throw that touchdown pass again because your last shot was blurry from a slow shutter speed. This is why it's important to know what those speeds represent in terms of their abilities to stop the action and deliver a blur-free shot.

First, let's examine just how much control you have over the shutter speeds. The 7D Mark II has a shutter speed range from 1/8000 of a second all the way down to 30 seconds. With that much latitude, you should have enough control to capture almost any subject. The other thing to think about is that Tv mode is considered a "semiautomatic" mode. This means that you are taking control over one aspect of the total exposure while the camera handles the other. In this instance, you are controlling the shutter speed and the camera is controlling the aperture. This is important to know because there will be times when you want to use a particular shutter speed but your lens won't be able to accommodate your request.

For example, you might encounter this problem when shooting in low-light situations: If you're shooting a fast-moving subject that will blur at a shutter speed slower than 1/125 of a second but the largest aperture of your lens is f/3.5, you might see that your aperture display in your viewfinder and the rear LCD panel will begin to blink. This is your warning that there won't be enough light available for the shot—due to the limitations of the lens—so your picture will be underexposed (too dark).

Another case where you might run into this situation is when you are shooting moving water. To get that look of silky, flowing water, you'll usually find it necessary to use a shutter speed of at least 1/15 of a second, if not longer. If your waterfall is in full sunlight, you may get that blinking aperture display once again, because the lens you are using only closes down to f/22 at its smallest opening. In this instance, your camera is warning that you will be overexposing your image (too light). Workarounds exist for these problems, and we will discuss them later (see Chapter 5, "Landscape Photography"), but you should know that there can be limitations when you're using Tv mode.

Setting up and shooting in Tv mode

1. Turn your camera on, and then turn the mode dial to align the Tv with the indicator line.
2. Select your ISO by pressing the ISO button on top of the camera and then turning the Main dial (the ISO selection will appear in the rear LCD panel).

3. Point the camera at your subject, and then activate the camera meter by depressing the shutter button halfway.
4. View the exposure information in the bottom area of the viewfinder or by looking at the rear LCD panel.
5. While the meter is activated, use your index finger to roll the Main dial left and right to see the changed exposure values. Roll the dial to the right for faster shutter speeds and to the left for slower speeds.

Av: Aperture Priority Mode

You wouldn't know it from its name, but Av mode is one of the most useful and popular modes in the Creative Zone. Av stands for Aperture Value and, like Time Value, it's another term that you'll seldom hear a photographer toss around. The mode is one of my personal favorites, though, and I believe that it will quickly become one of yours as well. Av, more commonly referred to as Aperture Priority mode, is also deemed a semiautomatic mode because it allows you to once again control one factor of exposure while the camera adjusts for the other.

Why, you may ask, is this one of my favorite modes? It's because the aperture of your lens dictates depth of field. Depth of field, along with composition, is a major factor in how you direct attention to what is important in your image. It is the controlling factor of how much area in your image is in focus. If you want to isolate a subject from the background, such as when shooting a portrait, you can use a large aperture to keep the focus on your subject and make both the foreground and background blurry. If you want to keep the entire scene sharply focused, such as with a landscape scene, then using a small aperture will render the greatest amount of depth of field possible.

When to use Aperture Priority (Av) mode

Here's a guide to help you decide when to use Aperture Priority (Av) mode:

- When shooting portraits or wildlife (**Figure 3.9**)
- When shooting most landscape photography (**Figure 3.10**)
- When shooting macro, or close-up, photography (**Figure 3.11**)
- When shooting architectural photography, which often benefits from a large depth of field (**Figure 3.12**)

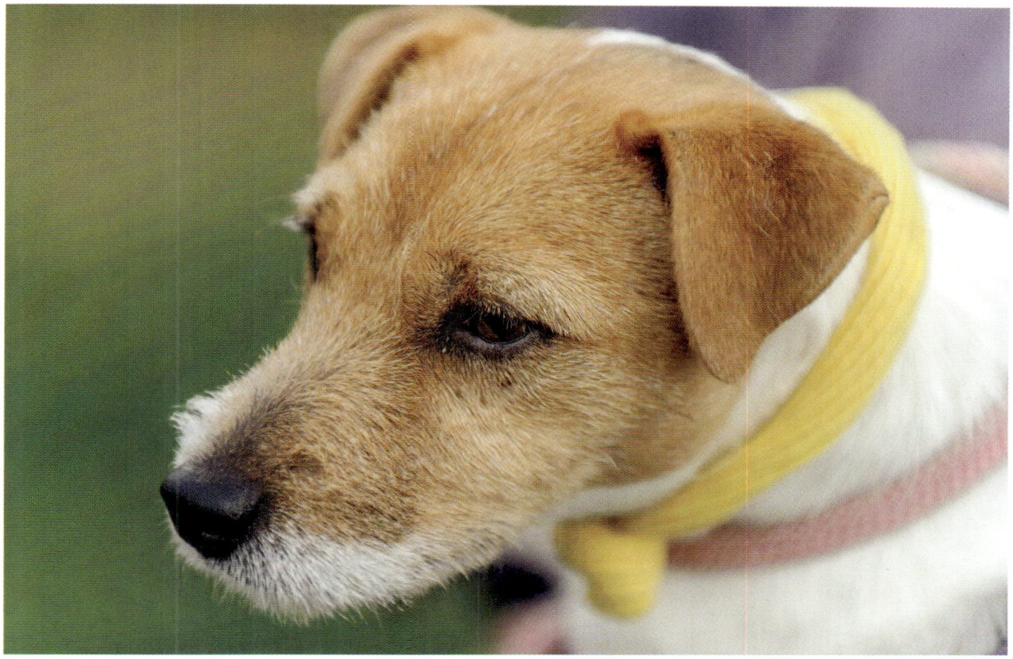

Figure 3.9

A fairly large aperture combined with a long focal length created a blurry background, so all the emphasis was left on the subject.

ISO 400 • 1/3200 sec. • f/2.8 • 200mm lens

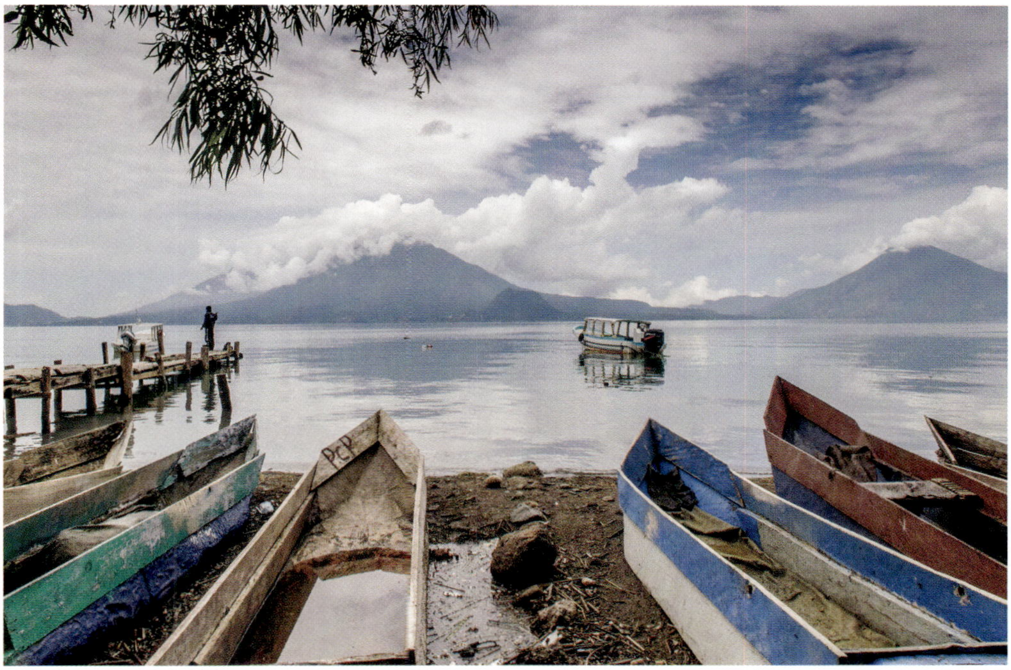

Figure 3.10

The smaller aperture setting brings sharpness to near and far objects.

ISO 200 • 1/160 sec. • f/16 • 17mm lens

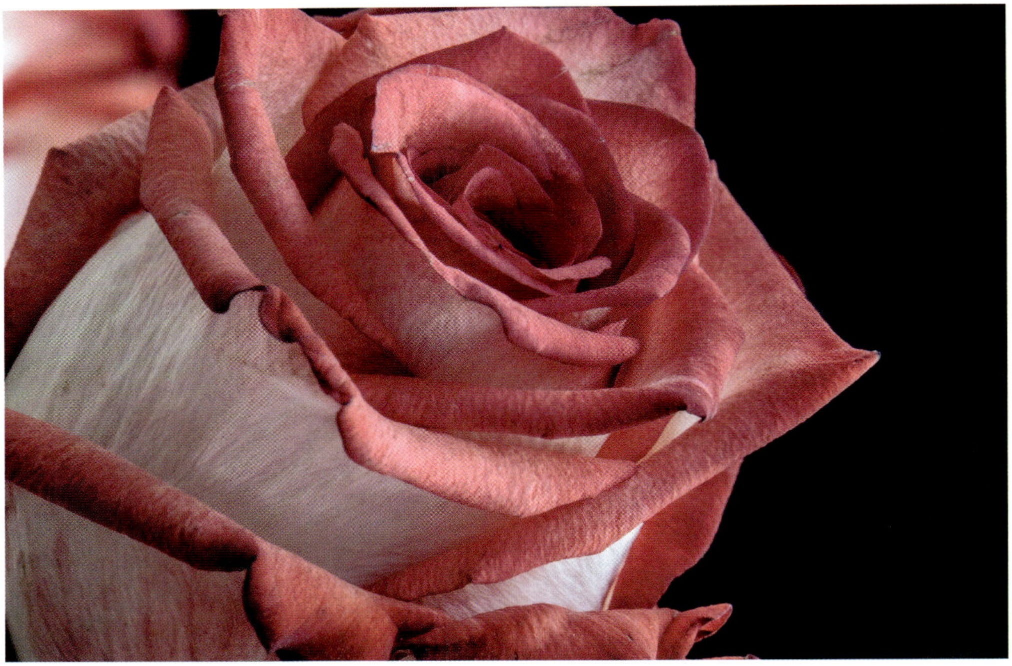

Figure 3.11
Small apertures give more sharpness in macro images.
ISO 2500 • 1/5 sec. • f/22 • 135mm lens

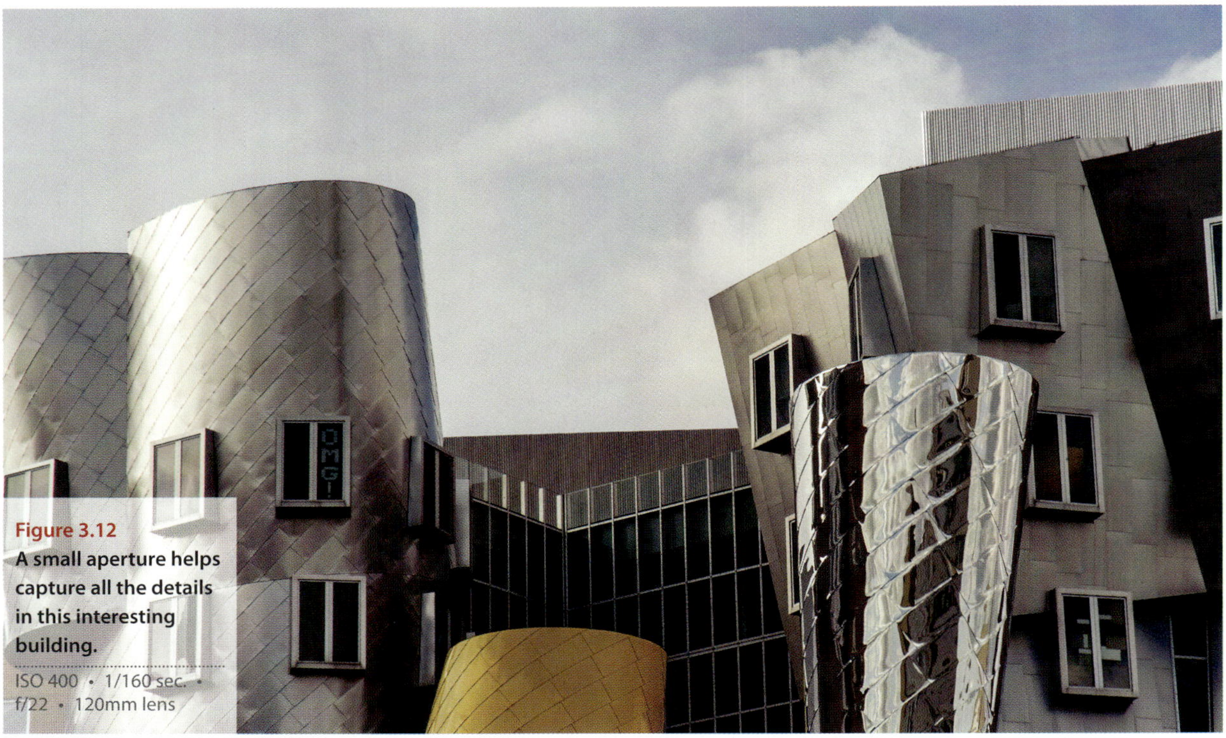

Figure 3.12
A small aperture helps capture all the details in this interesting building.
ISO 400 • 1/160 sec. • f/22 • 120mm lens

F-stops and aperture

As discussed earlier, when referring to the numeric value of your lens aperture, you will find it described as an *f-stop*. The f-stop is one of those old photography terms that, technically, relates to the focal length of the lens (e.g., 200mm) divided by the effective aperture diameter. These measurements are defined as "stops" and work incrementally with your shutter speed to create proper exposure. Older camera lenses used 1-stop increments to assist in exposure adjustments, such as 1.4, 2, 2.8, 4, 5.6, 8, 11, 16, and 22. Each stop represents about half the amount of light entering the lens iris as the larger stop before it. Today, most lenses don't have f-stop markings, since all adjustments to this setting are performed via the camera's electronics. The stops are also now typically divided into 1/3-stop increments to allow much finer adjustments to exposures, as well as to match the incremental values of your camera's ISO settings, which are also adjusted in 1/3-stop increments.

We have established that Aperture Priority (Av) mode is highly useful in controlling the depth of field in your image. But it's also pivotal in determining the limits of available light that you can shoot in. Different lenses have different maximum apertures. The larger the maximum aperture, the less light you need to achieve a properly exposed image. You will recall that, when in Tv mode, there is a limit at which you can handhold your camera without introducing movement or hand shake, which causes blurriness in the final picture. If your lens has a larger aperture, you can let in more light all at once, which means that you can use faster shutter speeds. This is why lenses with large maximum apertures, such as f/1.4, are called "fast" lenses.

On the other hand, bright scenes require the use of a small aperture (such as f/16 or f/22), especially if you want to use a slower shutter speed. That small opening reduces the amount of incoming light, and this reduction of light requires that the shutter stay open longer.

Setting up and shooting in Av mode

1. Turn your camera on, and then turn the mode dial to align the Av with the indicator line.
2. Select your ISO by pressing the ISO button on top of the camera and then turning the Main dial.
3. Point the camera at your subject, and then activate the camera meter by depressing the shutter button halfway.
4. View the exposure information in the bottom area of the viewfinder or by looking at the rear display panel.
5. While the meter is activated, use your index finger to roll the Main dial left and right to see the changed exposure values. Roll the dial to the right for a smaller aperture (higher f-stop number) and to the left for a larger aperture (smaller f-stop number).

Zoom lenses and maximum apertures

Some zoom lenses (like the 18–135mm kit lens) have a variable maximum aperture. This means that the largest opening will change depending on the zoom setting. In the example of the 18–135mm zoom, the lens has a maximum aperture of f/3.5 at 18mm and only f/5.6 when the lens is zoomed out to 135mm. Fixed-aperture zoom lenses maintain the same maximum aperture throughout the zoom range. They are typically much more expensive than their variable maximum aperture counterparts.

M: Manual Mode

Once upon a time, long before digital cameras and program modes, there was manual mode. In those days it wasn't called "manual mode" because there were no other modes. It was just photography. In fact, many photographers, including myself, cut their teeth on completely manual cameras. Let's face it—if you want to learn the effects of aperture and shutter speed on your photography, there is no better way to learn than by setting these adjustments yourself. However, today, with the advancement of camera technology, many new photographers never give this mode a second thought. That's truly a shame. Not only is it an excellent way to learn your photography basics, but it's also an essential tool to have in your photographic bag of tricks.

When you have your camera set to Manual (M) mode, the camera meter will give you a reading of the scene you are photographing. It's your job, though, to set both the f-stop (aperture) and the shutter speed to achieve a correct exposure. If you need a faster shutter speed, you will have to make the reciprocal change to your f-stop. Using any other mode, such as Tv or Av, would mean that you just have to worry about one of these changes, but Manual mode means you have to do it all yourself. This can be a little challenging at first, but after a while you will have a complete understanding of how each change affects your exposure, which will, in turn, improve the way that you use the other modes.

When to use Manual (M) mode

Here's a guide to help you decide when to use Manual (M) mode:

- When you need to maintain exposures between different frames for a panorama (**Figure 3.13**)
- When your environment is fooling your light meter and you need to maintain a certain exposure setting (**Figure 3.14**)
- When shooting silhouetted subjects, which requires overriding the camera's meter readings (**Figure 3.15**)

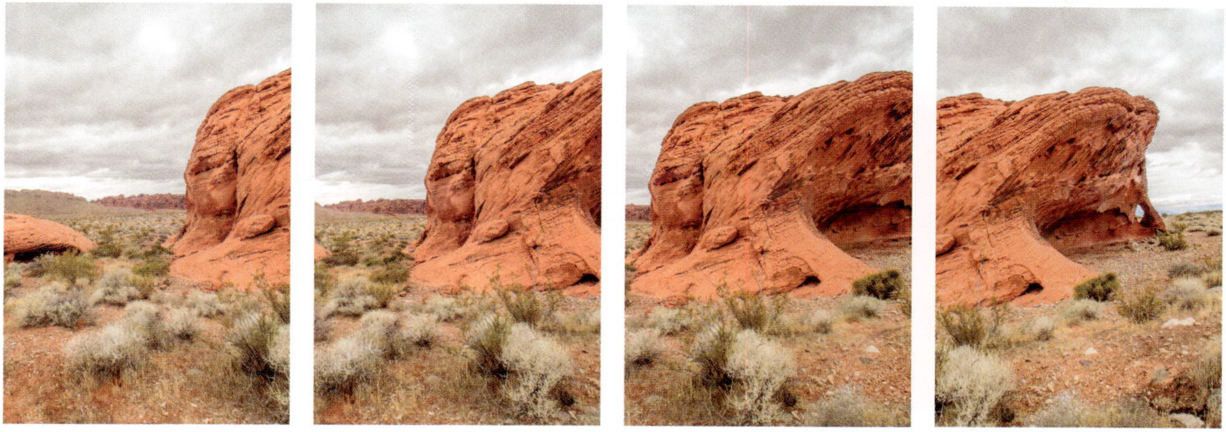

Figure 3.13

Setting the camera on Manual for panorama shots helps to keep the exposure consistent.

ISO 200 • 10 sec. • f/22 • 24mm lens

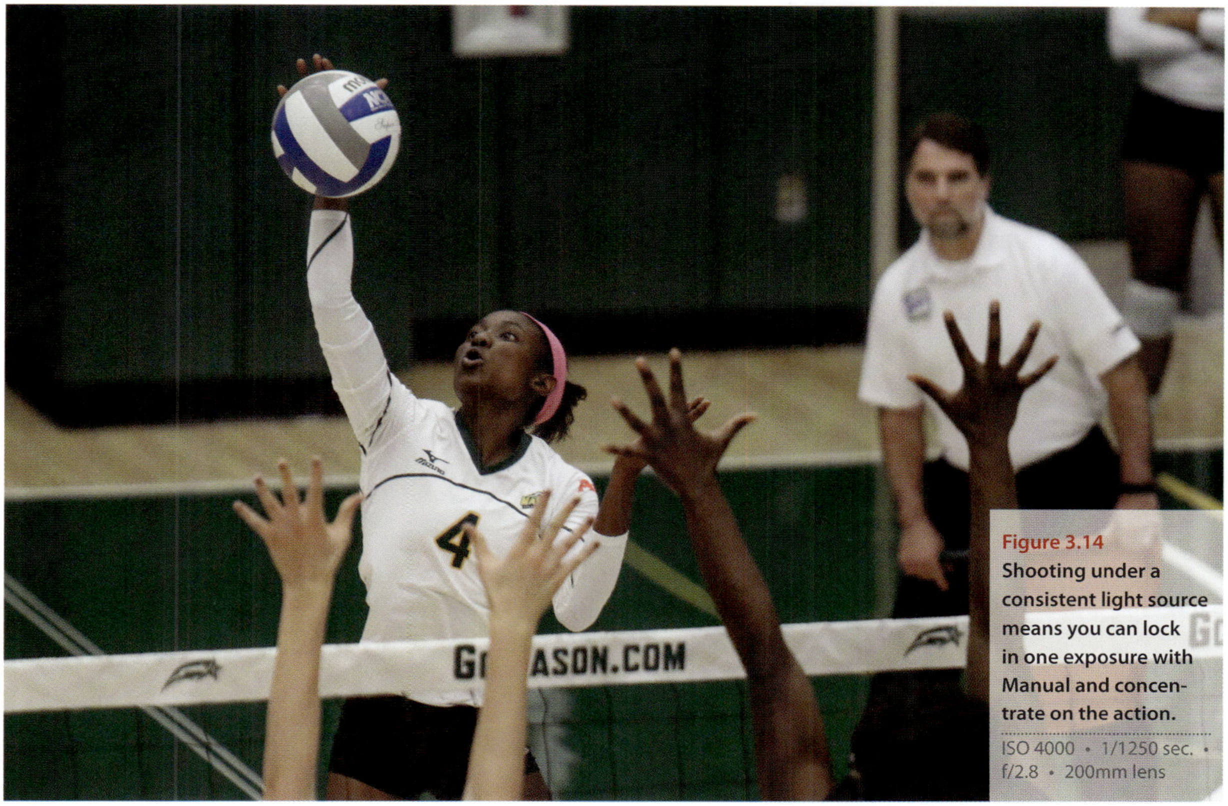

Figure 3.14

Shooting under a consistent light source means you can lock in one exposure with Manual and concentrate on the action.

ISO 4000 • 1/1250 sec. • f/2.8 • 200mm lens

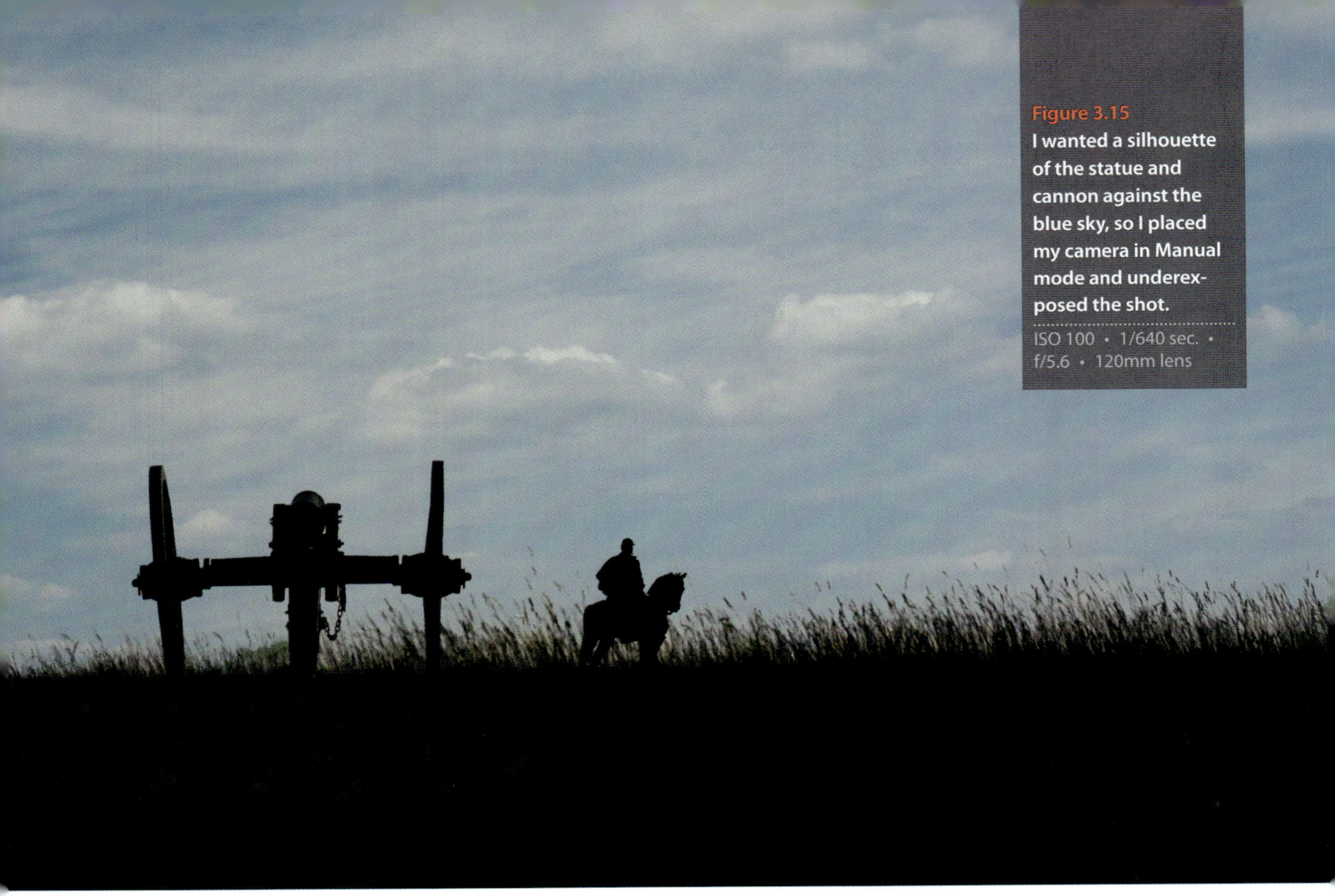

Figure 3.15
I wanted a silhouette of the statue and cannon against the blue sky, so I placed my camera in Manual mode and underexposed the shot.

ISO 100 • 1/640 sec. • f/5.6 • 120mm lens

Setting up and shooting in Manual mode

1. Turn the mode dial to align the M with the indicator line.
2. Select your ISO by pressing the ISO button on top of the camera and then turning the Main dial.
3. Point the camera at your subject, and then activate the camera meter by depressing the shutter button halfway.
4. View the exposure information in the bottom area of the viewfinder or by looking at the top or rear display panel.
5. While the meter is activated, use your index finger to roll the Main dial left and right to change your shutter speed value until the exposure mark is lined up with the zero mark. The exposure information is displayed on a scale along the right side of the viewfinder.
6. To set your exposure using the aperture, depress the shutter release button until the meter is activated. Then, using your thumb, hold in the Av button on the back of the camera, and then use your index finger to turn the Main dial right for a smaller aperture (large f-stop number) or left for a larger aperture (small f-stop number).

A "proper" exposure will line up the small mark with the arrow in the middle of the scale. As the indicator moves down the scale, it is a sign that you will be underexposing (not enough light is hitting the sensor to provide adequate exposure). Move the indicator above center and you will be providing more exposure than the camera meter calls for. This is overexposure. You can also refer to the scale on the rear LCD panel, which will indicate over- and underexposure using a plus and minus scale. As you become more familiar with your exposure settings, you will be able to move away from what the camera meter determines is correct and begin making corrections based on the result you want to achieve.

How I Shoot: A Closer Look at the Camera Settings I Use

The great thing about working with a DSLR camera is that I can always feel confident that some things will remain unchanged from camera to camera. For me, these are the Aperture Priority (Av) and Shutter Priority (Tv) shooting modes. Although I like to think of myself as a generalist in terms of my photography, I do tend to lean heavily on the landscape and urban photography genres. Working in these areas means that I'm almost always going to be concerned with my depth of field. Whether it's isolating my subject with a large aperture or trying to maximize the overall sharpness of a sweeping landscape, I keep an eye on my aperture setting.

If I have a need to control the action, I use Shutter Priority. If I'm trying to create a silky waterfall effect, I can depend on Tv to provide that long shutter speed. Maybe I am shooting a motocross jumper. I definitely need the fast shutter speeds that will freeze the fast-moving action. Although the other camera modes have their place, I think you will find that you will use the Av and Tv modes for 90 percent of your shooting.

The other concern that I have when setting up my camera is just how low I can keep my ISO. I raise the ISO only as a last resort, because each increase in sensitivity is an opportunity for more digital noise to enter my image. To that end, I always have the High ISO Speed Noise Reduction feature turned on Standard (see Chapter 6, "Say Cheese!").

To make quick changes while I shoot, I often use the Exposure Compensation feature (covered in Chapter 6) so that I can make small over- and underexposure changes. This is different than changing the aperture or shutter; it is more like fooling the camera meter into thinking the scene is brighter or darker than it actually is.

One of the reasons I change my exposure is to make corrections when I see the "blinkies" while looking at my images on the rear LCD. Blinkies are the warning signal that part of my image has been overexposed to the point that I no longer have any detail in the highlights. The highlight alert will flash wherever the potential exists for overexposure (**Figure 3.16**). The alert can be turned on as covered in Chapter 1 and is then visible in all of the preview screens. If you see any area of the preview blinking black, you are probably overexposing that part of the image. If I think that the overexposed area is important to the image, I will change the exposure compensation to underexpose enough to bring detail back to the blinking area.

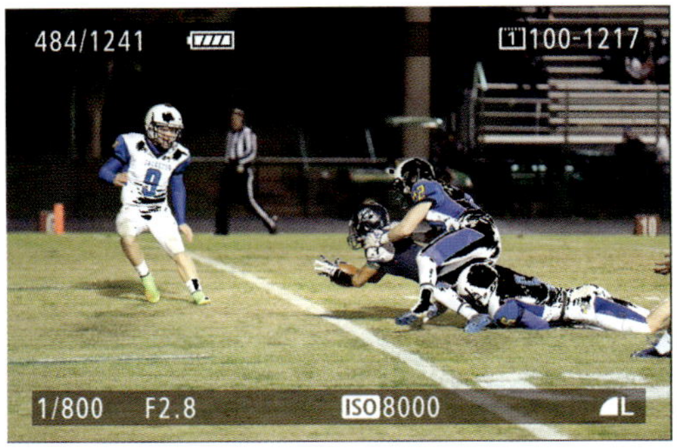

Figure 3.16
The white uniforms are blinking black in areas that are overexposed.

As you work your way through the coming chapters, you will see other tips and tricks I use in my daily photography, but the most important tip I can give is that you take the time to understand the features of your camera so that you can leverage the technology in a knowledgeable way. Doing so will result in better photographs.

Chapter 3 Assignments

The information in this chapter defines how you work with your camera from this point on. There may be times that you just want to grab some quick pictures and will resort to Intelligent Auto mode, but to get serious with your photography, you should learn the modes in the Creative Zone.

Starting off with Program mode

Set your camera on Program mode and start shooting. Become familiar with the adjustments you can make to your exposure by turning the Main dial. While shooting, keep an eye on your ISO.

Learning to control time with the Tv mode

Find some moving subjects, and then set your camera to Tv mode. Have someone ride their bike back and forth, or you can even just photograph cars as they go by. Begin with a slow shutter speed of around 1/30 of a second, and then start shooting with faster and faster shutter speeds. Keep shooting until you can freeze the action. Now find something that isn't moving, like a flower. Begin with a fast shutter speed, something like 1/500 of a second, and then work your way down to about 1/4 of a second. The point is to see how well you can handhold your camera before you start introducing hand shake into the image.

Controlling depth of field with the Av mode

The name of the game with Av mode is depth of field. Set up three items at different distances from you. You can use chess pieces or something similar. Now focus on the middle item and set your camera to the largest aperture that your lens allows (remember, large aperture means a small number like f/3.5). Now, while still focusing on the middle subject, start shooting with ever-smaller apertures until you are at the smallest f-stop for your lens. If you have a zoom lens, try doing this exercise with the lens at the widest lens setting, like 18mm, and then the longest telephoto setting, like 55mm or 135mm. Now move up to subjects that are farther away, like telephone poles, and shoot them in the same way. The idea is to get a feel for how each aperture setting and lens focal length affects your depth of field.

Giving and taking with Manual mode

Go outside on a sunny day and, using the camera in Manual mode, set your ISO to 100, your shutter speed to 1/125 of a second, and your aperture to f/16. Now press your shutter release button to get a meter reading. You should be pretty close to that zero mark. If not, make small adjustments to one of your settings until it hits that mark. This is where the fun begins. Start moving your shutter speed slower, to 1/60, and then set your aperture to f/22. Now go the other way. Set your aperture on f/8 and your shutter speed to 1/500. Review your images. If all went well, all the exposures should look the same. This is because you balanced the light with reciprocal changes to the aperture and shutter speed. Now go back to your original setting of 1/125 at f/16 and try moving the shutter speed without changing the aperture. Just make 1/3-stop changes (1/125 to 1/100 to 1/80 to 1/60), and then review your images to see what a 1/3 stop of overexposure looks like. Then do the same thing going in the opposite way. It's hard to know if you want to over- or underexpose a scene until you've done it and seen the results.

Share your results with the book's Flickr group!
Join the group here: flickr.com/groups/7dmarkii_fromsnapshotstogreatshots

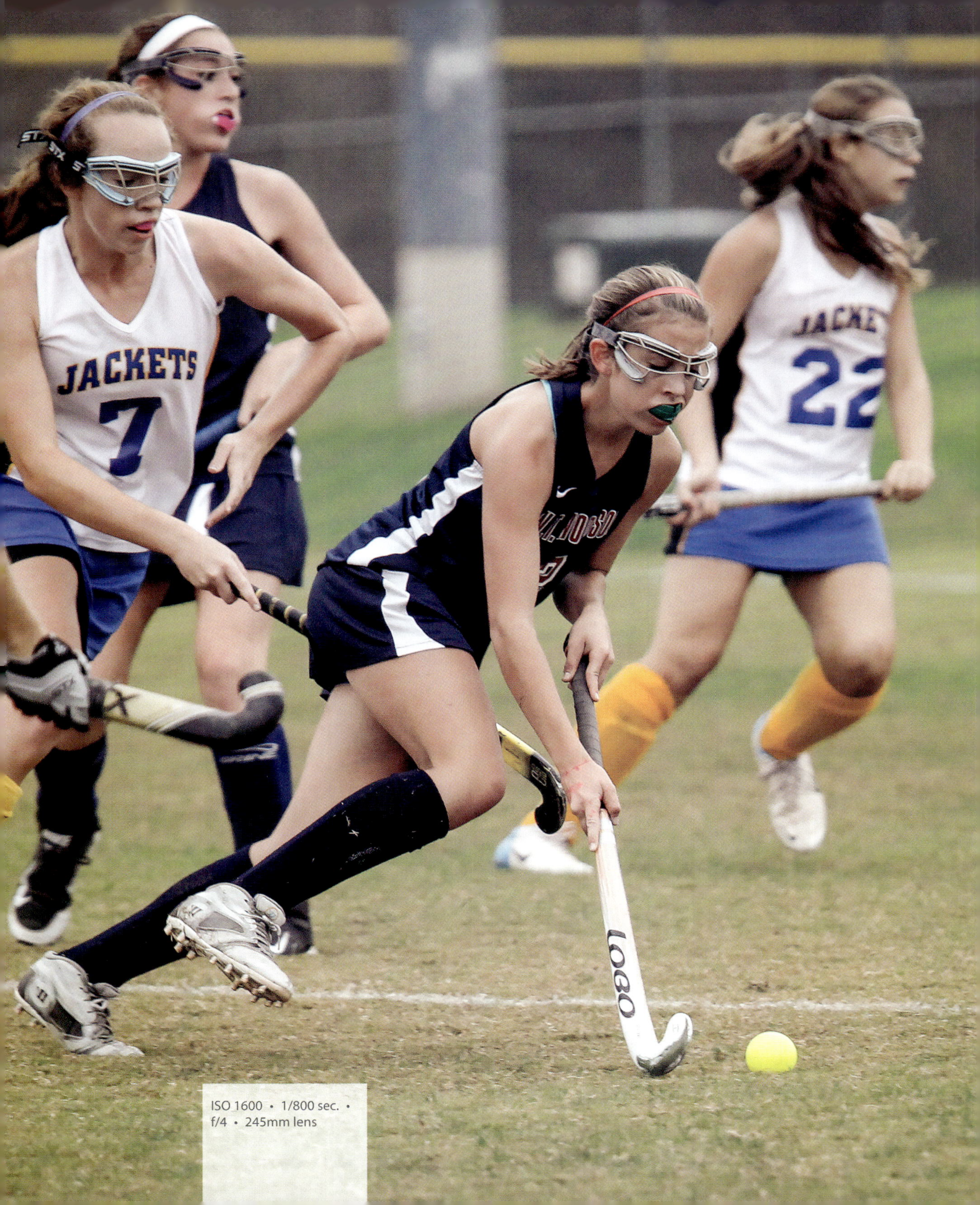

ISO 1600 • 1/800 sec. • f/4 • 245mm lens

4

Moving Target

The Tricks to Shooting Sports and More

When Canon announced the details of the 7D Mark II, it was pretty clear that the company had created the camera with a specific purpose in mind: sports and wildlife photography. That's not to say that it won't perform flawlessly in other genres, because it absolutely does. Rather, there are enhancements to this particular DSLR that set it apart from other models on the market, specifically the frame rate and high ISO ability. Those two combinations provide the perfect mix for photographing your favorite sporting event or capturing that elusive wildlife shot. Pair those features with a groundbreaking new focusing system and you have one amazing speed demon of a camera that is rivaled only by cameras costing several thousands more.

Poring Over the Picture

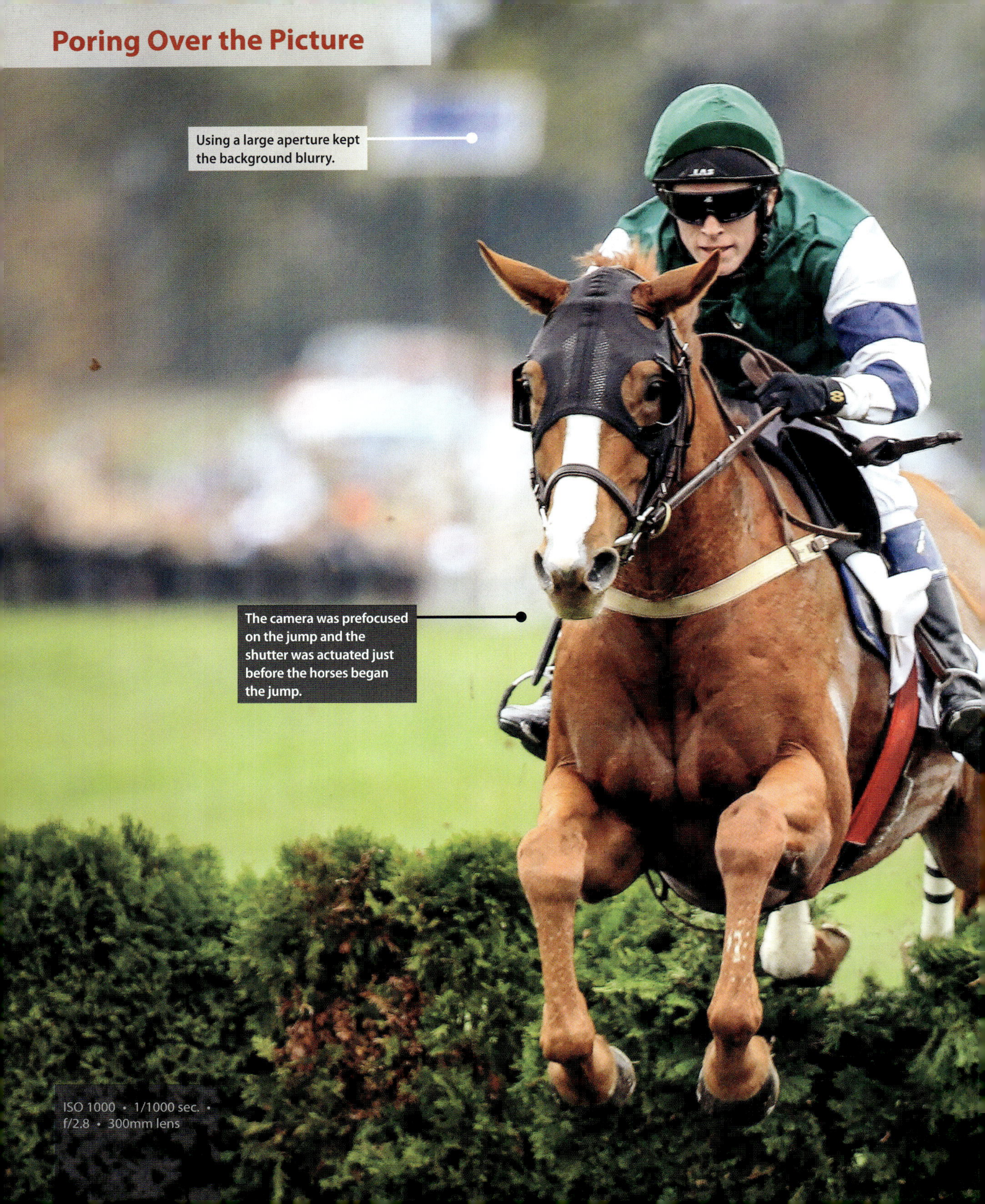

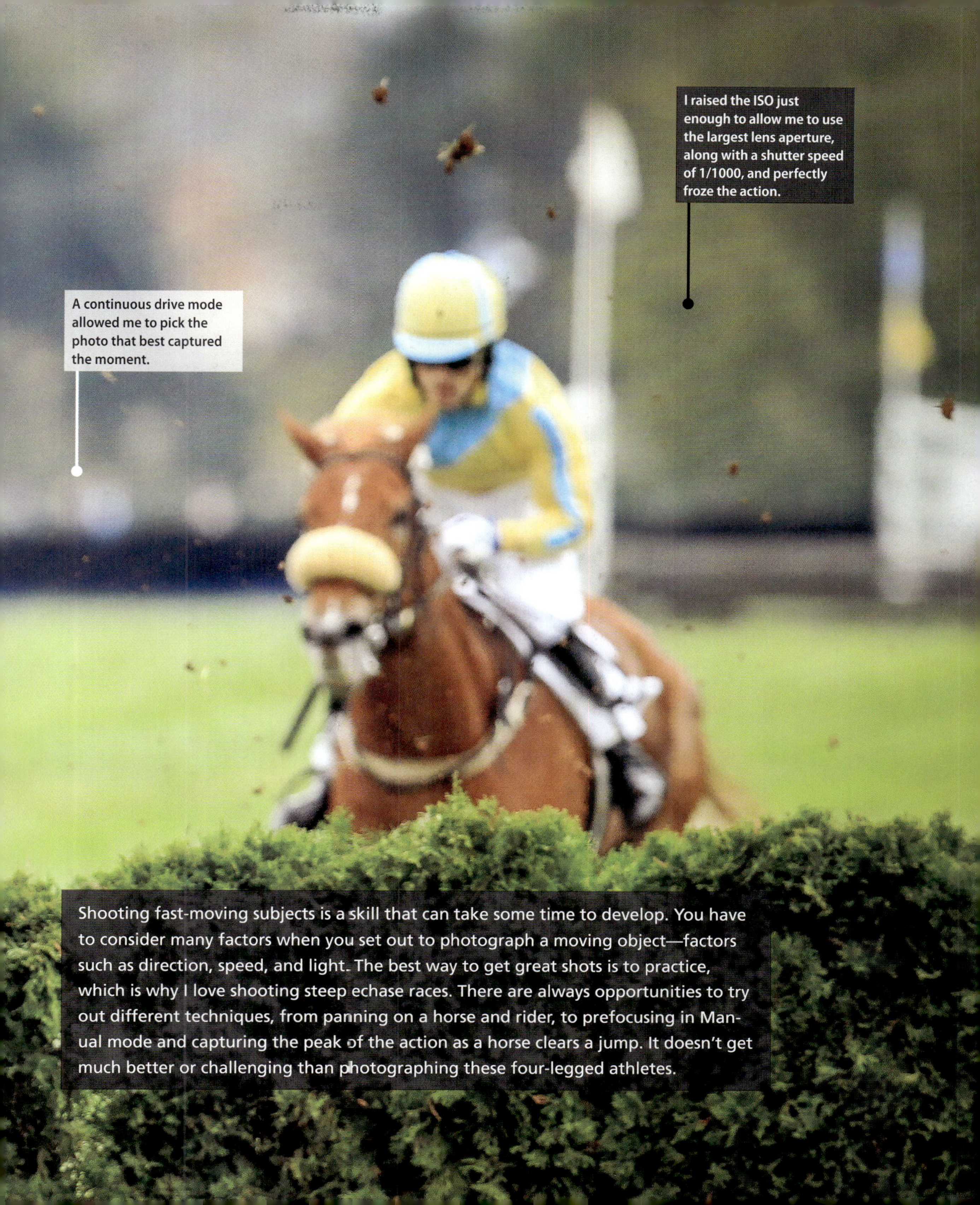

Shooting fast-moving subjects is a skill that can take some time to develop. You have to consider many factors when you set out to photograph a moving object—factors such as direction, speed, and light. The best way to get great shots is to practice, which is why I love shooting steep echase races. There are always opportunities to try out different techniques, from panning on a horse and rider, to prefocusing in Manual mode and capturing the peak of the action as a horse clears a jump. It doesn't get much better or challenging than photographing these four-legged athletes.

Stop Right There!

Shutter speed is the main tool in the photographer's arsenal for capturing great action shots. The ability to freeze a moment in time often makes the difference between a good shot and a great one. To take advantage of this concept, you should have a good grasp of the relationship between shutter speed and movement. When you press the shutter release button, your camera goes into action by opening the shutter curtain and then closing it after a predetermined length of time. The longer you leave your shutter open, the longer your subject will appear within the frame, so common sense dictates that the first thing to consider is just how fast your subject is moving.

Typically, you will be working in fractions of a second. How many fractions depends on several factors. Subject movement, though simple in concept, is actually based on three factors. The first is the direction of travel. Is the subject moving across your field of view (left to right) or traveling toward or away from you? The second consideration is the actual speed at which the subject is moving. There is a big difference between a moving sports car and a child on a bicycle. Finally, the distance from you to the subject has a direct bearing on how fast the action seems to be taking place. Let's take a brief look at each of these factors to see how they might affect your shooting.

Direction of travel

Typically, the first thing that people think about when taking an action shot is how fast the subject is moving, but in reality the first consideration should be the direction of travel. Where you are positioned in relation to the subject's direction of travel is critically important in selecting the proper shutter speed. When you open your shutter, the lens gathers light from your subject and records it on the camera sensor. If the subject is moving across your viewfinder, you need a faster shutter speed to keep that lateral movement from being recorded as a streak across your image. Subjects that are moving perpendicular to your shooting location do not move across your viewfinder and appear to be more stationary. This allows you to use a slightly slower shutter speed (**Figure 4.1**). A subject that is moving in a diagonal direction—both across the frame and toward or away from you—requires a shutter speed in between the two.

Subject speed

Once the angle of motion has been determined, you can then assess the speed at which the subject is traveling. The faster your subject moves, the faster your shutter speed needs to be in order to "freeze" that subject (**Figure 4.2**). A person walking across your frame might only require a shutter speed of 1/60 of a second, whereas a cyclist traveling in

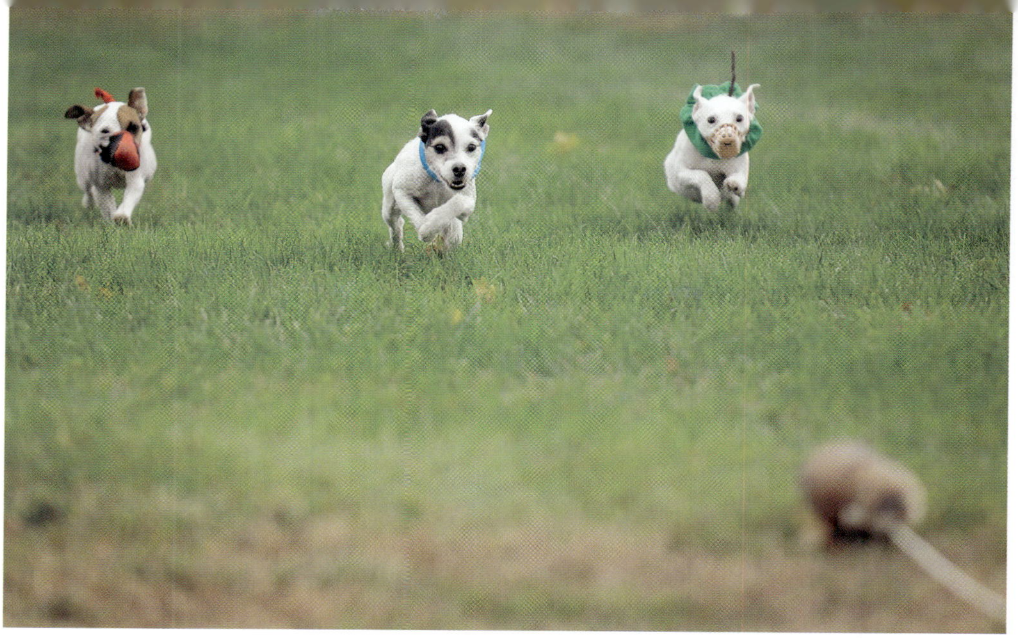

Figure 4.1
Action coming toward the camera can be captured with slower shutter speeds.
ISO 400 • 1/1000 sec. • f/4 • 300mm lens

the same direction would require 1/500 of a second or faster. That same cyclist traveling toward you at the same rate of speed, rather than across the frame, might only require a shutter speed of 1/250 of a second. You can start to see how the relationship of speed and direction comes into play in your decision-making process.

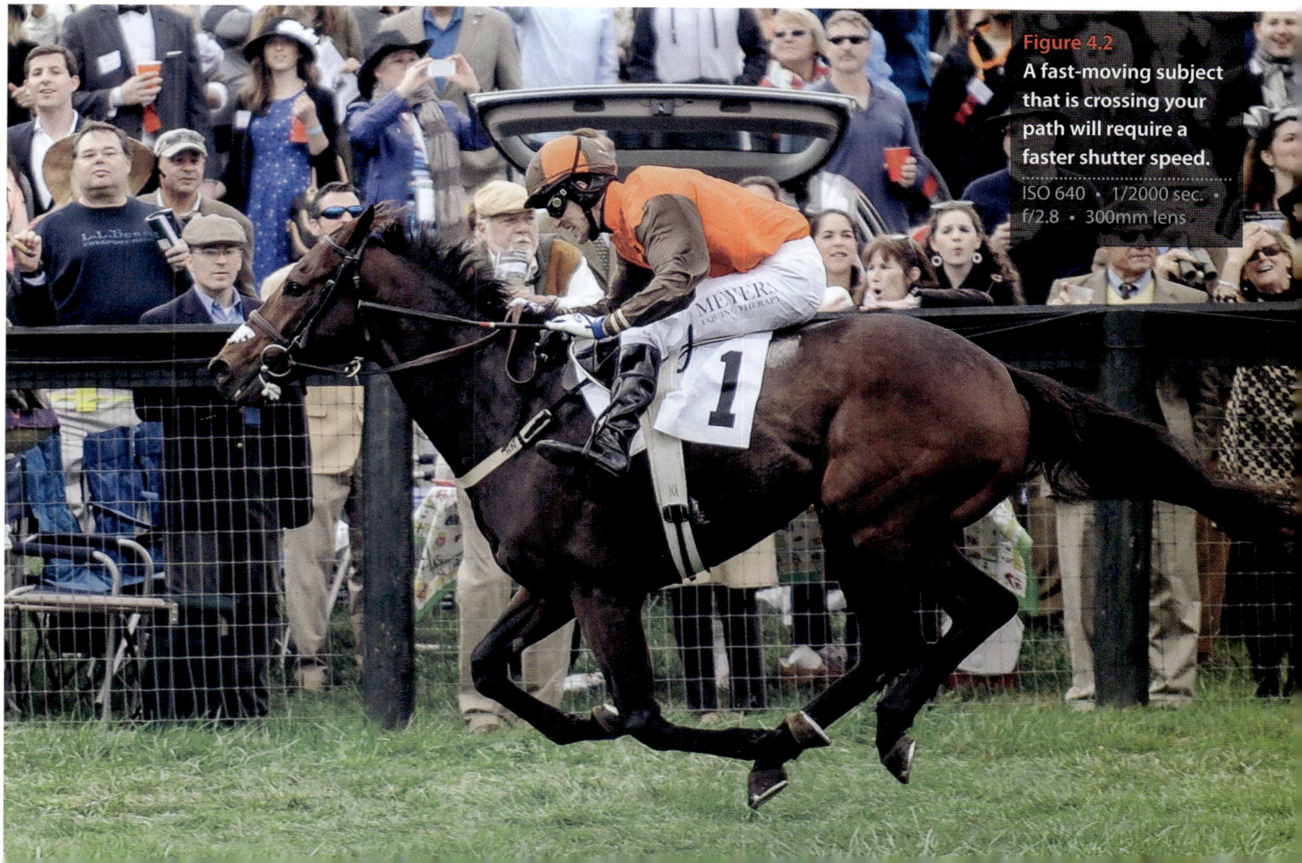

Figure 4.2
A fast-moving subject that is crossing your path will require a faster shutter speed.
ISO 640 • 1/2000 sec. • f/2.8 • 300mm lens

Subject-to-camera distance

So now you know both the direction and the speed of your subject. The final factor to address is the distance between you and the action. Picture yourself looking at a highway full of cars from up in a tall building a quarter of a mile from the road. As you stare down at the traffic moving along at 55-plus miles per hour, the cars and trucks seem to be slowly moving along the roadway. Now imagine yourself standing in the median of that same road as the same traffic flies by.

Although the traffic is moving at the same speed, the shorter distance between you and the traffic makes the cars seem like they are moving much faster. This is because your field of view is much narrower; therefore, the subjects are not going to present themselves within your field of view for the same length of time. The concept of distance applies to the length of your lens as well (**Figure 4.3**). If you are using a wide-angle lens, you can probably get away with a slower shutter speed than if you were using a telephoto, which puts you in the heart of the action. It all has to do with your field of view. That telephoto gets you "closer" to the action—and the closer you are, the faster your subject will be moving across your viewfinder.

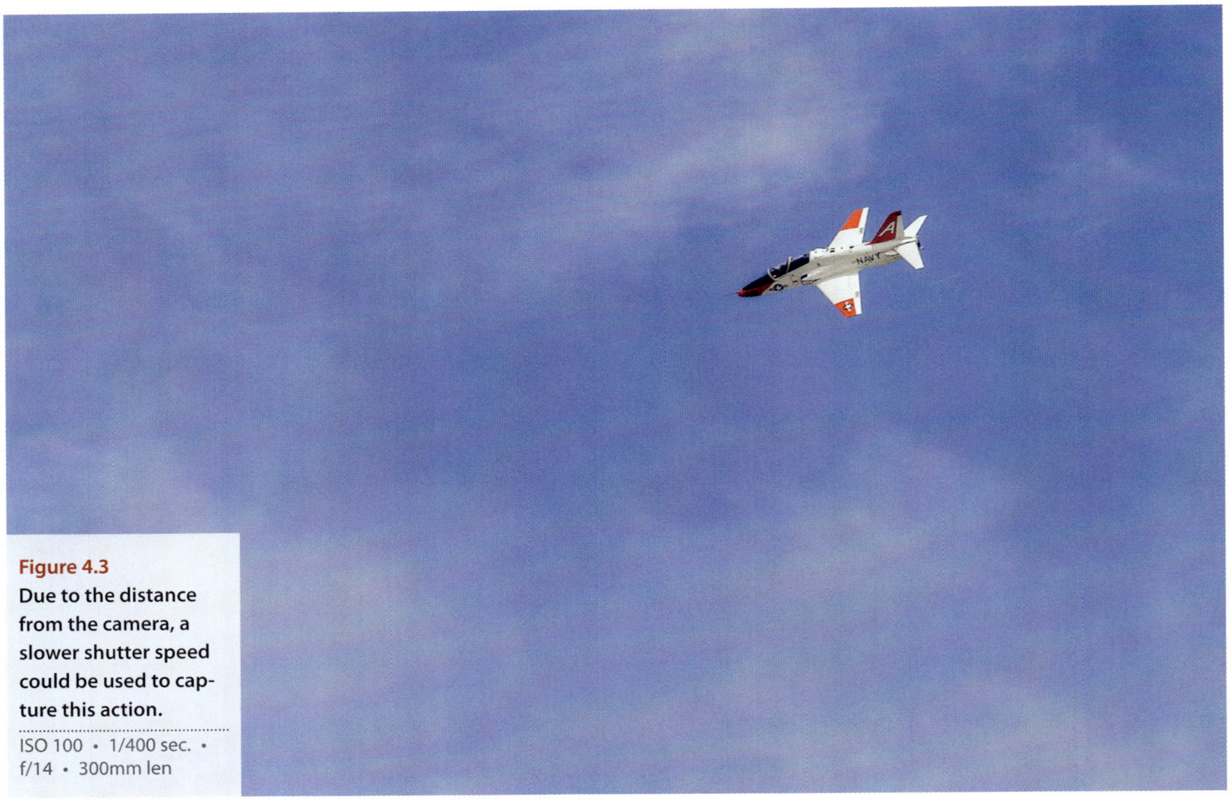

Figure 4.3
Due to the distance from the camera, a slower shutter speed could be used to capture this action.

ISO 100 • 1/400 sec. • f/14 • 300mm len

Zoom in to be sure

When reviewing your shots on the LCD, don't be fooled by the display. The smaller your image is, the sharper it will look. To ensure that you are getting sharp, blur-free images, zoom in on your LCD display.

To zoom in on your images, press the Image Review button, located to the lower left of the LCD display, and then press the Magnify Image button just above it to zoom in (**Figure 4.4**). Use the Main dial to increase the zoom ratio.

To zoom back out, roll the Main dial in the opposite direction. To get back to the full view, simply press either the Magnify or the Image Review button a second time. In Chapter 10, "Advanced Techniques," I will show you a little customization trick to make zooming in even faster.

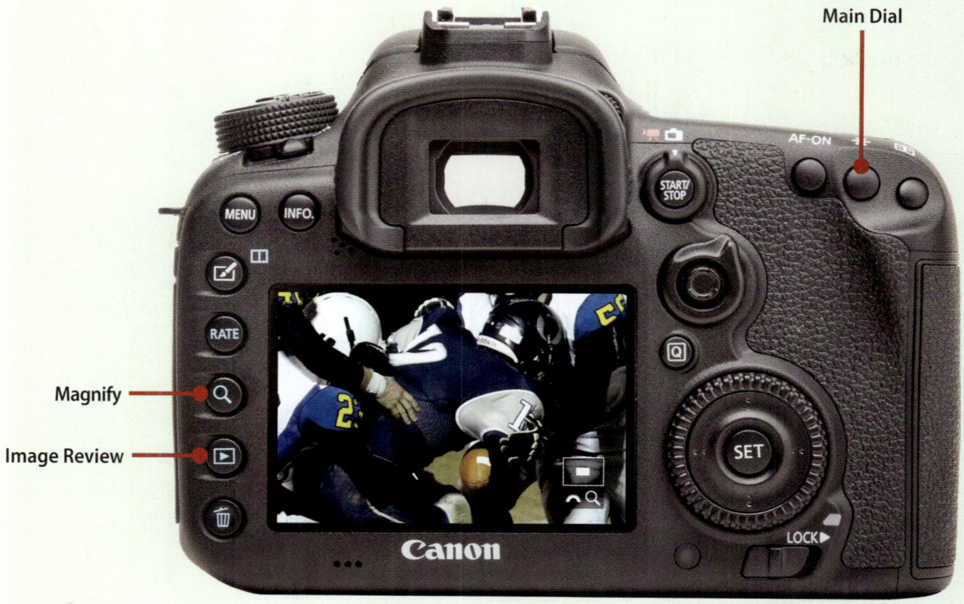

Figure 4.4
Zooming in on your image helps you confirm that the image is really sharp.

Using Shutter Priority (Tv) Mode to Stop Motion

In Chapter 3, "Camera Shooting Modes," you were introduced to the various shooting modes. Hopefully, you recall that the mode that gives you ultimate control over shutter speed is Tv mode, where you are responsible for selecting the shutter speed while handing over the aperture selection to the camera. The ability to concentrate on just one exposure factor helps you quickly make changes on the fly while staying glued to your viewfinder and your subject.

You need to take a couple of things into account when using Tv mode, both of which have to do with the amount of light available when shooting. Although you have control over which shutter speed you select in Tv mode, the range of shutter speeds available to you depends largely on how well your subject is lit.

Typically, when shooting fast-paced action you will be working with very fast shutter speeds. This means that your lens will probably be set to its largest aperture. If the light is not sufficient for the shutter speed selected, you will need to do one of two things: select a lens that offers a larger working aperture or raise the ISO of the camera. Working off the assumption that you have only one lens available, let's concentrate on balancing your exposure using the ISO.

Let's say you are shooting a baseball game at night, and you want to get some great action shots. You set your camera to Tv mode and, after testing out some shutter speeds, determine that you need to shoot at 1/500 of a second to freeze the action on the field. When you place the viewfinder to your eye and press the shutter button halfway, you notice that the f-stop readout is blinking at f/4.5. This is your camera's way of telling you that the lens has now reached its maximum aperture and you are going to be underexposed if you shoot your pictures at the currently selected shutter speed. You could slow your shutter speed down until the aperture reading stops blinking, but then you would get images with too much motion blur.

The alternative is to raise your ISO to a level that is fast enough for a proper exposure. The key here is to always use the lowest ISO that you can get away with. That might mean ISO 200 in bright sunny conditions or ISO 6400 (or higher) for an indoor or night situation (**Figure 4.5**). Just remember that the higher the ISO, the greater the amount of noise in your image. This is the reason you see professional sports photographers using those mammoth lenses perched atop a monopod: they could use a smaller lens, but to get those very large apertures they need a huge piece of glass on the front of the lens. The larger the glass on the front of the lens, the more light it gathers, and the larger the aperture for shooting. For the working pro, the large aperture translates into low ISO (and thus low noise), shallow depth of field, fast shutter speeds, and razor-sharp action.

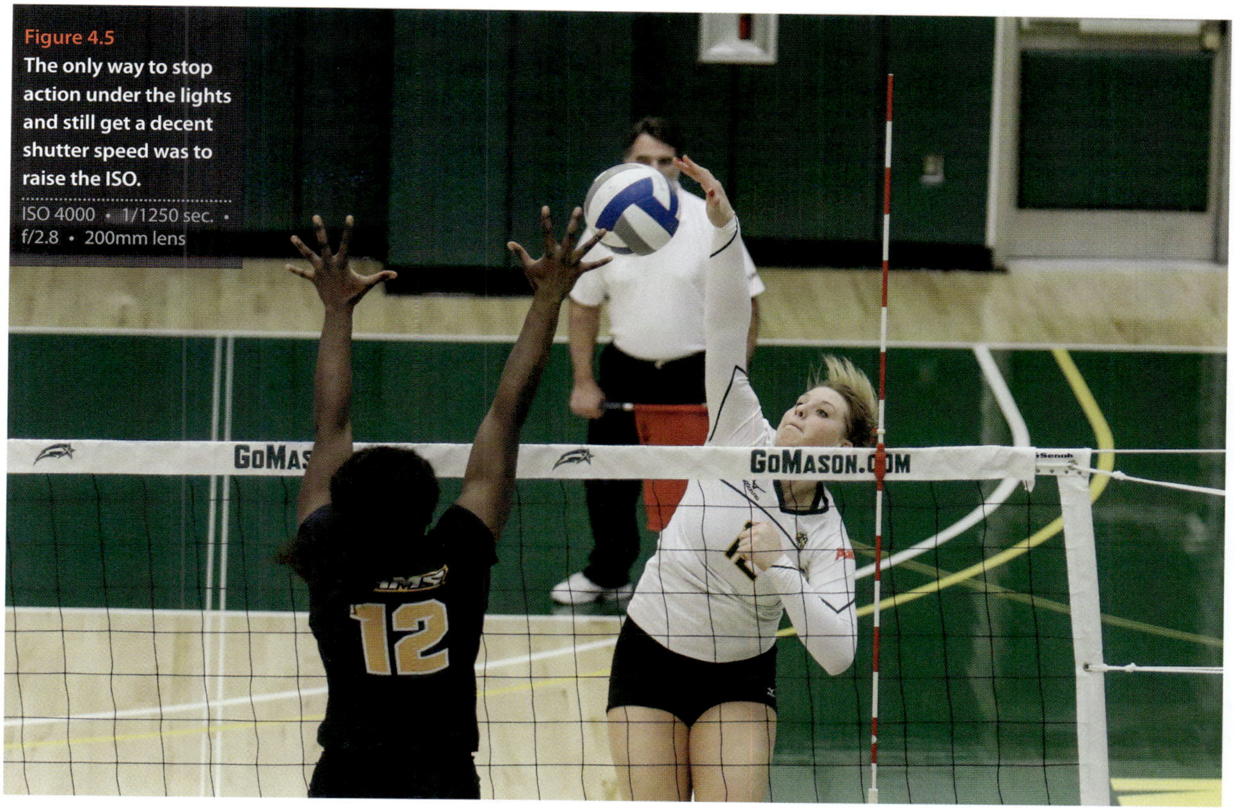

Figure 4.5
The only way to stop action under the lights and still get a decent shutter speed was to raise the ISO.
ISO 4000 • 1/1250 sec. • f/2.8 • 200mm lens

Adjusting your ISO on the fly

1. Check for the blinking aperture readout in the bottom-right portion of your viewfinder.
2. If it is blinking, move your index finger back from the shutter button and press the ISO button.
3. Move your finger forward to the Main dial and raise the ISO to the next highest level by turning it to the right.
4. Lightly press the shutter button and check to see if the aperture is still blinking.
5. If it's not blinking, shoot away. If it is, repeat steps 2–4 until it is set correctly.

Using Aperture Priority (Av) Mode to Isolate Your Subject

One of the benefits of working in Tv mode with fast shutter speeds is that, more often than not, you will be shooting with the largest aperture available on your lens. Shooting with a large aperture allows you to use faster shutter speeds, but it also narrows your depth of field.

To isolate your subject in order to focus your viewer's attention on it, a larger aperture is required. The larger aperture reduces the foreground and background sharpness: the larger the aperture, the more blurred your foreground and background will be.

I bring this up here because when you are shooting most sporting events, the idea is to isolate your main subject by having it in focus, while the rest of the image has some amount of blur. This sharp focus draws the viewer of your image right to the subject. Studies have shown that the eye is drawn to sharp areas before moving on to the blurry areas. Also, depending on what your subject matter is, you can get distracted by a busy background if everything in the photo is equally sharp. Without a narrow depth of field, it might be difficult for the viewer to establish exactly what the main subject is in your picture.

Let's look at how to use depth of field to bring focus to your subject. In the previous section, you learned that you should use Tv mode for getting those fast shutter speeds to stop action. Generally speaking, Tv mode will be the mode you most often use for shooting sports and other action, but occasionally you want to ensure you are getting the narrowest depth of field possible in your image. The way to do this is by using Aperture Priority mode.

So how do you know when you should use Av mode as opposed to Tv mode? It's not a simple answer, but your LCD screen can help you make this determination. The best scenario for using Av mode is a brightly lit scene where maximum apertures will still give you plenty of shutter speed to stop the action.

Let's say you are shooting a soccer game in the midday sun. If you have determined you need something between 1/500 and 1/1250 of a second for stopping the action, you could set your camera to a high shutter speed in Tv mode and just start shooting. But you also want to be using an aperture of, say, f/4.5 to get that narrow depth of field. Here's the problem: If you set your camera to Tv and select 1/1000 of a second as a nice compromise, you might get that desired f-stop—but you might not. As the meter is trained on your moving subject, the light levels could rise or fall, which might change that desired f-stop to something higher, like f/5.6, or even f/8. Now the depth of field is extended, and you will no longer get that nice isolation and separation you want.

To rectify this, switch the camera to Av mode and select f/4.5 as your aperture. Now as you begin shooting, the camera holds that aperture and makes exposure adjustments with the shutter speed (**Figure 4.6**). As I said before, this works well when you have lots of light—enough light so that you can have a high-enough shutter speed without introducing motion blur.

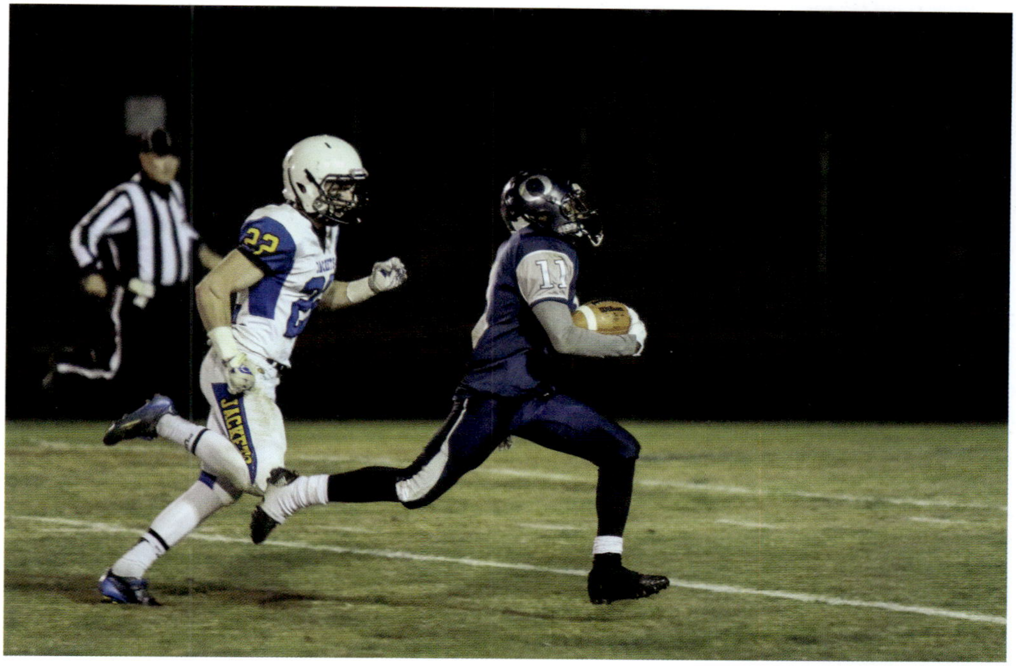

Figure 4.6
Selecting a large aperture setting ensures that the subjects are nicely separated from the background clutter.
ISO 8000 • 1/800 sec. • f/2.8 • 200mm lens

Keep Them in Focus with AI Servo and Auto AF Focus Point Selection

With the exposure issue handled for the moment, let's move on to a subject of equal importance: focusing. If you have browsed your manual, you know that there are several focus modes to choose from in the 7D Mark II. To get the greatest benefit from each of them, you must understand how they work and the situations where each mode will give you the best opportunity to grab a great shot. Because we are discussing subject movement, our first choice is going to be the AI Servo mode (the AI stands for Artificial Intelligence). AI Servo is a continuous focus operation. As long as you hold down the shutter release button, it will continually try to lock in focus, which is very helpful when your subject is moving about. When you have the camera set to use the 65-point auto selection mode, the camera will continually track subjects as long as they remain within the focus point areas.

Selecting and shooting in AI Servo focus mode

1. Press the Drive/AF button ("AF" for Automatic Focus) on the top of the camera.
2. Use your index finger to rotate the Main dial until AI Servo is selected on the rear LCD panel.
3. Locate your subject in the viewfinder; then press and hold the shutter button half-way to activate the focus mechanism.
4. Maintain the half press on the shutter release to track your subject, and then fully press the button when you are ready to take the photo. The focus will be set at the time that you take the photo.

Generally speaking, when you are using the 65-point automatic selection AF, the camera uses all 65 focus points for maintaining sharp focus (**Figure 4.7**). The camera will maintain focus on your subject as long as the subject remains within one of the focus points in the viewfinder or until you take a picture. When you are pressing the shutter button, you will see the focus points illuminate over the subject that is being focused on. Multiple points mean that focus is being achieved at more than one location. If you would like to improve the accuracy of the point selection, you can change the AF point and/or the AF point area, depending on your needs.

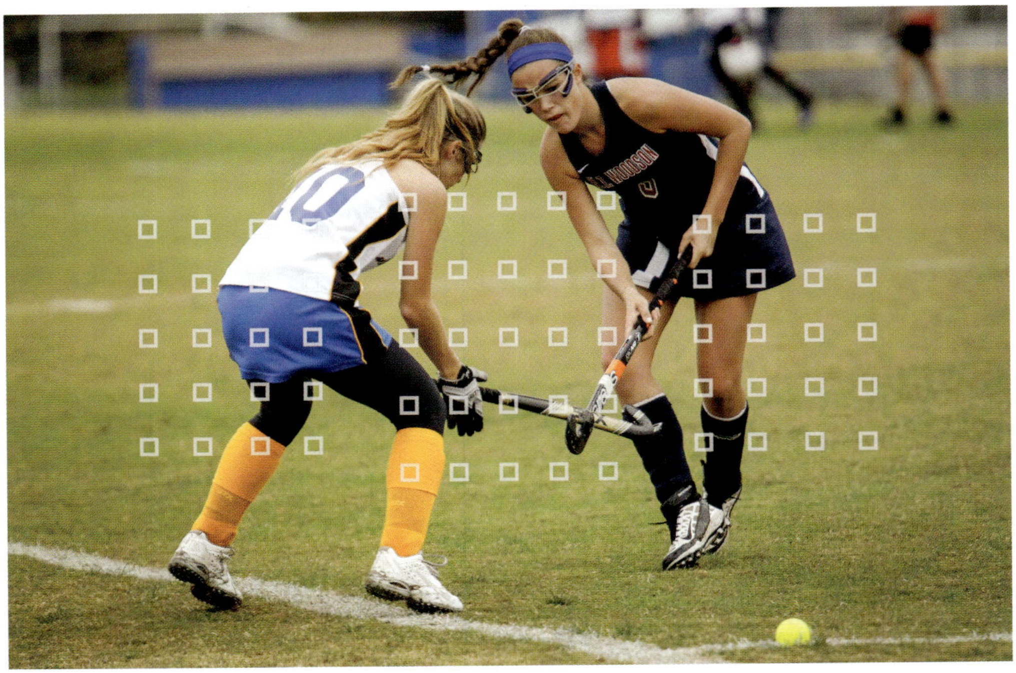

Figure 4.7
The Automatic Focus (AF) points are 65 small rectangular boxes arranged in three sections in your viewfinder.

We discussed the 65-point automatic selection area, but there are many more combinations available to choose from. By pressing the AF Point Selection button on the top-right area of the camera back, you will activate the point selection screen, which is visible on the rear LCD as well as through the viewfinder. Once active, you can use the AF Area Selection lever to change the focus point mode.

There are seven different modes to choose from, starting with the Spot AF mode (**A**), which allows for precise focus point selection to the fully automatic 65-point area (**B**), which does the point selection for you. In between those two are the Single-point AF (**C**); AF point expansion (5 points) (**D**); AF point expansion (9 points) (**E**); Zone AF (15 points in 9 different zones) (**F**); and the Large zone AF (dividing the points into left, middle, and right zones) (**G**).

When using AI Servo mode, you have the choice of using the Automatic Focus (AF) point mode in automatic, which uses the center point in the viewfinder, or you can select one of the autofocus points as your starting point.

A

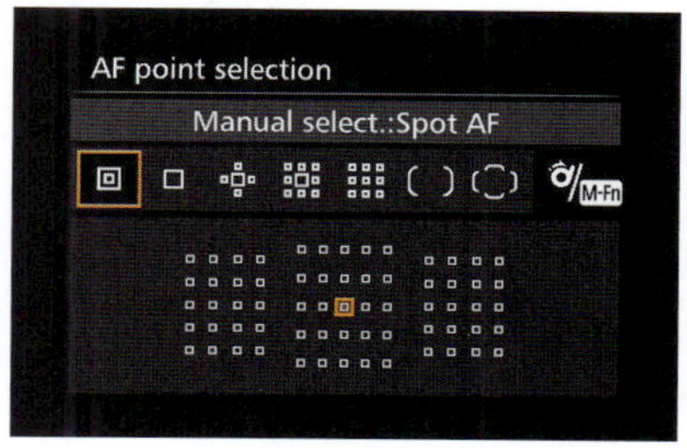

B

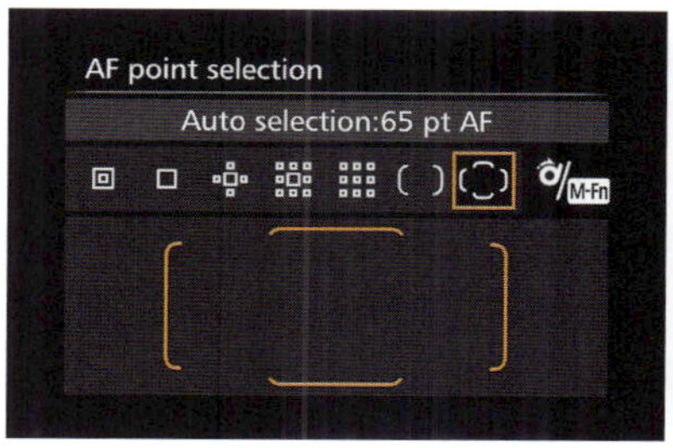

C

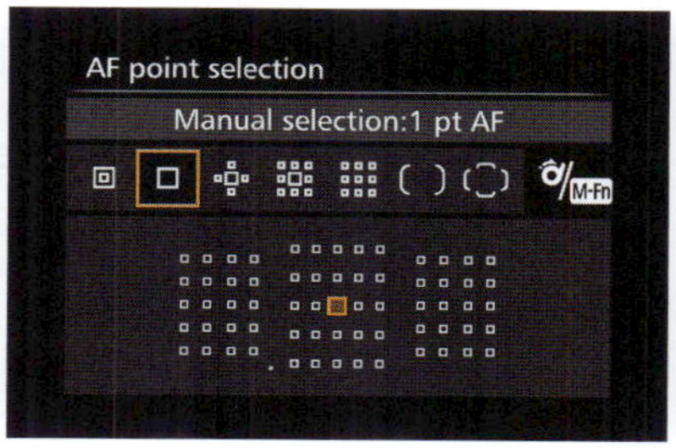

D

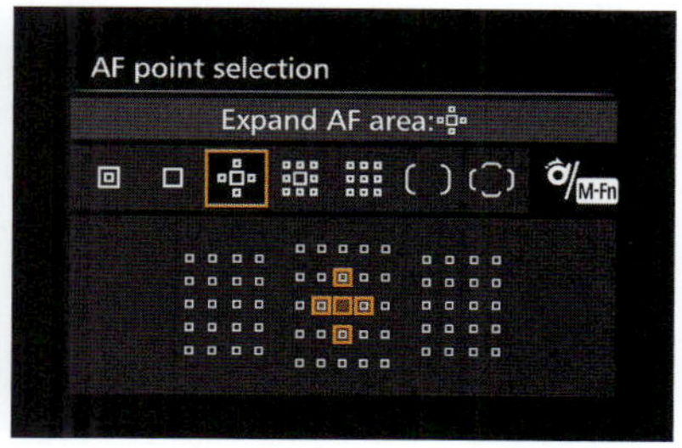

E

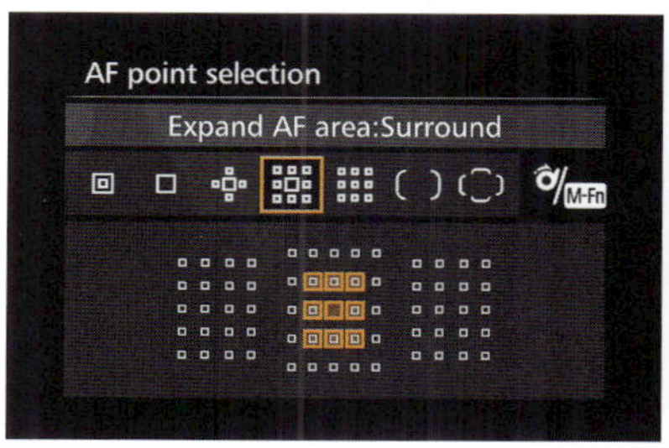

F

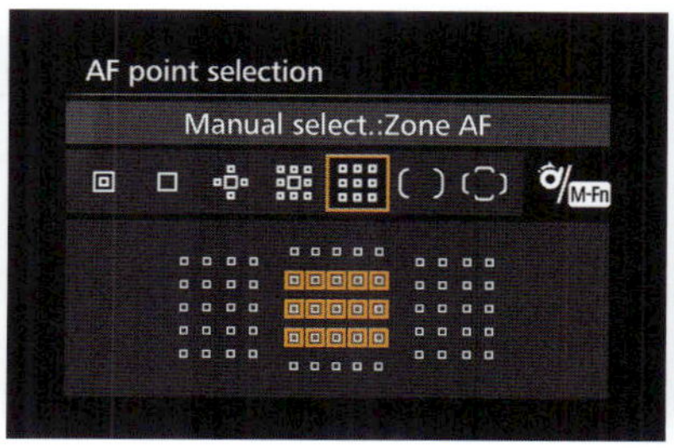

G

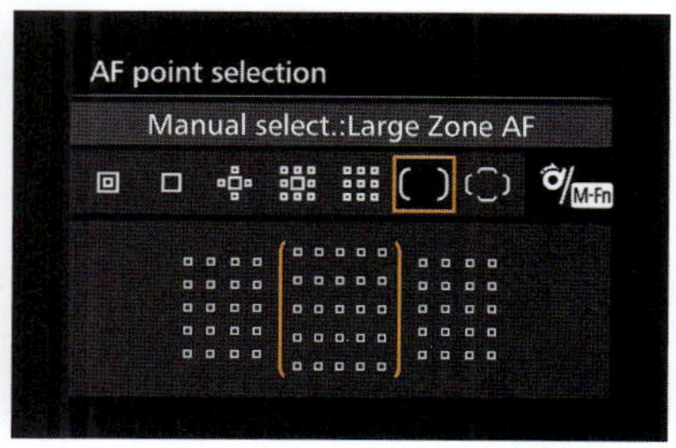

Selecting focus points or the Automatic Focus point mode

1. Press the Focus Point Selection button on the back of the camera.
2. Use the AF area selection lever or the Multi-function button on top of the camera to switch between the different focus point modes.
3. If you select anything other than the automatic point select mode, you can control the location of the points by using the Multi-controller button on the back of the camera.

Stop and Go with AI Focus AF

If you are going to be changing between a moving target and one that is still, consider using the AI Focus mode. This mode mixes both the One Shot and AI Servo modes for shooting a subject that goes from stationary to moving, without having to adjust your focus mode.

When you have a stationary subject, place your selected focus point on your subject and the camera will focus on it. If your subject begins to move out of focus, the camera will switch to AI Servo mode and track the movement, keeping a sharp focus.

For example, suppose you are shooting a football game. The quarterback has brought the team to the line and he is standing behind the center, waiting for the ball to be hiked. If you are using the AI Focus AF mode, you can place your focus point on the quarterback and start taking pictures of him as he stands at the line. As soon as the ball is hiked and the action starts, the camera will switch to AI Servo mode and track his movement within the frame. This technique can be a little tricky at first, but once you master it, it will make your action shooting effortless. Using this mode, you can identify your subject for the camera so that it knows exactly which subject to maintain as the priority for your focus selection.

To select AI Focus, follow the same steps listed for selecting AI Servo, but instead select the AI Focus mode (**Figure 4.8**).

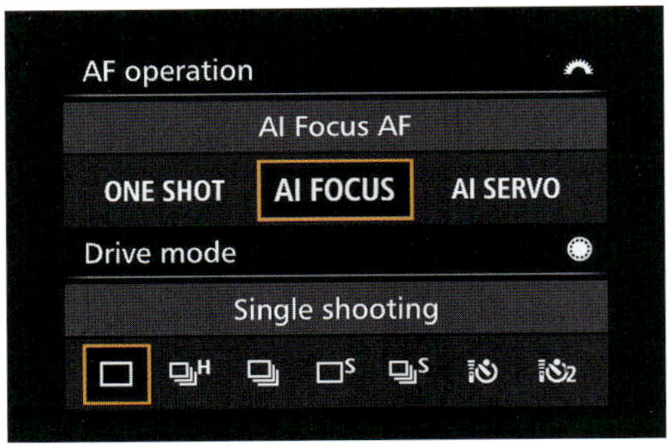

Figure 4.8
Setting your focus mode to AI Focus.

Choosing a focus mode

Selecting the proper focus mode depends largely on what type of subject you are photographing. One Shot is typically best for stationary subjects. It allows you to determine exactly where you want your focus to be, and then recompose your image while holding the focus in place. If you are taking pictures of an active subject that is moving quickly, trying to set a focus point with One Shot can be difficult, if not impossible. This is when you will want to rely on the AI modes to quickly assess the subject distance and set your lens focus. My preference is to use the AI Servo mode paired with the expanded AF area for point selection. This mode gives you a primary point to use for focus, with the addition of a point to either side as well as above and below the main point. This is very accurate and gives the camera a starting point for establishing focus.

Making a Case for Autofocus

Canon understands that there are a lot of choices for using autofocus, and figuring out the best options might get a little difficult. This is why Canon has created six different shooting scenarios, which the company calls Case 1–6, and these scenarios are available in the first AF configuration menu screen.

The cases are based on different sporting scenarios, ranging from tennis to rhythmic gymnastics. Each case has a setting for tracking sensitivity, acceleration and deceleration of objects, and autofocus point-switching sensitivity. Each of these settings can be fine-tuned, or you can just use the base settings for each case. Of course, you might not be shooting the same sport described for each of the different cases, but you can use the one that best matches the activity that you are shooting.

Selecting an AF case

1. Press the Menu button and turn the Main dial to get to the first AF configuration menu screen.
2. Use the Quick Control dial to select one of the six different cases (**A**).

A

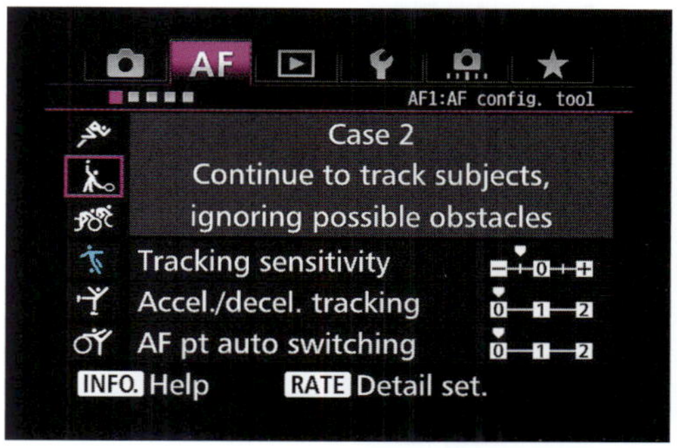

3. Press the Info button to see a description of the settings for the selected case (**B**).
4. To modify any of the settings for the case, press the Rate button to select the setting you want to change, and press Set (**C**).
5. Use the Quick Control dial to change the parameter, and then press Set once again to lock in the change (**D**).

B

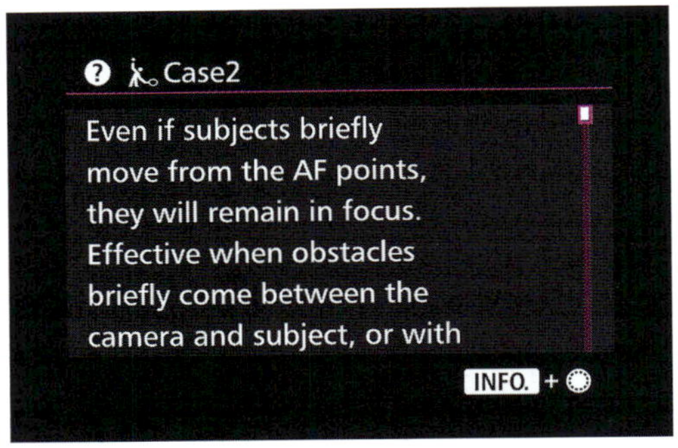

C

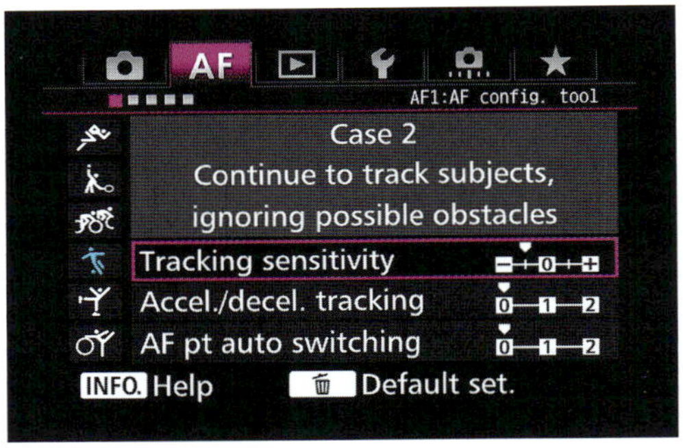

D

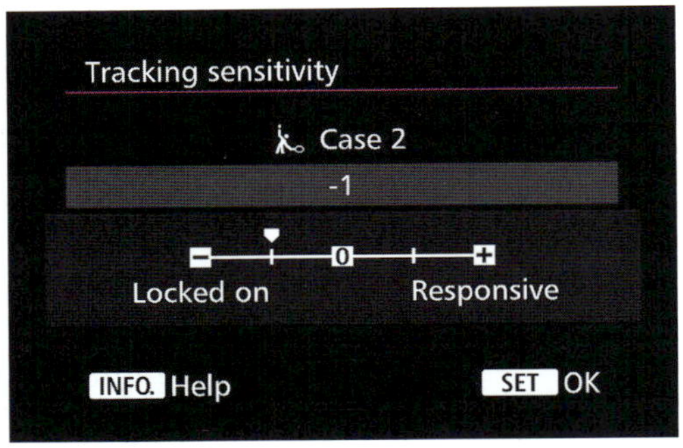

6. Press the Shutter Release button to exit the menu and start shooting.

Manual Focus for Anticipated Action

Although I use the autofocus modes for the majority of my shooting, sometimes I like to fall back on manual focus—usually when I know when and where the action will occur and I want to capture the subject as it crosses a certain plane of focus. Using manual focus is effective in sports like motocross or auto racing, where the subjects are on a defined track. By prefocusing the camera, you just have to wait for the subject to approach your point of focus, and then start firing the camera.

In **Figure 4.9**, the horses in the steeplechase race were traveling directly toward me from behind the hedge jump, so tracking the action with AI Servo would have been difficult, if not impossible. To get my shot, I focused on the front of the hedge and waited for the horses to come into range. As they began their jump over the hedge, I started shooting and captured the horses and riders at the height of the action.

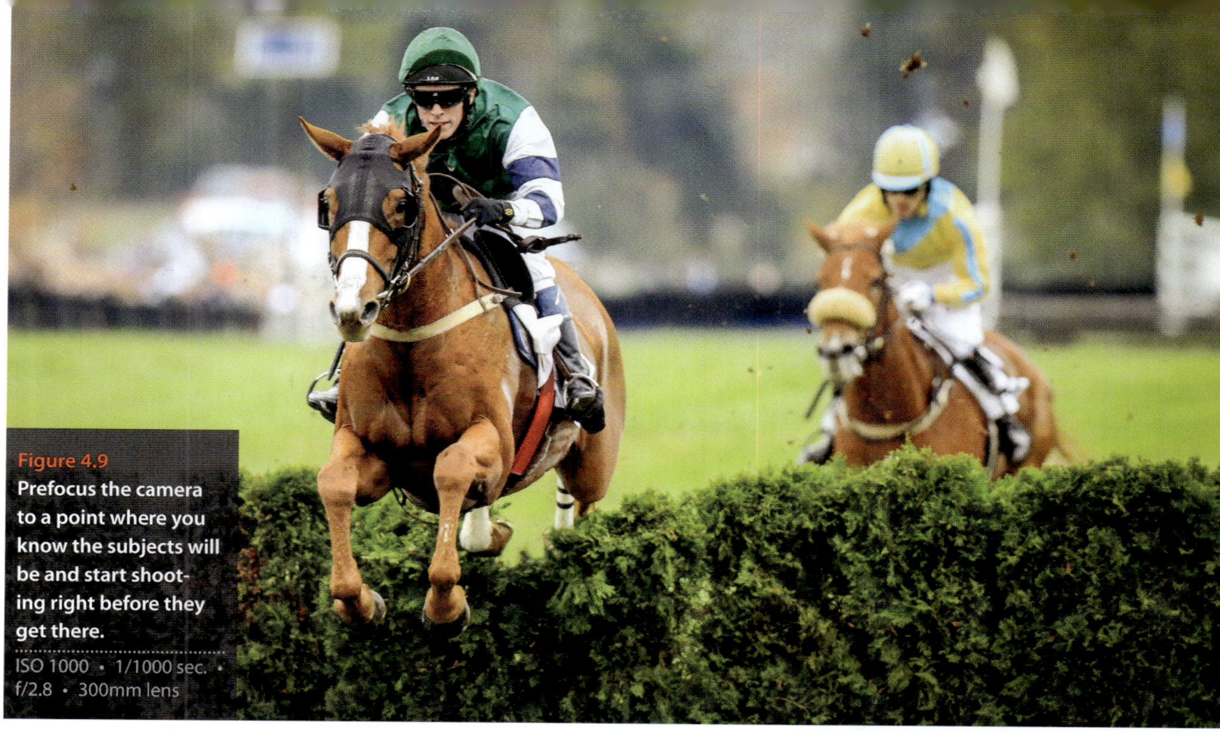

Figure 4.9
Prefocus the camera to a point where you know the subjects will be and start shooting right before they get there.

ISO 1000 • 1/1000 sec. • f/2.8 • 300mm lens

Drive modes

The drive mode determines how fast your camera will take pictures. Single-shooting mode is for taking one photograph at a time. With every full press of the shutter, the camera will take a single image. The Continuous mode allows for a more rapid capture rate. When you are using the Continuous mode, the camera continues to take pictures as long as the shutter release button is held down (or until the memory buffer fills up).

Keeping Up with the Continuous Shooting Mode

Getting great focus is one thing, but capturing the best moment on the sensor can be difficult if you are shooting just one frame at a time. In the world of sports, and in life in general, things move pretty fast. If you press the shutter button at the wrong time, you might miss your shot. This is the hazard of shooting in Single shooting drive mode. Fortunately, your 7D Mark II comes equipped with a Continuous shooting—or "burst"—mode that lets you capture a series of images at up to 10 frames per second (**Figure 4.10**). I say *up to* because there are actually three burst modes to choose from. There is the high-speed burst, which works at the stated 10 frames per second, plus a low-speed mode for 3 frames per second. There is also a silent continuous mode that reduces shutter noise but slows the frame rate to 4 frames per second.

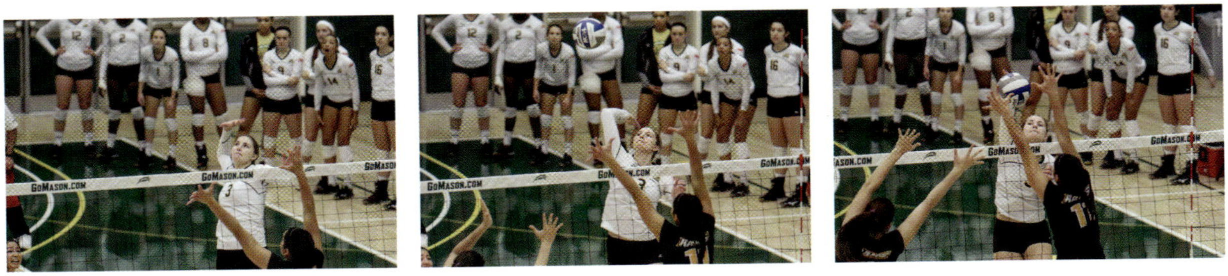

Figure 4.10 Using the Continuous drive mode means that you are sure to capture the peak of the action.

ISO 4000 • 1/1250 sec. • f/2.8 • 160mm lens

Setting up and shooting in the Continuous drive mode

1. Press the Drive/AF button on the top of the camera.
2. Rotate the Quick Control dial while looking at the rear LCD screen to select the desired mode.
3. Press the shutter release button slightly to return to shooting mode.
4. To shoot, press the shutter button and hold until the desired number of frames has been captured.
5. Your camera has an internal memory, called a buffer, where images are stored while they are being processed prior to being moved to your memory card. Depending on the image format you are using, the buffer might fill up, and the camera will stop shooting until space is made in the buffer for new images. If this happens, you will see the word Busy appear in the viewfinder and on the rear LCD panel. The camera readout in the viewfinder tells you how many frames you have available before the buffer is full.

Manual Callout

The number of actual frames that you can capture during continuous shooting varies, depending on the image format that you are using (JPEG, RAW, RAW+JPEG). Three factors can limit your number of continuous frames. One is the buffer, which is a temporary memory for holding images, and another is the processors, which convert the image data on the camera sensor into a file for storage. The final factor is the speed of the memory card you are using. To find out the frame rates, as well as the maximum number of frames that you can take in one continuous burst, check out page 151 of your camera manual.

A Sense of Motion

Shooting action isn't always about freezing the action. There are times when you want to convey a sense of motion so that the viewer can get a feel for the movement and flow of an event. Two techniques you can use to achieve this effect are panning and motion blur.

Panning

Panning has been used for decades to capture the speed of a moving object as it moves across the frame. It doesn't work well for subjects that are moving toward or away from you. Panning is achieved by following your subject across your frame, moving your camera along with the subject, and using a slower-than-normal shutter speed so that the background (and sometimes even a bit of the subject) has a sideways blur, but the main portion of your subject is sharp and blur-free. The key to a great panning shot is selecting the right shutter speed: too fast and you won't get the desired blurring of the background; too slow and the subject will have too much blur and will not be recognizable. Practice the technique until you can achieve a smooth motion with your camera that follows along with your subject. I usually begin around 1/30 of a second, and then make changes depending on the results. The other thing to remember when panning is to follow through even after the shutter has closed. This will keep the motion smooth and give you better images.

In **Figure 4.11**, I used the panning technique to follow this motocross rider as he rode in front of me. I set the camera drive mode to Continuous shooting, and I used Tv mode to select a shutter speed of 1/40 of a second while the focus mode was on AI Servo. It's important to shoot a continuous sequence, because you are more likely to get at least one good frame from the burst.

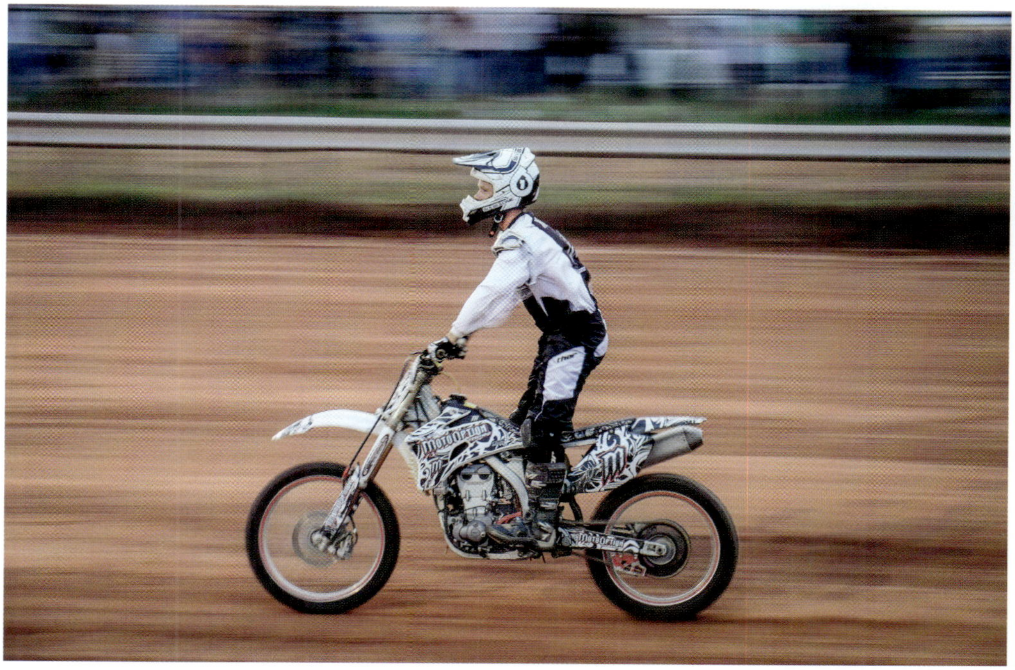

Figure 4.11
Following the subject as it moves across the field of view allows for a slower shutter speed and adds a sense of motion to the shot.

ISO 2000 • 1/40 sec. • f/9 • 116mm lens

Motion blur

Another way to let the viewer in on the feel of the action is to include some blur in the image. I don't mean accidental blur from choosing the wrong shutter speed. This blur is more exaggerated, and it tells a story. In **Figure 4.12**, I was interested in capturing the movement of the kayaker as he paddled through the fast-moving water. A fast shutter speed would have surely frozen the action, but it would not have told the story of the movement. Instead of moving with the action, I let the movement of the kayaker and the water create the blur as I held the camera in a stationary position.

Just as in panning, there is no preordained shutter speed to use for this effect. It is a matter of trial and error until you have a look that conveys the action. I usually try to get some area of the subject that is frozen. The key to this technique is the correct shutter speed combined with keeping the camera still during the exposure. You are trying to capture the motion of the subject, not the photographer or the camera, so use a good shooting stance or even a tripod. Also, try shooting in Continuous drive mode and capture several consecutive exposures. Chances are, your first one may not look good, but one of the images in the series will have just the look you are after.

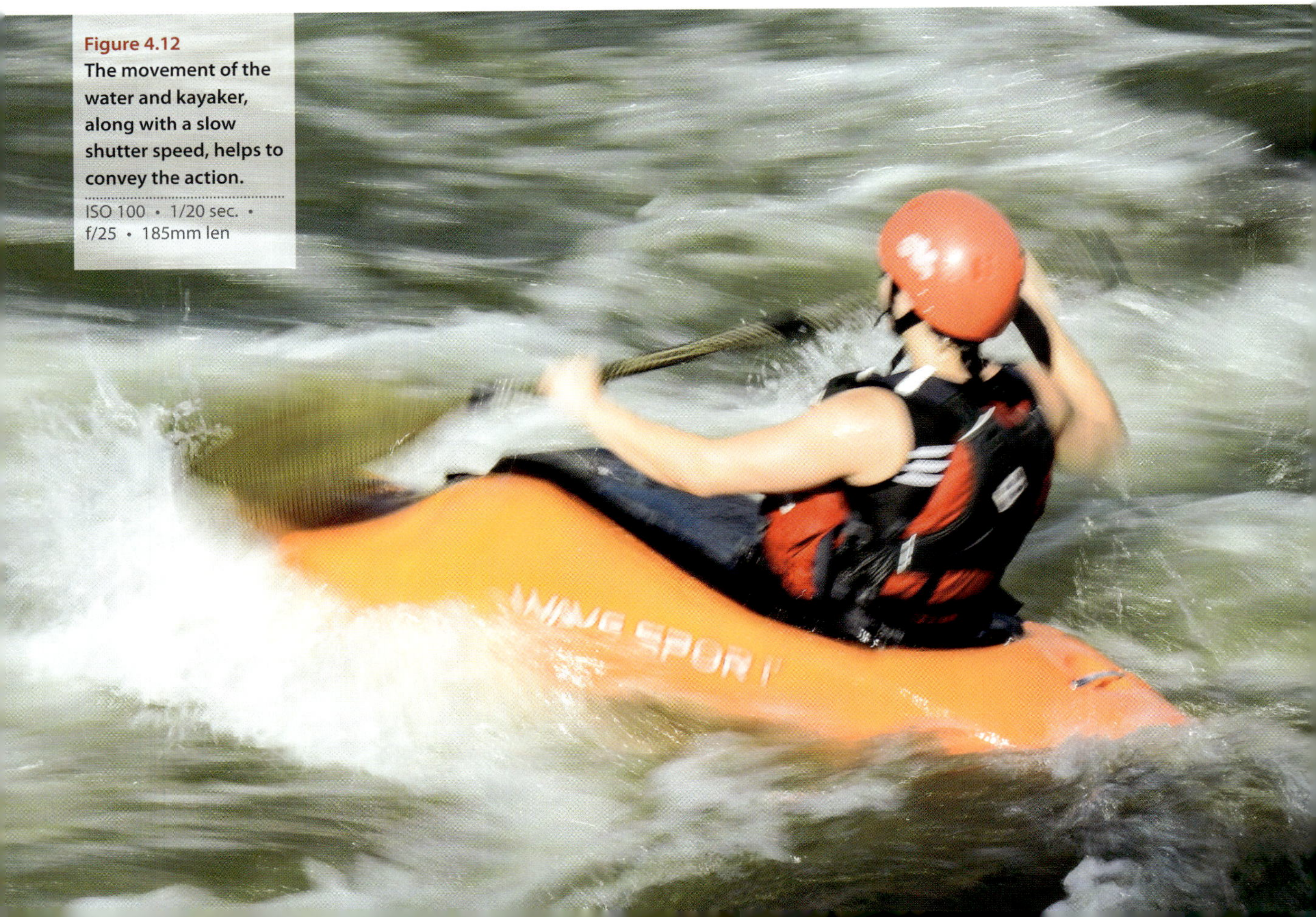

Figure 4.12
The movement of the water and kayaker, along with a slow shutter speed, helps to convey the action.

ISO 100 • 1/20 sec. • f/25 • 185mm len

Chapter 4 Assignments

Shooting sports or action of any type is a little challenging at first. It can be difficult to put all the pieces together at just the right time. These exercises will help you tackle the fundamentals so that you will know exactly how to set your camera to get the image you want and capture the moment before it's gone.

The mechanics of motion

For this first assignment, you need to find some action. Explore the relationship between the speed of an object and its direction of travel. Use the same shutter speed to record your subject moving toward you and across your view. Try using the same shutter speed for both to compare the difference made by the direction of travel.

Getting a feel for focusing modes

We discussed two ways to use autofocus for action: AI Servo and AI Focus. Starting with AI Servo mode, find a moving subject and use the mode to become familiar with the way the mode works. Change from autofocus point selection to a single-point selection. Now repeat the process using the AI Focus mode. The point of the exercise is to become familiar enough with the two modes to decide which one to use for the situation you are photographing.

Anticipating the spot using manual focus

Find a subject that you know will cross a specific line that you can prefocus on. A street with moderate traffic works well for this. Focus on a spot on the street that the cars will travel across (don't forget to set your lens for manual focus). To do this right, you need to set the drive mode on the camera to the Continuous mode. Now when a car approaches the spot, start shooting. Try shooting in 3- or 4-frame bursts.

Following the action

Panning is a great way to show motion. To begin, find a subject that will move across your path at a steady speed and practice following it in your viewfinder from side to side. Now, with the camera in Tv mode, set your shutter speed to 1/30 of a second and the focus mode to AI Servo. Pan along with the subject and shoot as it moves across your view. Experiment with various shutter speeds and focal lengths. Panning is one of those skills that takes some time to get a feel for, so try it with different types of subjects moving at different speeds.

Feeling the movement

Instead of panning with the motion, use a stationary camera position and adjust the shutter speed until you get a blurred effect that gives the sense of motion while still being able to identify the subject. There is a big difference between a slightly blurred photo that looks like you just picked the wrong shutter speed and one that looks intentional for the purpose of showing motion. As with panning, you will have to experiment to find just the right shutter speed to achieve the desired effect.

Share your results with the book's Flickr group!
Join the group here: flickr.com/groups/7dmarkii_fromsnapshotstogreatshots

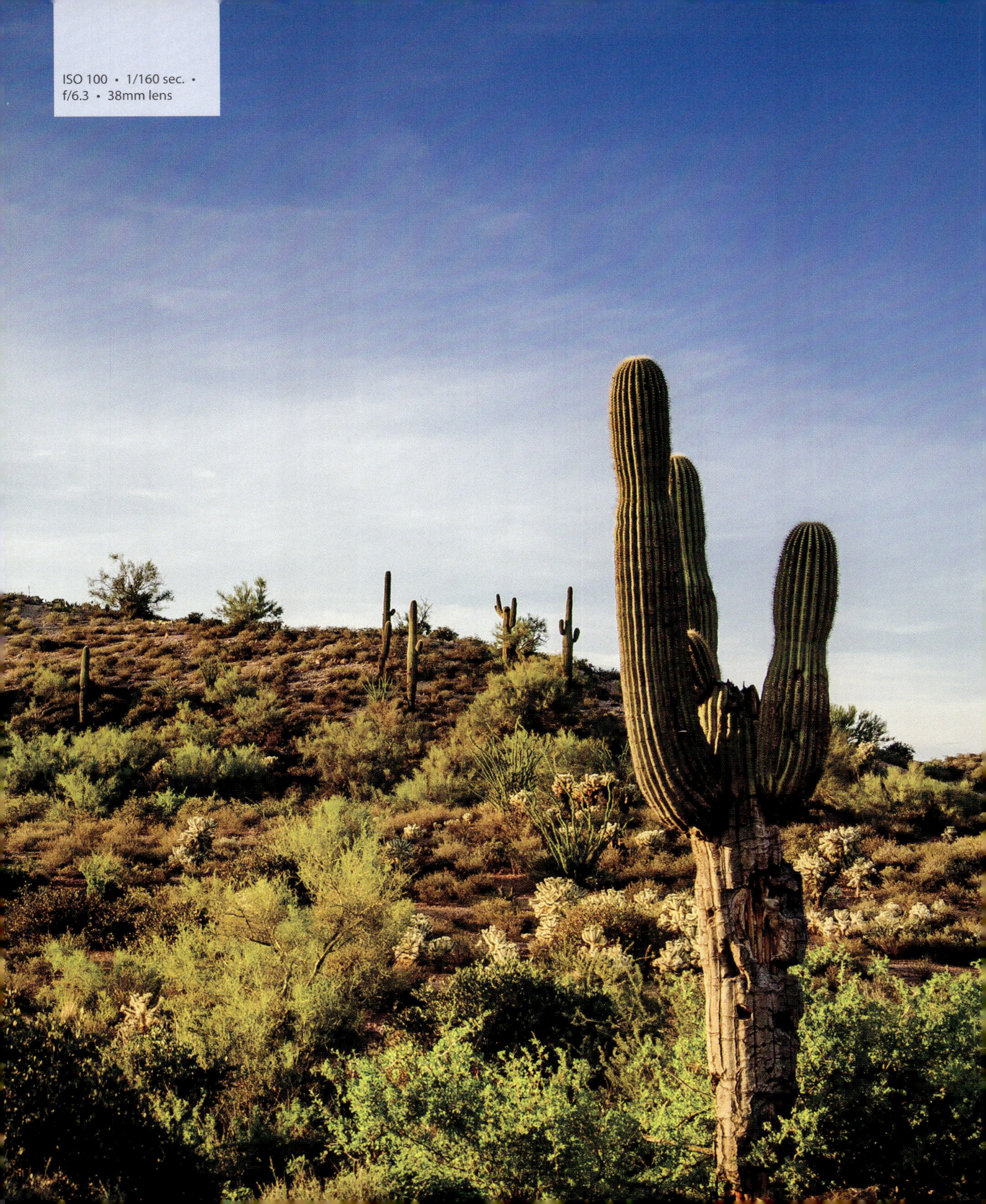

ISO 100 • 1/160 sec. • f/6.3 • 38mm lens

5

Landscape Photography

Tips, Tools, and Techniques to Get the Most Out of Your Landscape Photography

It's really funny how people can react to new technology. When the 7D Mark II was first announced I would see so many people commenting in forums about how nice the camera is for sports shooters but that they like to shoot landscapes, so it's obviously not the right camera for them. Allow me to let you in on a little secret that these photographers obviously don't know: You don't need a special camera for shooting landscapes. In fact, I would put the 7D Mark II up against almost any other camera out there when it comes to capturing great scenic images because it's not so much about the camera but rather how you use it that counts.

In this chapter, we will explore some of the features of the 7D Mark II that not only improve the look of your landscape photography, but also make it easier to take great shots. We will also explore some typical scenarios and discuss methods to bring out the best in your landscape work. You don't even have to tell anyone that you took that awesome shot with a "sports" camera.

Poring Over the Picture

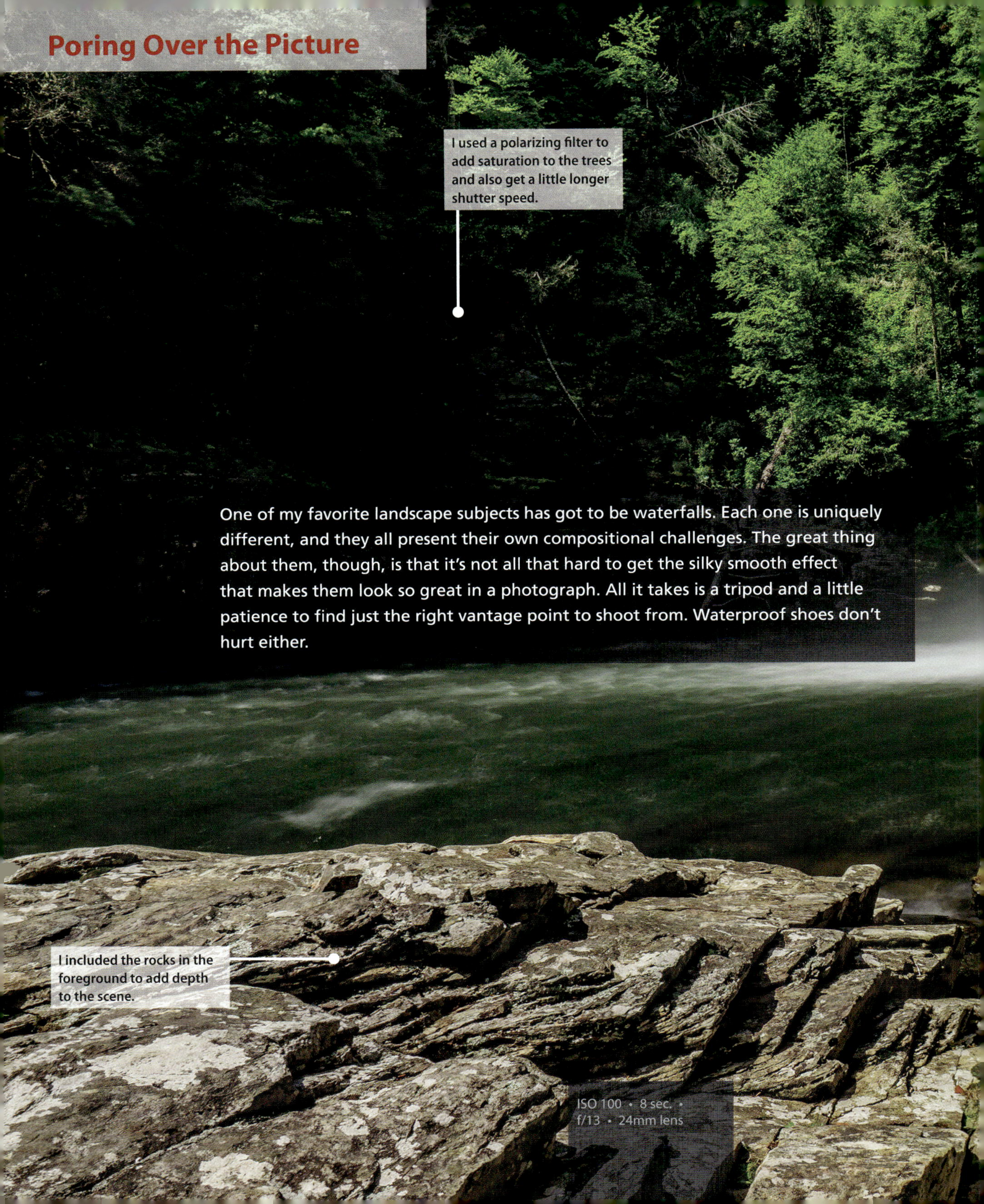

One of my favorite landscape subjects has got to be waterfalls. Each one is uniquely different, and they all present their own compositional challenges. The great thing about them, though, is that it's not all that hard to get the silky smooth effect that makes them look so great in a photograph. All it takes is a tripod and a little patience to find just the right vantage point to shoot from. Waterproof shoes don't hurt either.

ISO 100 • 8 sec. • f/13 • 24mm lens

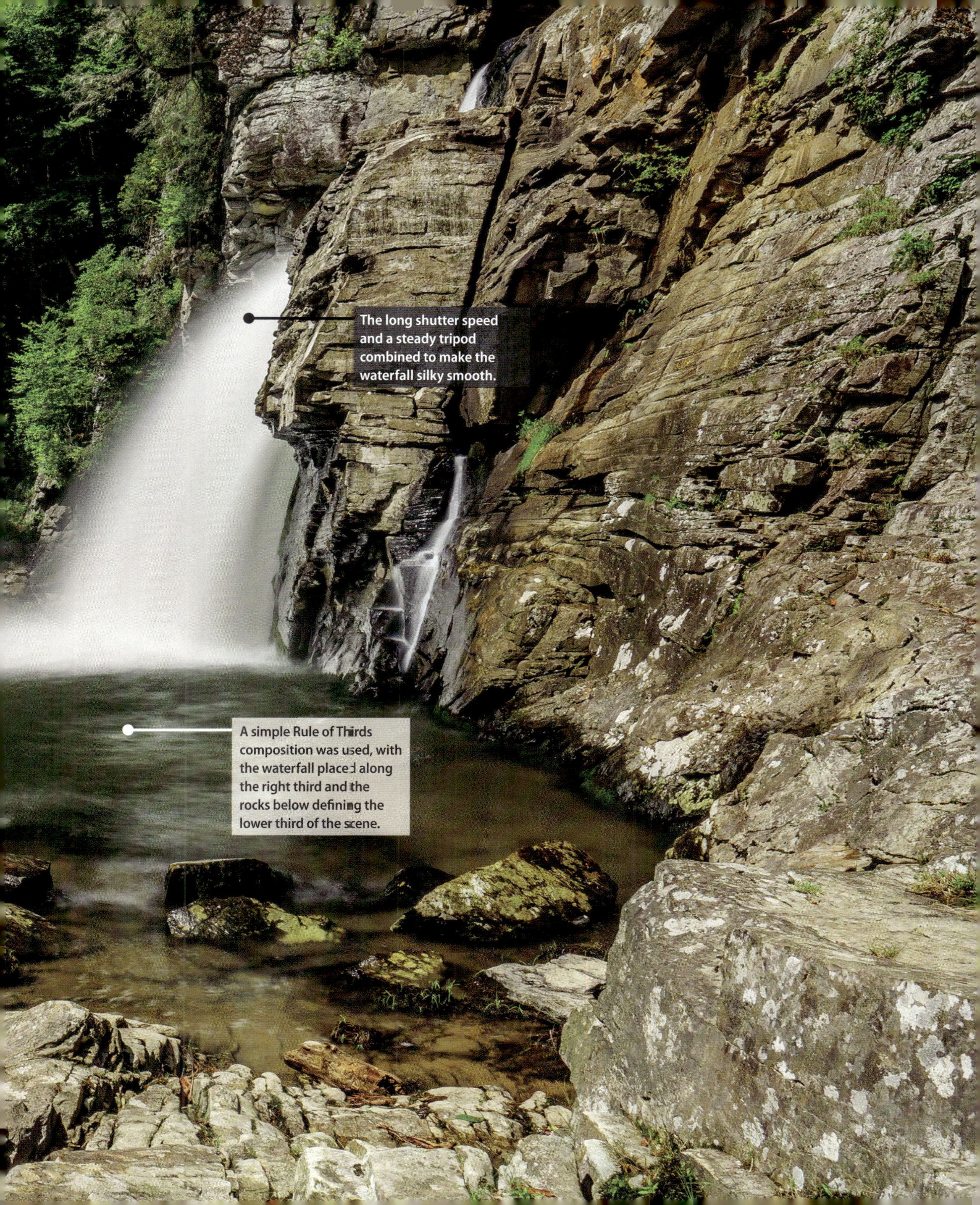
The long shutter speed and a steady tripod combined to make the waterfall silky smooth.
A simple Rule of Thirds composition was used, with the waterfall placed along the right third and the rocks below defining the lower third of the scene.

Sharp and in Focus: Using Tripods

There are a lot of great features in the 7D Mark II that we will discuss to help you capture great images, but when it comes to landscape photography, I would be remiss if I didn't cover one crucial piece of gear that is essential for creating an exceptional image: the tripod. Tripods are critical to your landscape work for a couple of reasons. The first relates to the time of day that you will be working. For reasons that will be explained later, the best light for most landscape work happens at sunrise and just before sunset. Although this is the best time to shoot, it's also kind of dark. That means you'll be working with slow shutter speeds. Slow shutter speeds mean camera shake when you are trying to handhold the camera. Camera shake equals bad photos.

The second reason is also related to the amount of light that you're gathering with your camera. When taking landscape photos, you will usually want to be working with very small apertures, as they give you lots of depth of field (DOF). This also means that, once again, you will be working with slower-than-normal shutter speeds.

Slow shutter = camera shake = bad photos.

Do you see where I'm going with this? The one tool that you can turn to in order to truly defeat the camera-shake issue and ensure tack-sharp photos is a steady tripod (**Figure 5.1**).

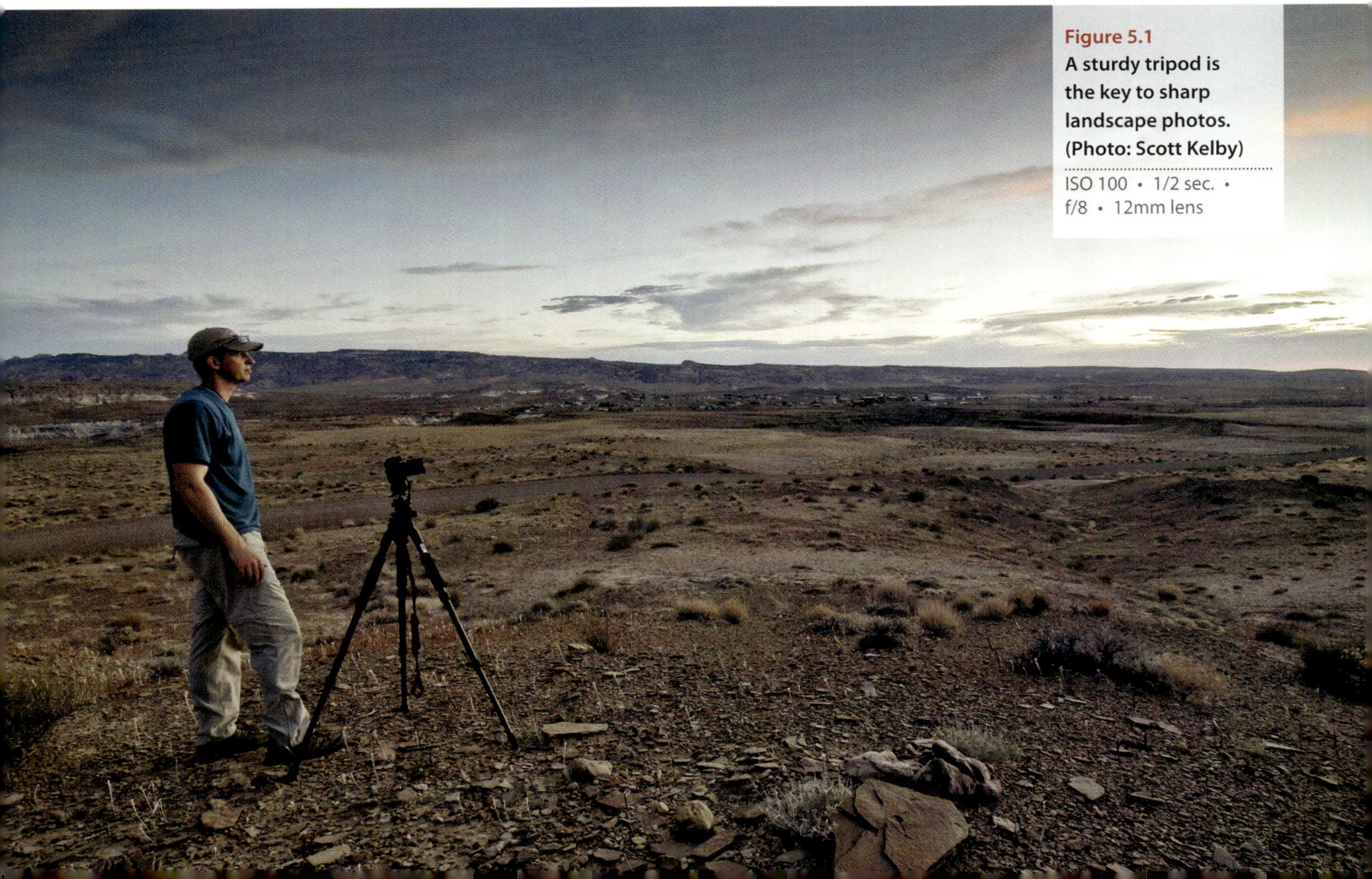

Figure 5.1
A sturdy tripod is the key to sharp landscape photos. (Photo: Scott Kelby)

ISO 100 • 1/2 sec. • f/8 • 12mm lens

So what should you look for in a tripod? Well, first make sure it is sturdy enough to support your camera and any lens you might want to use. Next, check the height of the tripod. Your day will end much better if you haven't been bent over looking through your viewfinder for the better part of the day. Finally, think about getting a tripod that uses a quick-release head. This type of tripod usually employs a plate that screws into the bottom of the camera and then quickly snaps into place on the tripod. A quick-release head will be especially handy if you are going to move between shooting by hand and using the tripod. You can find more information on tripods in Chapter 11, "Pimp My Ride."

Tripod stability

Most tripods have a center column that allows the user to extend the height of the camera above the point where the tripod legs join together. This might seem like a great idea, but the reality is that the higher you raise that column, the less stable your tripod becomes. Think of a tall building that sways near the top. To get the most solid base for your camera, always try to use it with the center column at its lowest point so that your camera is right at the apex of the tripod legs.

IS lenses and tripods don't mix

If you are using image stabilization (IS) lenses on your camera, remember to turn this feature off when you use a tripod (**Figure 5.2**). This is because the image stabilization can, while trying to minimize camera movement, actually *create* movement when the camera is already stable. To turn off the IS feature, just slide the Stabilizer selector switch on the side of the lens to the Off position.

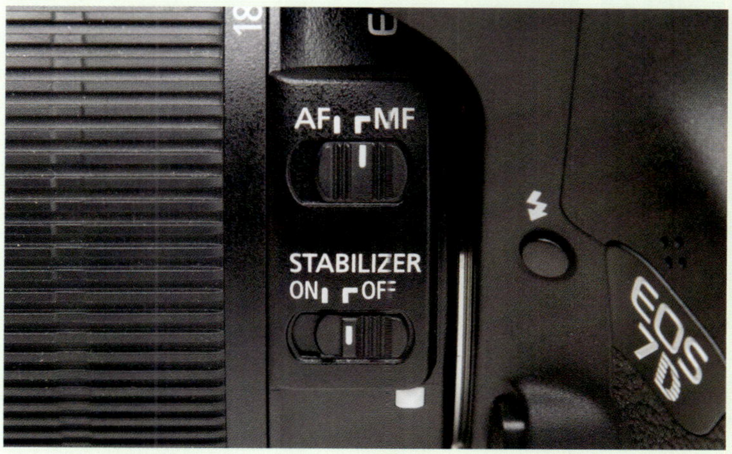

Figure 5.2
Turn off the Image Stabilization feature when using a tripod.

Selecting the Proper ISO

One of the biggest drawbacks of the Intelligent Auto mode is the inability to change exposure settings. When you are shooting most landscape scenes, the ISO is the one factor that should be changed only as a last resort. Although it is easy to select a higher ISO to get a smaller aperture, the noise introduced into your images from a high ISO setting can be quite harmful (**Figure 5.3** and **Figure 5.4**). The noise is not only visible as large grainy artifacts; it can also be multicolored, which further degrades the image quality. Take a look at the image in Figure 5.4, which was taken with an ISO of 1600. The purpose was to shorten the shutter speed and still use a small aperture setting of f/22.

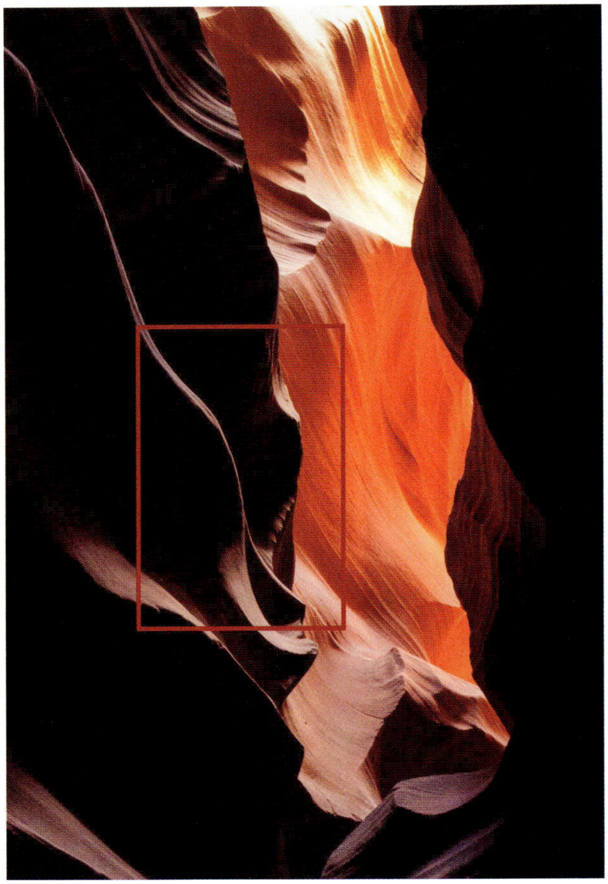

Figure 5.3
A high ISO setting created a lot of digital noise in the shadows.

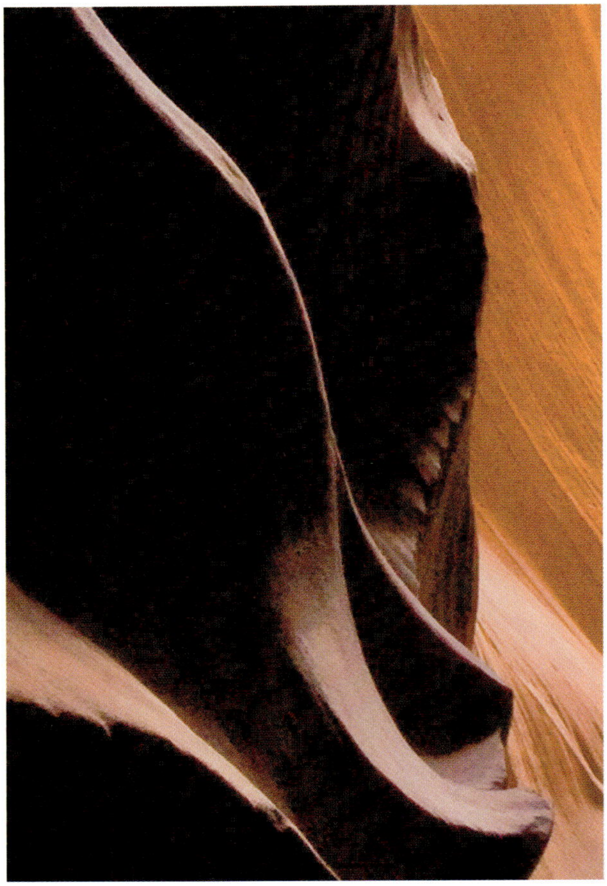

Figure 5.4
When the image is enlarged, the noise is even more apparent.

ISO 1600 • 2 sec. • f/22 • 24mm lens

The problem is that the noise level is so high that, in addition to being distracting, it is obscuring fine details in the canyon wall.

Now check out another image that was taken in the same canyon light but with a much lower ISO setting (**Figure 5.5** and **Figure 5.6**). As you can see, the noise levels are much lower, which means that blacks look black and the fine details are beautifully captured.

When shooting landscapes, be sure to use one of the Creative modes like Av or Tv and set your ISO to the lowest possible setting at all times. Between the use of image-stabilization lenses (if you are shooting handheld) and a good tripod, there should be few circumstances where you would need to shoot landscapes with anything above an ISO of 400.

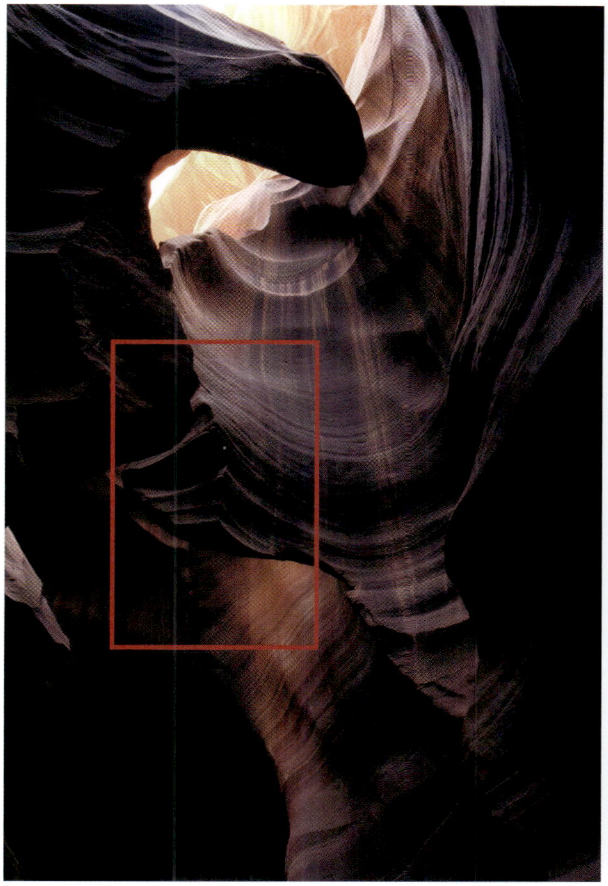

Figure 5.5

By lowering the ISO to 100, I avoided the noise and captured a clean image.

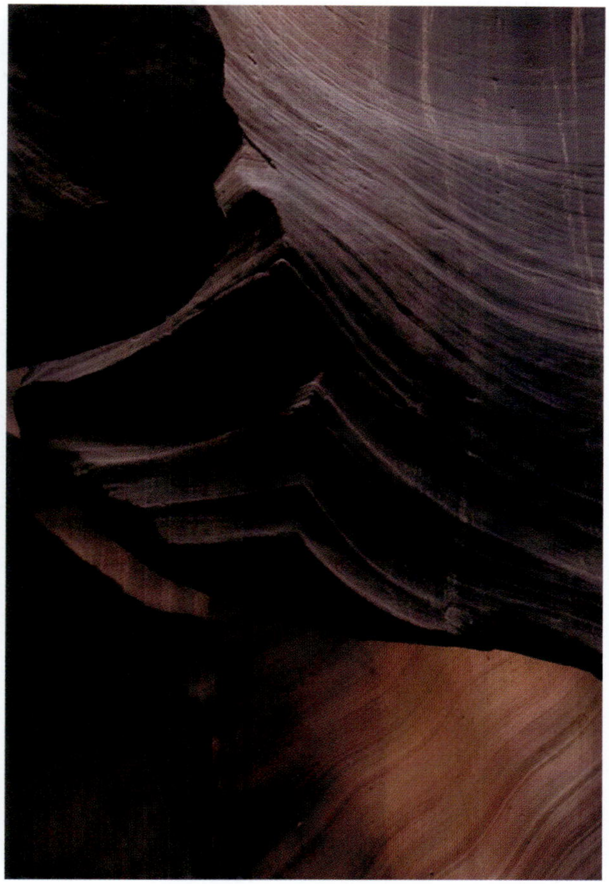

Figure 5.6

Zooming in shows that the noise levels for this image are almost nonexistent.

ISO 100 • 30 sec. • f/22 • 24mm lens

Using Noise Reduction

Both canyon images were taken with a tripod, but the image set to an ISO of 100 required four more stops of shutter speed (30 seconds at ISO 100) than the high ISO image (2 seconds at ISO 1600). The temptation to use higher ISOs should always be avoided, because the end result will be more image noise and less detail.

You can also encounter issues when using low ISO settings: Extremely long shutter speeds can also introduce noise into your image. This noise is a result of the heating of the camera sensor as it is being exposed to light. This effect is not visible in short exposures, but as you start shooting with shutter speeds that exceed 1 second in length, the level of image noise can increase. Your camera has a couple of features that you can turn on to combat noise from long exposures and high ISOs.

Setting up noise reduction

1. Press the Menu button; then use the Main dial to access the third shooting menu, highlight the High ISO Speed NR option, and press Set (**A**).
2. The default setting is Standard, but use the High setting for really high ISOs (**B**).

A

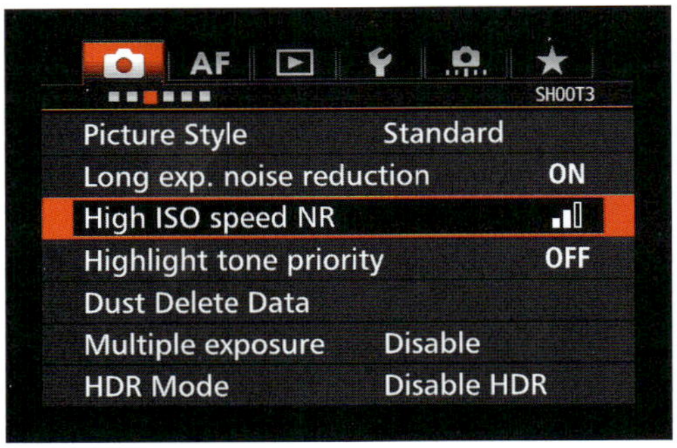

B

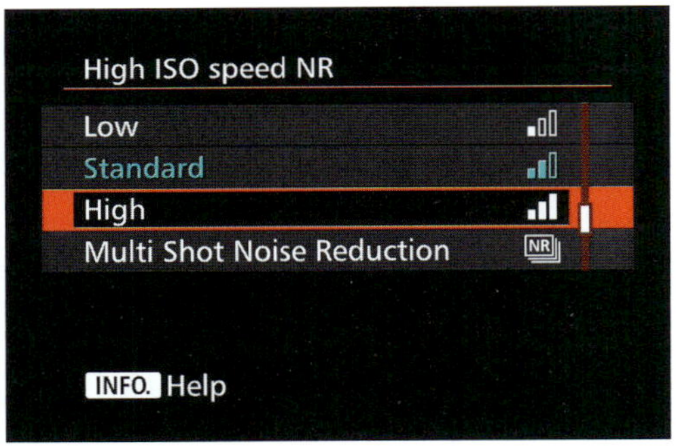

3. Press the Menu button to return to the shooting menu, and then select Long Exp. Noise Reduction. Press the Set button to change the options (**C**).

C

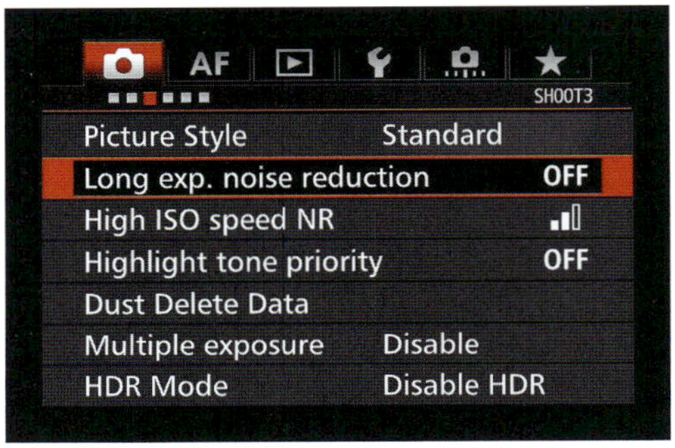

4. The default setting is Auto, which will handle most scenarios. If you know you are going to be making extremely long exposures, you should probably go ahead and set it to On (**D**).

D

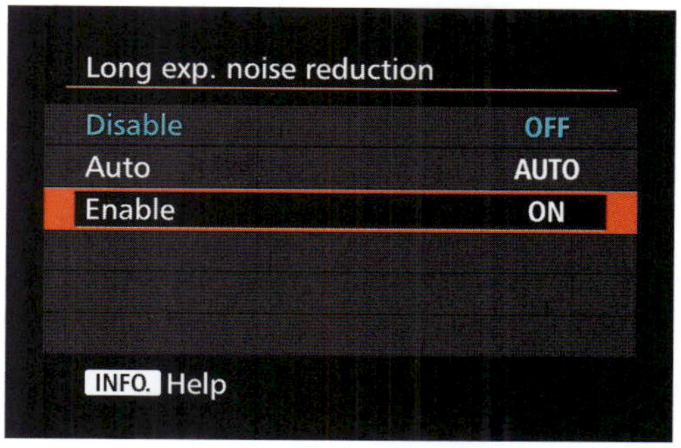

Selecting a White Balance

This probably seems like a no-brainer: If it's sunny, select Daylight. If it's overcast, choose the Shade or Cloudy setting. Those choices wouldn't be wrong for those circumstances, but why limit yourself? Sometimes you can change the mood of the photo by selecting a white balance that doesn't quite fit the light for the scene you are shooting. **Figure 5.7** is an example of a correct white balance. It was late afternoon and the sun was starting to move low in the sky, giving everything that warm afternoon glow. I set the white balance for this image to Cloudy to add a bit of warmth. But what if I wanted to make the scene look like it was shot in the predawn hours of early morning? Simple; I could just change the white balance to Fluorescent, which is a much cooler setting (**Figure 5.8**).

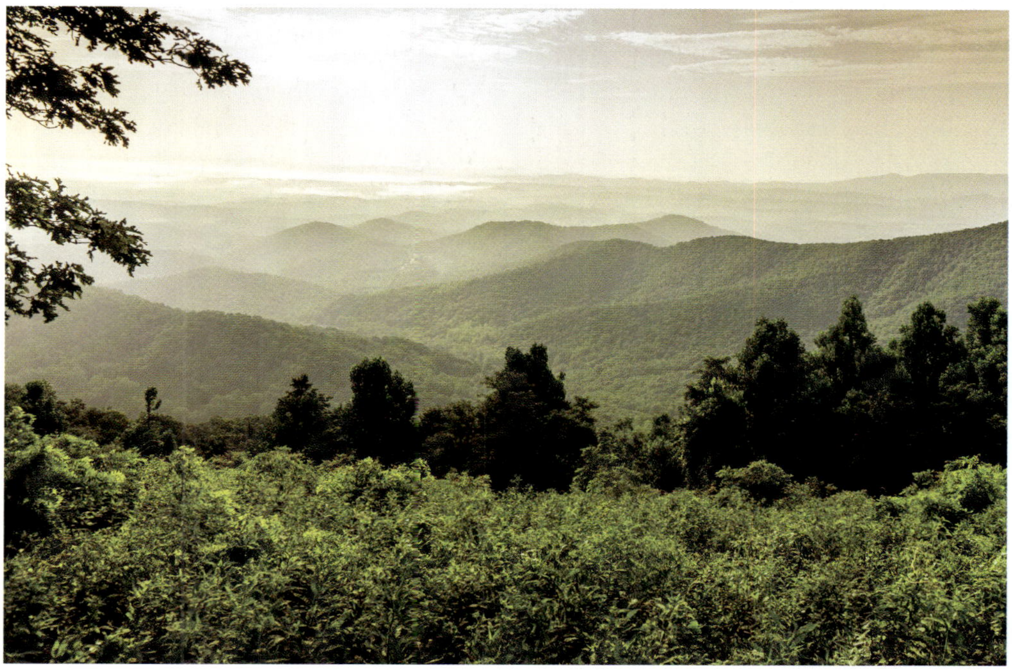

Figure 5.7
Using the "proper" white balance yields predictable results.

ISO 100 • 1/30 sec. • f/8 • 95mm lens

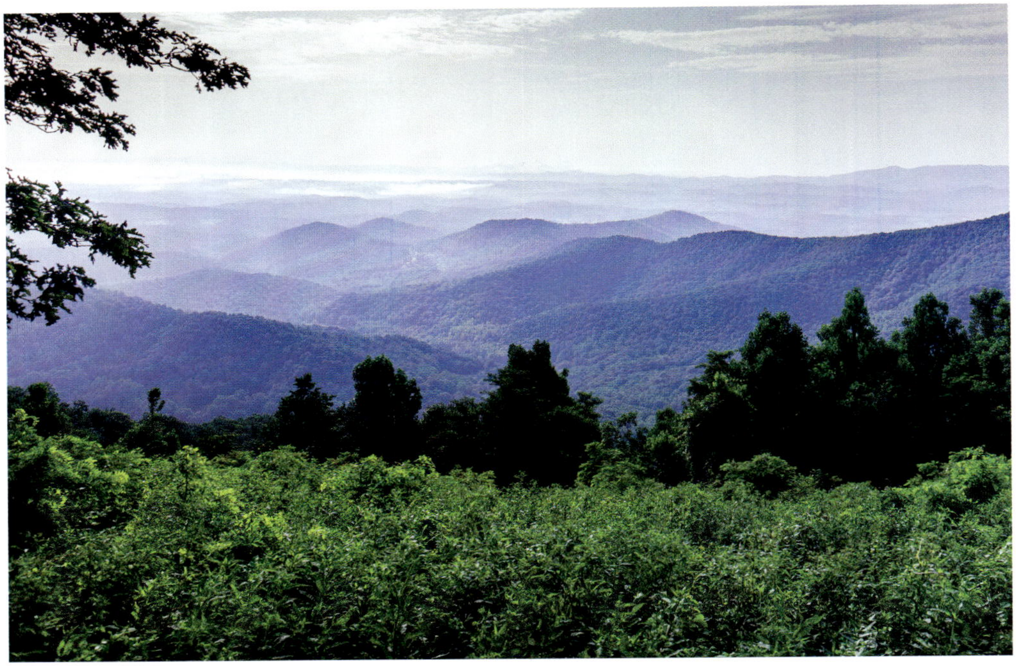

Figure 5.8
Changing the white balance to Fluorescent gives the impression that the picture was taken at a different time of day than it really was.

ISO 100 • 1/30 sec. • f/8 • 95mm lens

You can select the most appropriate white balance for your shooting conditions in a couple of ways. The first way is to just take a shot, review it on the LCD, and keep the one you like. Of course, you would need to take one for each white balance setting, which means that you will have to take about seven different shots to see which is most pleasing. The second method, and my personal favorite, doesn't require taking a single shot. Instead, it uses Live View to get perfectly selected white balances. Live View gives instant feedback as you scroll through all of the white balance settings and displays them for you right on the LCD. Even better, you can choose a custom setting that will let you dial in exactly the right look for your image. (See Chapter 6, "Say Cheese!" for more on Live View.)

Using Live View to preview different white balance settings

1. Press the Live View button located to the right of the rear LCD screen.
2. With Live View activated, press the Q button, which will bring up the Live View options on the sides of the screen.
3. Use the Multi-controller to highlight the White Balance icon (the middle one on the right side of the screen), and then rotate the Quick Control dial to change the white balance.

4. Select the white balance setting that looks most appropriate for your scene; then press the Q button to lock in your change and resume shooting.
5. Press the Live View button once again to exit Live View mode.

Using the Landscape Picture Style

When shooting landscapes, I always look for great color and contrast. This is one of the reasons that so many landscape shots are taken in the early morning or during sunset. The light is much more vibrant and colorful at these times of day and adds a sense of drama to an image. You can help boost this effect, especially in the less-than-golden hours of the day, by using the Landscape picture style (**Figure 5.9** and **Figure 5.10**). By using the Landscape picture style, you can set up your landscape shooting so that you capture images with increased sharpness and a slight boost in blues and greens. This style will add some pop to your landscapes without the need for additional processing in any software.

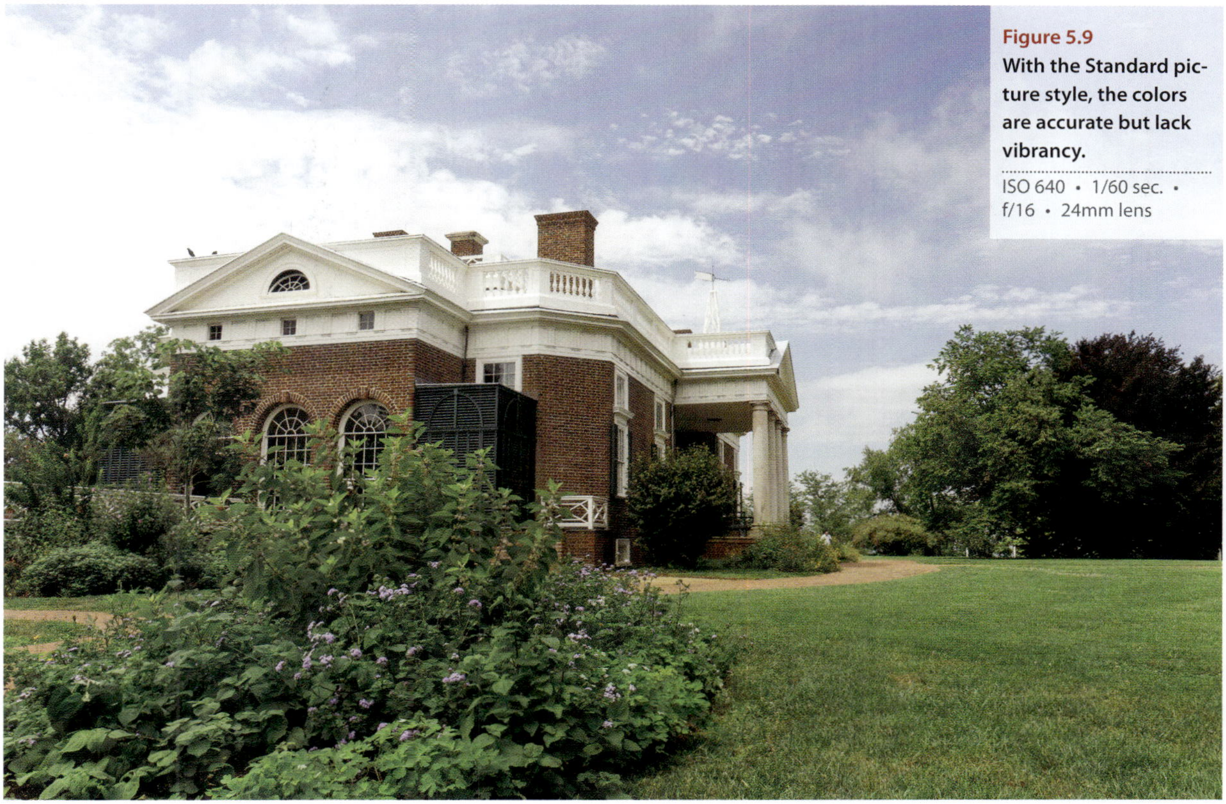

Figure 5.9
With the Standard picture style, the colors are accurate but lack vibrancy.

ISO 640 • 1/60 sec. • f/16 • 24mm lens

Figure 5.10
Using the Landscape picture style adds sharpness, a little contrast, and color boost to skies and vegetation.

ISO 640 • 1/60 sec. • f/16 • 24mm lens

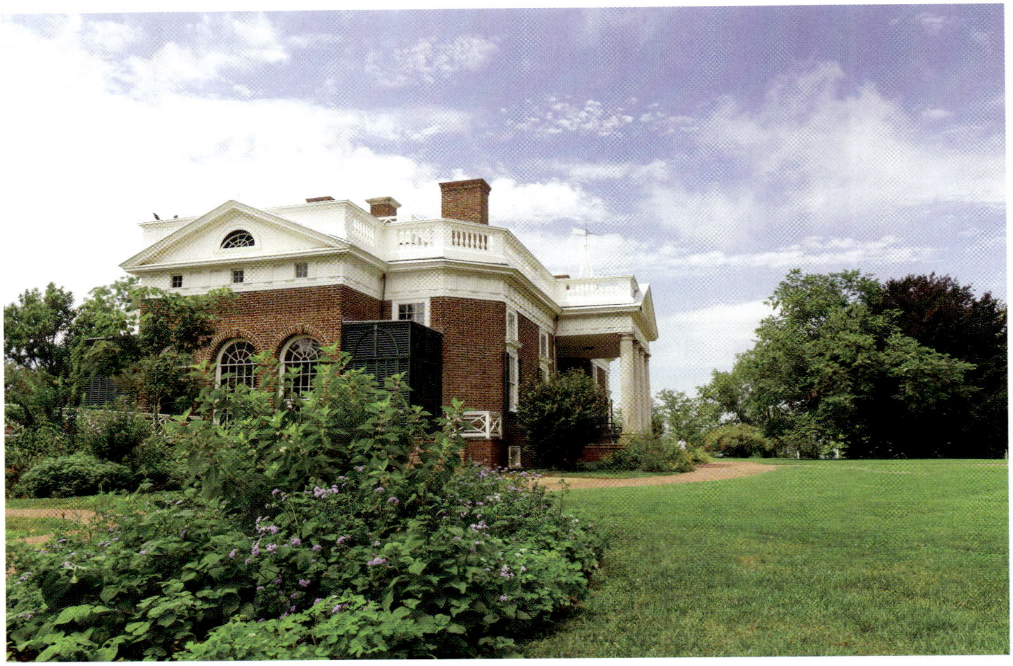

Setting up the Landscape Picture Style

1. Press the Creative Photo button on the back of the camera (it's just below the menu button).
2. Highlight the Picture Style icon, and press the Set button (**A**).

A

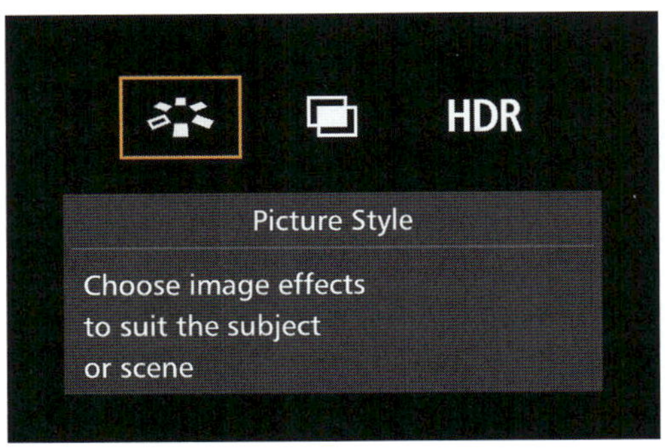

B

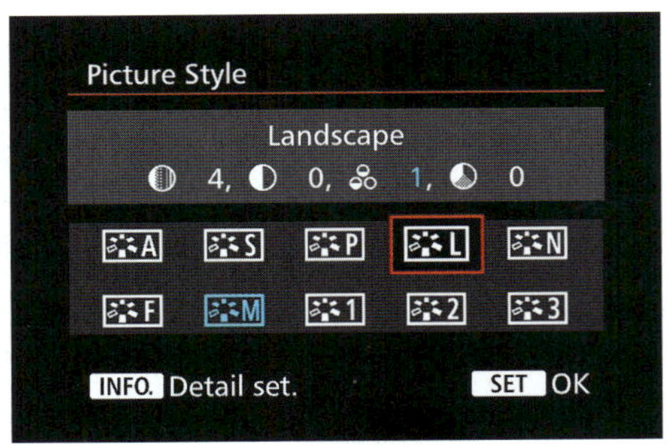

3. Use the Quick Control dial to highlight the Landscape setting, and then press the Set button to lock in your change (**B**).

If you are shooting raw, your images will look like they have the Picture Style applied when you are viewing them on the back of the camera, but the style will go away once you open the images in your postprocessing software. You will need to add the Picture Style back as part of your postprocessing. Only JPEGs have the Picture Style applied as part of the final image processing in-camera. You can also choose to have the best of both worlds by saving both a RAW and a JPEG at the time of capture.

Taming Bright Skies with Exposure Compensation

Balancing exposure in scenes that have a wide contrast in tonal ranges can be extremely challenging. The one thing you should try not to do is overexpose your skies to the point of blowing out your highlights (unless, of course, that's the look you're going for). It's one thing to have white clouds, but it's a completely different and bad thing to have no detail at all in those clouds. This usually happens when the camera is trying to gain exposure in the darker areas of the image (**Figure 5.11**).

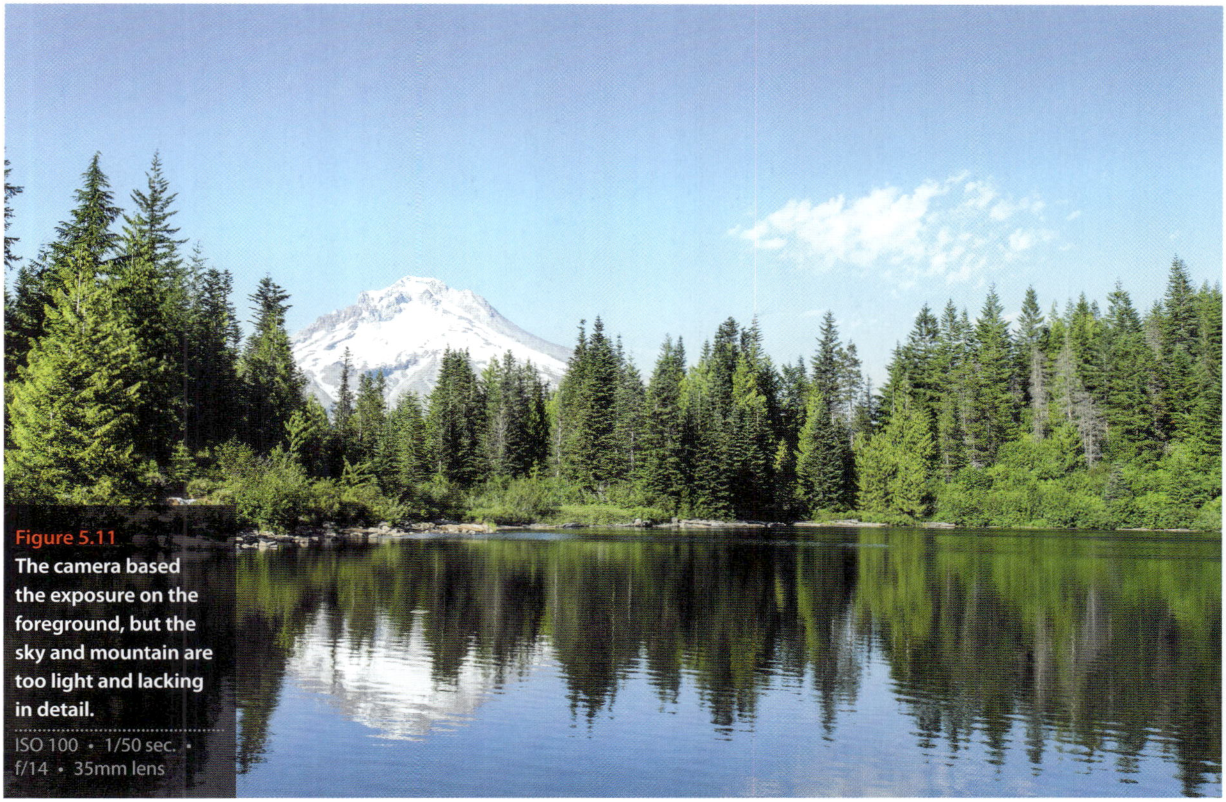

Figure 5.11
The camera based the exposure on the foreground, but the sky and mountain are too light and lacking in detail.
ISO 100 • 1/50 sec. • f/14 • 35mm lens

The one way to tell if you have blown out your highlights is to check the Highlight Alert, or "blinkies," feature on your camera (see the "How I Shoot" section in Chapter 3, "Camera Shooting Modes"). When you take a shot where the highlights are exposed beyond the point of having any detail, that area will blink in your LCD display. It is up to you to determine whether that particular area is important enough to regain detail by altering your exposure. If the answer is yes, then the easiest way to go about it is to use some exposure compensation.

With this feature, you can force your camera to choose an exposure that ranges, in 1/3-stop increments, from 5 stops over to 5 stops under the metered exposure (**Figure 5.12**).

A quick way to gauge for overexposure is to keep the highlight alert turned on. When you take a photo, you will be alerted to the overexposed skies by the blinking areas in the preview. When you see them, follow the subsequent steps to dial in some compensation. Just remember that not everything in your photo is meant to have detail, and sometimes it won't matter how much compensation you use because those areas will never have detail—for example, the sun or really bright, white clouds.

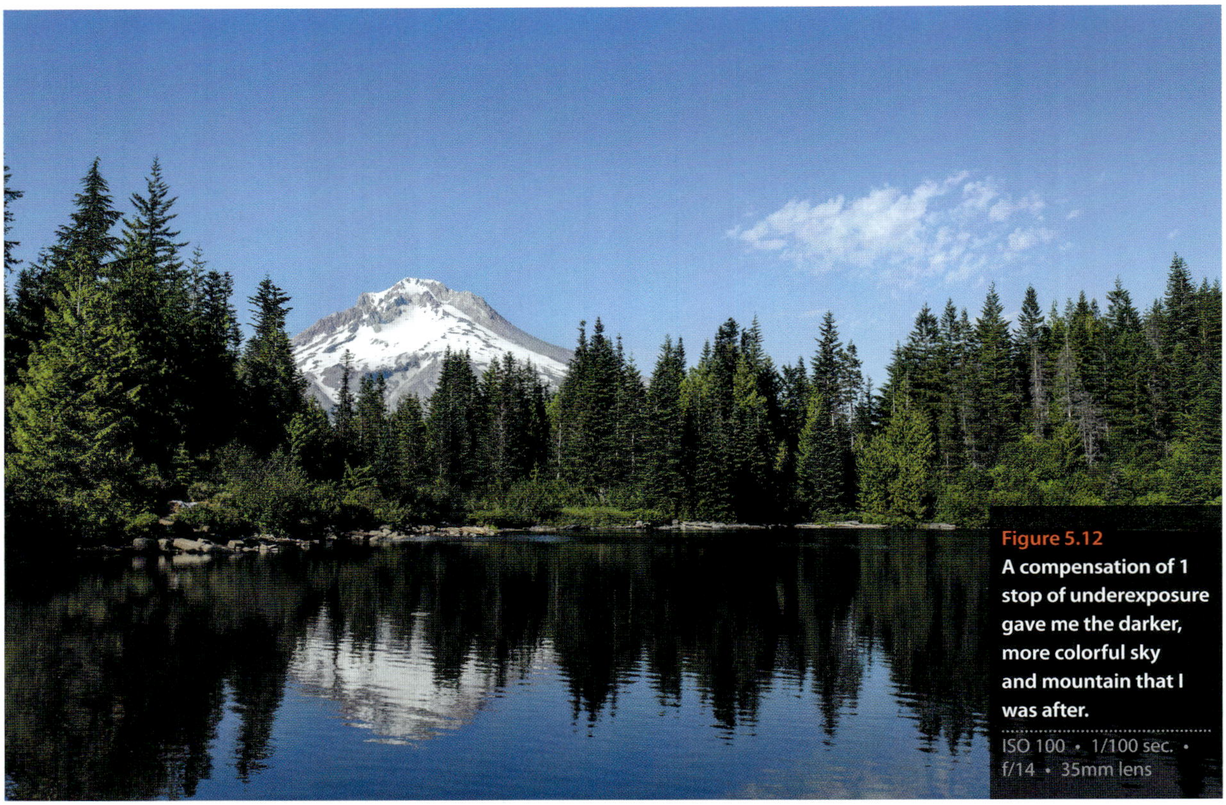

Figure 5.12
A compensation of 1 stop of underexposure gave me the darker, more colorful sky and mountain that I was after.

ISO 100 • 1/100 sec. • f/14 • 35mm lens

Using Exposure Compensation to regain detail in highlights

1. Activate the camera meter by lightly pressing the shutter release button.
2. Use the Quick Control dial to set the amount of over- or underexposure that you desire.
3. Take a photo.
4. If the blinkies are gone, you are good to go. If not, keep subtracting from your exposure by 1/3 of a stop until you have a good exposure in the highlights.

I generally keep my camera set to –1/3 stop for most of my landscape work unless I am working with a location that is very dark or low-key.

High-key and low-key images

When you hear someone refer to a subject as being *high key*, it usually means that the entire image consists of a very bright subject with very few shadow areas—think snow or beach. It makes sense, then, that a *low-key* subject has very few highlight areas and a predominance of shadow areas. Think of a cityscape at night as an example of a low-key photo.

Shooting Beautiful Black-and-White Landscapes

Nothing is as timeless as a beautiful black-and-white landscape photo. For many, it is the purest form of photography. The genre conjures up thoughts of Ansel Adams in Yosemite Valley, capturing stunning monoliths with his 8x10-view camera. Well, just because you are shooting with a digital camera doesn't mean you can't create your own stunning photos using the power of the Monochrome picture style (**Figure 5.13**). Not only can you shoot in black and white, you can also apply built-in filters to lighten or darken different elements within your scene, as well as add contrast and definition.

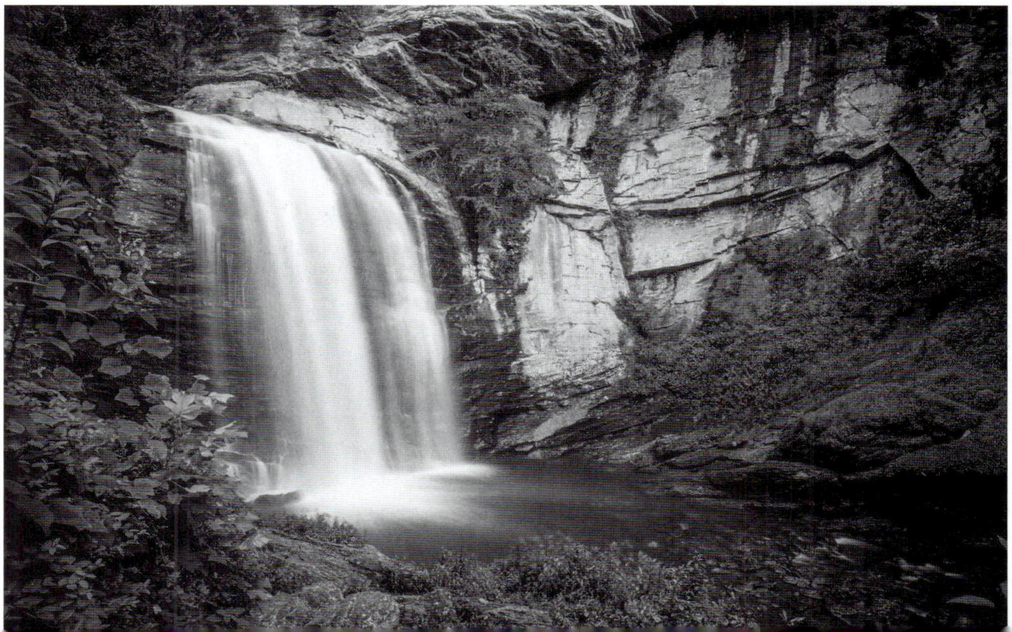

Figure 5.13
Capturing black-and-white images is as simple as turning on the Monochrome picture style.

ISO 100 • 2 sec. • f/20 • 24mm lens

The four filter colors are yellow, orange, red, and green. The most typically used filters in black-and-white photography are red and yellow. This is because the color of the filter will darken opposite colors and lighten similar colors. So if you want to darken a blue sky, you use a yellow filter because blue is the opposite of yellow. To darken green foliage, you use a red filter. Check out the series of shots in **Figure 5.14** with different filters applied to a color chart.

You can see that no real difference in contrast exists between the color and the black-and-white image with no filter, but there is a definite loss of tonal value between many of the different colors. For instance, the light violet and chartreuse appear to be the same shade of gray in the black-and-white image with no filters applied. This is the same for many of the colors, which would normally be fairly contrasting in their appearance. You can regain some of this tonal contrast by applying a colored filter effect to the monochrome picture style. There are four different colors to choose from—yellow, orange, red, and green. Each will lighten subjects of the same color while darkening colors on the opposite side of the spectrum. For example, the red filter makes reds lighter and cyan darker; the yellow filter makes yellow objects lighter while making blue objects darker. So if you have a blue sky, you might want to try the yellow or orange filter to make it look a bit darker in your image. Experiment with the different options to get the best result for the scene that you are photographing.

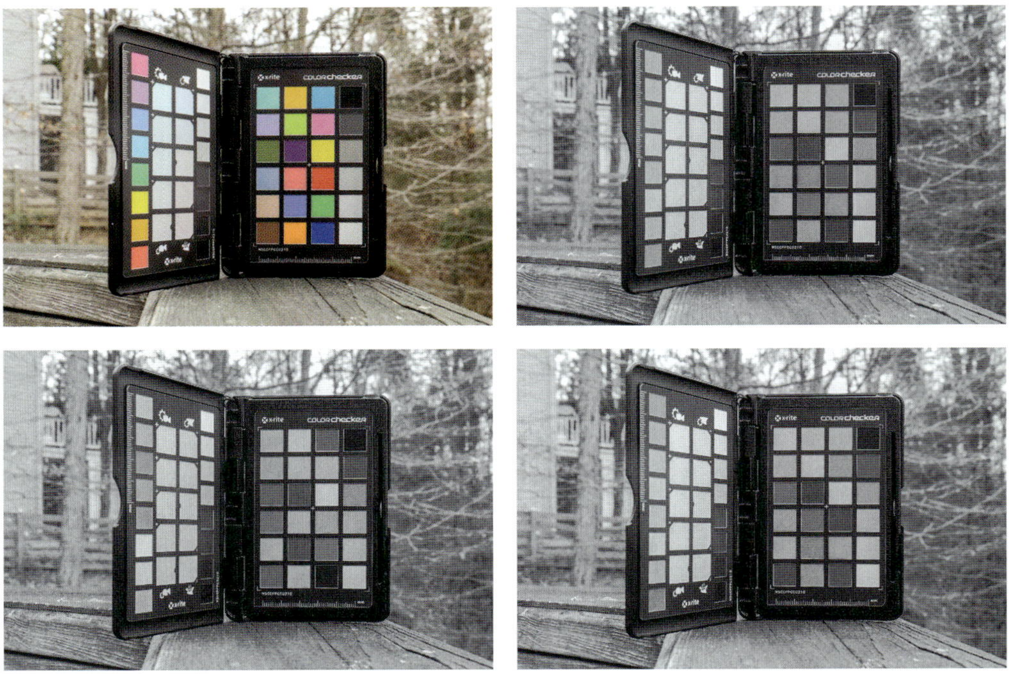

Figure 5.14
Adding color filter settings to the Monochrome picture style allows you to brighten or darken elements in your scene based on their color. The top-right image has no filter applied to it. The bottom-left image has a green filter, and the bottom-right image has a red filter.

ISO 800 • 1/60 sec. • f/11 • 24mm lens

Other options in the Monochrome picture style enable you to adjust the sharpness and contrast, and even add some color toning to the final image. This information is covered in the "Classic Black-and-White Portraits" section of Chapter 6. I like to have Sharpness set to 5 and Contrast set to 1 for my landscape images. This gives an overall look to the black-and-white image that is reminiscent of the classic black-and-white films. Experiment with the various settings to find the combination that is most pleasing to you.

Monochrome and RAW

The Picture Styles are only applied to the image when you are shooting in JPEG mode. This is due to the fact that RAW files are unprocessed, allowing for more advanced image enhancement in a postprocessing program. To get the best of both worlds, try shooting black-and-whites with the RAW+JPEG file option. This allows you to capture a JPEG with all of the Picture Style adjustments as well as the RAW file that you can process differently later.

The Golden Light

If you ask professional landscape photographers what their favorite time of day to shoot is, chances are they will tell you it's the hours surrounding daybreak and sunset (**Figure 5.15** and **Figure 5.16**). That's because the light is coming from a very low angle to the landscape, which creates shadows and gives depth and character. There is also a quality to the light that seems cleaner and is more colorful than the light you get when shooting at midday. One thing that can dramatically improve any morning or evening shot is the presence of clouds. The sun will fill the underside of the clouds with a palette of colors and add drama to your skies.

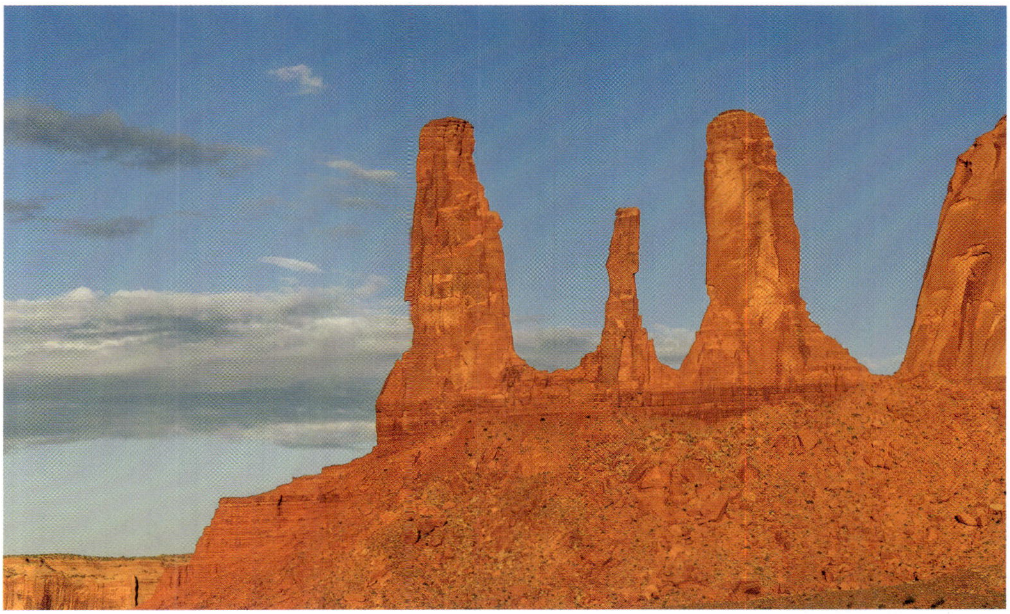

Figure 5.15
The right subject can come alive with color during the first few minutes of sunrise.

ISO 100 • 1/400 sec. • f/5 • 58mm lens

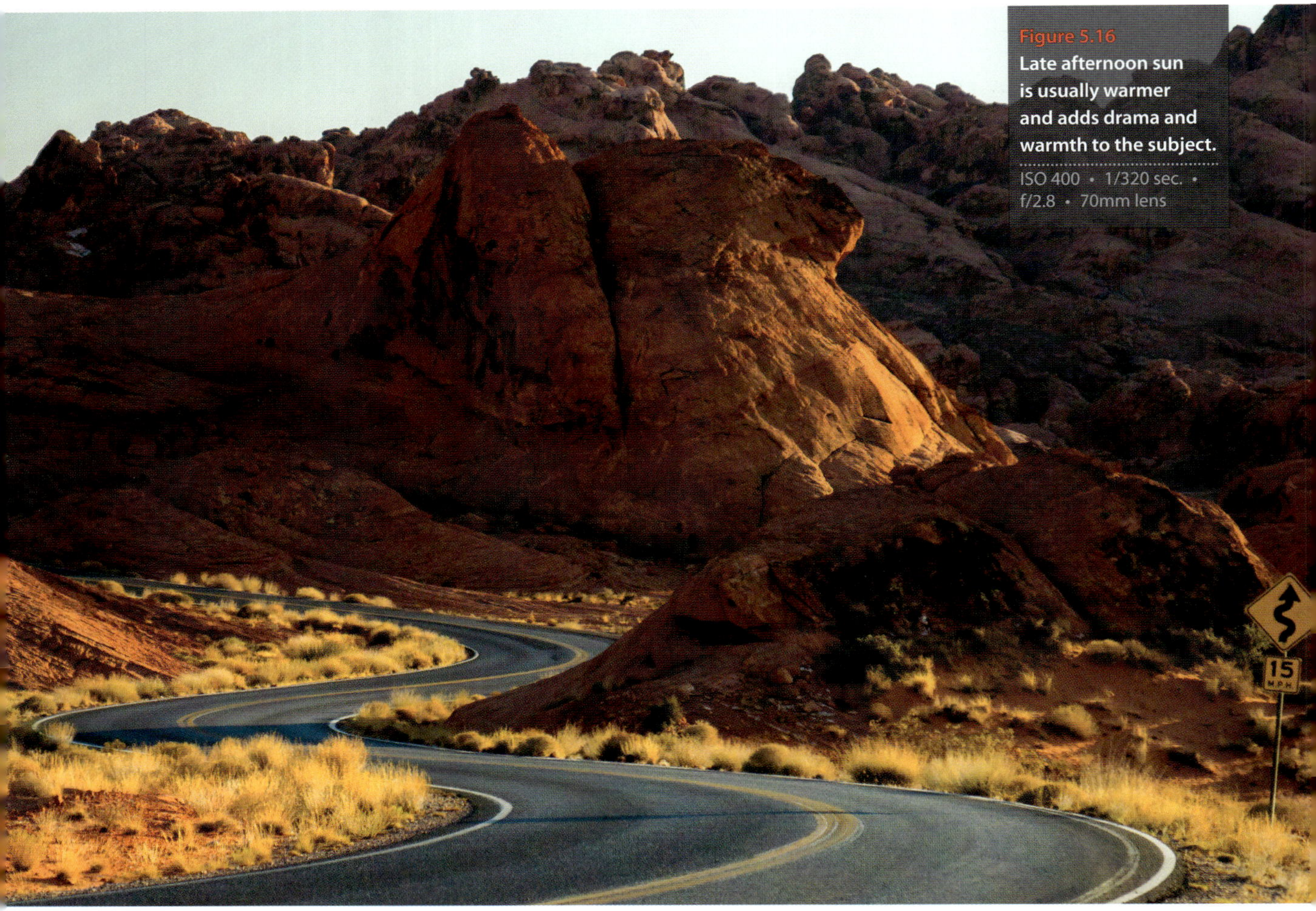

Figure 5.16
Late afternoon sun is usually warmer and adds drama and warmth to the subject.
ISO 400 • 1/320 sec. • f/2.8 • 70mm lens

Warm and cool color temperatures

These two terms are used to describe the overall color cast of an image. Reds and yellows are said to be *warm*, which is usually the look that you get from the late afternoon sun. Blue is usually the predominant color when talking about a *cool* cast.

Where to Focus

Large landscape scenes are great fun to photograph, but they can present a problem: Where exactly do you focus when you want everything to be sharp? Since your goal is to create a great landscape photo, you will need to concentrate on how to best create an image that is tack sharp, with a depth of field that renders great focus throughout the scene.

I have stressed the importance of a good tripod when shooting landscapes. The tripod lets you concentrate on the aperture portion of the exposure without worrying how long your shutter will be open. This is because the tripod provides the stability to handle any shutter speed you might need when shooting at small apertures. I find that, for most of my landscape work, I set my camera to Aperture Priority mode and the ISO to 100 (for a clean, noise-free image).

However, shooting with the smallest aperture on your lens doesn't necessarily mean that you will get the proper sharpness throughout your image. The real key is knowing where in the scene to focus your lens to maximize the depth of field for your chosen aperture. To do this, you must use something called the "hyper focal distance" of your lens.

Hyper focal distance (HFD) is the point of focus that will give you the greatest acceptable sharpness from a point near your camera all the way out to infinity. If you combine good HFD practice with a small aperture, you will get images that are sharp to infinity.

You have a couple of ways to do this, and the one that is probably the easiest, as you might guess, is the one most widely used by working pros. When your shot is all set up and composed, focus on an object that is about one-third of the distance into your frame (**Figure 5.17**). It is usually pretty close to the proper distance and will render favorable results. When you have the focus set, use your Depth Of Field Preview button to check the sharpness of all the objects in your scene. This button is located just under the lens release button and is activated once you have depressed the shutter button partway (**Figure 5.18**).

When the Depth Of Field Preview button is depressed, it will cause the lens to close down to the selected aperture and let you preview the depth of field directly through your viewfinder. You can also use this feature during Live View mode to see the depth of field directly on your LCD display.

Tack sharp

As one of those terms that photographers like to throw around, *tack sharp* refers not only to the focus of an image but also to the overall sharpness of the image. This usually means that there is excellent depth of field in terms of sharp focus for all elements in the image. It also means that there is no sign of camera shake, which can give soft edges to subjects that should look nice and crisp. To get your images tack sharp, use a small depth of field, don't forget your tripod, use the self-timer to activate the shutter if no cable release is handy, and practice achieving good HFD when picking your point of focus.

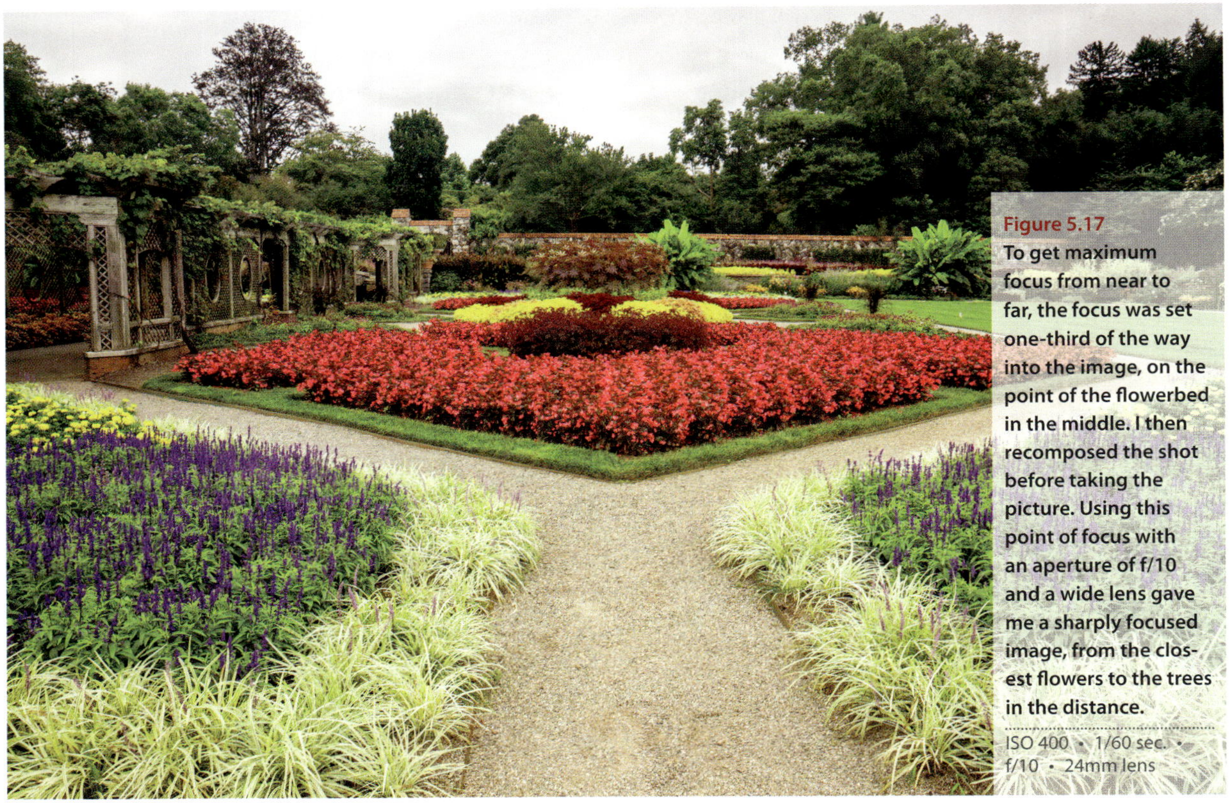

Figure 5.17
To get maximum focus from near to far, the focus was set one-third of the way into the image, on the point of the flowerbed in the middle. I then recomposed the shot before taking the picture. Using this point of focus with an aperture of f/10 and a wide lens gave me a sharply focused image, from the closest flowers to the trees in the distance.

ISO 400 • 1/60 sec. • f/10 • 24mm lens

Figure 5.18
Using the Depth Of Field Preview button can help you ensure that the image is sharp.

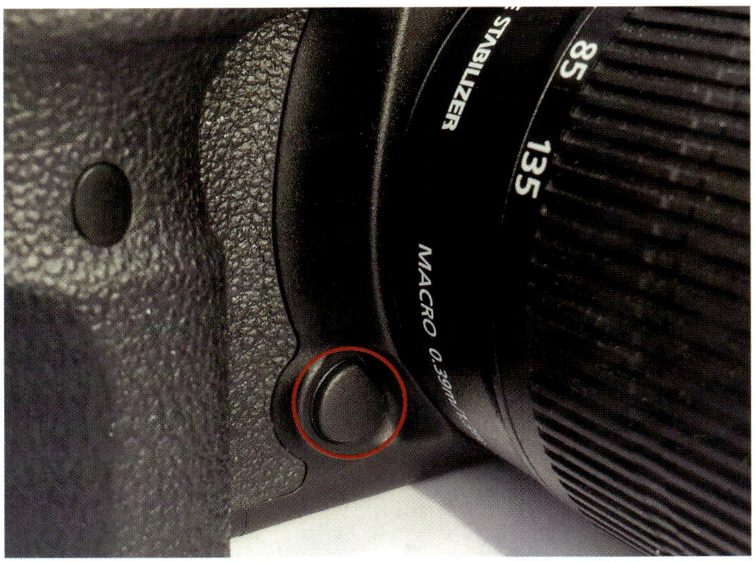

One thing to remember is that, as your lens gets wider in focal length, your HFD will be closer to the camera position. This is because the wider the lens, the greater depth of field you can achieve—yet another reason why a good wide-angle lens is indispensable to the landscape shooter.

Easier Focusing

There's no denying that the automatic focus features on the 7D Mark II are great, but sometimes it pays to turn them off and go manual. This is especially true if you are shooting on a tripod: Once you have your shot composed in the viewfinder and you are ready to focus, there is a chance that the area you want to focus on is not going to be in the area of one of the focus points. Often this is the case when you have a foreground element that is fairly low in the frame. You could use a single focus point set low in your viewfinder, and then pan the camera down until it rests on your subject. But then you would have to press the shutter button halfway to focus the camera, and then try to recompose and lock down the tripod. It's no easy task.

But you can have the best of both worlds by having the camera focus for you, and then switching to manual focus to comfortably recompose your shot (**Figure 5.19**).

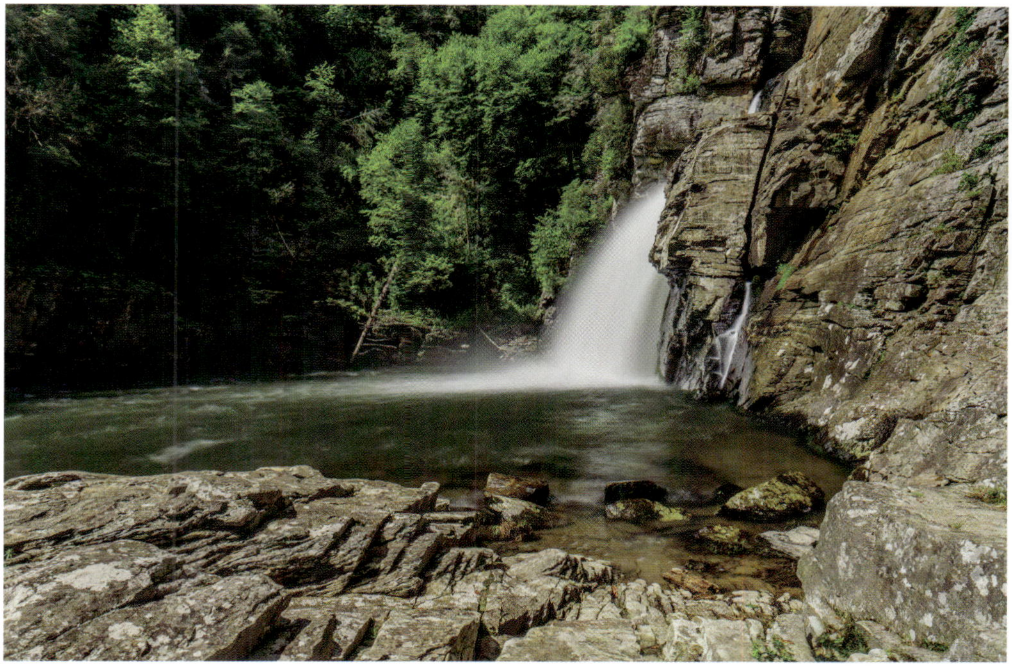

Figure 5.19
Using the HFD one-third rule, I focused on the rocks in the lower portion of the image, and then switched the lens to manual focus before recomposing for the final shot.

ISO 100 • 8 sec. • f/13 • 24mm lens

Getting focused while using a tripod

1. Set up your shot and find the area that you want to focus on.
2. Pan your tripod head so that your active focus point is on that spot.
3. Press the shutter button halfway to focus the camera, and then remove your finger from the button.
4. Switch the camera to manual focus by sliding the switch on the lens barrel from AF to MF.
5. Recompose the composition on the tripod, and then take the shot.

The camera will fire without trying to refocus the lens. This technique works especially well for wide-angle lenses, which can be difficult to focus in manual mode.

Making Water Fluid

For the landscape shooter, nothing is quite as satisfying as capturing a silky waterfall shot. Creating the smooth-flowing effect is as simple as adjusting your shutter speed to allow the water to be in motion while the shutter is open. The key is to have your camera on a stable platform, such as a tripod, so that you can use a shutter speed that's long enough to work (**Figure 5.20**). To achieve a great effect, use a shutter speed that is at least 1/15 of a second or longer.

Setting up for a waterfall shot

1. Attach the camera to your tripod; then compose and focus your shot.
2. For the best quality, make sure the ISO is set to 100.
3. Using Av mode, set your aperture to the smallest opening (such as f/22 or f/36).
4. Press the shutter button halfway so the camera takes a meter reading.
5. Check to see if the shutter speed is 1/15 of a second or slower.
6. Take a photo, and then check the image on the LCD.

If the water is blinking on the LCD, indicating a loss of detail in the highlights, use the Exposure Compensation feature (as discussed earlier in this chapter) to bring details back into the waterfall. You will need to have the Highlight Alert feature turned on to check for overexposure (see "How I Shoot" in Chapter 3).

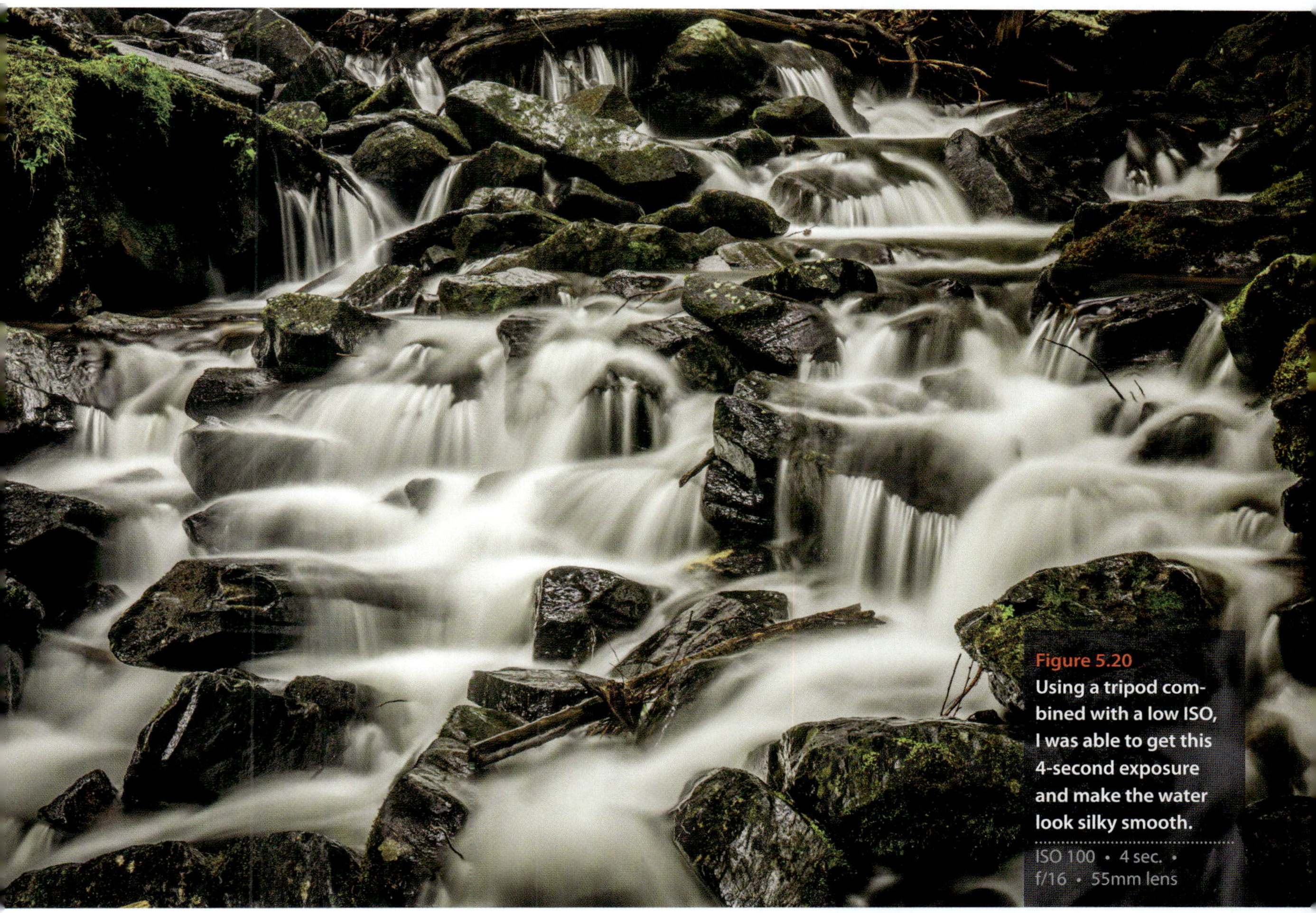

Figure 5.20
Using a tripod combined with a low ISO, I was able to get this 4-second exposure and make the water look silky smooth.

ISO 100 • 4 sec. • f/16 • 55mm lens

It's possible you will not be able to have a shutter speed long enough to capture a smooth, silky effect, especially if you are shooting in bright daylight conditions. To overcome this obstacle, you need a filter for your lens—either a polarizing filter or a neutral density filter. The polarizing filter redirects wavelengths of light to create more vibrant, accurate colors; reduce reflections; and darken blue skies. It is a handy filter for landscape work. The neutral density filter is typically just a dark piece of glass that serves to darken the scene by one, two, or three stops. This filter allows you to use slower shutter speeds during bright conditions. Think of it as sunglasses for your camera lens. You will find more discussion on filters in Chapter 11, "Pimp My Ride."

Directing the Viewer: A Word About Composition

As a photographer, it's your job to lead the viewer through your image. You accomplish this by using the principles of composition, which is the arrangement of elements in the scene that draws the eye through your image and holds your viewer's attention. As the director of this viewing, you need to understand how people see, and then use that information to focus their attention on the most important elements in your image.

There is a general order at which we look at elements in a photograph. The first is brightness. The eye wants to travel to the brightest object within a scene. So if you have a bright sky, it's probably the first place the eye will travel to. The second order of attention is sharpness. Sharp, detailed elements will get more attention than soft, blurry areas. Finally, the eye will move to vivid colors while leaving the dull, flat colors for last. It is important to know these essentials in order to grab—and keep—the viewer's attention and then direct the eye through the frame.

In **Figure 5.21**, the eye is drawn to the bright flowers in the bottom of the page. They are also the sharpest and most colorful objects in the image, which helps to focus attention on them as the main subject. From there, the eye moves to the less colorful and slightly out-of-focus house in the background. Finally, the view is moved to the sky and dark trees, which then leads back to the flowers. The elements within the image all help to keep the eye moving but never leave the frame.

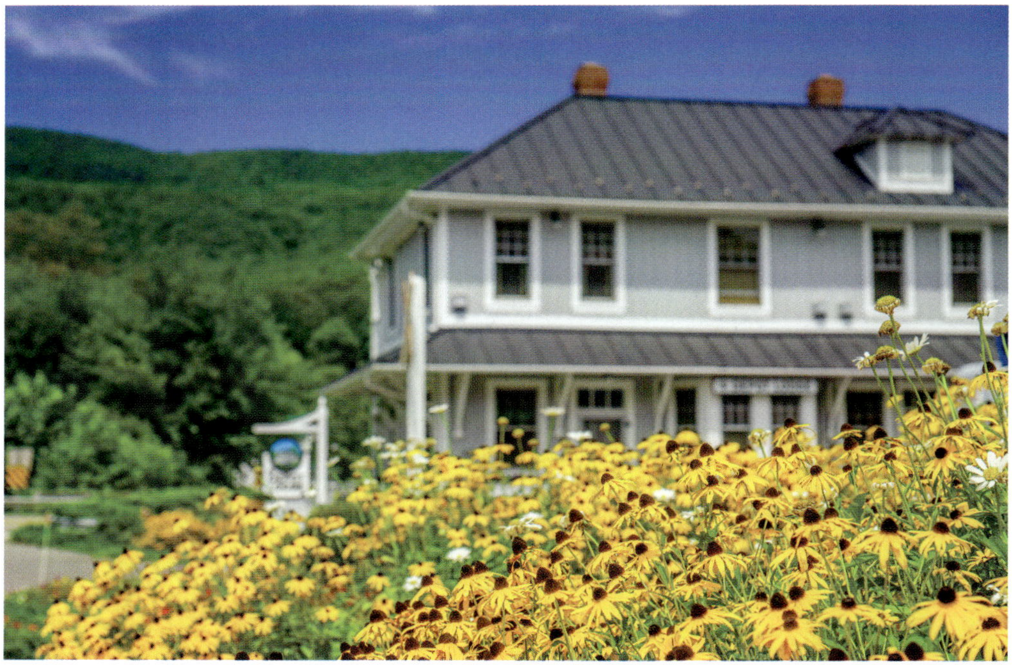

Figure 5.21
The composition of the elements pulls the viewer's eyes around the image, leading from one element to the next.
ISO 200 • 1/500 sec. • f/5.6 • 55mm lens

Rule of thirds

There are, in fact, quite a few philosophies concerning composition. The easiest one to begin with is known as the "rule of thirds." Using this principle, you simply divide your viewfinder into thirds by imagining two horizontal and two vertical lines that divide the frame equally.

The key to using this method of composition is to have your main subject located at or near one of the intersecting points (**Figure 5.22**).

By placing your subject near these intersecting lines, you are giving the viewer space to move within the frame. The one thing you don't want to do is place your subject smack-dab in the middle of the frame. Doing so is sometimes referred to as "bull's-eye" composition, and it requires the right subject matter for it to work. Using bull's-eye composition is not always wrong, but it will usually be less interesting and may not hold the viewer's focus.

Speaking of the middle of the frame: The other general rule of thirds deals with horizon lines. Generally speaking, you should position the horizon one-third of the way up or down in the frame. Splitting the frame in half by placing your horizon in the middle of the picture is akin to placing the subject in the middle of the frame; it doesn't lend a sense of importance to either the sky or the ground.

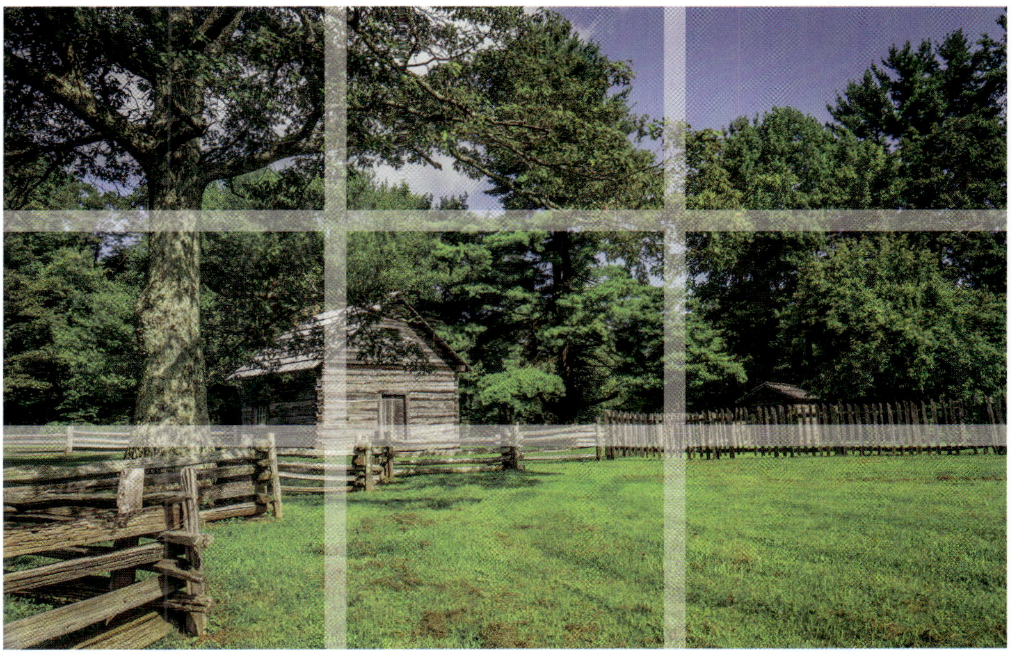

Figure 5.22
If you laid a rule-of-thirds grid atop this image, you would see that I composed the shot so that the fence line runs along the bottom third and the cabin is near the bottom-left intersection.

ISO 100 • 1/60 sec. • f/14 • 35mm lens

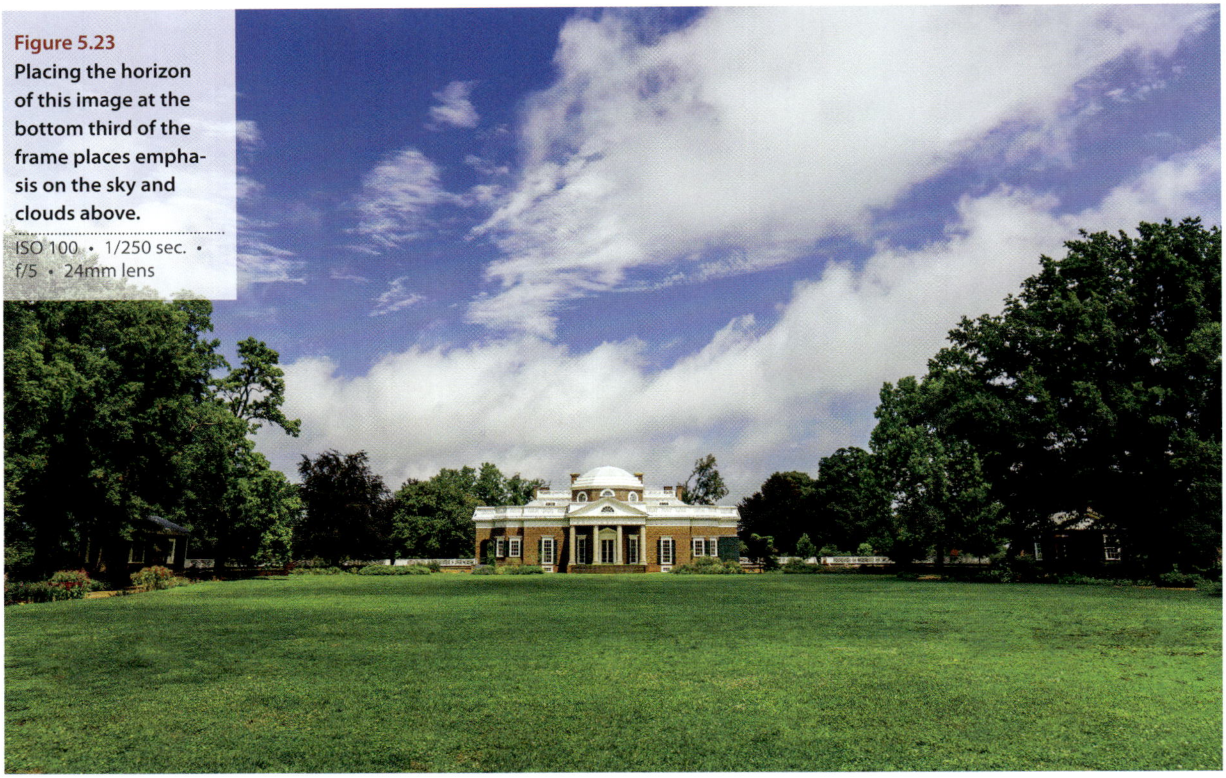

Figure 5.23
Placing the horizon of this image at the bottom third of the frame places emphasis on the sky and clouds above.
ISO 100 • 1/250 sec. • f/5 • 24mm lens

In **Figure 5.23**, I incorporated the rule of thirds by aligning my horizon in the top third of the frame and the group of cacti near the bottom third. In doing so, I have created a sense of depth in the image. By selecting the correct focal length for the lens (18mm, in this instance) and the right vantage point, I was able to place my horizon line so that it gives the greatest emphasis on the subject.

Creating depth

Because a photograph is a flat, two-dimensional space, you need to create a sense of depth, as mentioned earlier, by using the elements in the scene to create a three-dimensional feel. You accomplish this by including different and distinct spaces for the eye to travel: a foreground, middle ground, and background. By using these three spaces, you draw the viewer in and render depth to your image.

The lake in Northern Carolina shown in **Figure 5.24** illustrates this principle well. The grassy area at the bottom strongly defines the foreground area. The lake is a great middle area that provides transition from the foreground to the background. The small mountain, trees, and sky complete the image by adding some distant depth to the scene.

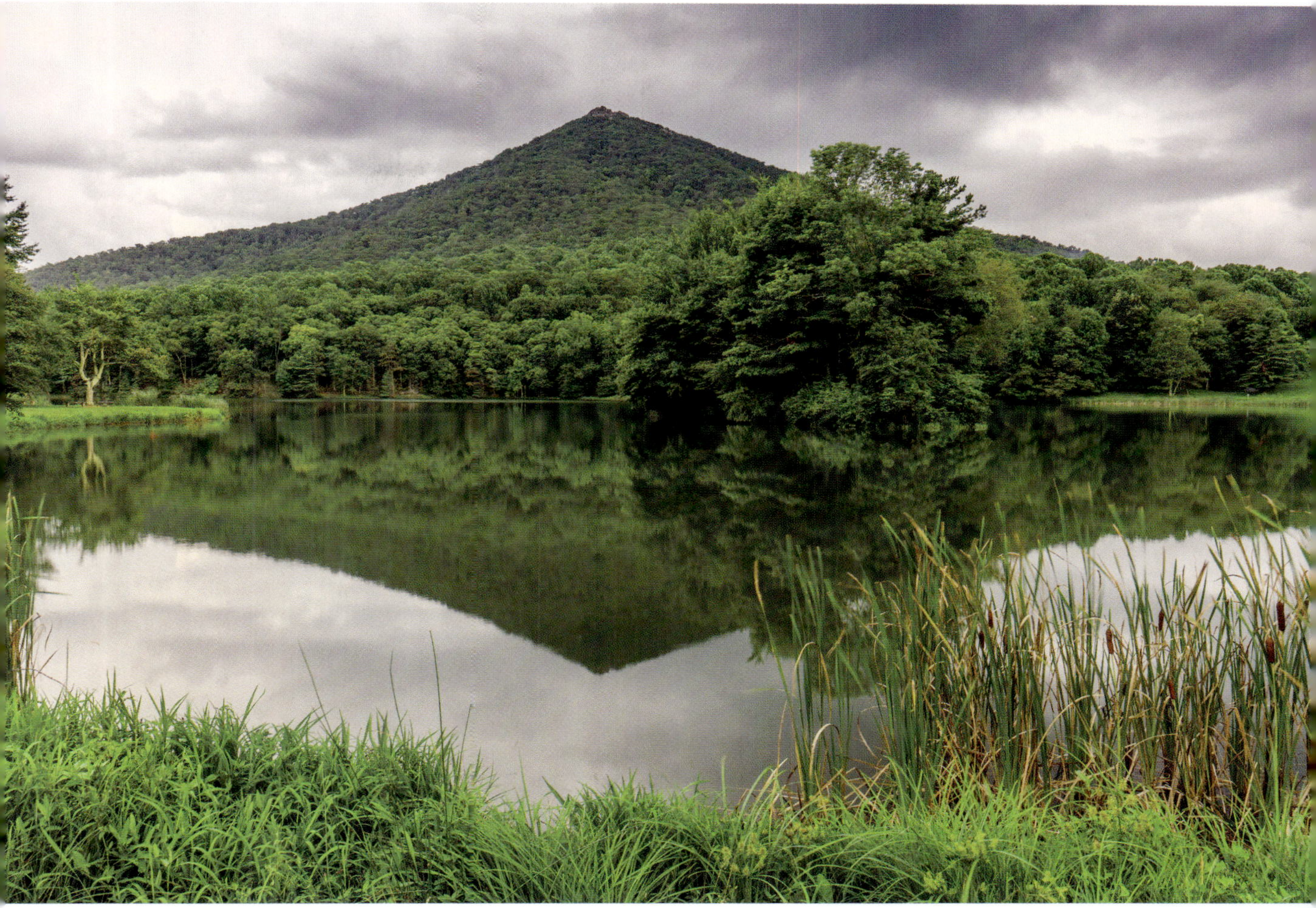

Figure 5.24

The grass, lake, trees, mountain, and sky all add to the feeling of depth in the image.

ISO 200 • 0.8 sec. • f/16 • 26mm lens

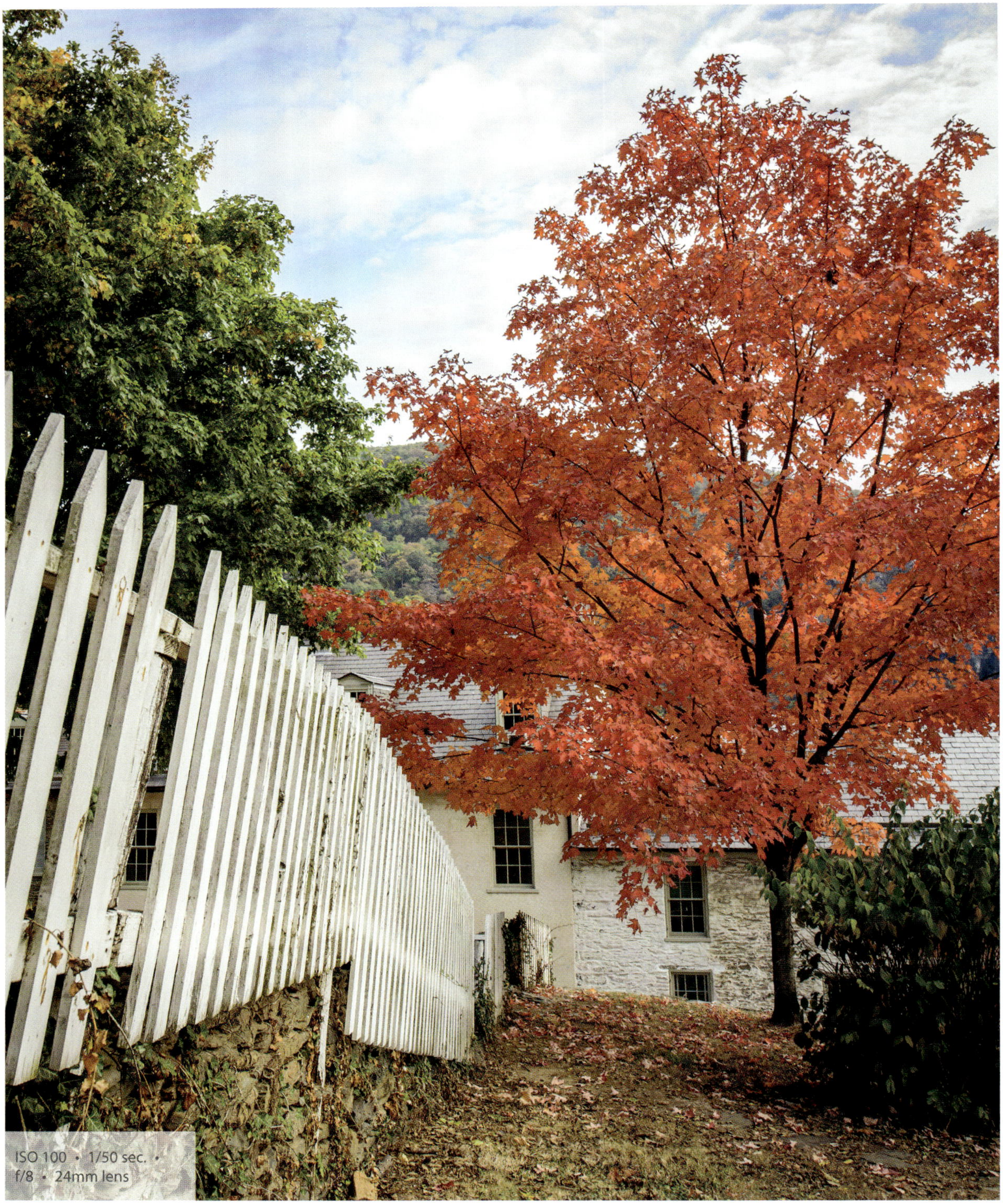

ISO 100 • 1/50 sec. • f/8 • 24mm lens

Chapter 5 Assignments

We've covered a lot of ground in this chapter, so it's definitely time to put this knowledge to work in order to get familiar with these new camera settings and techniques.

Comparing depth of field: wide angle vs. telephoto

You should practice using the hyper focal distance of your lens to maximize the depth of field. You can do this by picking a focal length to work with on your lens. If you have a zoom lens, try using the longest length. Compose your image and find an object to focus on. Set your aperture to f/22 and take a photo.

Now do the same thing with the zoom lens at its widest focal length. Use the same aperture and focus point.

Review the images and compare the depth of field when using wide angle as opposed to a telephoto lens. Try this with a large aperture as well.

Applying hyper focal distance to your landscapes

Once again, pick a scene that has objects that are near the camera position and something that is clearly defined in the background. Try using a wide to medium-wide focal length for this (18–35mm). Use a small aperture and focus on the object in the foreground; then recompose and take a shot. Without moving the camera position, use the object in the background as your point of focus and take another shot. Finally, find a point that is one-third of the way into the frame from near to far and use that as the focus point. Compare all of the images to see which method delivered the greatest range of depth of field.

Shooting black-and-white landscapes

The 7D Mark II gives you so much shooting flexibility when it comes to landscapes. Some of the most iconic landscapes ever captured were in black and white, so you should definitely give this picture style a try. Find a colorful scene; then try capturing the scene with a normal black-and-white look and then with different color filter effects. Don't forget to switch back to the Landscape picture style when you are done.

Share your results with the book's Flickr group!
Join the group here: flickr.com/groups/7dmarkii_fromsnapshotstogreatshots

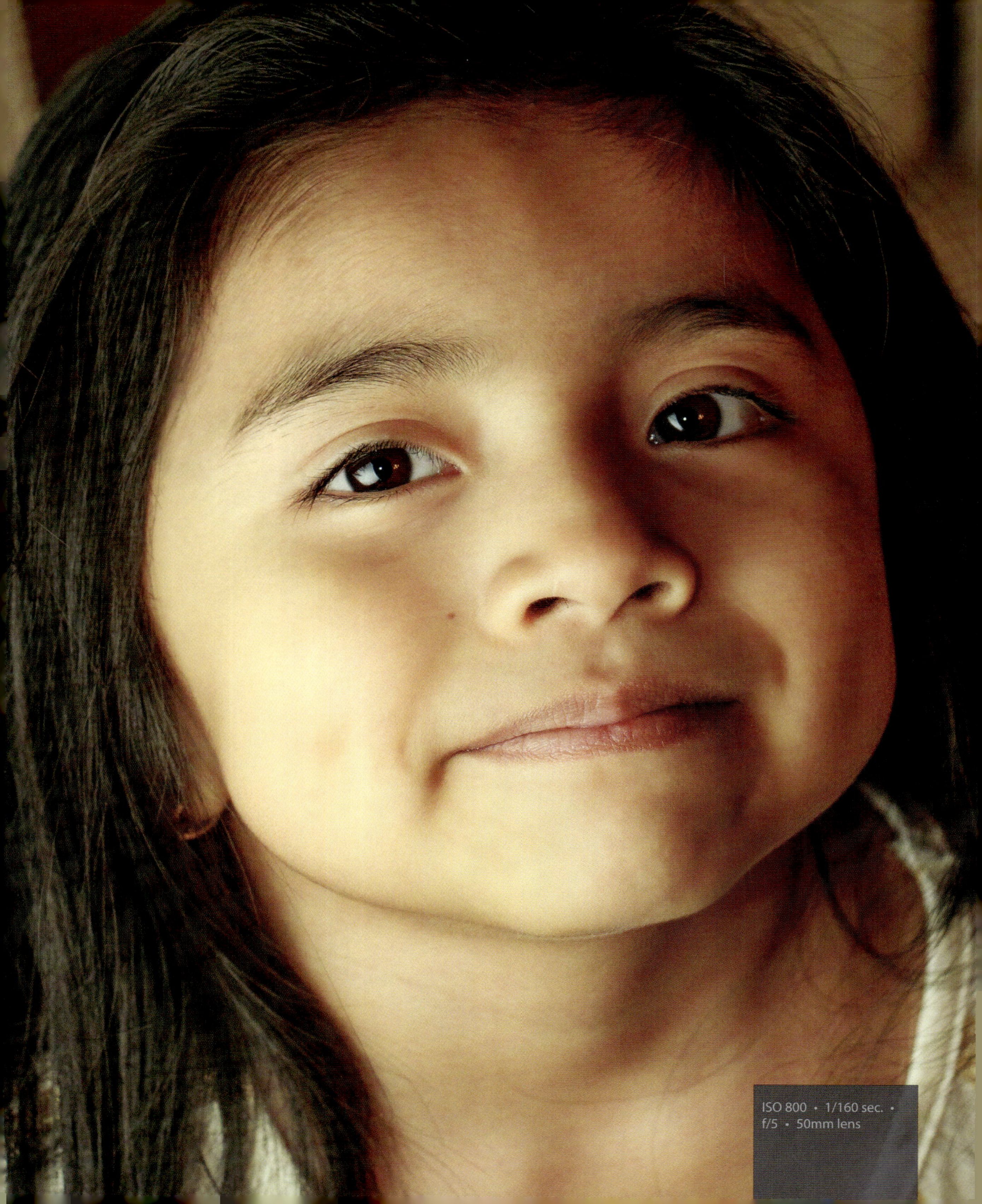

ISO 800 • 1/160 sec. • f/5 • 50mm lens

6

Say Cheese!

Settings and Features to Make Great Portraits

Taking pictures of people is one of the great joys of photography. You will experience a great sense of accomplishment when you capture the spirit and personality of someone in a photograph. At the same time, you have a great responsibility because the person in front of the camera is depending on you to make them look good. You can't always change how someone looks, but you can control the way you photograph that individual. In this chapter, we will explore camera features and techniques that can help you create great portraits.

Poring Over the Picture

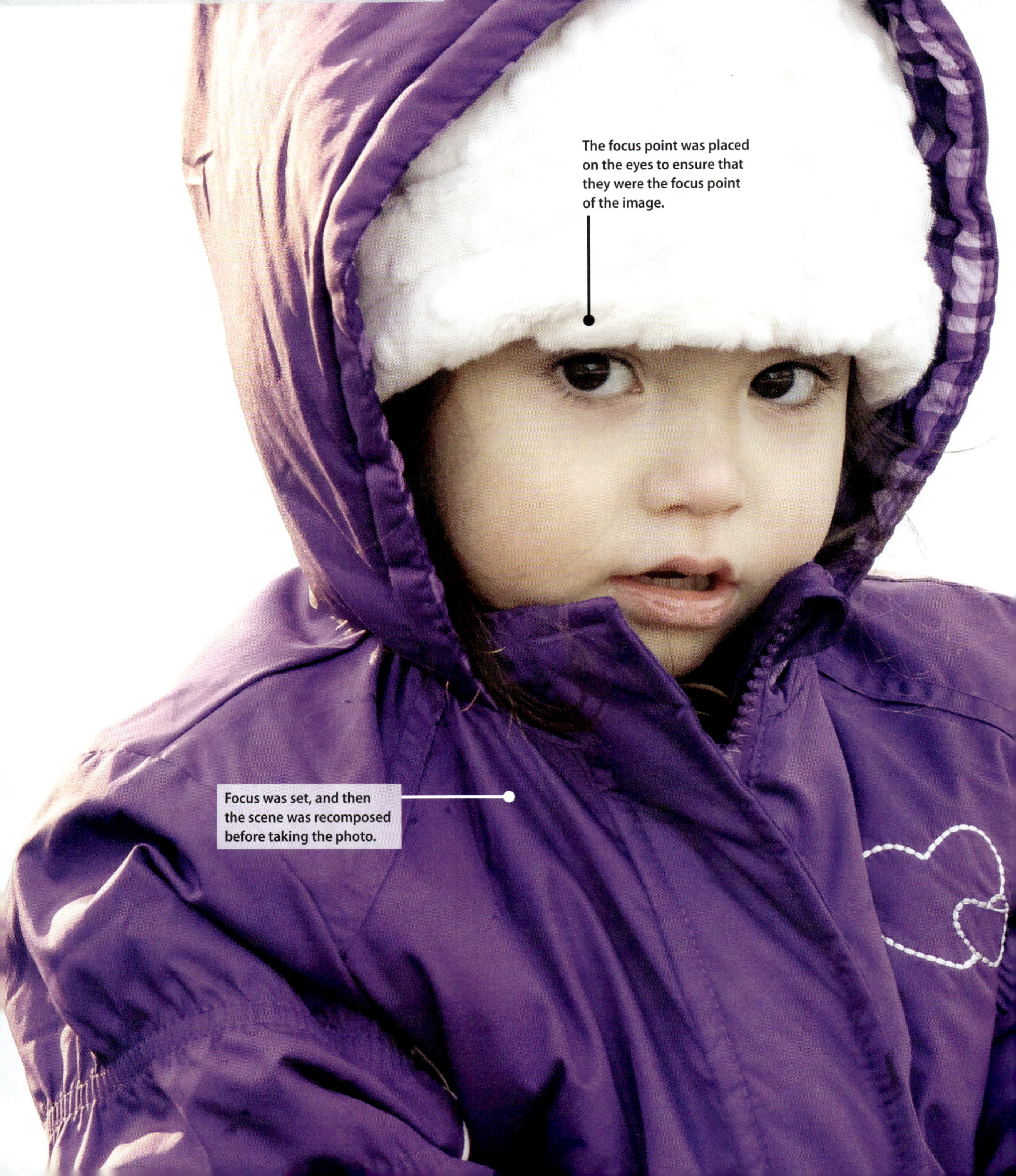

ISO 400 • 1/100 sec. •
f/5.6 • 120mm lens

The bright snow meant that I needed to dial in some overexposure to brighten things up.

Taking photographs of children can be challenging, to say the least. Throw in an interesting scene like snow and you get a whole new set of issues to deal with that can test your skill. This is when it pays to know how your camera works and how to quickly make adjustments on the fly. A little knowledge goes a long way in capturing those special moments, no matter where they occur.

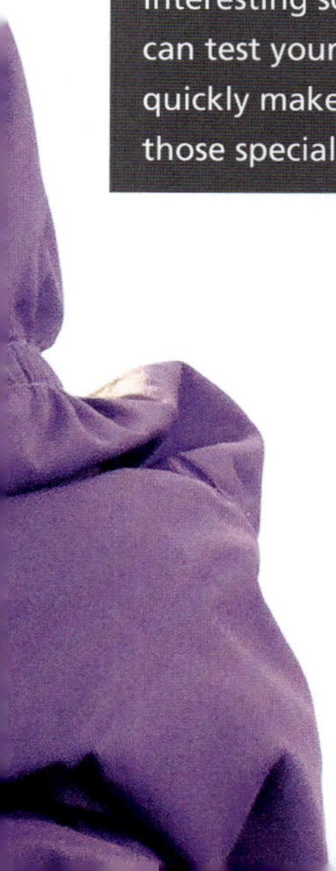

A shallow depth of field was achieved by using a large aperture.

Using Aperture Priority Mode

If you took a poll of portrait photographers to see which shooting mode was most often used for portraits, the answer would certainly be Aperture Priority (Av) mode. Selecting the right aperture is important for placing the most critically sharp area of the photo on your subject, while simultaneously blurring all of the distracting background clutter (**Figure 6.1**). Not only will a large aperture give the narrowest depth of field, it will also allow you to shoot in lower light levels at lower ISO settings.

This isn't to say that you have to use the largest aperture on your lens. A good place to begin is f/5.6. This will give you enough depth of field to keep the entire face in focus, while providing enough blur to eliminate distractions in the background. This isn't a hard-and-fast setting; it's just a good, all-around number to start with. Your aperture might change depending on the focal length of the lens you are using and on the amount of blur you want for your foreground and background elements.

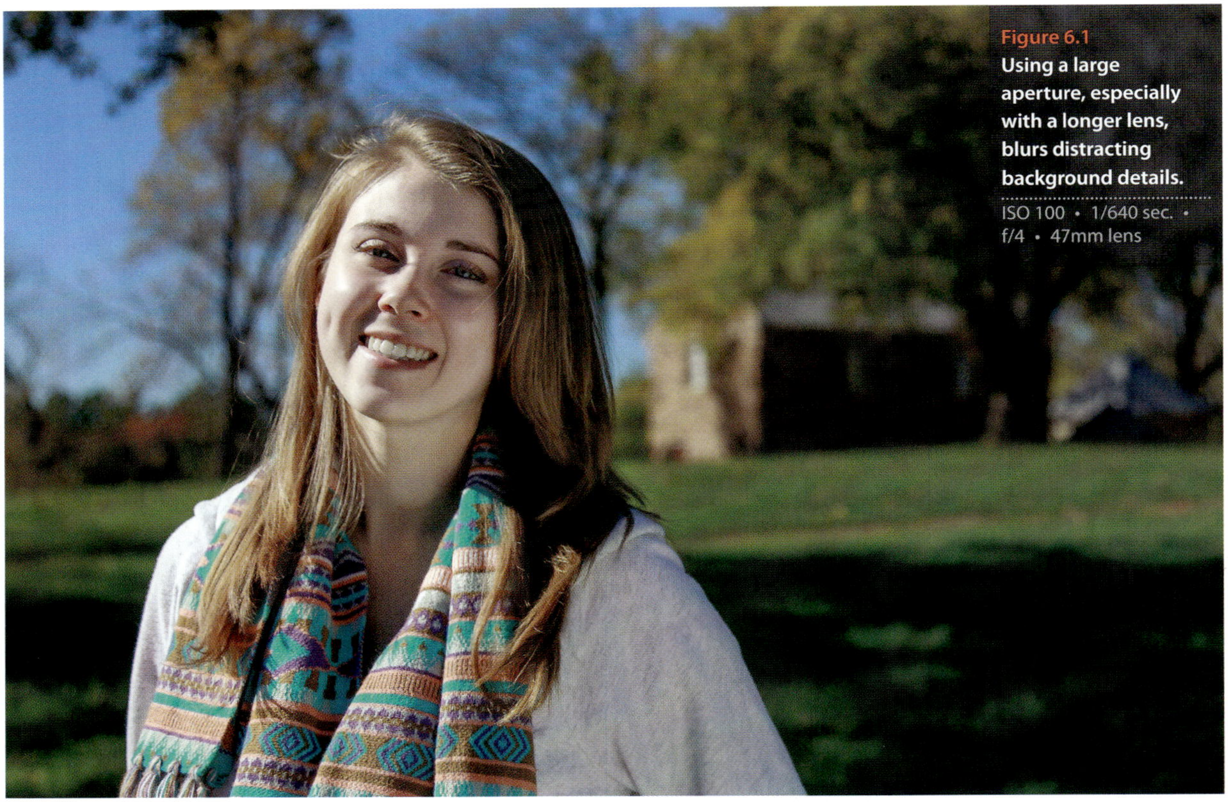

Figure 6.1
Using a large aperture, especially with a longer lens, blurs distracting background details.

ISO 100 • 1/640 sec. • f/4 • 47mm lens

Go wide for environmental portraits

Occasionally, your subject's environment is of great significance to the story you want to tell. This might mean using a smaller aperture to get more detail in the background or foreground. Once again, by using Av mode, you can set your aperture to a higher f-stop, such as f/8 or f/11, and include the important details of the scene that surrounds your subject.

Using a wider-than-normal lens can also assist in getting more depth of field as well as showing the surrounding area. A wide-angle lens requires less stopping down of the aperture to achieve an acceptable depth of field. This is because wide-angle lenses are covering a greater area, so the depth of field appears to cover a greater percentage of the scene.

A wider lens might also be necessary to relay more information about the scenery (**Figure 6.2**). Select a lens length that is wide enough to tell the story but not so wide that you distort the subject. There's nothing quite as unflattering as giving someone a big, distorted nose (unless you are going for that sort of look). When shooting a portrait with a wide-angle lens, keep the subject away from the edge of the frame. This will reduce the distortion, especially in very wide focal lengths. As the lens length increases, distortion will be reduced. I generally don't like to go wider than about 24mm for portraits. For standard portraits, I prefer a 55mm lens setting.

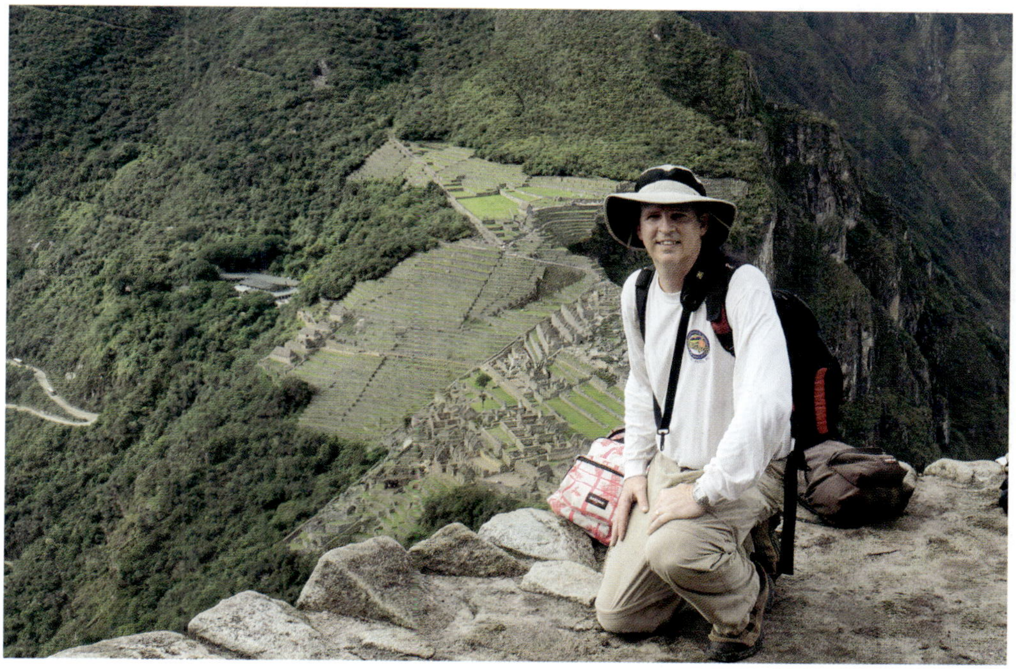

Figure 6.2
A wide-angle lens allows you to capture more of the environment in the scene without having to increase the distance between you and the subject.

ISO 400 • 1/250 sec. • f/9 • 24mm lens

Metering basics

There are multiple metering modes in your camera, but the way they work is very similar. A light meter measures the amount of light being reflected off your subject, and then renders a suggested exposure value based on the brightness of the subject and the ISO setting of the sensor. To establish this value, the meter averages all of the brightness values to come up with a middle tone, sometimes referred to as 18 percent gray. The exposure value is then rendered based on this middle-gray value. This means that a white wall would be underexposed and a black wall would be overexposed in an effort to make each one appear gray. To assist with special lighting situations, the 7D Mark II has four metering modes: Evaluative (**Figure 6.3**), which uses the entire frame; Partial (**Figure 6.4**), which uses the middle 9 percent of the frame; Spot (**Figure 6.5**), which takes specific readings from small areas (often used with a gray card); and Center-Weighted (**Figure 6.6**), which looks at the entire frame but places most of the exposure emphasis on the center of the frame.

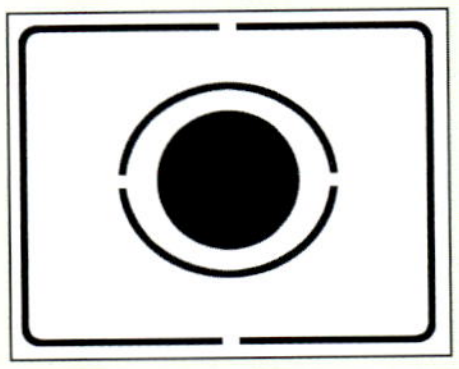

Figure 6.3 The Evaluative metering mode uses the entire frame.

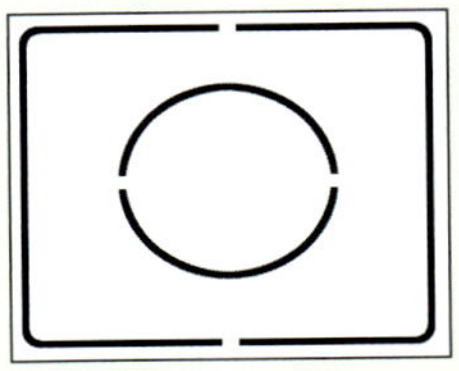

Figure 6.4 The Partial metering mode uses the middle of the frame.

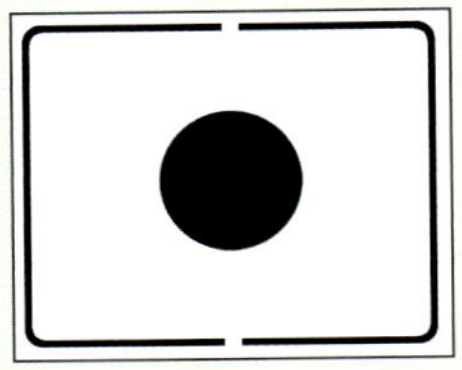

Figure 6.5 The Spot metering mode uses a very small area of the frame.

Figure 6.6 The Center-Weighted metering mode looks at the entire frame but emphasizes the center of it.

Metering Modes for Portraits

For most portrait situations, the Evaluative metering mode is ideal. (For more on how metering works, see the "Metering basics" sidebar.) This mode measures light values from all portions of the viewfinder, and then establishes a proper exposure for the scene. The only problem you might encounter when using this metering mode is when you have very light or dark backgrounds in your portrait shots.

In these instances, the meter might be fooled into using the wrong exposure information because it will be trying to lighten or darken the entire scene based on the prominence of dark or light areas (**Figure 6.7**). You can deal with this in one of two ways. You can use the Exposure Compensation feature, which we covered in Chapter 5, "Landscape

Photography," to dial in adjustments for over- and underexposure. Or you can change the metering mode from Evaluative to Partial or Center-Weighted metering. The Partial metering mode uses only the center area of the viewfinder (about 9 percent) to get its exposure information. This is the best way to achieve proper exposure for most portraits; metering off of skin tones, averaged with hair and clothing, will often give a more accurate exposure (**Figure 6.8**). You'll also want to use this metering mode when your subject is strongly backlit.

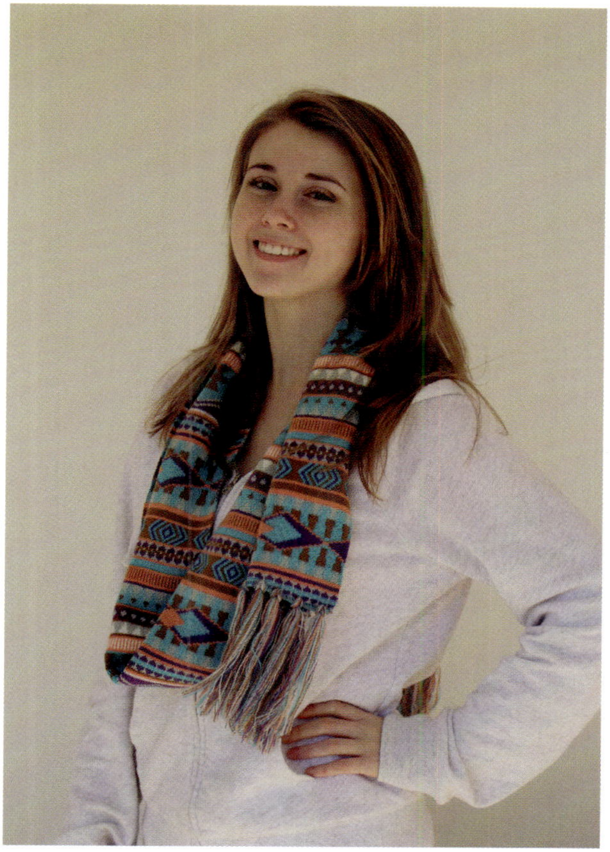

Figure 6.7
The light background color and clothing fooled the meter into choosing a slightly underexposed setting for the photo.

ISO 200 • 1/1600 sec. • f/32.8 • 70mm lens

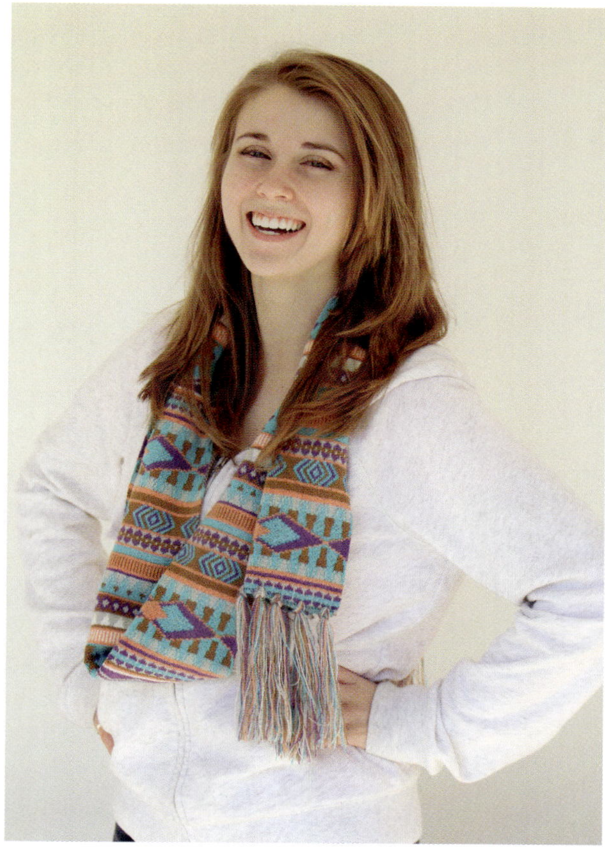

Figure 6.8
When I switch to either the Partial or the Center-Weighted metering mode, the camera will ignore much of the background and add a little more time to the exposure.

ISO 200 • 1/640 sec. • f/2.8 • 70mm lens

Setting your metering mode to Partial metering

1. Press the WB/Meter button on the top of the camera to open the meter option screen.
2. Use the Main dial to scroll through the metering modes until you find the symbol for Partial metering mode. The names of the different modes will appear near the bottom of the screen. If you press the Set button a second time, you can see all of the available metering modes (**Figure 6.9**).
3. Press the Set button to return to shooting mode.

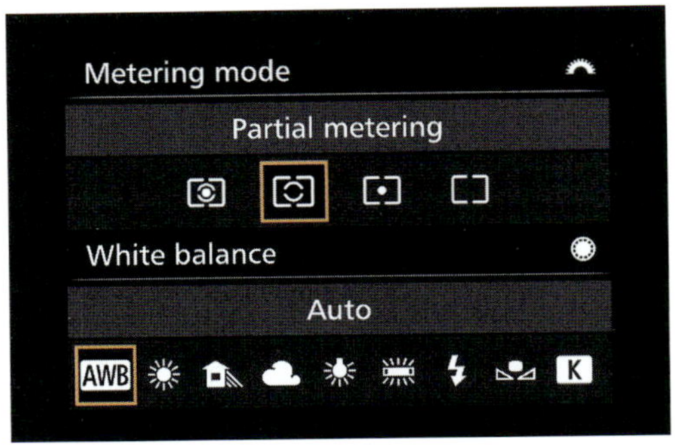

Figure 6.9
Setting the meter mode to Partial puts emphasis on the middle of the viewfinder.

Using the AE Lock Feature

There will often be times when your subject is not in the center of the frame but you still want to use the Partial metering mode. So how can you get an accurate reading if the subject isn't in the center? Try using the AE (Auto Exposure) Lock feature to hold the exposure setting while you recompose.

AE Lock lets you use the exposure setting from any portion of the scene that you think is appropriate, and then lock that setting regardless of how the scene looks when you recompose. An example of this would be when you're shooting a photograph of someone and a large amount of blue sky appears in the picture. Normally, the meter might be fooled by all that bright sky and try to reduce the exposure. Using AE Lock, you can establish the correct metering by zooming in on the subject (or even pointing the camera toward the ground), taking the meter reading and locking it in with AE Lock, and then recomposing and taking your photo with the locked-in exposure.

Shooting with the AE Lock feature

1. Find the AE Lock (✱) button on the back of the camera and place your thumb on it.
2. While looking through the viewfinder, place the center focus point on your subject.
3. Press the Shutter Release button halfway to activate the camera and get a meter reading.

4. Press the AE Lock button to lock in the exposure. A star will appear in your viewfinder, letting you know that the exposure has been locked.
5. Recompose your shot, and then take the photo.
6. To take more than one photo without having to take another meter reading, just hold down the AE Lock button until you are done using the meter setting.

Focusing: The Eyes Have It

It has been said that the eyes are the windows to the soul, and nothing could be truer when you are taking a photograph of someone (**Figure 6.10**). You could have the perfect composition and exposure, but if the eyes aren't sharp, the entire image suffers. Although you have many different focusing modes to choose from on your 7D Mark II, for portrait work you can't beat One Shot mode using a single focusing point. One Shot focusing will establish a single focus for the lens and then hold it until you take the photograph; the other focusing modes continue focusing until the photograph is taken. The single-point selection lets you place the focusing point right on your subject's eye and set that spot as the critical focus point. Using One Shot mode lets you get that focus and recompose all in one motion.

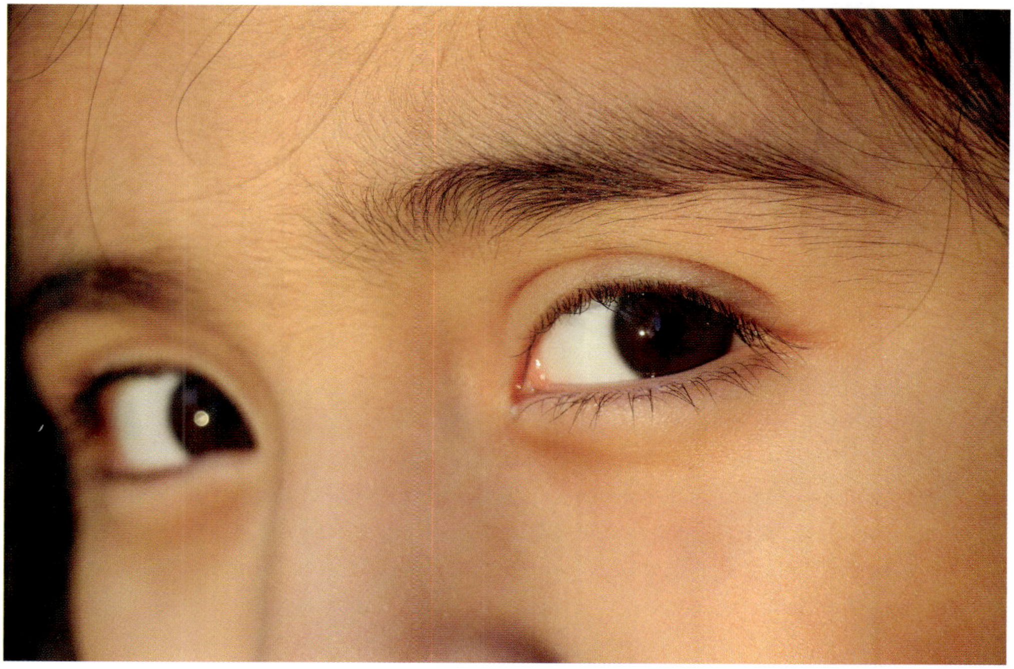

Figure 6.10
When photographing people, you should almost always place the emphasis on the eyes.

ISO 800 • 1/320 sec. • f/5.6 • 132mm lens

Setting up for One Shot focusing mode

1. Press the Drive/AF button on the top of the camera.
2. Rotate the Main dial to change the focusing mode to One Shot; then press the Set button.
3. Press the Shutter Release button to activate the camera meter, lock focus and computer, and then take the photo.
4. You will need to press, release, and repeat to take additional photos.

Setting your focus to a single point

1. Press the Focus Point Selection button (at the top right on the back of the camera), and then look in your viewfinder or the rear LCD screen.
2. Use the AF Area selection lever to toggle through the different focus modes. Select the Spot AF Point or the Single point mode.
3. Use the Multi-controller to move the focus point to one of the 65 available points.
4. Now, to shoot using this focus point, place that point on your subject's eye, and press the shutter button halfway until the focus point locks in and you hear the chirp. While still holding the shutter button down halfway, recompose and take your shot.

I typically use the center point for focus selection. I find it easier to place that point directly on the location where my critical focus should be established, and then recompose the shot. Even though the single point can be selected from any of the focus points, it typically takes longer to figure out where that point should be in relation to my subject. By using the center point, I can quickly establish focus and get on with my shooting.

Classic Black-and-White Portraits

There is something timeless about a black-and-white portrait. It eliminates the distraction of color and puts all the emphasis on the subject. To get great black and whites without having to resort to any image-processing software, set your picture style to Monochrome (**Figure 6.11**). You should know that the picture styles are automatically applied when shooting with the JPEG file format. If you are shooting in RAW, the picture that shows up on your rear LCD display will look black and white, but it will appear as a color image when you open it in your Digital Photo Professional software. You can use the software to apply the Monochrome, or any other style, to your RAW image within the image-editing software.

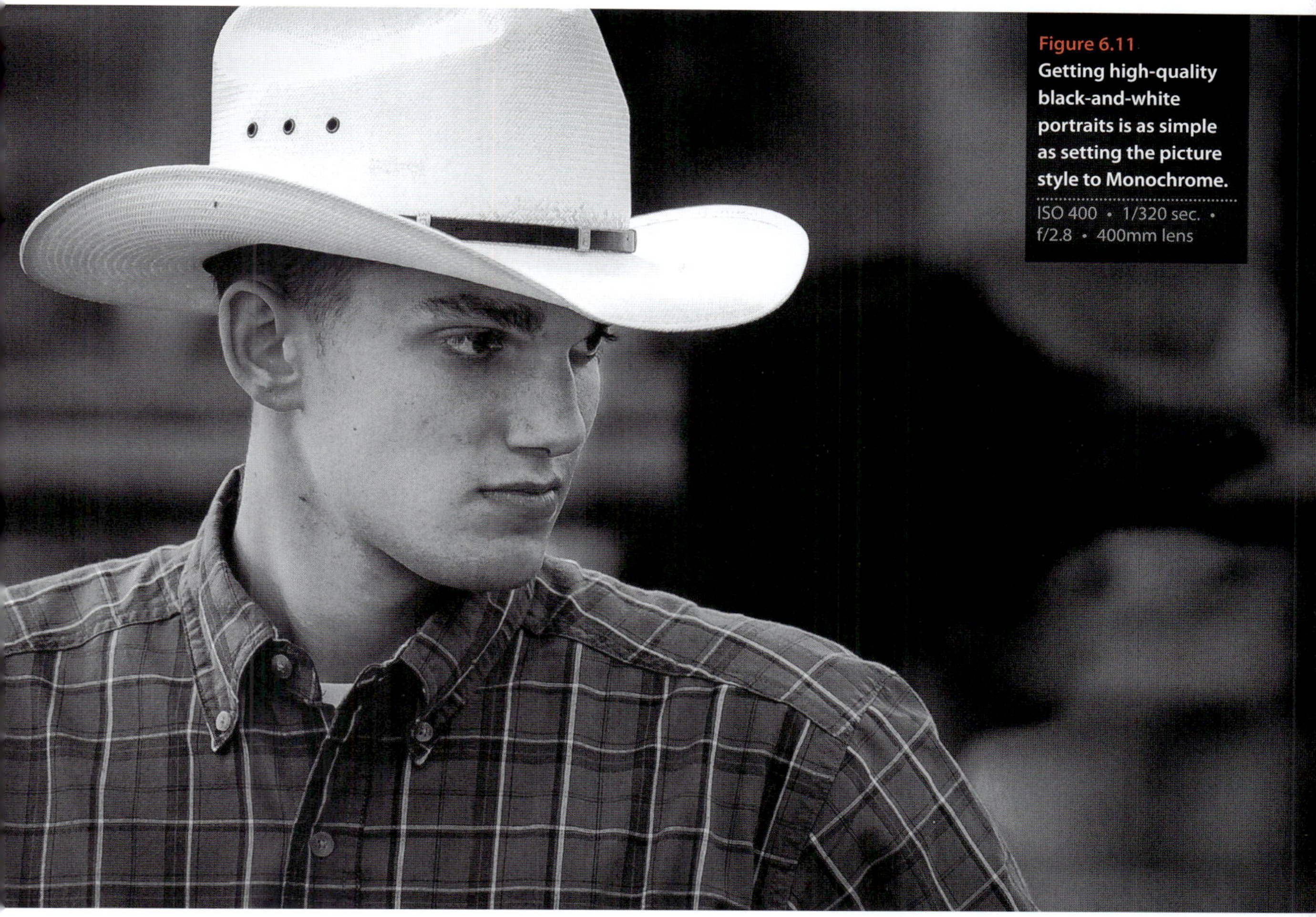

Figure 6.11
Getting high-quality black-and-white portraits is as simple as setting the picture style to Monochrome.
ISO 400 • 1/320 sec. • f/2.8 • 400mm lens

The real key to using the Monochrome picture style is to customize it for your portrait subject. The style can be changed to alter the sharpness and contrast. For women, children, puppies, and anyone else who should look somewhat soft, set the Sharpness setting to 0 or 1. For old cowboys, longshoremen, and anyone else you want to look really detailed, try a setting of 6 or 7. I typically like to leave Contrast at a setting of around –1 or –2. This gives me a nice range of tones throughout the image.

The other adjustment that you should try is to change the picture style's Filter effect from None to one of the four available settings (Yellow, Orange, Red, or Green). Using the filters will have the effect of either lightening or darkening the skin tones. The Red and Yellow filters usually lighten skin, whereas the Green filter can make skin appear a bit darker. Experiment to see which one works best for your subject.

Setting your picture style to Monochrome

1. Start by pressing the Creative Photo button located just under the Menu button.
2. Use the Quick Control dial to select the Picture Style icon (second from the left), and press the Set button (**A**).
3. Using the Quick Control dial, highlight the Monochrome setting, and lock it in by pressing the Set button again (**B**).

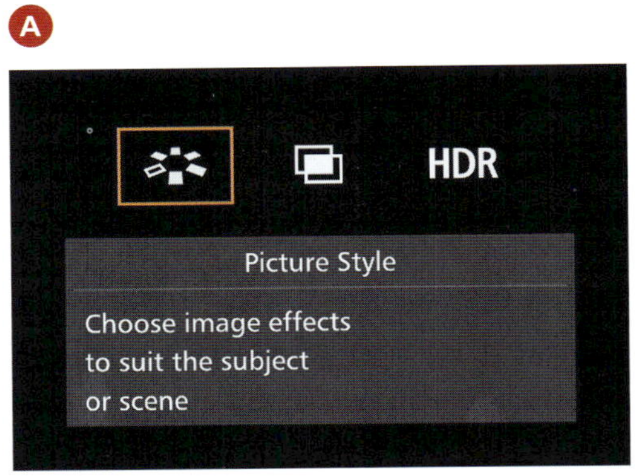

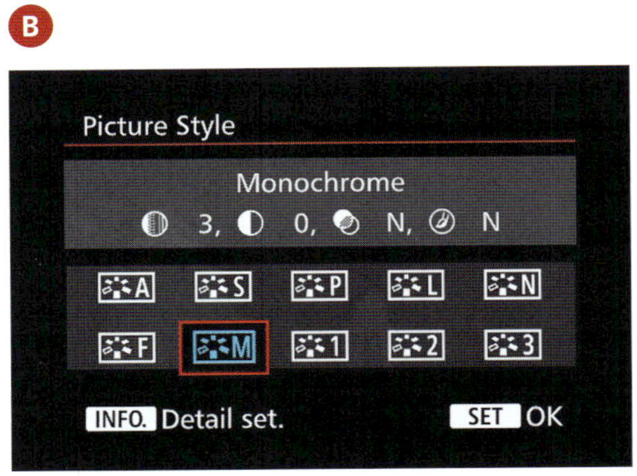

Your camera will continue to shoot with the Monochrome picture style until you change it to another setting.

Customizing the picture style settings

1. When you're in the Picture Style section of the menu where you have Monochrome selected, press the Info button located to the left of your viewfinder.
2. Use the Multi-controller to highlight the setting you would like to change, and press the Set button.
3. Use the Quick Control dial to move the cursor to a new position on the scale (the default setting will remain marked with a gray arrow) or to select a different filter, and press the Set button (**A**, **B**).

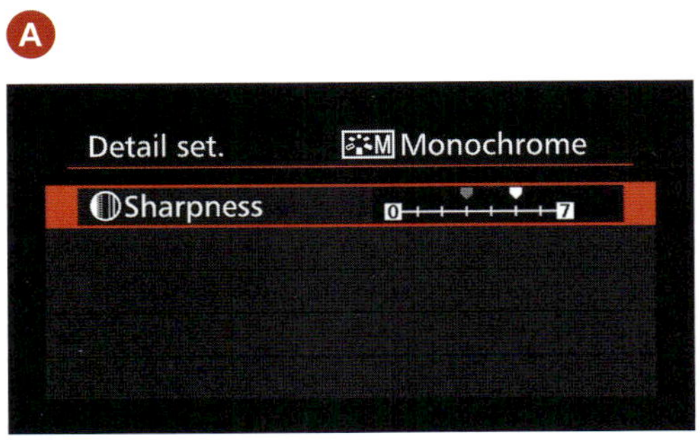

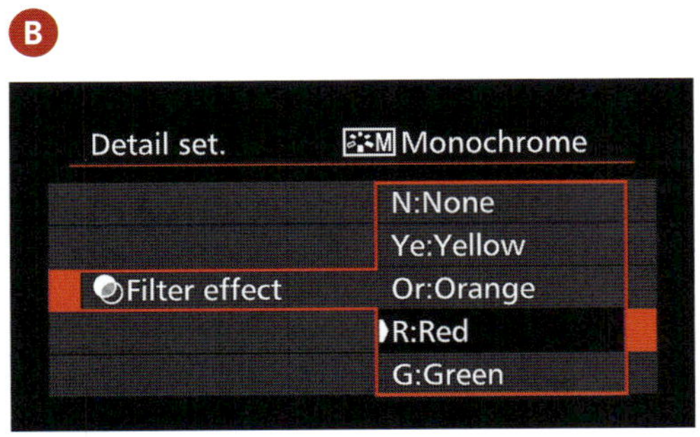

4. Perform the same process for the other options; then press the Menu button to return to the regular menu screen. You can now start shooting with your new settings.

The Portrait Picture Style for Better Skin Tones

As long as we are talking about picture styles for portraits, there is another style on your 7D Mark II that has been tuned specifically for this type of shooting. As you might guess, it's called Portrait. To set this style on your camera, follow the same directions as earlier, except this time select the Portrait style instead of Monochrome. The Portrait style provides individual options that, like the Monochrome style, include sharpness and contrast. You can also change the saturation (how intense the colors will be) and color tone (which lets you change the skin tones from more reddish to more yellowish). I prefer brighter colors, so I like to boost the Saturation setting to +2 and leave everything else at the defaults. You won't be able to use the same adjustments for everyone, especially when it comes to color tone, so do some experimenting to see what works best.

Detect Faces with Live View

Face detection in digital cameras has been around for a few years, but it's still a fairly new concept in the world of the DSLR. Your 7D Mark II has three different autofocus modes for Live View: FlexiZone-Multi, FlexiZone-Single, and my personal favorite, Face+Tracking. These modes are different from the standard focus modes used in regular shooting like One Shot, AI Servo, and AI Focus. Face+Tracking mode is probably the slowest of the Live View focusing modes, so I use it mostly when I am working with a tripod or when my subjects are going to remain fairly still. When you turn on Live View with Face+Tracking focusing, the camera does an amazing thing: It zeroes in on any face appearing on the LCD and places a box around it (**Figure 6.12**).

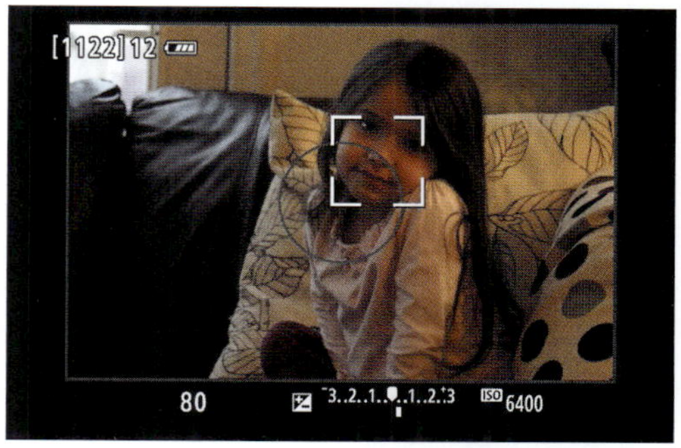

Figure 6.12
The Live View Face Detection mode can lock in on your subject's face for easy focusing.

If more than one face is in the frame, the box will appear over just one of them, but it will have little arrows to the side of it. Press the Multi-controller from side to side to make the box jump from one face to the other until you have selected the one that you want to focus on.

> **Manual Callout**
>
> There is a complete chapter in your manual that is dedicated to using Live View mode. It can be found in your manual on pages 285–311.

Setting up and shooting with Live View and Face Detection focusing

1. Press the Menu button and use the Main dial to highlight the fourth shooting menu screen. Then highlight the Live View Shoot. option and make sure it is set to Enable (**A**).
2. Next, move down one menu item to the AF Method option, and press Set (**B**).

A

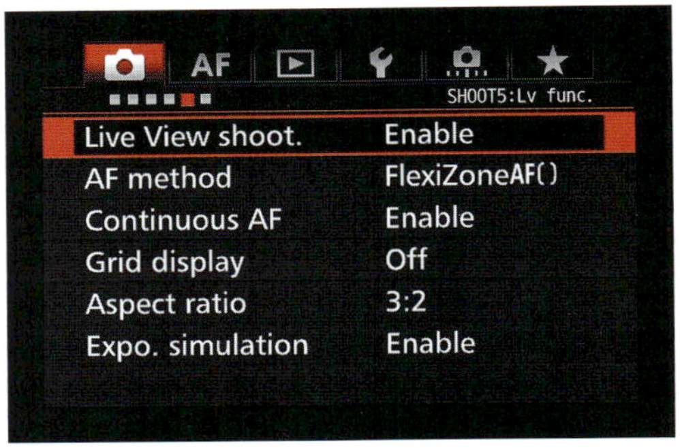

B

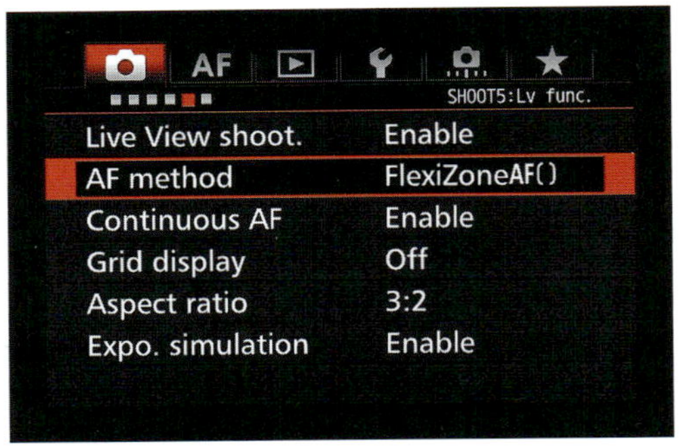

3. Select the Face+Tracking option, and press Set (**C**).
4. Press the Menu button to exit the menu mode and get ready for shooting.
5. Activate the Live View function by pressing the Live View button located on the back of the camera, to the right of the viewfinder.
6. Point your camera at a person and watch as the frame appears over the face in the LCD.
7. Press and hold the shutter release button halfway to focus on the face and wait until you hear the confirmation chirp.
8. Press the shutter button fully to take the photograph.

C

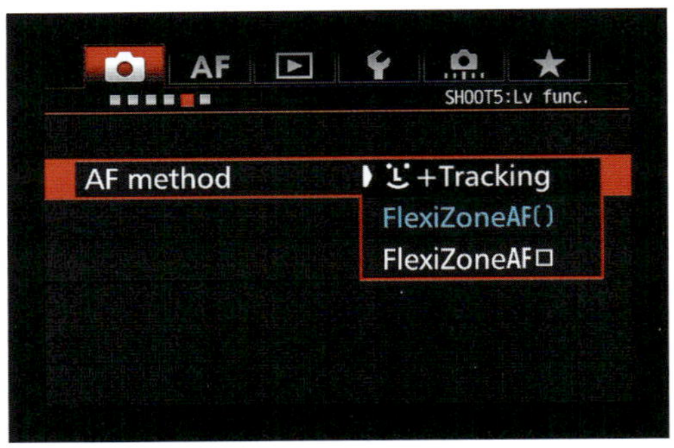

If you are having difficulty getting a face to focus, you can press the Q button (for the Quick Control screen) to activate the Live View options and make sure the AF option is highlighted. Then just turn the Main dial to switch from the Face Detection focusing mode to AF Live mode (**Figure 6.13**). This will bring up a focus point in the center of the screen that you can toggle to a new location.

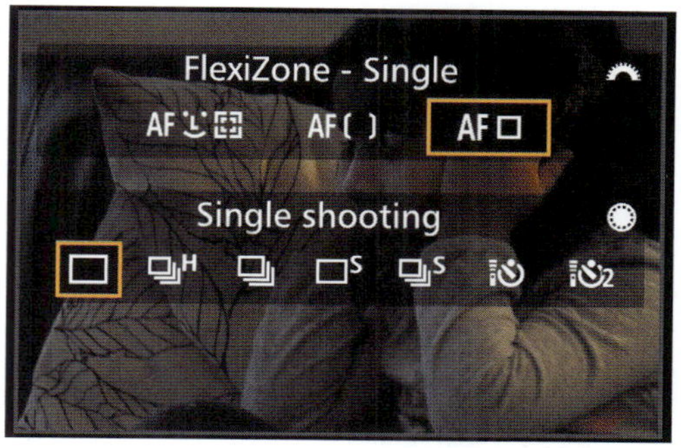

Figure 6.13
Change the focus mode if you can't get the camera to detect any faces.

Using Live View's grid overlay

Another benefit to using Live View is the Grid overlay. This feature places a grid over your image, dividing it into thirds, which can be of great benefit in properly composing your image.

Setting up Live View's Grid option

1. Press the Menu button, and then use the Main dial to get to the fifth shooting menu screen.
2. Using the Quick Control dial, scroll down to Grid Display and press Set (**A**).

A

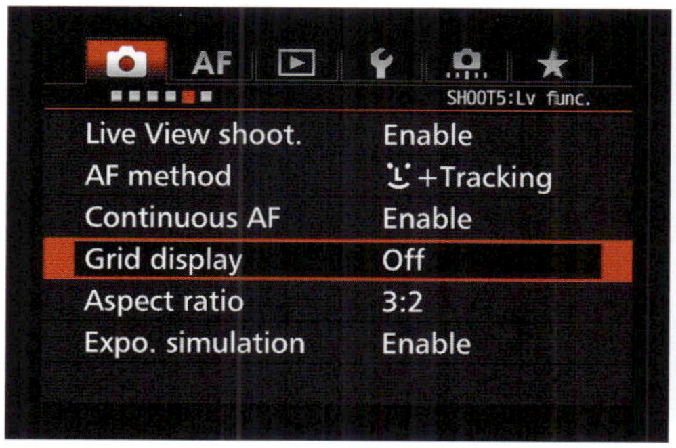

B

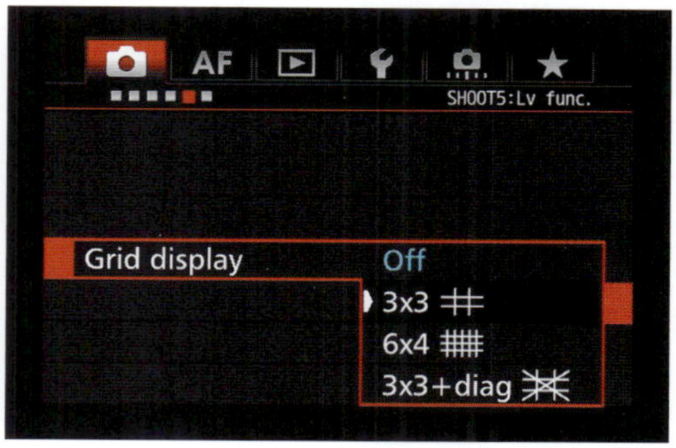

3. Scroll down to the 3x3 grid and press Set (**B**).

Now when you activate Live View, you will see the one-third grid overlay superimposed on the rear display (**Figure 6.14**). This effect shows up only on the display and will not be visible in your final image.

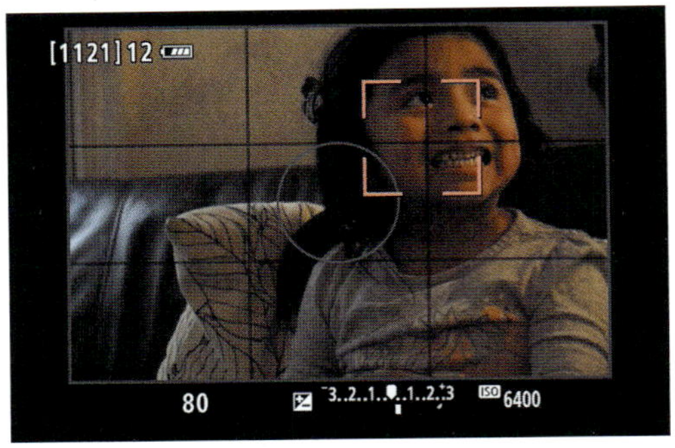

Figure 6.14
Using Live View's Grid option can help you compose your shots.

Use Fill Flash for Reducing Shadows

> **Catchlight**
>
> A *catchlight* is that little sparkle that adds life to the eyes. When you are photographing a person with a light source in front of them, you will usually get a reflection of that light in the eye, be it your flash, the sun, or something else brightly reflecting in the eye. The light is reflected off the surface of the eyes as bright highlights and serves to bring attention to the eyes.

A common problem when taking pictures of people outside, especially during the midday hours, is that the overhead sun can create dark shadows under the eyes and chin. You could have your subject turn his or her face to the sun, but that is usually considered cruel and unusual punishment. So how can you have your subject's back to the sun and still get a decent exposure of the face? Try turning on your flash to fill in the shadows. This also works well when you are photographing someone wearing a ball cap or someone who has a bright scene behind them (**Figure 6.15**). The fill flash helps lighten subjects so they don't appear in shadow, while providing a nice catchlight in the eyes.

The key to using the flash as a fill is to not use it on full power. If you do, the camera will try to balance the flash with the daylight, and you will get a very flat and featureless face.

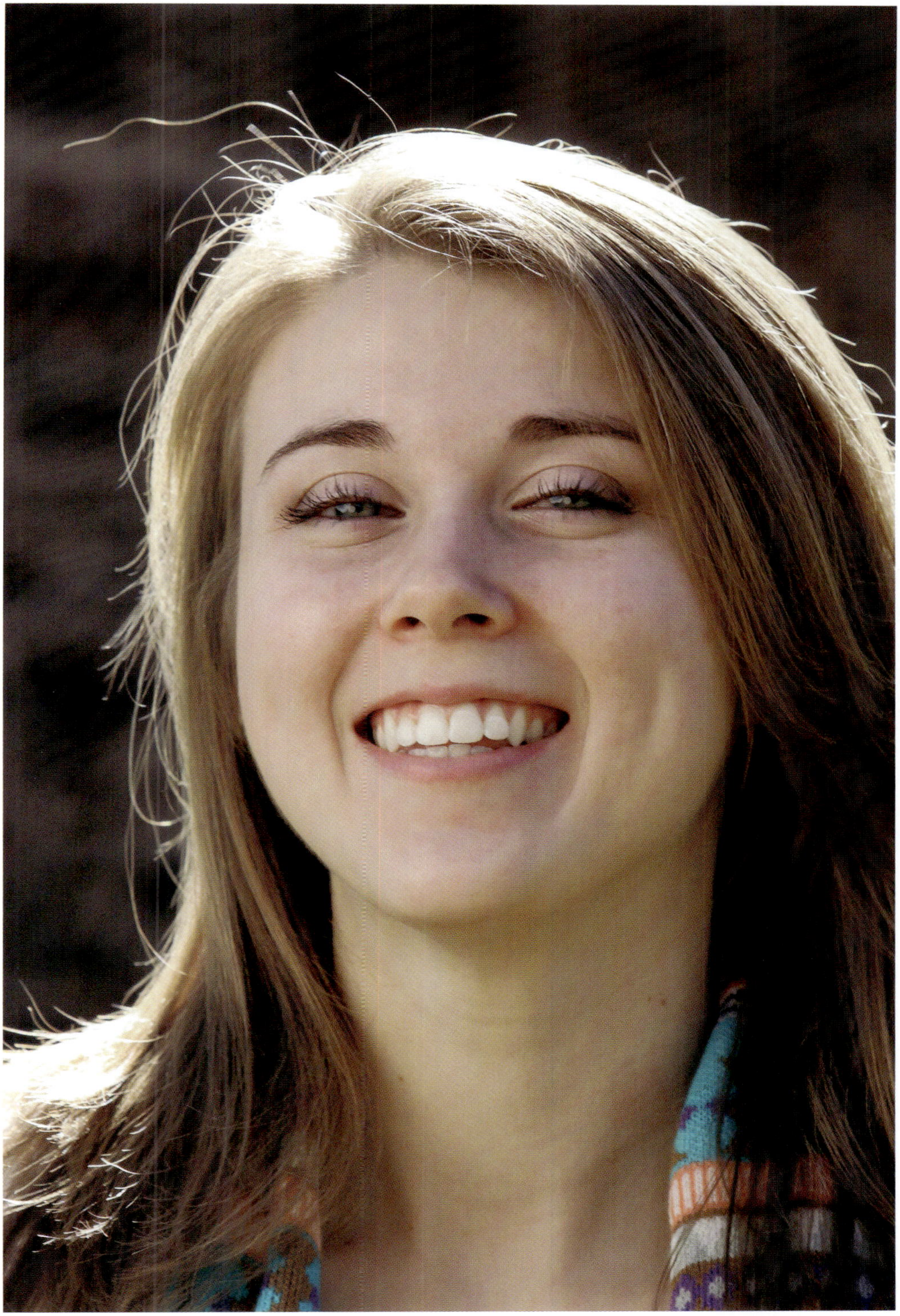

Figure 6.15
The subject was positioned with the sun at her back and some fill flash added to lighten her face.

ISO 200 • 1/160 sec. • f/9 • 160mm lens

Setting up and shooting with fill flash

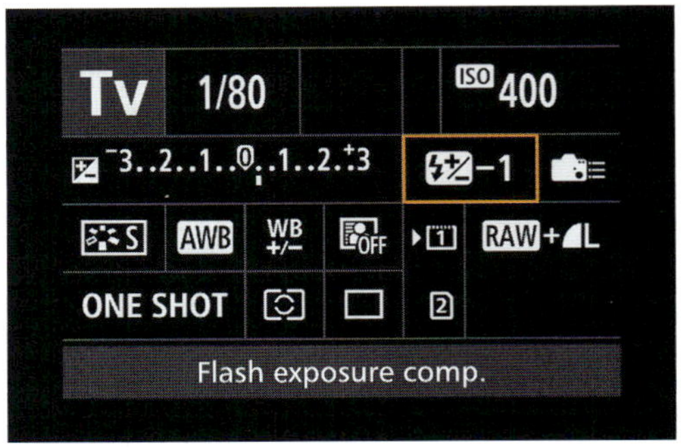

1. Press the pop-up flash button to raise your pop-up flash into the ready position.
2. Press the Q button to activate the Quick Control screen.
3. Use the Multi-controller to position the cursor over the Flash Exposure Comp. option.
4. Use the Main dial to select the desired amount of flash compensation.
5. Lightly press the shutter release button to exit the Quick Control screen.

One problem that can quickly surface when using the on-camera flash is red-eye. Not to worry, though—we will talk about that in Chapter 7, "Mood Lighting."

People on the Move

Not all portraits are shot with the subject sitting in a chair, posed and ready for the picture. Sometimes you might want to get an action shot that says something about the person, similar to an environmental portrait. Children, especially, just like to move. Why fight it? Set up an action portrait instead.

For the photo in **Figure 6.16**, I set my camera to Tv mode. I knew there would be a good deal of movement involved, and I wanted to make sure that I had a fairly high shutter speed to freeze the action, so I set it to 1/500 of a second. I used a Continuous focus mode, I had the drive mode set to Continuous, and I started firing off shots as my subject was swinging away from me. I had quite a few throwaway shots, but I was able to get one that captured the peak of the action.

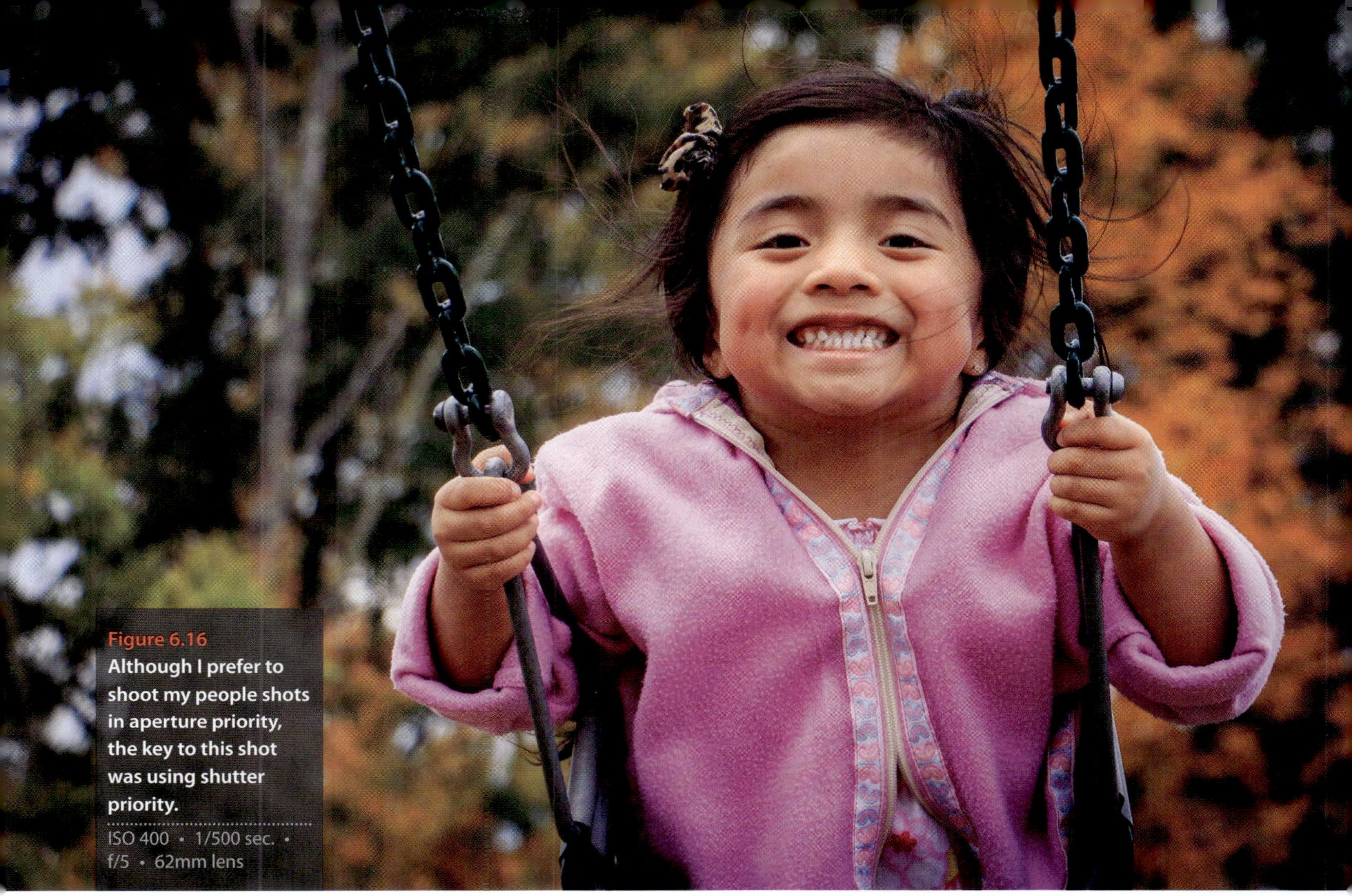

Figure 6.16
Although I prefer to shoot my people shots in aperture priority, the key to this shot was using shutter priority.
ISO 400 • 1/500 sec. • f/5 • 62mm lens

Tips for Shooting Better Portraits

Before we get to the assignments for this chapter, I want to leave you with a few extra pointers on shooting portraits that don't necessarily have anything specific to do with your camera. Entire books have been written that cover topics like portrait lighting, posing, and so on. But here are a few pointers that will make your people pics look a lot better.

Avoid the center of the frame

This falls under the category of composition. Placing your subject in the middle of the frame is usually a pretty boring way of composing your portraits (**Figure 6.17**). Try moving them off to the side using the rule-of-thirds trick and you will end up with a much more interesting image (**Figure 6.18**).

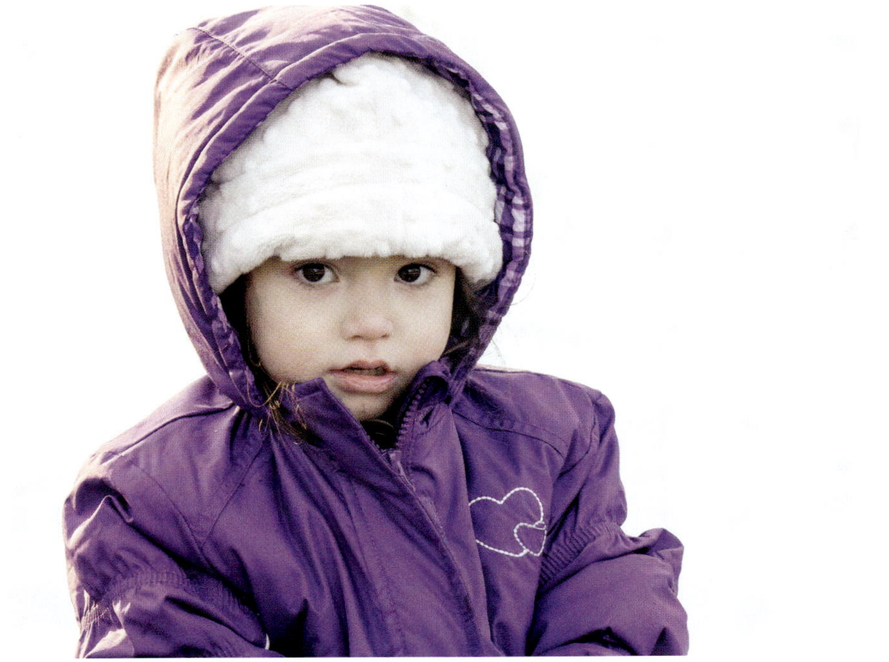

Figure 6.17
Having the subject in the middle of the frame with so much empty space on the sides can make for a less-than-interesting portrait.

ISO 400 • 1/100 sec. • f/5.6 • 120mm lens

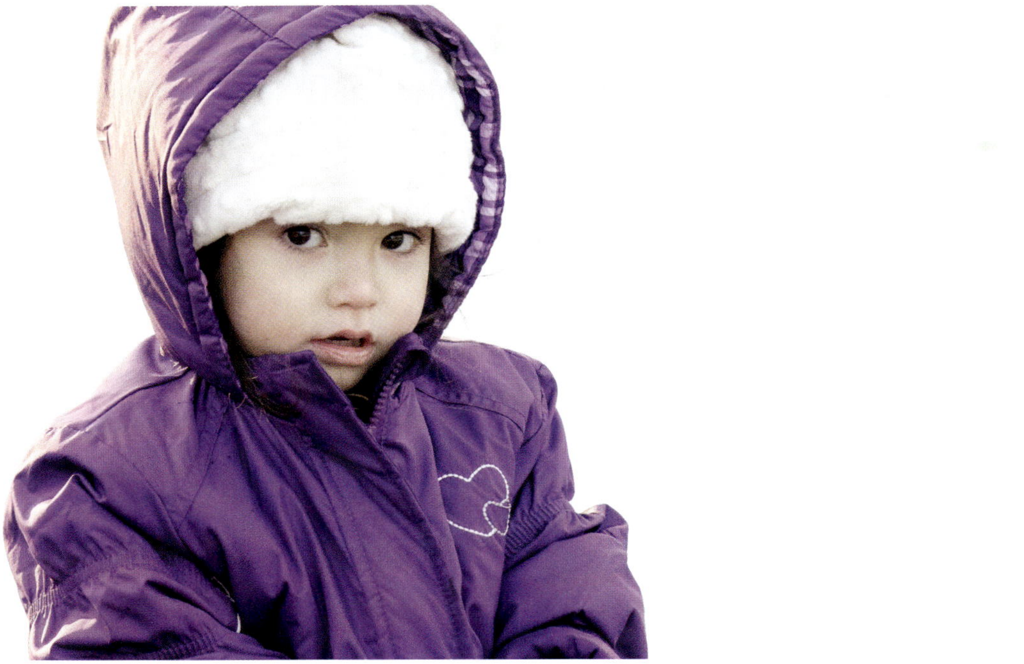

Figure 6.18
Try moving the subject off to the side for a more interesting composition.

ISO 400 • 1/80 sec. • f/5.6 • 120mm lens

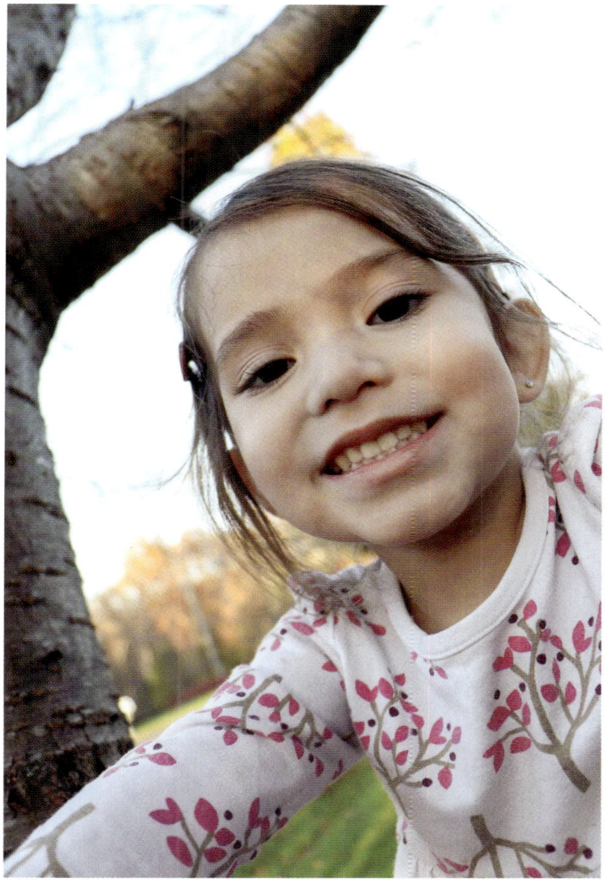

Figure 6.19
At this close distance, the 18mm lens is distorting the subject's face.

ISO 400 • 1/200 sec. • f/3.5 • 18mm lens

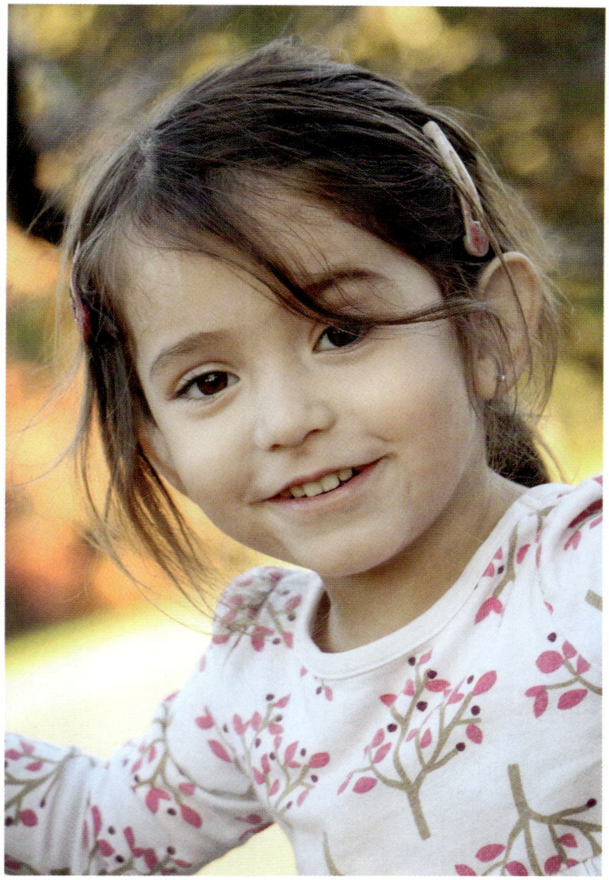

Figure 6.20
By zooming out to 135mm, I am able to remove the distortion for a much better photo.

ISO 800 • 1/80 sec. • f/5.6 • 135mm lens

Choose the right lens

Choosing the correct lens can make a huge impact on your portraits. A wide-angle lens can distort features of your subject, which can lead to an unflattering portrait (**Figure 6.19**). Select a longer focal length if you will be close to your subject (**Figure 6.20**).

Don't cut them off at the knees

There is an old rule about photographing people: Never crop the picture at a joint. This means no cropping at the ankles or the knees. If you need to crop at the legs, the proper place to crop is mid-shin or mid-thigh (**Figure 6.21**).

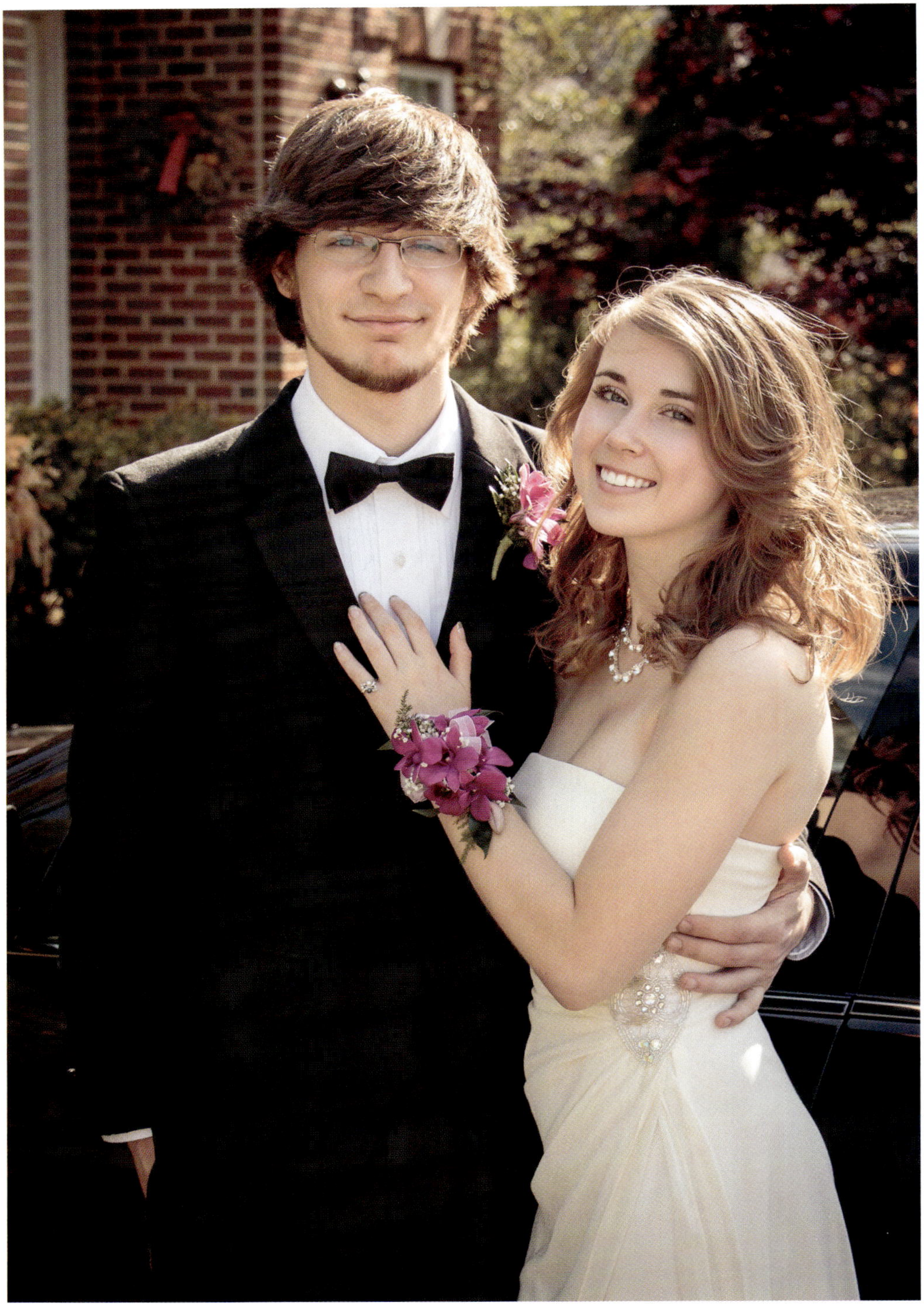

Figure 6.21
A good crop for people is when it intersects at mid-thigh or mid-shin.
ISO 400 • 1/640 sec. • f/6.3 • 300mm lens

Use the frame

Have you ever noticed that most people are taller than they are wide? Turn your camera vertically for a more pleasing composition (**Figure 6.22**).

Sunblock for portraits

The midday sun can be harsh and can do unflattering things to people's faces (**Figure 6.23**). If you can, find a shady spot out of the direct sunlight. You will get softer shadows, smoother skin tones, and better detail (**Figure 6.24**). This holds true for overcast skies as well. Just be sure to adjust your white balance accordingly.

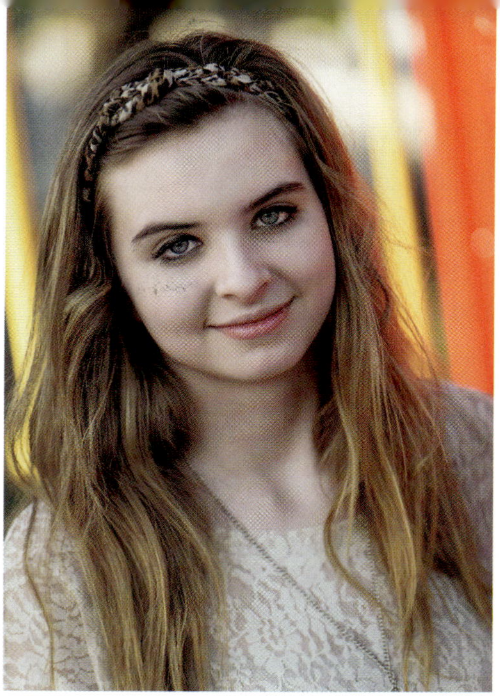

Figure 6.22
Get in the habit of turning your camera to a vertical position when shooting portraits. This is also referred to as portrait orientation.

ISO 100 • 1/400 sec. • f/3.2 • 135mm lens

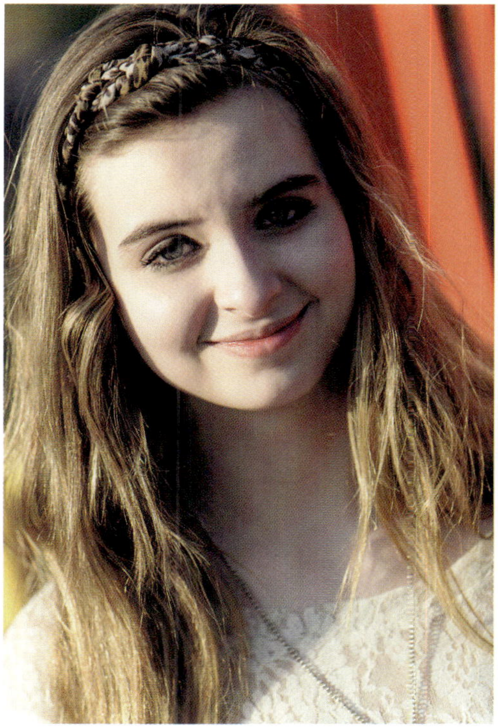

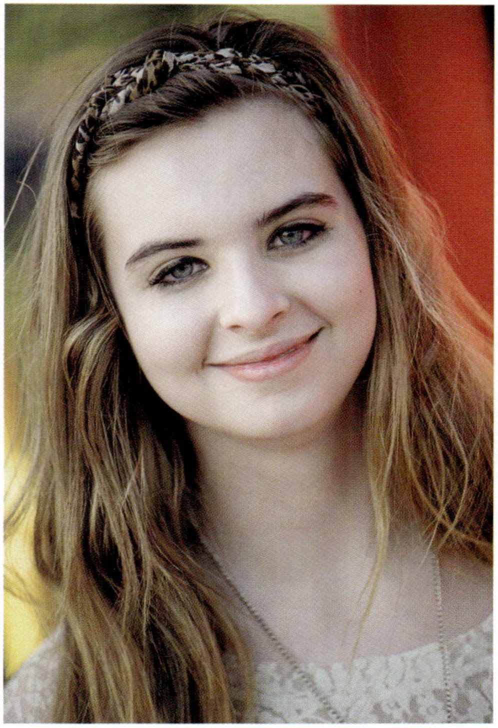

Figure 6.23
(left) The bright, direct sunlight looks too harsh on the subject's face.

ISO 100 • 1/800 sec. • f/3.2 • 180mm lens

Figure 6.24
By moving my subject over just a couple of feet, I was able to get her out of the direct sun and into a much more flattering situation.

ISO 100 • 1/640 sec. • f/3.2 • 180mm lens

Get down on their level

If you want better pictures of children, don't shoot from an adult's eye level. Getting the camera down to the child's level will make your images look more personal (**Figure 6.25**).

Don't be afraid to get close

When you are taking someone's picture, don't be afraid of getting close and filling the frame (**Figure 6.26**). This doesn't mean you have to get physically close to the subject. By using a long focal length lens, you can get a nice close-up without having to invade the subject's personal space.

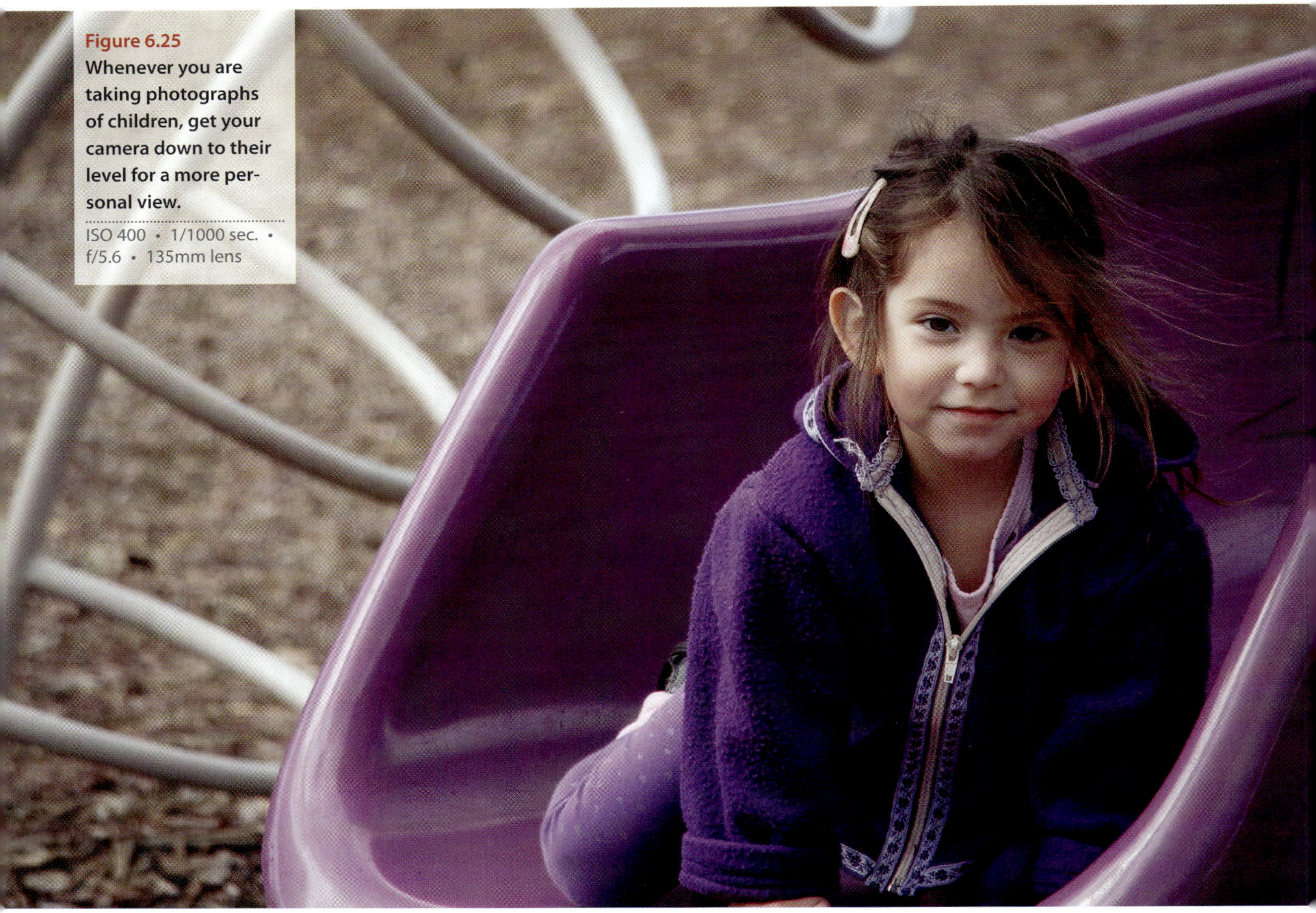

Figure 6.25
Whenever you are taking photographs of children, get your camera down to their level for a more personal view.
ISO 400 • 1/1000 sec. • f/5.6 • 135mm lens

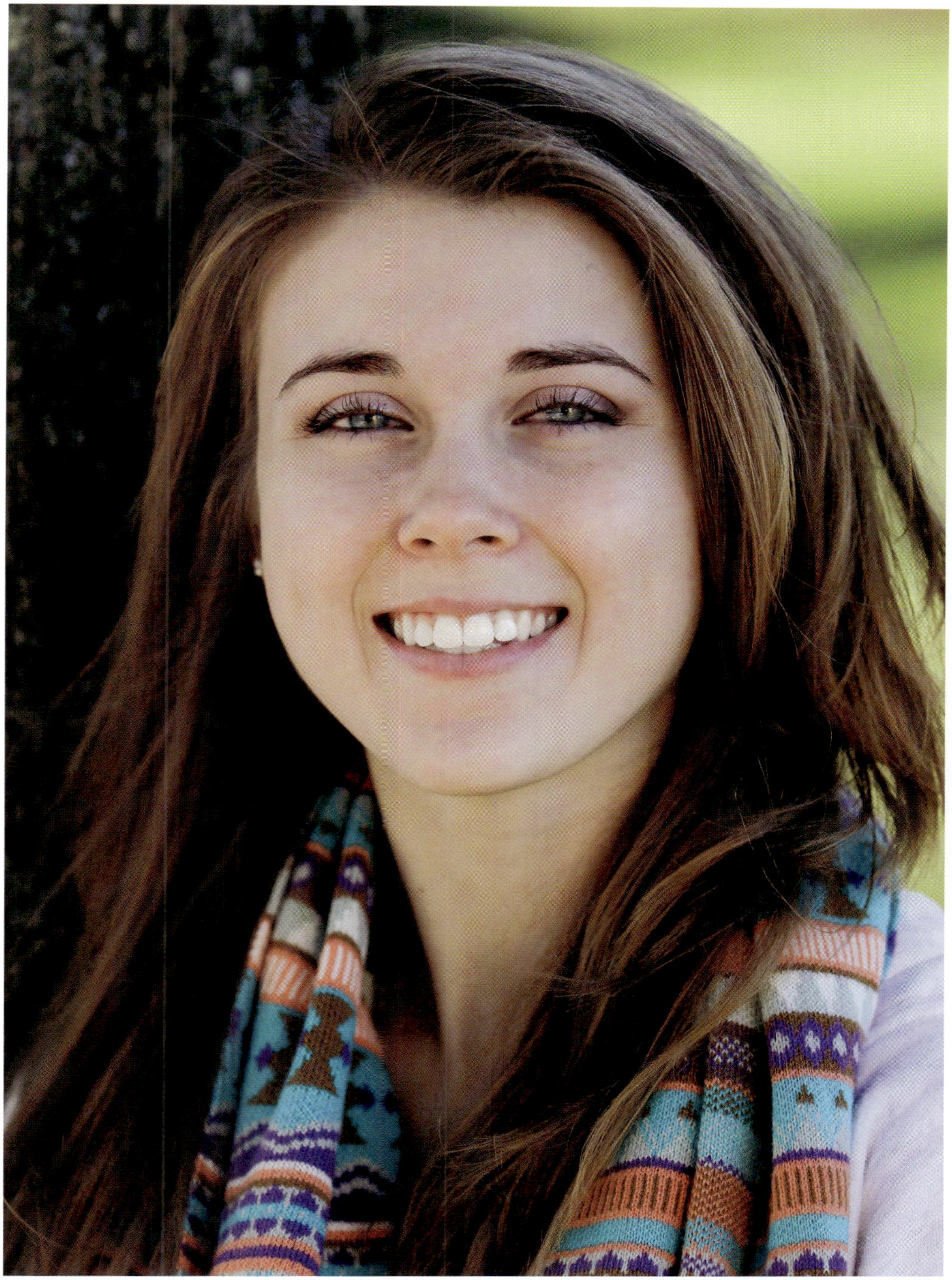

Figure 6.26
Filling the frame with the subject's face can lead to a much more intimate portrait.

ISO 400 • 1/800 sec. • f/2.8 • 105mm lens

Try a long lens for candid shots

Putting a camera in someone's face can elicit some unnatural results. People feel a need to pose, or they get nervous and stiff. If you want to capture some nice portraits with a candid feel, try shooting with a long lens (**Figure 6.27**). The distance will remove you and your camera from the equation and people will tend to react more normally with you around. If you are looking to be a street photographer, a long lens will be one of your best tools.

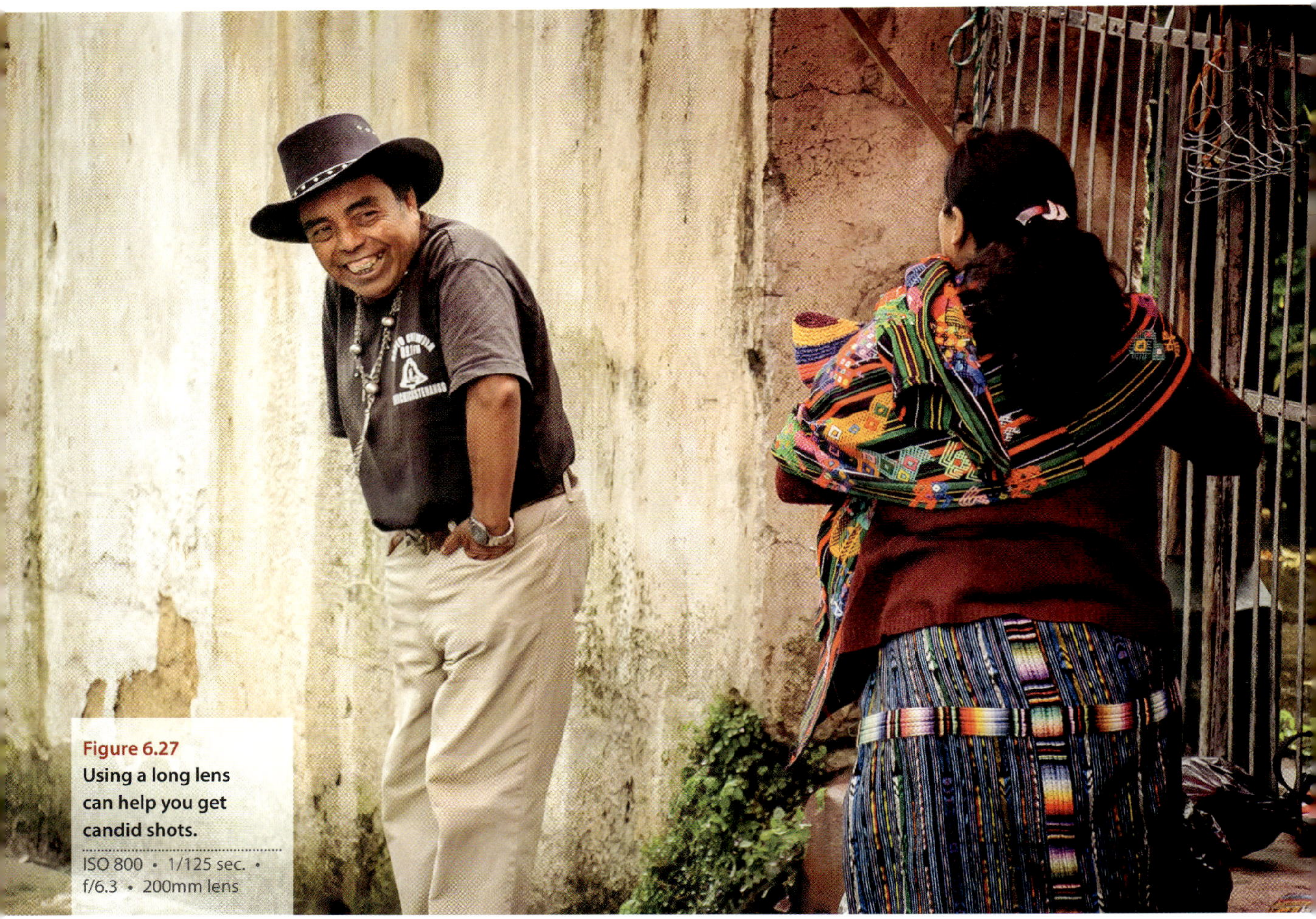

Figure 6.27
Using a long lens can help you get candid shots.
ISO 800 • 1/125 sec. • f/6.3 • 200mm lens

Chapter 6 Assignments

Great people photos begin with knowing how to apply some basic principles—and then practice, practice, practice. Find a willing subject and experiment with all the different techniques discussed in the chapter. Remember that it's your responsibility to make your subject look good, and that starts with practice.

Depth of field in portraits

Let's start with something simple. Grab your favorite person and start experimenting with using different aperture settings. Shoot wide open (the widest your lens goes, such as f/2.8 or f/4), and then stopped down (like f/22). Look at the difference in the depth of field and how it plays an important role in placing the attention on your subject. Make sure you don't have your subject standing against the background. Give some distance so that there is a good blurring effect of the background at the wide f-stop setting.

Discovering the qualities of natural light

Pick a nice sunny day and try shooting some portraits in the midday sun. If your subjects are willing, have them turn so the sun is in their face. If they are still speaking to you after blinding them, have them turn their back to the sun. Try this with and without the fill flash so you can see the difference. Finally, move them into a completely shaded spot and take a few more shots.

Picking the right metering method

Find a very dark or light background and place your subject in front of it. Take a couple of shots, giving a lot of space around your subject for the background to show. Now switch metering modes and use the AE Lock feature to get a more accurate reading of your subject. Notice the differences in exposure between the metering methods.

Picture styles for portraits

Have some fun playing with the various picture styles. Try the Portrait style as compared to the Standard style. Then try Monochrome and play with the color filter options to see how they affect skin tones.

Share your results with the book's Flickr group!
Join the group here: flickr.com/groups/7dmarkii_fromsnapshotstogreatshots

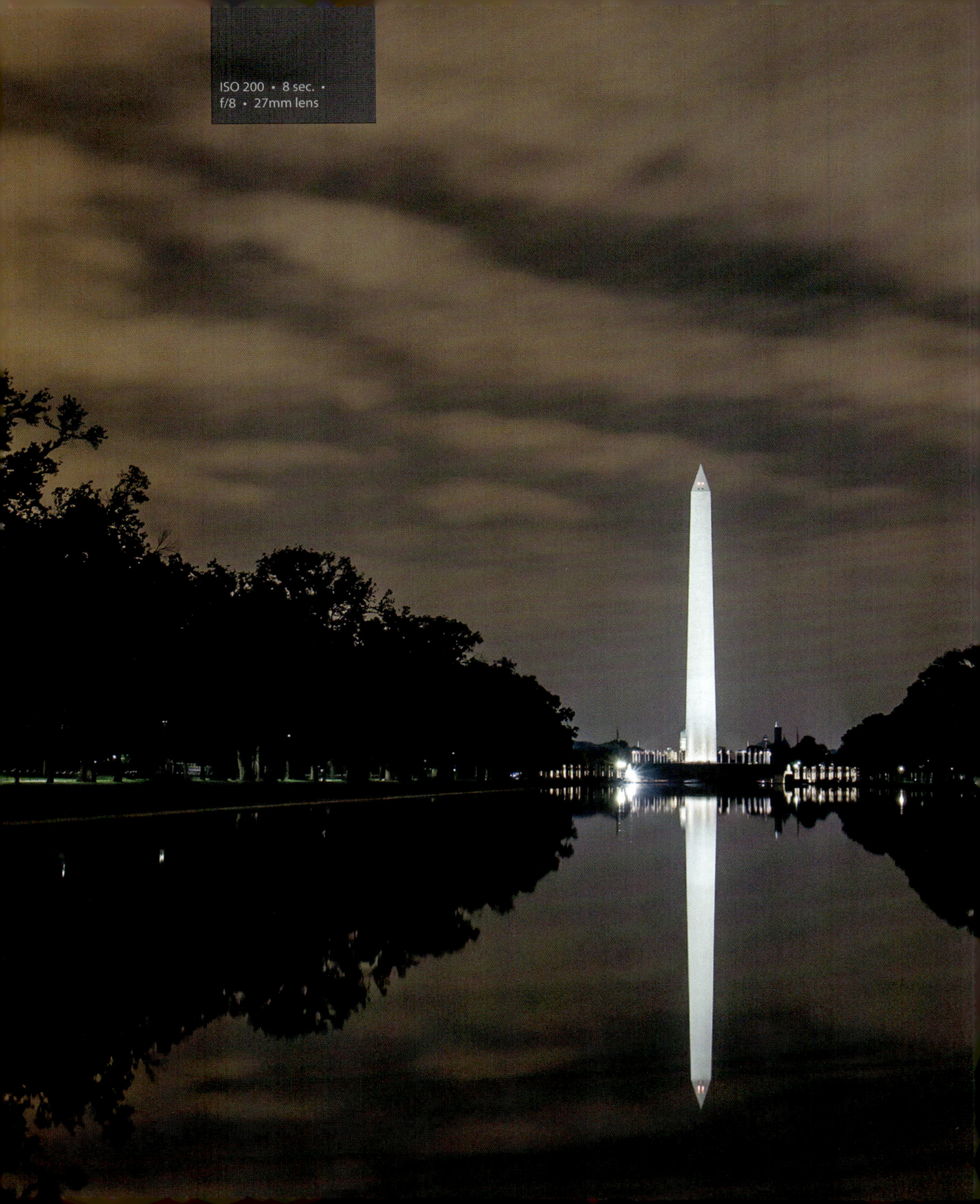

ISO 200 • 8 sec. • f/8 • 27mm lens

7

Mood Lighting

Shooting When the Lights Get Low

The sun going down is no reason to put your camera away. Your 7D Mark II has some great features that let you work with available light as well as the built-in flash. In this chapter, we will explore ways to push your camera's technology to the limit in order to capture great photos in difficult lighting situations. We will also explore the use of flash and how best to use your built-in flash features to improve your photography. But first, let's check out what we can do when working with low-level available light.

Poring Over the Picture

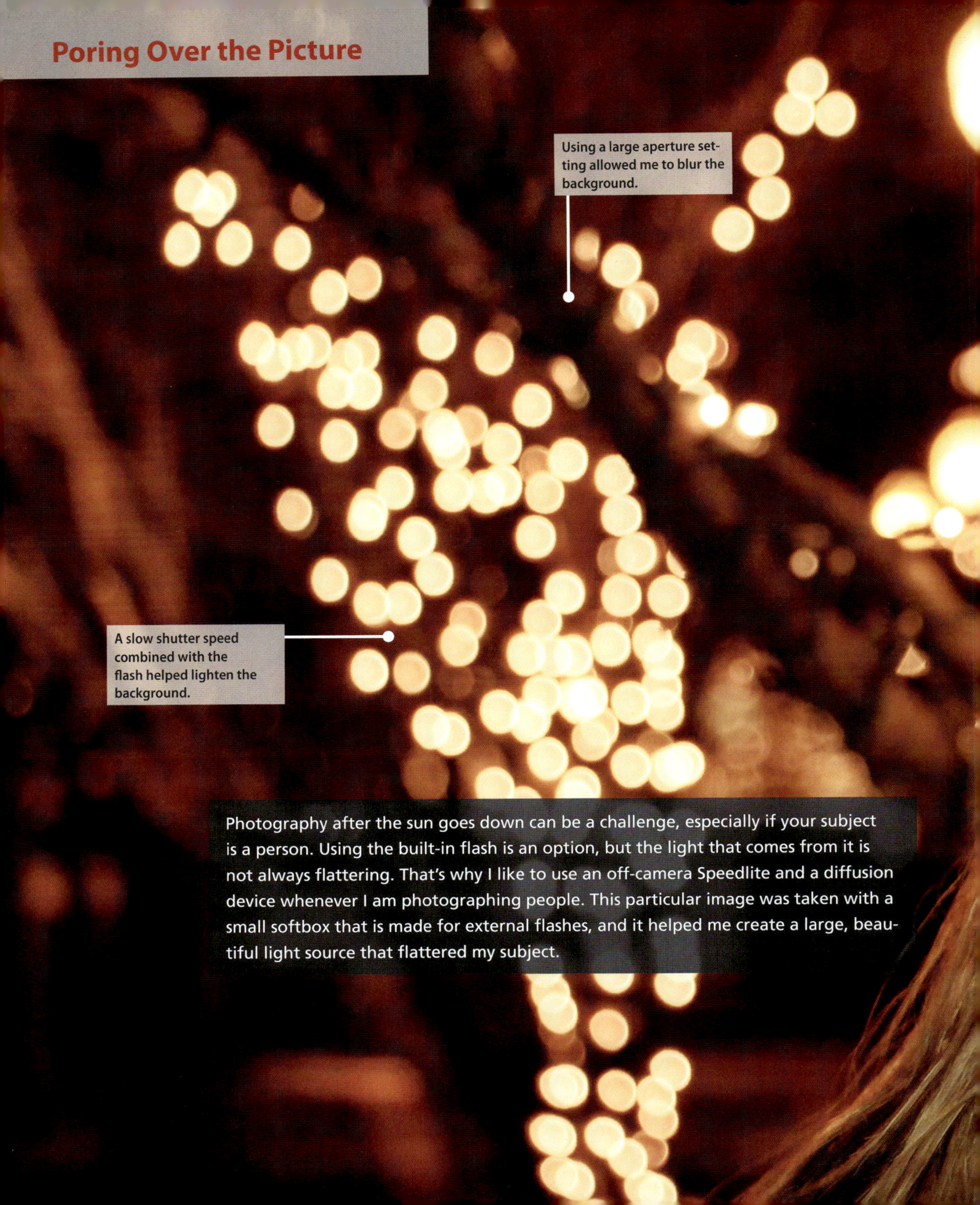

Photography after the sun goes down can be a challenge, especially if your subject is a person. Using the built-in flash is an option, but the light that comes from it is not always flattering. That's why I like to use an off-camera Speedlite and a diffusion device whenever I am photographing people. This particular image was taken with a small softbox that is made for external flashes, and it helped me create a large, beautiful light source that flattered my subject.

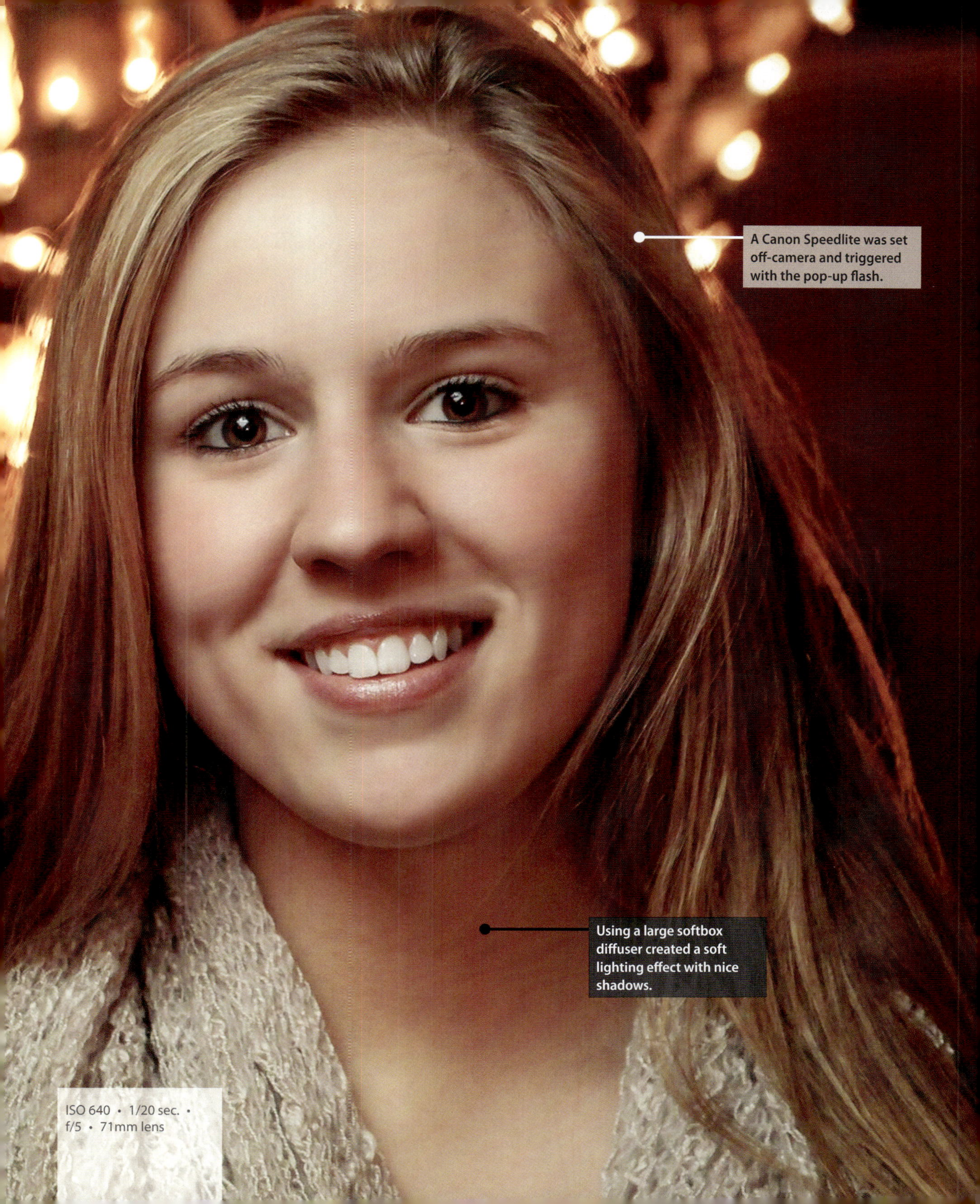
A Canon Speedlite was set off-camera and triggered with the pop-up flash.
Using a large softbox diffuser created a soft lighting effect with nice shadows.
ISO 640 • 1/20 sec. • f/5 • 71mm lens

Raising the ISO: The Simple Solution

Let's begin with the obvious way to keep shooting when the lights get low: raising the ISO (**Figure 7.1**). By now you know how to change the ISO: Just press the ISO button on the top of the camera and turn the Main dial to adjust. In typical shooting situations, you should keep the ISO in the 100–800 range. Doing so will keep your pictures nice and clean by holding the digital noise to a minimum. But as the available light gets low, you might find yourself working in the higher ranges of the ISO scale, which could lead to more noise in your image.

You could use the flash, but that has a limited range (15–20 feet) that might not work for you. Also, you could be in a situation where flash is prohibited, or at least frowned upon, such as at a wedding or in a museum.

And what about a tripod in combination with a long shutter speed? That is also an option, and we'll cover it a little later in the chapter. The problem with using a tripod and a slow shutter speed in low-light photography, though, is that it performs best when subjects aren't moving. Besides, try to set up a tripod in a Metro station or museum and see how quickly you grab the attention of the security guards.

So if the only choice to get the shot is to raise the ISO to 800 or higher, make sure that you turn on the High ISO Speed Noise Reduction feature. This menu function is set to

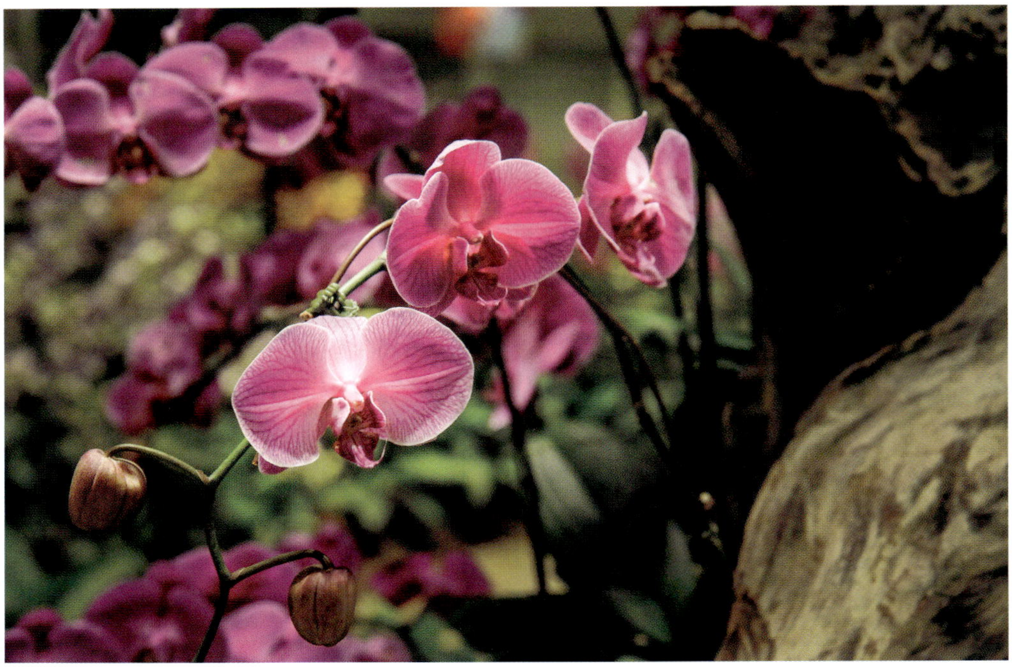

Figure 7.1
The light inside this orchid house was fairly dim and forced me to raise the ISO to get the shot without having to use a flash.

ISO 5000 • 1/80 sec. • f/8 • 80mm lens

Standard by default, but as you start using higher ISO values, you might want to consider changing it to the Strong setting. (See Chapter 5, "Landscape Photography," to learn about setting the noise-reduction features.)

To see the effect of High ISO Speed Noise Reduction, you need to zoom in and take a closer look (**Figure 7.2** and **Figure 7.3**).

Raising the noise reduction to the Strong setting slightly increases the processing time for your images, so if you are shooting in Continuous drive mode, you might see a little reduction in the speed of your frames per second.

One important thing to note about the use of Noise Reduction is that it only applies when you are shooting in JPEG mode. If you are capturing your images in a RAW format, you will need to apply noise reduction in your image-editing software.

Noise reduction saves space

When shooting at very high ISO settings, running High ISO Speed NR at the Standard or Strong setting can save you space on your memory card. If you are saving your photos as JPEGs, the camera will compress the information in the image to take up less space. When you have excessive noise, you can literally add megabytes to the file size. This is because the camera has to deal with more information: It views the noise in the image as photo information and, therefore, tries not to lose that information during the compression process. That means more noise equals bigger files. So not only will turning on the High ISO Speed NR feature improve the look of your image, it will also save you some space so you can take a few more shots.

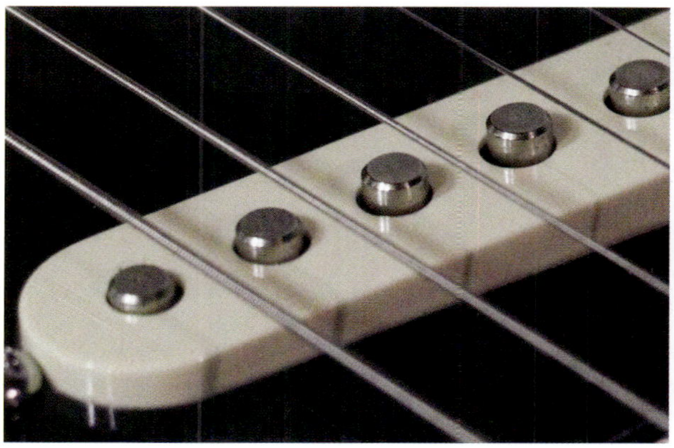

Figure 7.2

Here is a 100 percent enlargement of an image without any ISO noise reduction.

ISO 6400 • 1/125 sec. • f/5.6 • 88mm lens

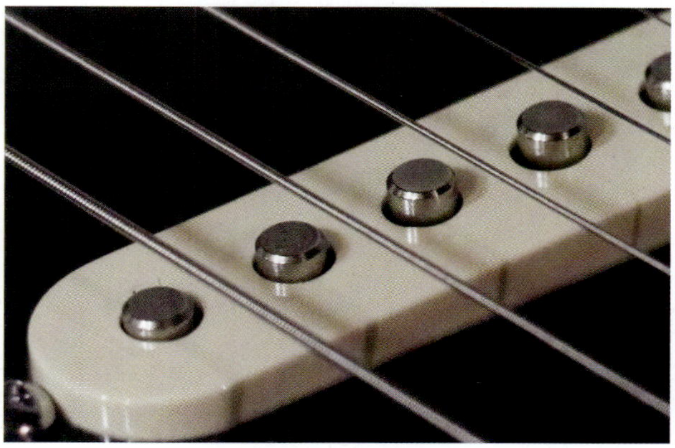

Figure 7.3

Here is the same scene with noise reduction set to Strong.

ISO 6400 • 1/125 sec. • f/5.6 • 88mm lens

Using Very High ISOs

Is ISO 16000 just not enough for you? Well, in that case, you will need to expand the ISO to H1 or H2. This will open up another 2 stops of ISO, raising the new limit to an incredible 25600 for H1 and 51200 for H2. These settings are grayed out in your ISO setting screen until you unlock them in the menu.

Setting up the ISO Expansion feature

1. Press the Menu button and navigate to the second shooting menu screen.
2. Highlight the ISO Speed Settings option, and press Set (**A**).
3. Use the Quick Control dial to highlight the ISO Speed Range option, and press Set (**B**).

A

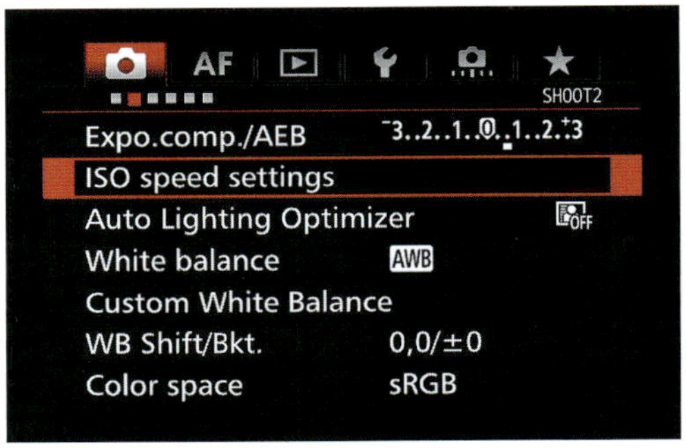

B

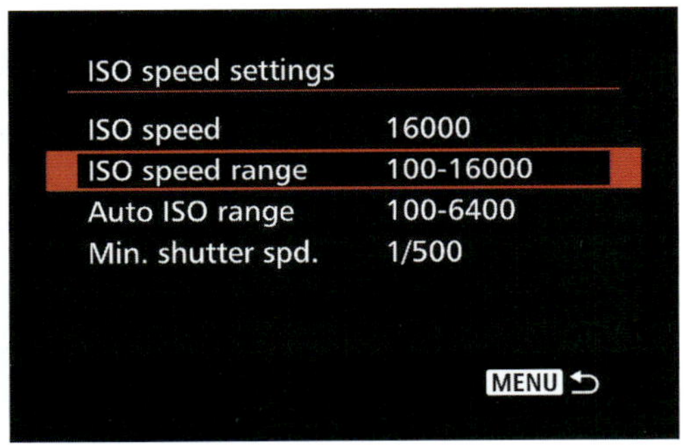

4. Using the Quick Control dial, highlight the Maximum setting, press Set, and then rotate the dial to change the maximum setting to H1 or H2 and press Set again (**C**).
5. The final step is to highlight the OK option and press the Set button to lock in the change.

C

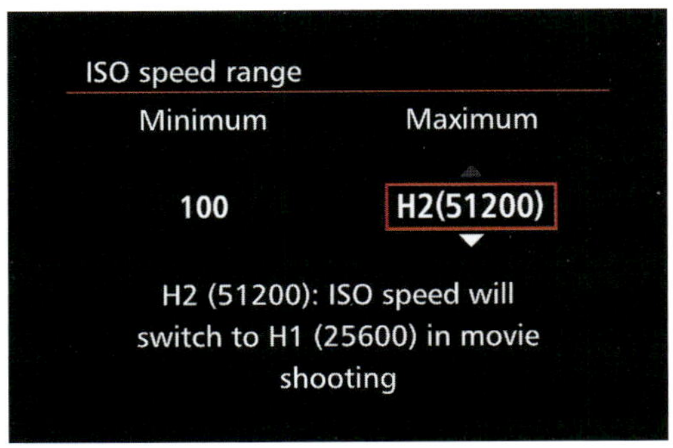

Now when you press the ISO button you will see that you have the higher ISO options available to use as needed.

A word of warning about the expanded ISO settings: Although it's great to have high ISO settings available during low-light shooting, they should always be your last resort.

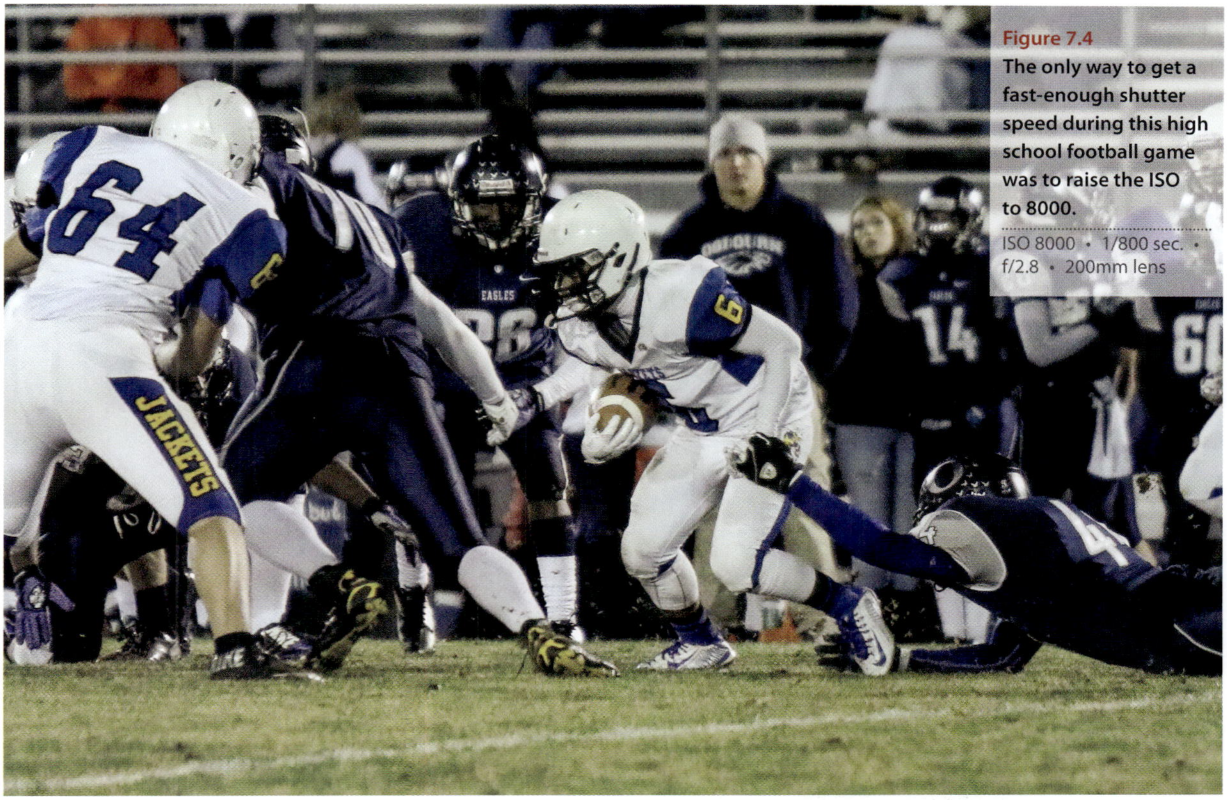

Figure 7.4
The only way to get a fast-enough shutter speed during this high school football game was to raise the ISO to 8000.

ISO 8000 • 1/800 sec. • f/2.8 • 200mm lens

Even with the High ISO Speed NR turned on, the amount of visible noise will be extremely high. I can't think of a situation where I ever need to use the 25600 (H1) setting, but you might find yourself at a nighttime sporting event under the lights, which could require ISOs of 6400 or 8000 to improve your shutter speeds and capture the action (**Figure 7.4**).

Using Multi Shot Noise Reduction

Using high ISO settings is sometimes unavoidable, and using the highest setting on the high ISO noise reduction can lead to a softer look to your images. If you are photographing a nonmoving subject, you might want to try out the Multi Shot Noise Reduction option (**Figure 7.5**). This works by taking four consecutive exposures, aligning them, and then averaging out the random noise in each image to create one high-quality shot that has much less noise than you would get from just using the standard noise reduction (**Figure 7.6**).

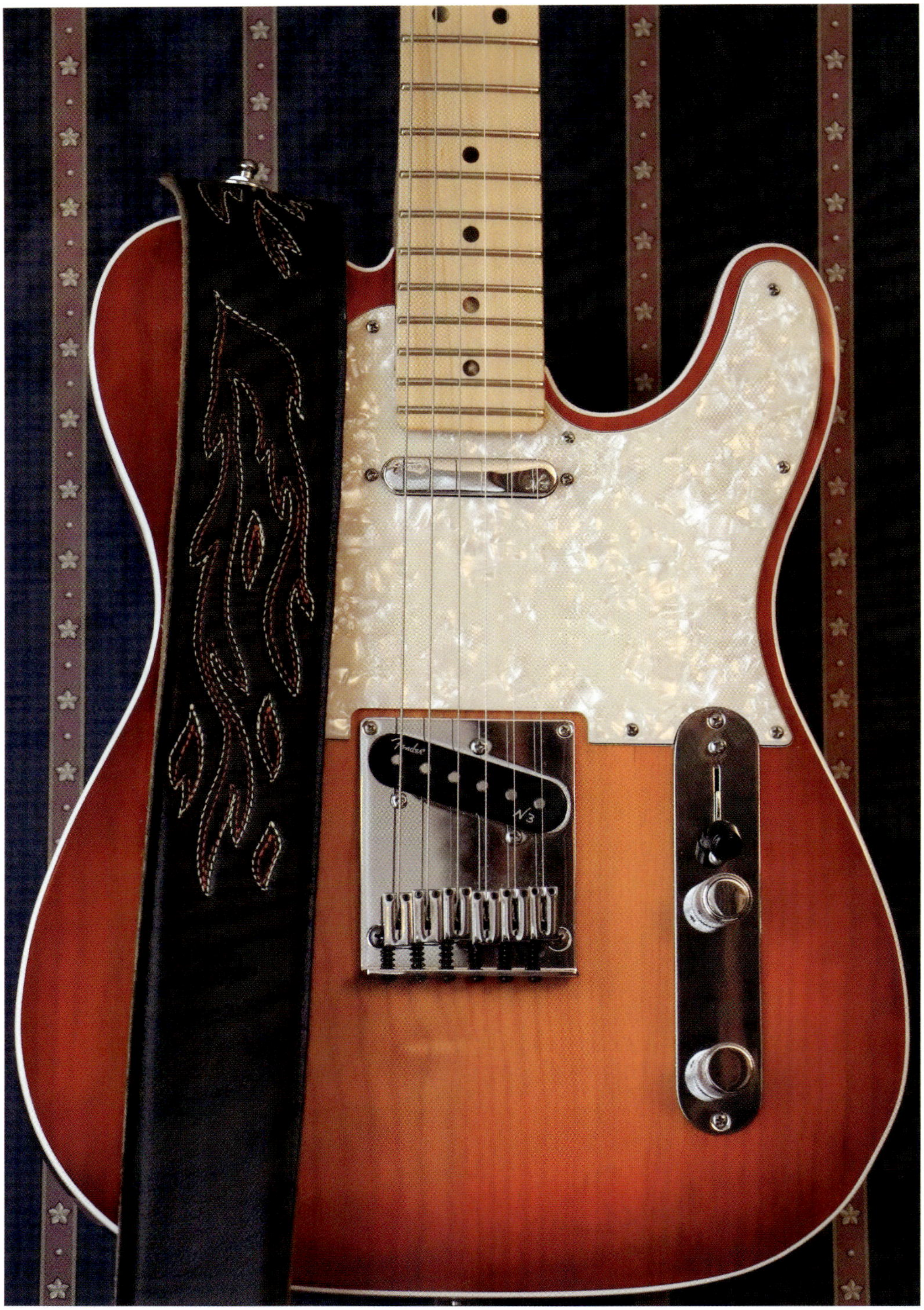

Figure 7.5
You can get high-quality images with high ISO settings using the Multi Shot Noise Reduction option.

ISO 16000 • 1/100 sec. • f/5 • 67mm lens

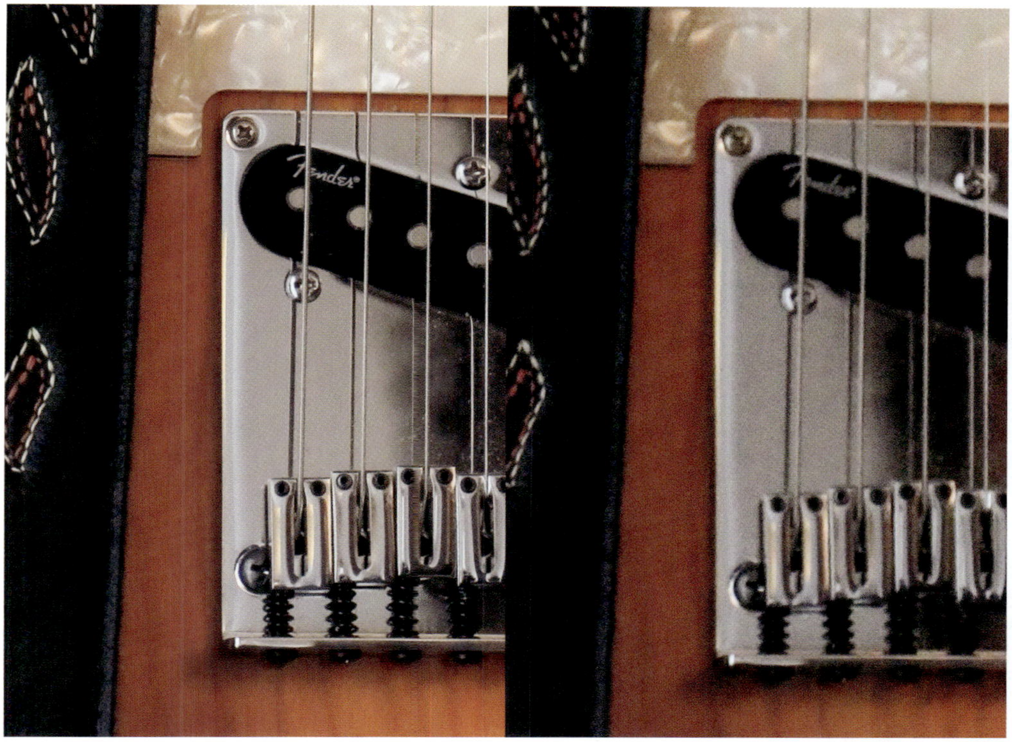

Figure 7.6
The image on the left was created with the Multi Shot Noise Reduction option. The noisier image on the right was created with standard noise-reduction settings. The exposure settings were exactly the same for both images.

Setting up the Multi Shot Noise Reduction option

1. Press the Menu button; then navigate to the third shooting menu, select High ISO Speed NR, and press set (**A**).
2. Select the Multi Shot Noise Reduction option, and press set (**B**).

A

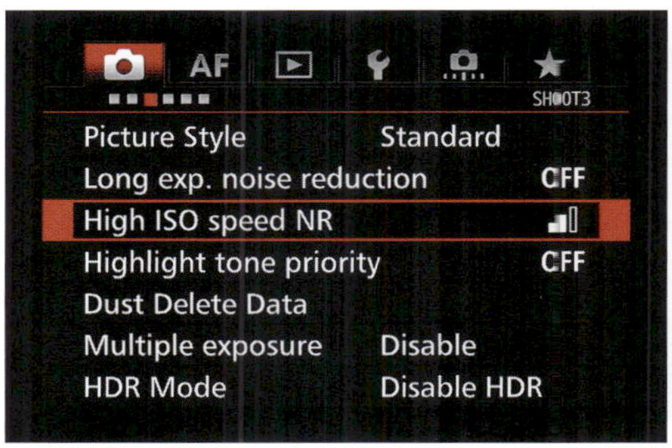

B

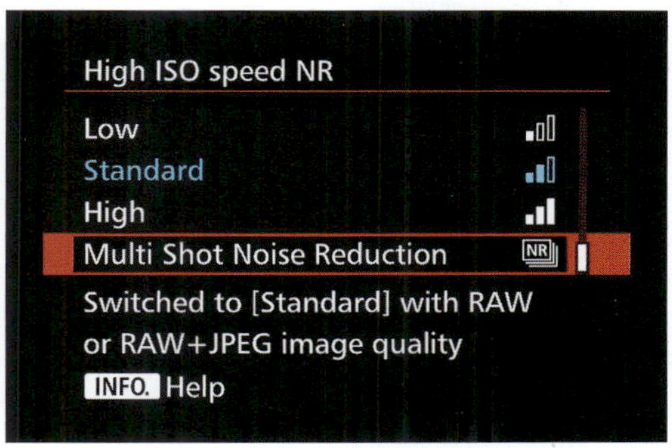

3. Adjust the camera to your desired exposure settings.
4. Press and hold the shutter release button once and the camera will take the four exposures and then display the resulting JPEG image.
5. Be sure to set the noise reduction back to a normal setting, or just turn the camera off to have it reset to the Standard setting.

Stabilizing the Situation

> **Self-timer**
>
> Whether you are shooting with a tripod or even resting your camera on a wall, you can increase the sharpness of your pictures by taking your hands out of the equation. Whenever you use your finger to depress the shutter release button, you are increasing the chance that there will be a bit of shake in your image. To eliminate this possibility, try setting up your camera to use the self-timer. To turn on the self-timer, press the Drive/AF button and use the Quick Control dial to select one of the two self-timer modes. I generally use the 2-second mode to cut down on time between exposures.

If you purchased your camera with one of the new image stabilization (IS) lenses, you already own a great tool to squeeze two stops of exposure out of your camera when shooting without a tripod (**Figure 7.7**). Typically, the average person can handhold a camera down to about 1/60 of a second before blurriness results due to hand shake. As the length of the lens is increased (or zoomed), the ability to handhold at slow shutter speeds (1/60 and slower) and still get sharp images is further reduced.

The Canon IS lenses contain small gyro sensors and servo-actuated optical elements, which correct for camera shake and stabilize the image. The IS function is so good that it is possible to improve your handheld photography by two or three stops, meaning that if you are pretty solid at a shutter speed of 1/60, the IS feature lets you shoot at 1/15, and possibly even 1/8 of a second (**Figure 7.8** and **Figure 7.9**).

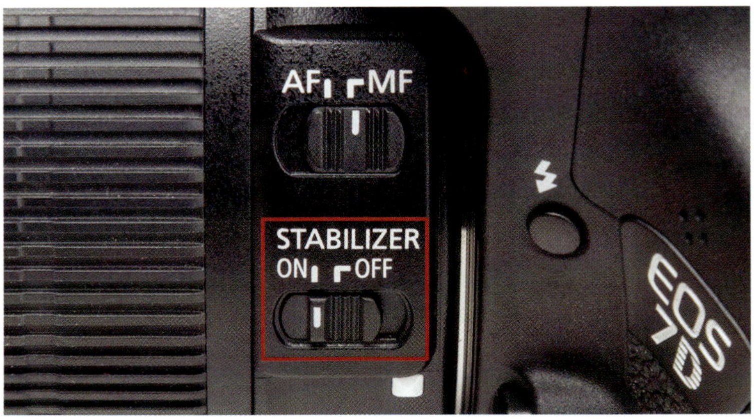

Figure 7.7
Set the Stabilizer to the On position when using longer shutter speeds while handholding your camera.

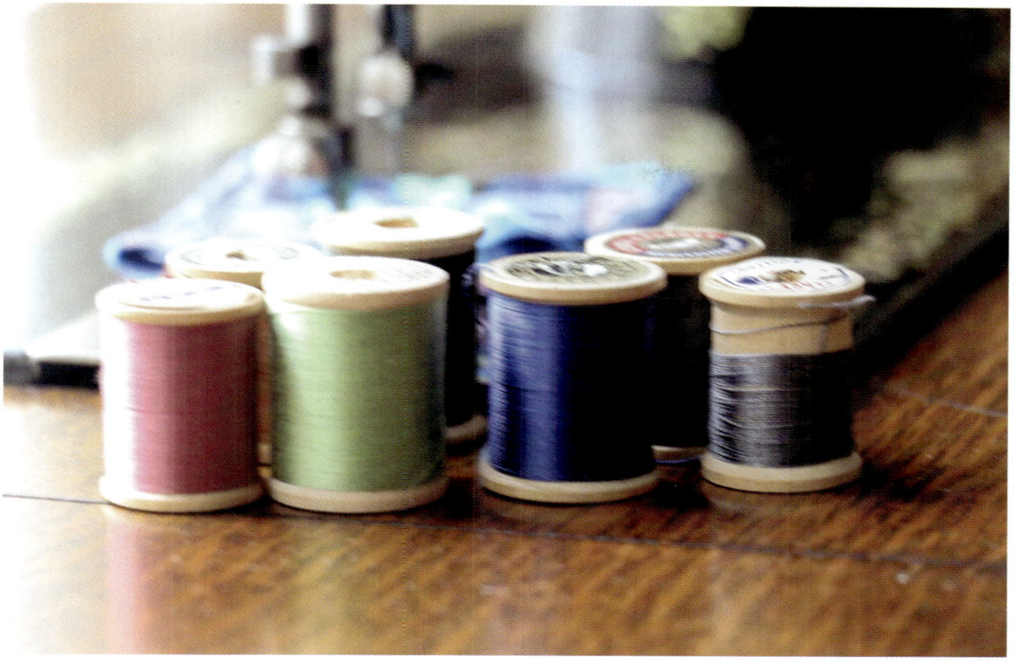

Figure 7.8
This image was handheld with the IS turned off.

ISO 400 • 1/4 sec. • f/5.6 • 135mm lens

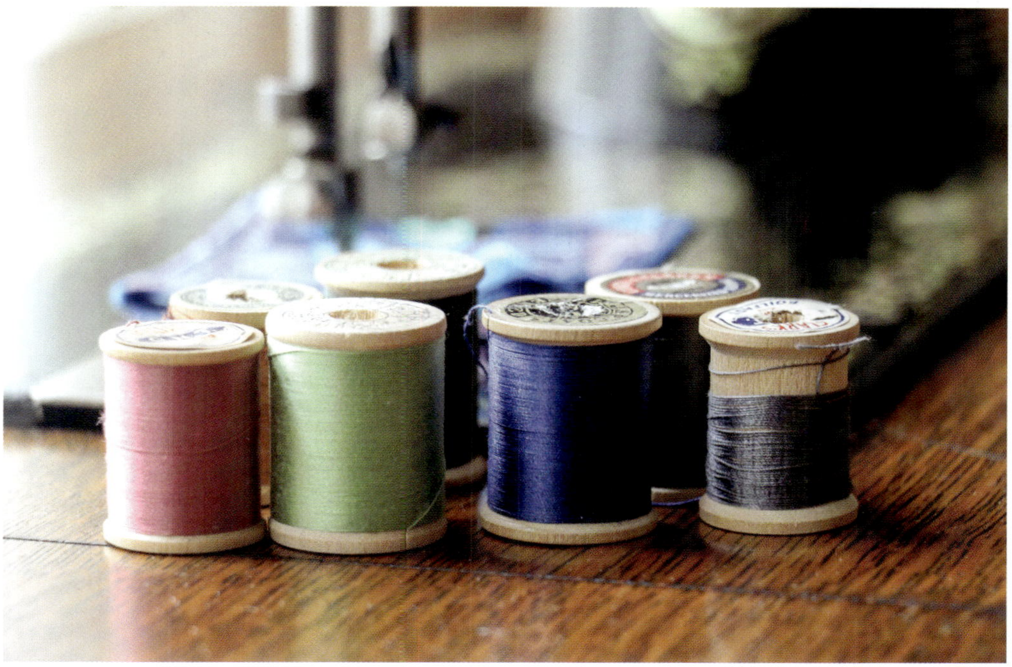

Figure 7.9
Here is the same subject shot with the same settings, but this time with IS turned on.

Focusing in Low Light

The 7D Mark II has a great focusing system, but occasionally the light levels might be too low for the camera to achieve an accurate focus. You can overcome this obstacle in a few ways.

First, you should know that the camera uses contrast in the viewfinder to establish a point of focus. This is why your camera will not be able to focus when you point it at a white wall or a cloudless sky. It simply can't find any contrast in the scene to work with. Knowing this, you might be able to use a single focus point in One Shot mode to find an area of contrast that is of the same distance as your subject. You can then hold that focus by pressing the shutter button halfway and recomposing your image.

Occasionally, there just isn't anything for you to focus on. A perfect example of this would be a fireworks display. If you point your lens to the night sky in any automatic focus (AF) mode, it will just keep searching for—and not finding—a focus point. In this case, you can turn off the autofocus feature and manually focus the lens (**Figure 7.10**). Look for the AF/MF switch on the side of the lens and slide it to the MF position.

Don't forget to put it back in AF mode at the end of your shoot.

Focus Assist

Another way to ensure good focus is to enable the 7D Mark II's Focus Assist mode. Focus Assist uses a short burst from your pop-up flash to shine some light on the scene, which assists the autofocus system in locating more detail. This feature is automatically activated when shooting in the Scene Intelligent Auto mode. Focus Assist should be enabled by default, but you can check the menu just to make sure.

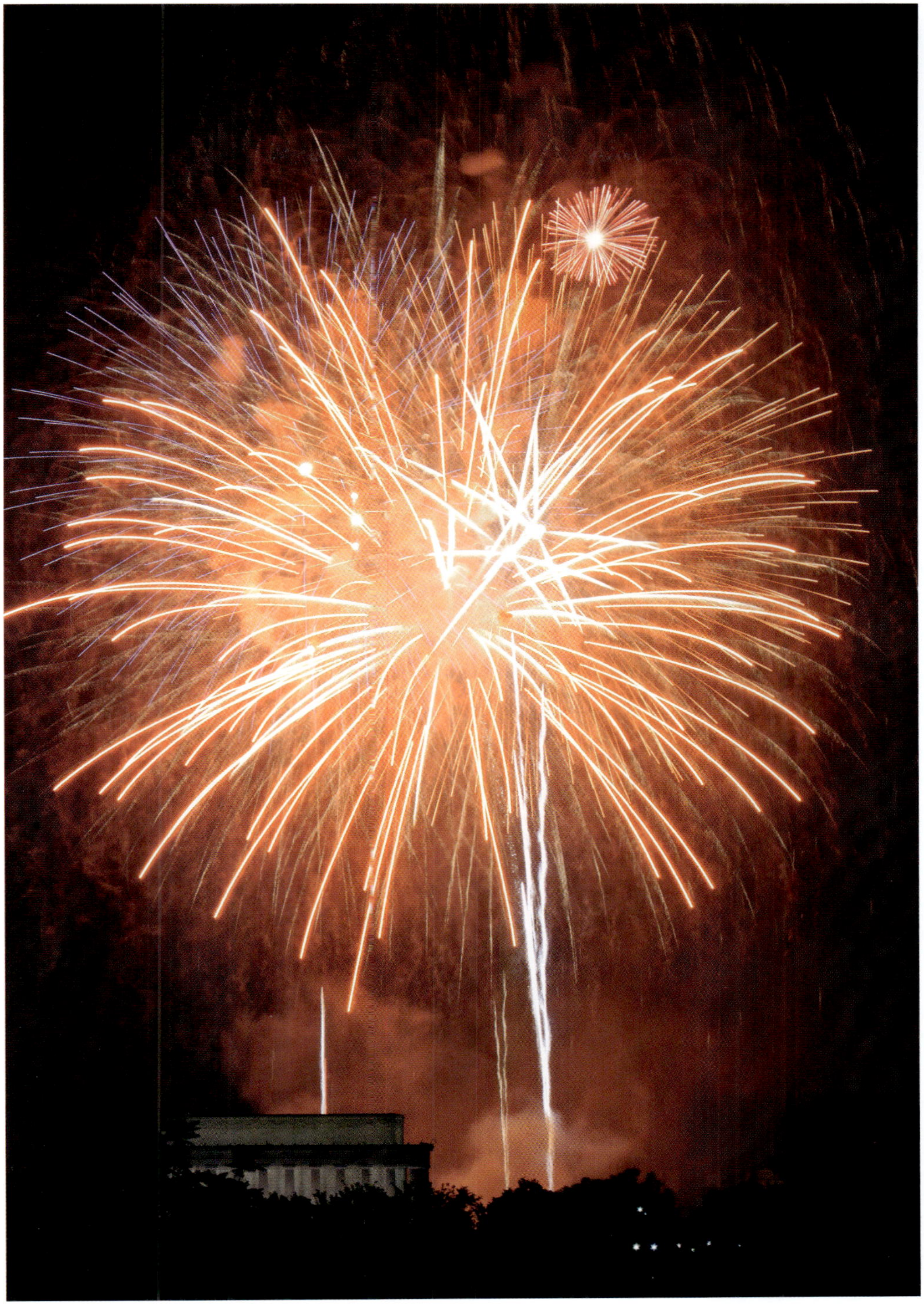

Figure 7.10
Focusing on the night sky is best done in manual focus mode.

ISO 100 • 2 sec. • f/13 • 110mm lens

Turning on the Focus Assist feature

1. Press the Menu button; then use the Main dial to get to the third AF menu tab, highlight AF-Assist Beam Firing (**A**).
2. If it is not enabled, press the Set button, highlight Enable, and press the Set button again (**B**).

A

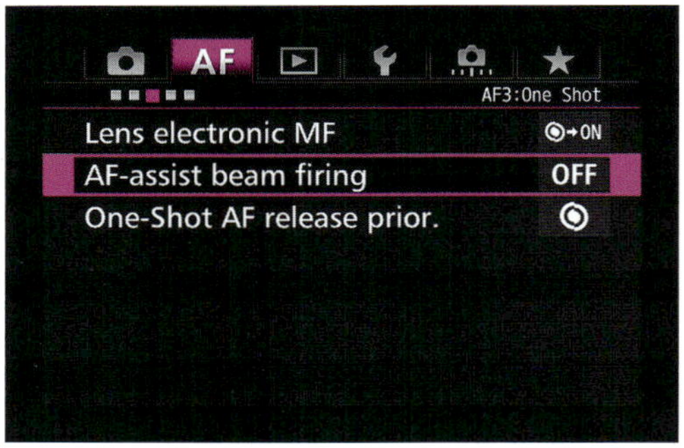

B

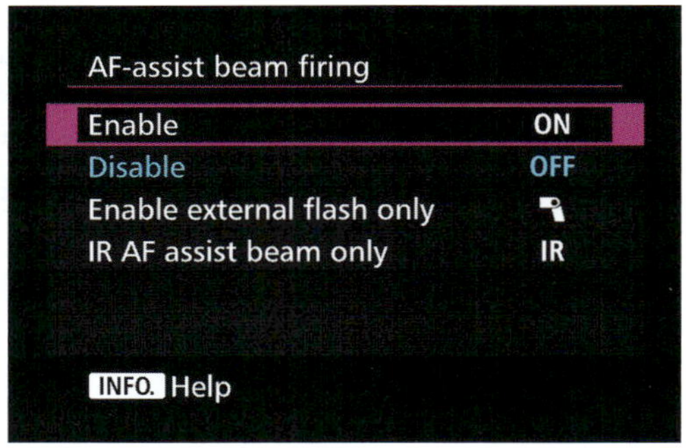

3. To use it when while shooting, press the flash button to raise the pop-up flash.
4. With the flash in the "up" position, press the shutter button to focus and Focus Assist will activate if necessary.

If you don't want the flash to fire during the actual exposure, you must first disable the flash. This lets Focus Assist function while keeping the flash from going off during the actual exposure.

Disabling the flash

1. Press the Menu button, and then scroll the Main dial to highlight the first shooting menu (far left).
2. Scroll down to Flash Control, and press the Set button (**A**).

A

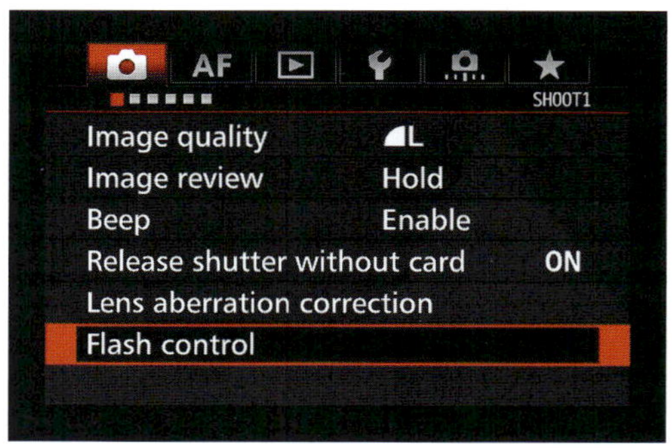

3. Select Flash Firing, and press the Set button (**B**).

B

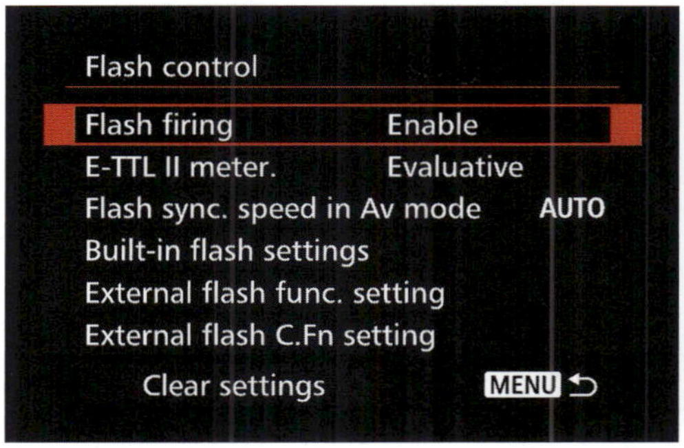

C

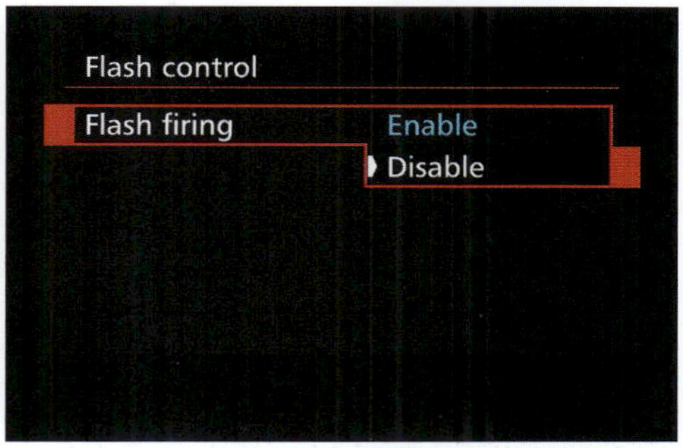

4. Set the Flash Firing option to Disable (**C**).

Shooting Long Exposures

We have covered some of the techniques for shooting in low light, so let's go through the process of capturing a night or low-light scene for maximum image quality (**Figure 7.11**). The first thing to consider is that in order to shoot in low light with a low ISO, you will need to use shutter speeds that are longer than you could possibly handhold (longer than 1/15 of a second). This will require the use of a tripod or stable surface for you to place your camera on. For maximum quality, the ISO should be low—somewhere at or below 400. Long Exp. Noise Reduction should be turned on to minimize the effects of exposing for longer durations. (To set this up, see Chapter 5.)

Once the noise reduction is turned on, set your camera to Aperture Priority (Av) mode. This way, you can concentrate on the aperture that you believe is most appropriate and let the camera determine the best shutter speed. If it is too dark for the autofocus to function properly, try manually focusing. Finally, consider using a cable release (see Chapter 11, "Pimp My Ride") to activate the shutter. If you don't have one, check out the "Self-timer" sidebar. Once you shoot the image, you may notice some lag time before it is displayed on the rear LCD. This is due to the noise-reduction process, which can take anywhere from a fraction of a second up to 30 seconds, depending on the length of the exposure.

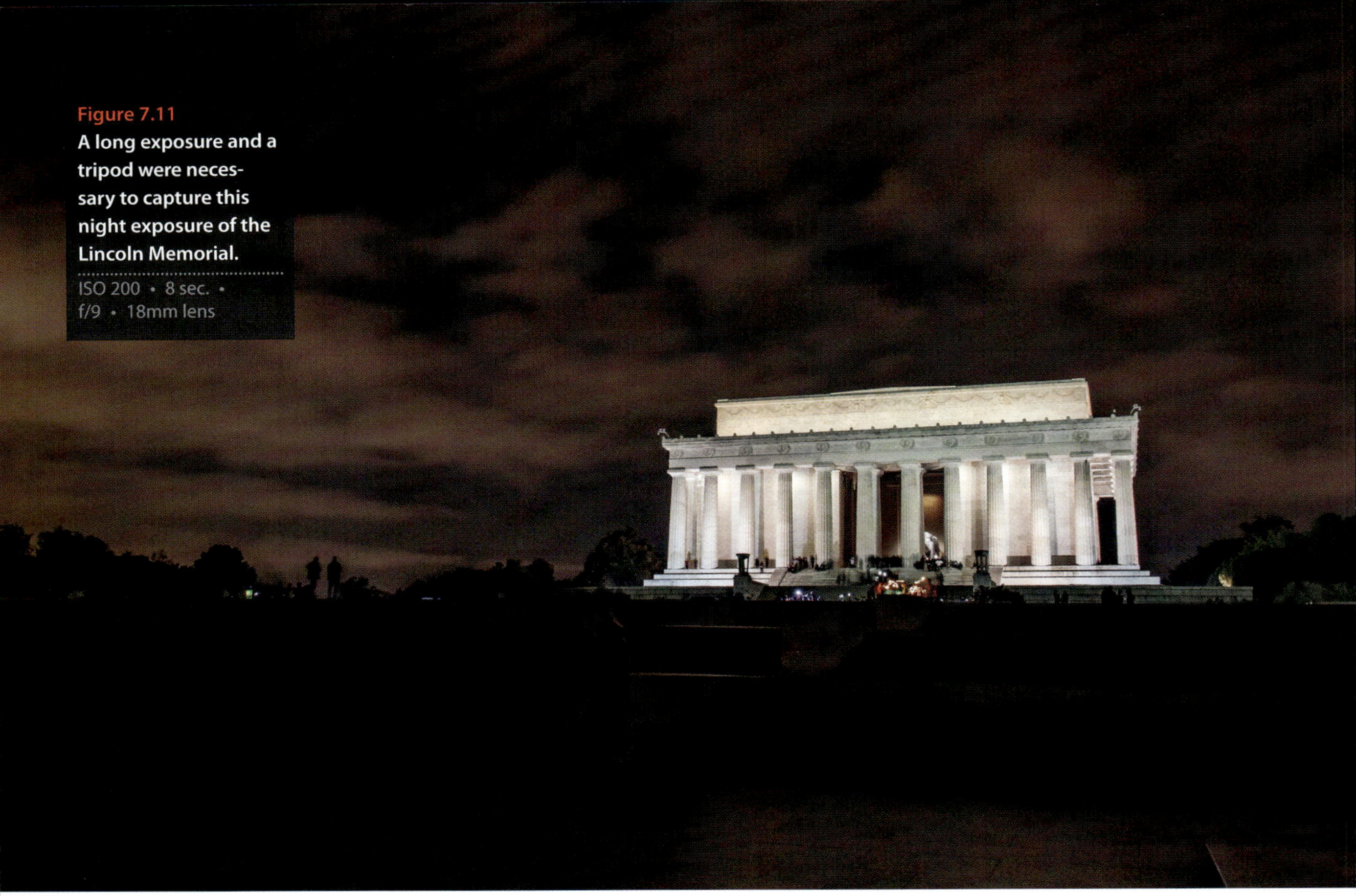

Figure 7.11
A long exposure and a tripod were necessary to capture this night exposure of the Lincoln Memorial.
ISO 200 • 8 sec. • f/9 • 18mm lens

Flash sync

The basic idea behind the term flash synchronization (flash sync for short) is that when you take a photograph using the flash, the camera needs to ensure that the shutter is fully open at the time the flash goes off. This is not an issue if you are using a long shutter speed, such as 1/15 of a second, but does become more critical for fast shutter speeds. To ensure that the flash and shutter are synchronized so that the flash is going off while the shutter is open, the 7D Mark II implements a top sync speed of 1/200 of a second. This means that when you are using the flash, you will not be able to have your shutter speed set any faster than 1/200. If you did use a faster shutter speed, the shutter would start closing before the flash fired, which would cause a black, underexposed area to appear in the frame where the light from the flash was blocked.

Using the Built-In Flash

There are going to be times when you have to turn to your camera's built-in flash to get the shot. The pop-up flash on the 7D Mark II is not extremely powerful, but with the camera's advanced metering system it does a pretty good job of lighting up the night… or just filling in the shadows.

With the exception of the Intelligent Auto mode, you will have to turn the flash on for yourself. To do this, just press the pop-up flash button located on the front of the camera (**Figure 7.12**). Once the flash is up, it is ready to go (**Figure 7.13**). It's that simple.

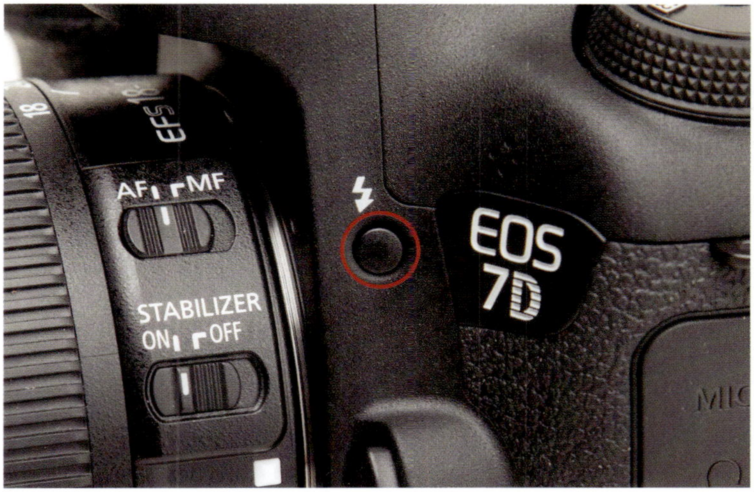

Figure 7.12
A quick press of the pop-up flash button will release the built-in flash to its ready position.

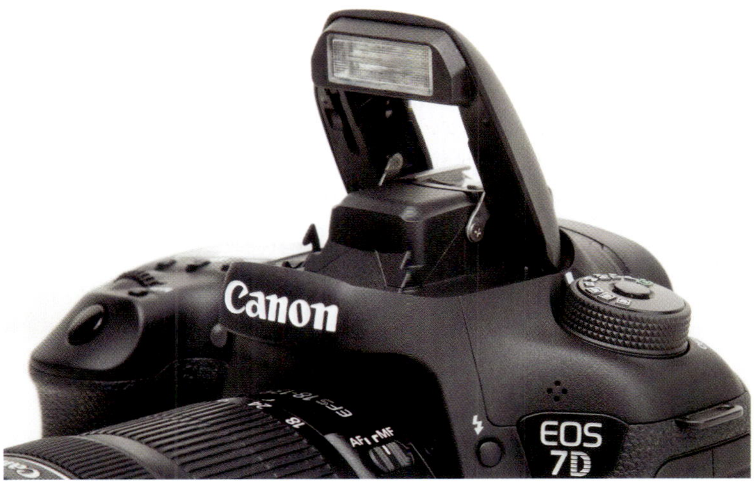

Figure 7.13
The pop-up flash in its ready position.

Shutter speeds

The standard flash synchronization speed for your camera is between 1/60 and 1/200 of a second. When you are working with the built-in flash in the Basic zone, the camera will typically use a shutter speed of 1/60 of a second. The exception to this is when you use the Night Portrait mode, which will fire the flash with a slower shutter speed so that some of the ambient light has time to record in the image.

The key to using the flash to get great pictures is to control the shutter speed. The goal is to balance the light from the flash with the existing light so that everything in the picture has an even illumination. Let's take a look at the shutter speeds for the modes in the Creative zone:

- **Program (P):** The shutter speed stays at 1/60 of a second. You can make changes to the aperture by rotating the Quick Control dial, but you risk over- or underexposing your image.
- **Shutter Priority (Tv):** You can adjust the shutter speed to as fast as 1/250 of a second all the way down to 30 seconds. The lens aperture will adjust accordingly, but typically at long exposures the lens will be set to its largest aperture.
- **Manual (M):** Manual mode works the same as Tv mode, with a range of 1/250 down to 30 seconds. The difference, of course, is that you must manually set the f-stop.
- **Aperture Priority (Av):** This mode has three custom settings for adjusting the shutter speed when using the flash, depending on your needs. The point of this setting is to allow you to use the aperture of your choice while still getting good flash exposures.

The default value is Auto, which adjusts from 1/200 all the way down to 30 seconds, depending on the available light. As the aperture gets smaller, the shutter speeds will get longer. There are also two speed-limiting settings to choose from. The first is 1/250–1/60 Sec. Auto. This limits the shutter speed to a maximum duration of 1/60 of a second.
If you have the aperture open to an f-stop that has a very small opening for a proper exposure, the shutter speed indicator will flash, letting you know that you are risking underexposure. For all other exposures, the camera will moderate the shutter speed to a selection that is within the 1/60–1/250 range. The other setting is 1/250 Sec. (Fixed). This setting maintains a shutter speed of 1/250 of a second no matter what the f-stop is set to. Your flash will try to vary its power output to meet the needs of the setting that you have selected.

Setting the sync speed when using flash in Av mode

1. Press the Menu button and go to the first shooting menu. Highlight Flash Control, and then press the Set button (**A**).
2. Select Flash Sync. Speed In Av Mode using the Cross keys, and press the Set button (**B**).

A

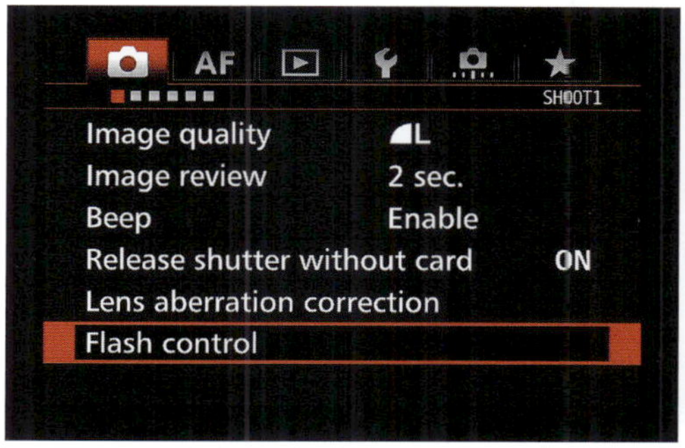

B

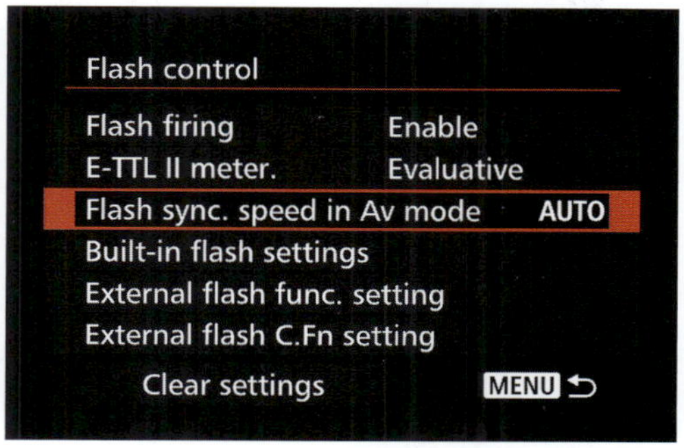

3. Select the Av sync speed that you desire using the Cross keys, and press Set once more (**C**).

C

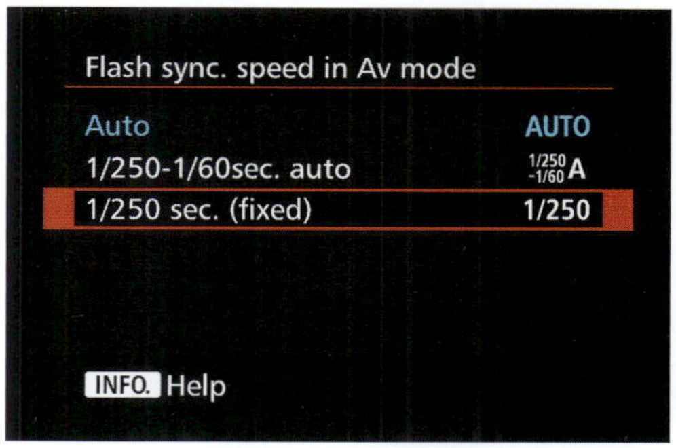

Metering modes

The built-in flash uses a technology called E-TTL II (Evaluative Through The Lens) metering to determine the appropriate amount of flash power to output for a good exposure. When you depress the shutter button, the camera quickly adjusts focus while gathering information from the entire scene to measure the amount of ambient light. As you press the shutter button down completely, a pre-flash occurs to meter the light off the subject from the flash, and a determination is made as to how much power is needed to balance the subject with the ambient light. This applies to all the modes with the exception of Manual mode.

The default setting for the flash meter mode is Evaluative. You can set the meter to Average mode, but you should probably avoid doing so. Your best results will come from the E-TTL mode.

But if you have special metering needs, such as a background that is very light or dark, you might consider using the Flash Exposure (FE) Lock to meter off your subject, and then recompose your image in the viewfinder.

This feature works much like the Automatic Exposure (AE) Lock function that we discussed in Chapter 6, "Say Cheese!"

Flash range

Because the pop-up flash is fairly small, it does not have enough power to illuminate a large space (**Figure 7.14**). The effective distance varies depending on the ISO setting. At ISO 100, the range is about 10 feet. This range can be extended to as far as 230 feet when the camera is set to an ISO of 51200. For the best image quality, your ISO setting should stay fairly low. Higher ISO settings could result in introducing excessive noise into your photos. Check out page 255 in your manual for a table of flash distances.

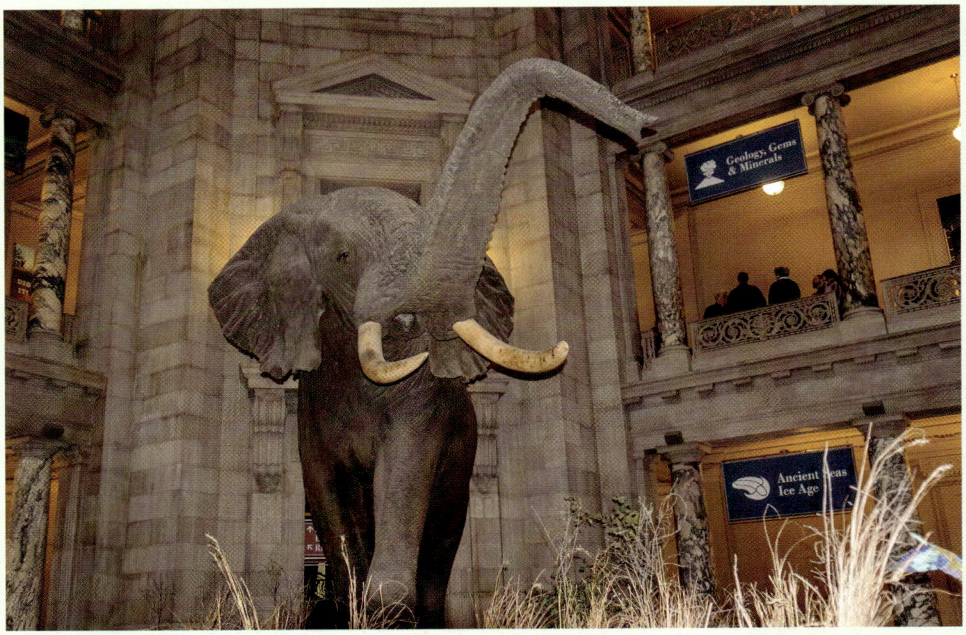

Figure 7.14

The pop-up flash was used to fill in shadows on the elephant, while the high ISO and long exposure time allowed the ambient light to illuminate the rest of the scene.

ISO 800 • 1/30 sec. • f/2.8 • 20mm lens

Using the FE Lock feature

1. Point the camera at the area that you want to base the flash exposure on. This is normally your subject.
2. Raise the flash into the ready position, and then press the M/Fn button to fire a pre-flash that will measure the flash exposure.
3. Recompose the scene as you like, and press the shutter button completely.

The FE Lock will cancel after each exposure, so you have to repeat these steps each time you need to lock the flash exposure.

Using the Average metering mode might also require that you tweak the flash output by using Flash Exposure Compensation. This is because the camera will be metering the entire scene to set the exposure, so you might have to add or subtract flash power to balance out the scene.

Compensating for the Flash Exposure

The E-TTL system will usually do an excellent job of balancing the flash and ambient light for your exposure, but it does have the limitation of not knowing what effect you want in your image. You may want more or less flash in a particular shot. You can achieve this by using the Flash Exposure Compensation feature.

Just as with exposure compensation, flash compensation allows you to dial in a change in the flash output in increments of 1/3 of a stop. You will probably use this most often to tone down the effects of your flash, especially when you are using the flash as a subtle fill light (**Figure 7.15** and **Figure 7.16**).

Using the Flash Exposure Compensation feature to change the flash output

1. Press the Flash Compensation/ISO button to activate the compensation control on the LCD screen.
2. Use the Quick Control dial to adjust the flash compensation in 1/3-stop increments (left to subtract and right to add).
3. Press the shutter button halfway to return to shooting mode, and then take a picture.
4. Review your image to see if more or less flash compensation is required, and repeat these steps as necessary.

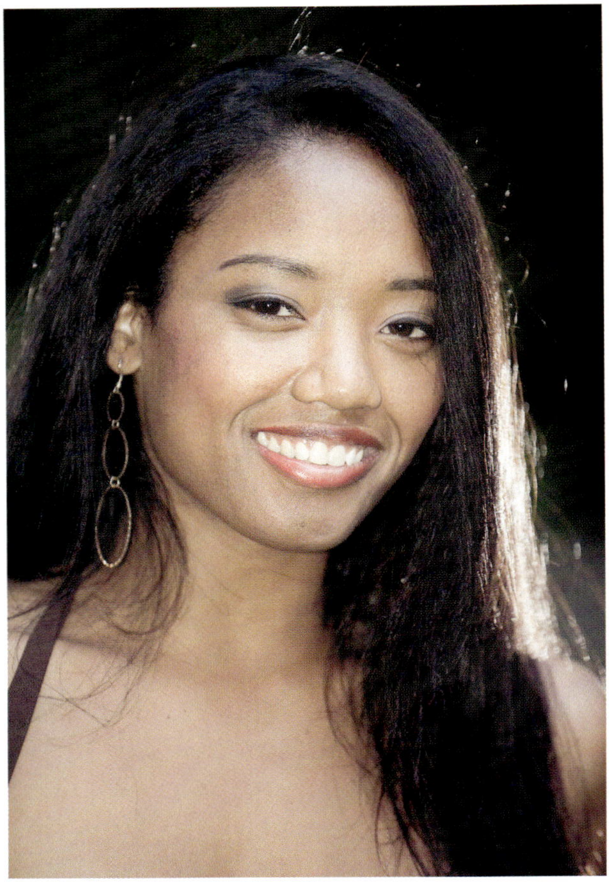

Figure 7.15

I took this shot with the pop-up flash set to normal power. As you can see, it was trying too hard to illuminate my subject.

ISO 400 • 1/60 sec. • f/4 • 200mm lens

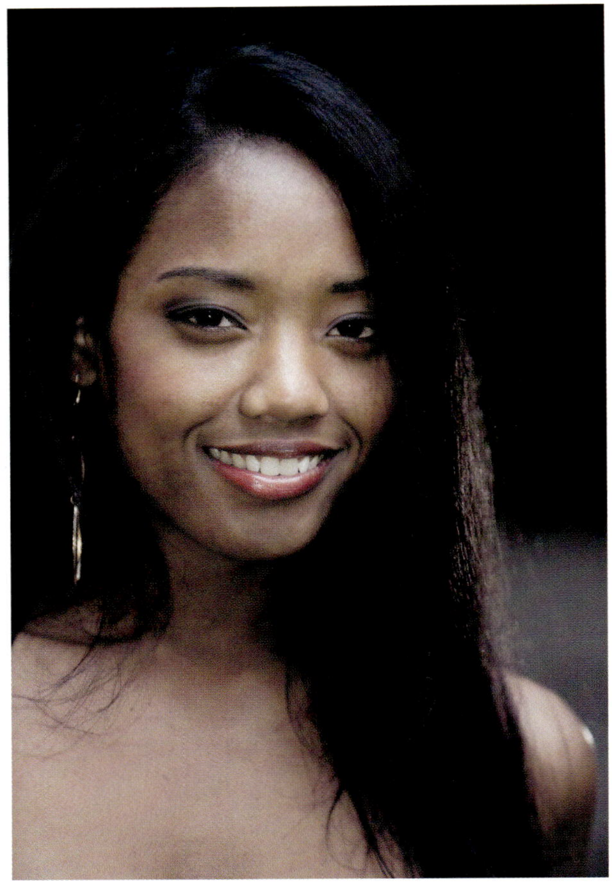

Figure 7.16

This image was made with the same camera settings. The difference is that the flash compensation was set to –1.3 stops.

ISO 400 • 1/60 sec. • f/4 • 200mm lens

The Flash Exposure Compensation feature does not reset itself when the camera is turned off, so whatever compensation you have set will remain in effect until you change it. Your only clue to knowing that the flash output is changed will be the presence of the Flash Exposure Compensation symbol on the rear LCD, so make sure you check it. It will disappear when there is zero compensation set.

Reducing Red-Eye

We've all seen the result of using on-camera flashes when shooting people: the dreaded red-eye! This demonic effect is the result of the light from the flash entering the pupil and then reflecting back as an eerie red glow. The closer the flash is to the lens, the greater the chance that you will get red-eye. This is especially true when it is dark and the subject's pupils are dilated. There are two ways to combat this problem. The first is to get the flash away from the lens. That's not an option if you are using the pop-up flash. Therefore, you will need to turn to the Red-Eye Reduction feature.

This is a simple feature that shines a light from the camera at your subjects, causing their pupils to shrink, thus eliminating or reducing the effects of red-eye (**Figure 7.17**).

The feature is set to Off by default, and you need to turn it on in the shooting menu.

Turn on the lights!

When you are shooting indoors, another way to reduce red-eye, or just shorten the length of time that the reduction lamp needs to be shining into your subject's eyes, is to turn on a lot of lights. The brighter the ambient light levels, the smaller the subject's pupils will be. This will reduce the time necessary for the red-eye reduction lamp to shine. It will also allow you to take more candid pictures because your subjects won't be required to stare at the red-eye lamp while waiting for their pupils to reduce.

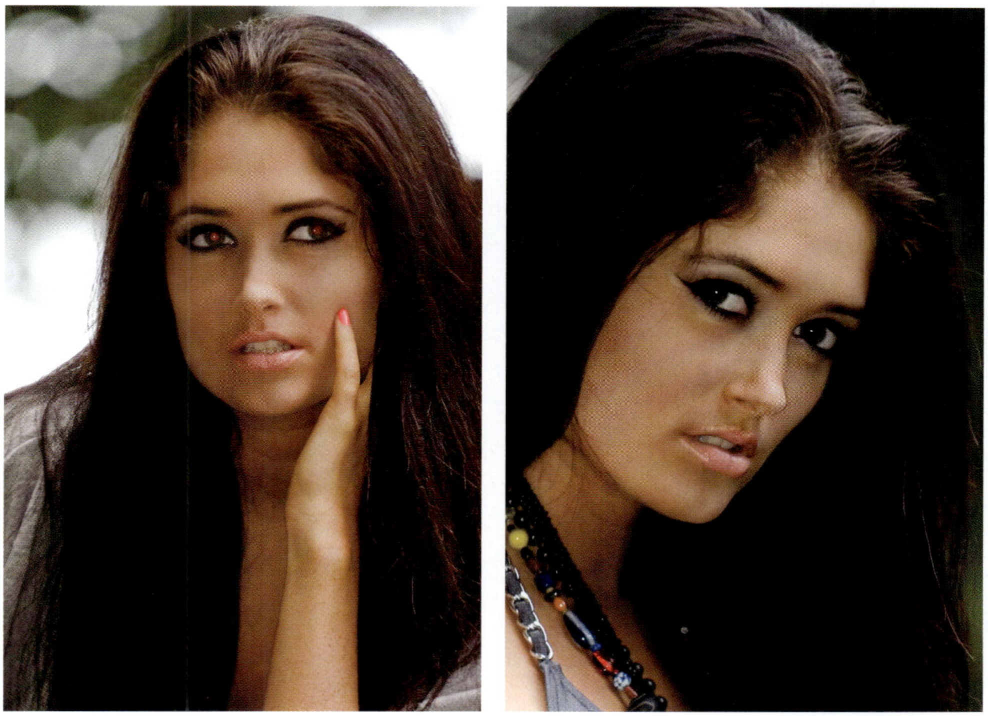

Figure 7.17
The picture on the left did not use Red-Eye Reduction, thus the glowing red eyes. Notice that the pupils on the image on the right, without red-eye, are smaller as a result of using the Red-Eye Reduction lamp.

ISO 800 • 1/60 sec. • f/5.6 • 200mm lens

Turning on the Red-Eye Reduction feature

1. Press the Menu button, and then turn the Main dial to get to the fourth shooting menu.
2. Use the Quick Control dial to highlight the Red-Eye Reduc. setting (**A**).
3. Press the Set button, and then select Enable and press the Set button (**B**).

A

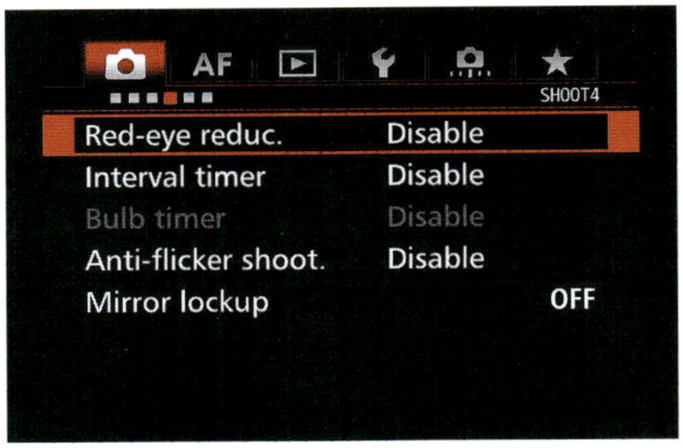

B

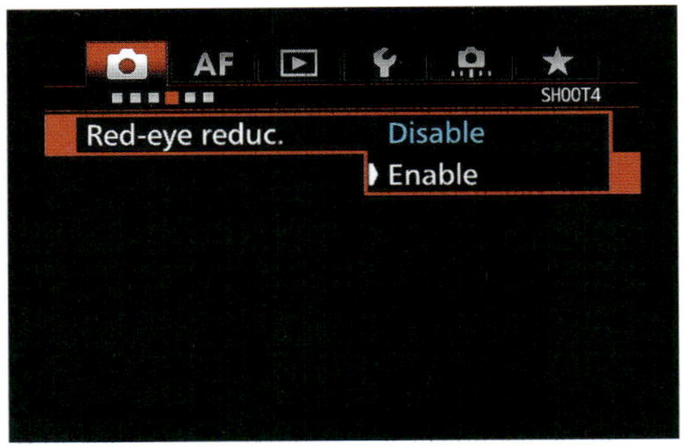

4. Press the Menu button twice or the shutter release button to return to shooting mode.

To get the full benefit from the Red-Eye Reduction feature, you should hold down the shutter button halfway, which causes the reduction light to shine into your subject's eyes. A small scale will appear in the viewfinder that shows how long to hold the shutter button before pressing completely. Once the countdown scale has reduced down to nothing, press the shutter button completely to take the picture.

Truth be told, I rarely shoot with red-eye reduction turned on because of the time it takes before being able to take a picture. If I am after candid shots and have to use the flash, I will take my chances on red-eye and try to fix the problem in my image-processing software. The Canon Image Browser software that comes with your 7D Mark II has a red-eye reduction feature that works really well.

Using an External Speedlite

One of the more exciting features of the 7D Mark II is its ability to control an off-camera flash by using the pop-up flash as the wireless controller. In years past, you needed to mount a controller flash unit on top of the camera (such as the ST-E2 transmitter), which meant spending additional money. Now you can simply purchase one of the wireless-enabled Speedlites like the 320EX and have complete control to move it away from the camera.

The biggest benefit to doing this is that you can get more natural-looking light by having the flash moved to the side of the camera. This gives you better and more natural shadows. You can also do things like fire the external flash through umbrellas, softboxes, or simple diffusion panels to make the quality of light much softer and complimentary to your subject (**Figure 7.18**).

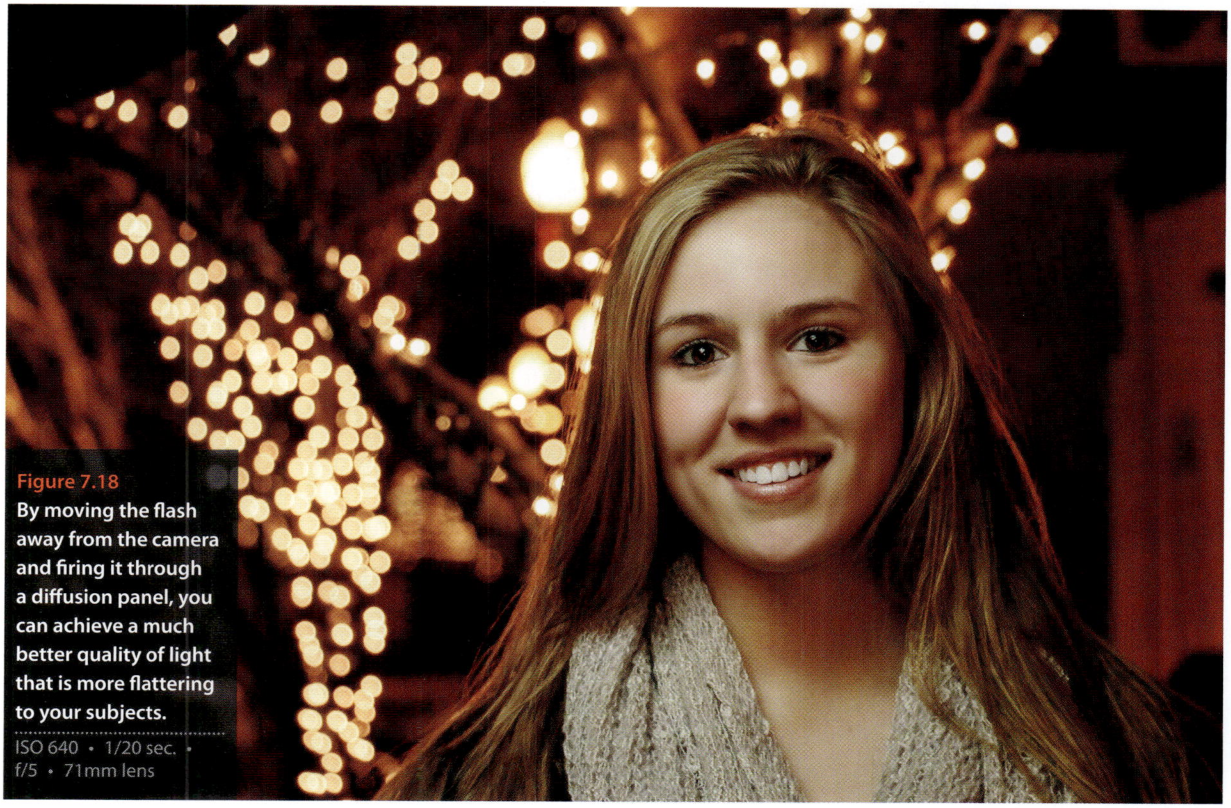

Figure 7.18
By moving the flash away from the camera and firing it through a diffusion panel, you can achieve a much better quality of light that is more flattering to your subjects.

ISO 640 • 1/20 sec. • f/5 • 71mm lens

Using off-camera flash

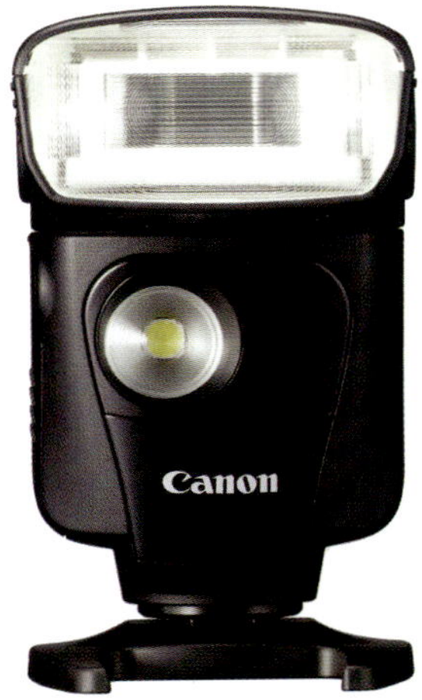

Figure 7.19
The 320EX is a great Speedlite for starting out with an off-camera flash.

To use an off-camera Speedlite, you need to do two things. First, purchase the Speedlite. There are several models that allow you to use the wireless feature, and they range in price from around $200 for the 320EX all the way up to the top-of-the-line model, the 600EX-RT with its nearly $500 price tag. Personally, I am a fan of the 320EX (**Figure 7.19**) because it allows me to use it off-camera but has the added benefit of having a built-in LED light that can be used as both a focus-assist lamp and a video-recording light. It also has a pivoting head that allows the light to be bounced off the ceiling to create softer, more flattering light.

Setting up off-camera flash

1. Press the Menu button, and then select the Flash Control option in the first shooting menu (**A**).
2. Use the Quick Control dial to select the Built-in Flash Settings option, and press Set (**B**).

A

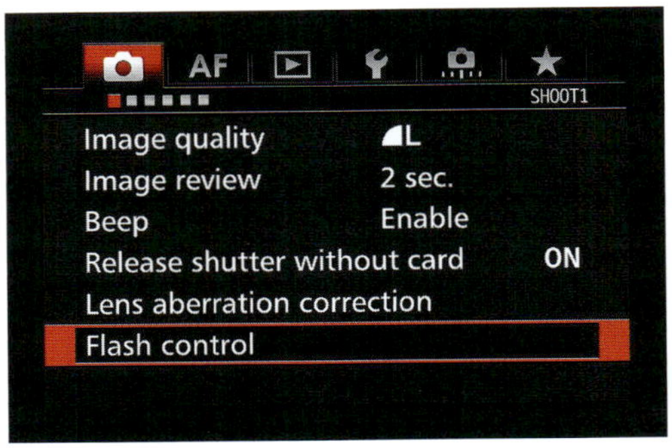

B

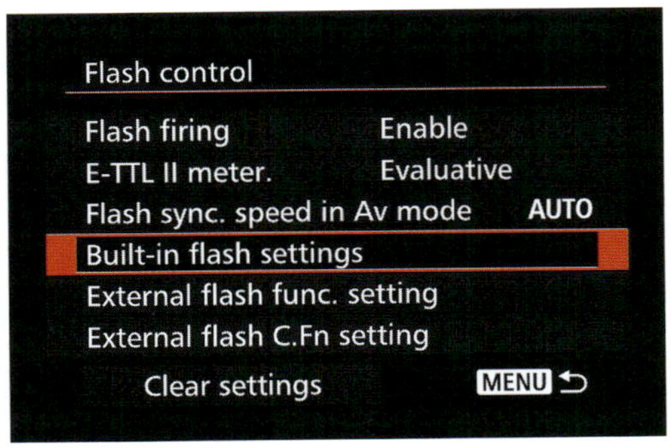

3. Choose the Wireless Func. option, and press Set (**C**).
4. Select the Single External Flash option, and press the Set button (**D**).

C

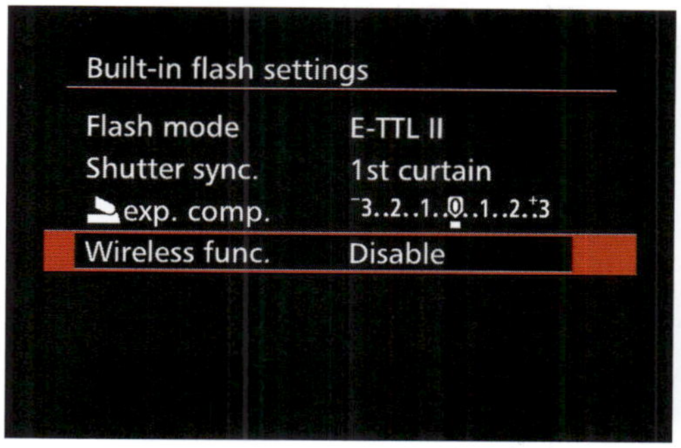

D

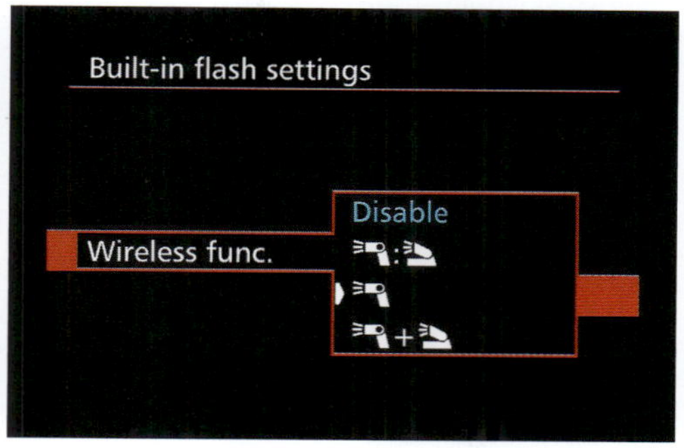

5. The default channel for the wireless flash is Channel 1. If you want to use a different channel, go to the Channel option, press Set, and change to the channel of your choice (**E**).
6. Turn on your external flash and set it up to be a remote flash with the same channel number that you just selected.
7. Open the pop-up flash, and then press the flash button again to open the flash options window on the rear LCD.
8. Press the INFO button to test the wireless flash.

E

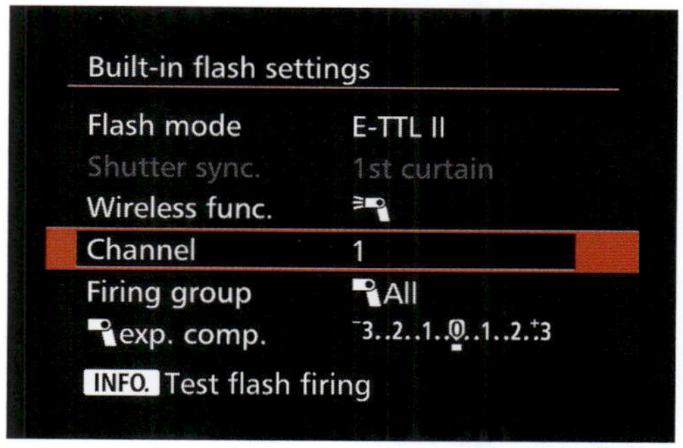

The external flash should be set to use the E-TTL option so that it is working with the camera's metering system to provide a balanced exposure. Just like the built-in flash, you can use flash compensation for the external off-camera flash to raise or lower the flash exposure as needed.

This is just a basic setup for using a wireless external flash, and there are a lot of different exposure options available to help you get even more creative with your flash photography. I use the method described here for the majority of my off-camera flash work with great results.

Manual Callout

Wireless flash photography is a lot of fun and lets you expand on the creative possibilities of your photography. You may find that you wish to add additional wireless flashes to your system, which is easily handled with the wireless technology built into your camera. If you want further direction and creative options, check out the Wireless Flash section of your manual (pages 262–283).

Flash and Glass

If you find yourself in a situation where you want to use your flash to shoot through a window or display case, try placing your lens right against the glass so that the reflection of the flash won't be visible in your image (**Figure 7.20** and **Figure 7.21**). This is extremely useful in museums and aquariums.

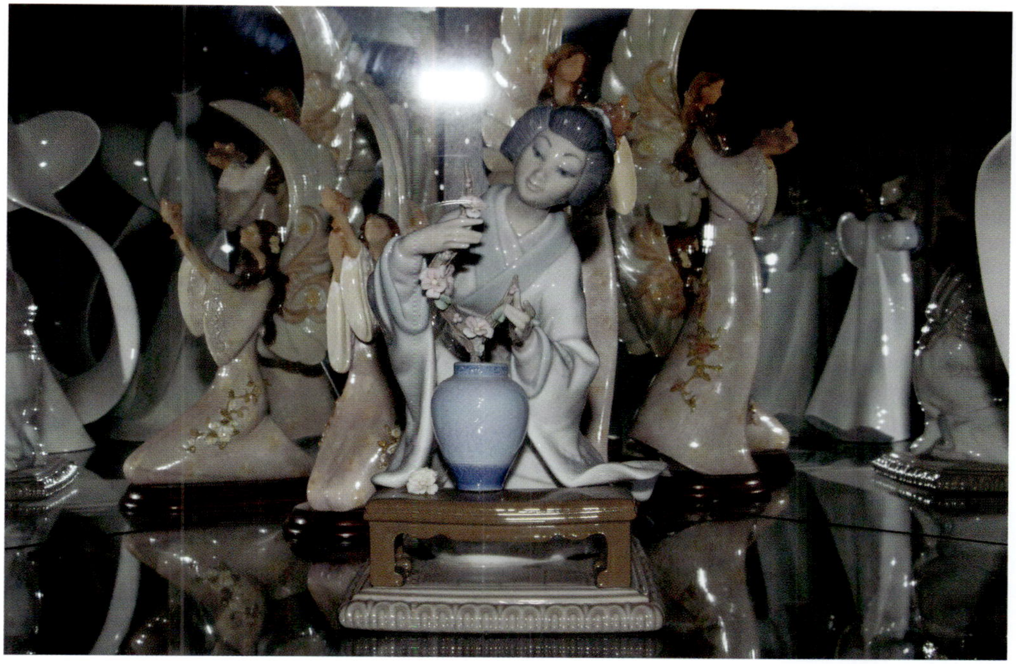

Figure 7.20
The bright spot at the top of the frame is a result of the flash reflecting off the display case.

ISO 640 • 1/250 sec. • f/16 • 35mm lens

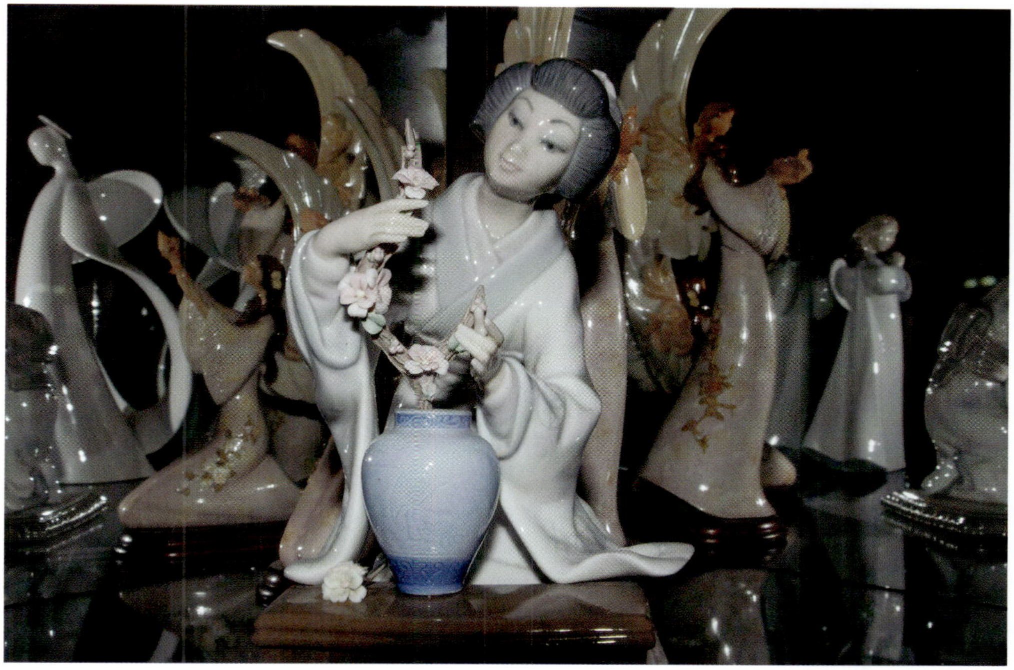

Figure 7.21
To eliminate the reflection, place the lens against the glass or as close to it as possible. This might also require zooming the lens out a little.

ISO 640 • 1/250 sec. • f/16 • 24mm lens

Chapter 7 Assignments

Now that we have looked at the possibilities of shooting after dark, it's time to put it all to the test. These assignments cover the full range of shooting possibilities, both with flash and without. Let's get started.

How steady are your hands?

It's important to know your limits in terms of handholding your camera and still getting sharp pictures. This will change depending on the focal length of the lens you are working with. Wider-angle lenses are more forgiving than telephoto lenses, so check this out for your longest and shortest lenses. Using an 18–200mm zoom as an example, set your lens to 200mm, and then, with the camera set to ISO 100 and the mode set to Tv, start taking pictures with lower and lower shutter speeds. Review each image on the LCD at a zoomed-in magnification to take note of when you start seeing visible camera shake in your images. It will probably be around 1/125 of a second for a 200mm lens.

Now do the same for the wide-angle setting on the lens. My limit is about 1/30 of a second. These shutter speeds are with the Image Stabilization feature turned off. If you have an IS lens, try it with and without the IS feature enabled to see just how slow you can set your shutter while getting sharp results.

Pushing your ISO to the extreme

Turn on the Expanded ISO feature. Now find a place to shoot where the ambient light level is low. This could be at night or indoors in a darkened room. Using the mode of your choice, start increasing the ISO from 100 until you get to 51200. Make sure you evaluate the level of noise in your image, especially in the shadow areas. Only you can decide how much noise is acceptable in your pictures. I can tell you from personal experience that I never like to stray above that ISO 800 mark.

Getting rid of the noise

Turn on the High ISO Speed Noise Reduction and repeat the previous assignment. Find your acceptable limits with the noise reduction turned on. Also pay attention to how much detail is lost in your shadows with this function enabled.

Long exposures in the dark

If you don't have a tripod, find a stable place to set your camera outside and try some long exposures. Set your camera to Av mode, and then use the self-timer to activate the camera (this will keep you from shaking the camera while pressing the shutter button).

Shoot in an area that has some level of ambient light, be it a streetlight or traffic lights, or even a full moon. The idea is to get some late-night, low-light exposures.

Reducing the noise in your long exposures

Repeat the last assignment with Long Exposure Noise Reduction set to On. Now look at the difference in the images that were taken before and after the noise reduction was enabled. For best results, perform this assignment and the previous assignment in the same shooting session using the same subject.

Testing the limits of the pop-up flash

Wait for the lights to get low, and then press that pop-up flash button to start using the built-in flash. Try using the different shooting modes to see how they affect your exposures. Use the Flash Exposure Compensation feature to take a series of pictures while adjusting from –2 stops all the way to +2 stops so that you become familiar with how much latitude you will get from this feature.

Getting the red out

Find a friend with some patience and a tolerance for bright lights. Have them sit in a darkened room or outside at night, and then take their picture with the flash. Now turn on the Red-Eye Reduction to see if you get better results. Don't forget to wait for the red-eye timer to completely extinguish before taking the picture.

Share your results with the book's Flickr group!
Join the group here: flickr.com/groups/7dmarkii_fromsnapshotstogreatshots

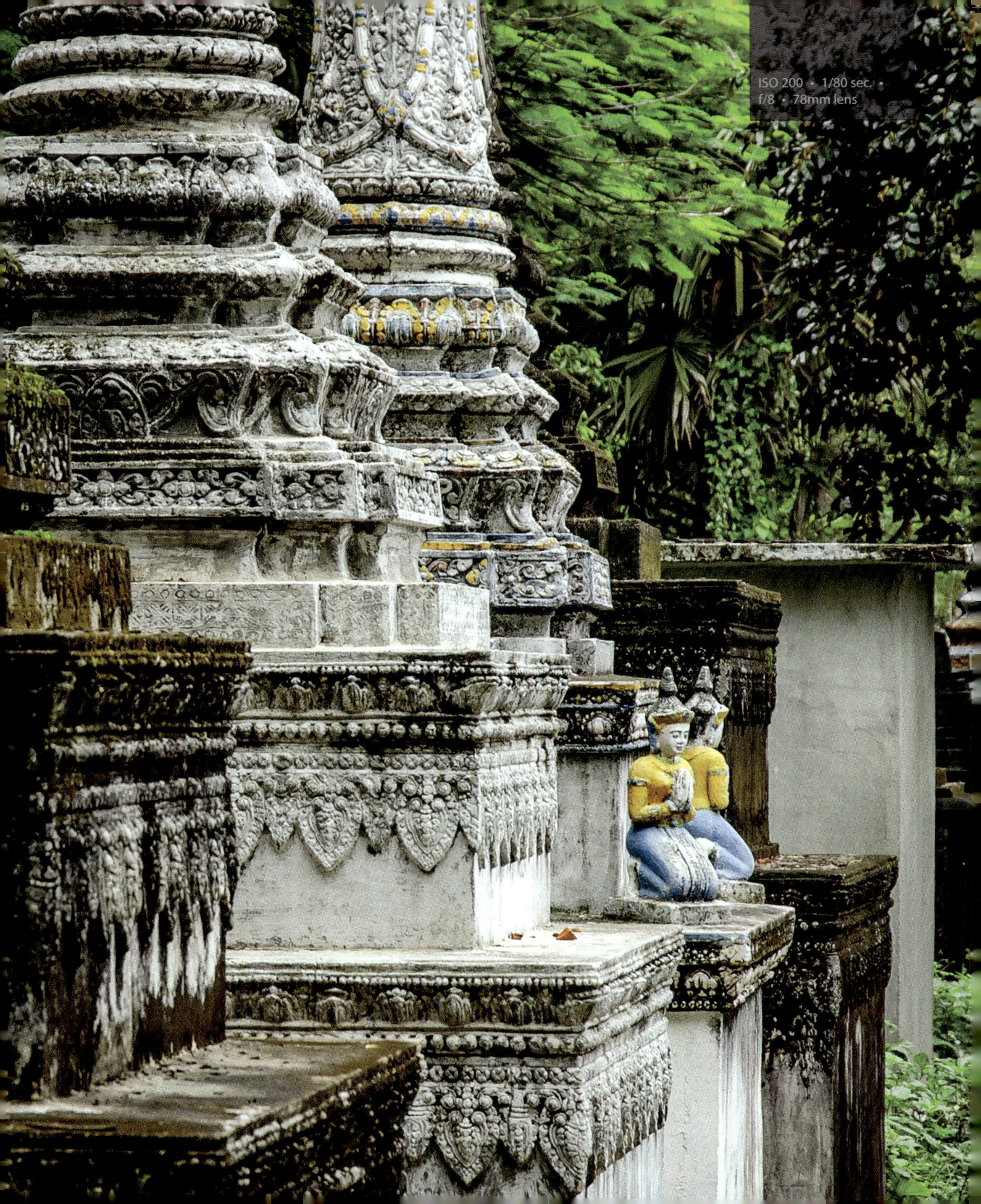
ISO 200 • 1/80 sec. • f/8 • 78mm lens

8

Creative Compositions

Improve Your Pictures with Sound Compositional Elements

Creating a great photograph takes more than just the right settings on your camera. To take your photography to the next level, you need to gain an understanding of how the elements within the frame come together to create a compositionally pleasing image. Composition is the culmination of light, shape, and, to borrow a word from the iconic photographer Jay Maisel, gesture. Composition is a way for you to pull your viewing audience into your image and guide them through the scene. Let's examine a few methods you can use to add interest to your photos by utilizing some common compositional elements.

Poring Over the Picture

You can have all of the right camera settings for a photograph, but if you don't pay attention to your composition you will never achieve anything more than an average-looking photo. It would have been easy for me to just put the mosque in the center of the frame, but it would have made for a very boring image of a beautiful building. Instead, I took the time to explore the area to find the right angle and lens choice to bring all the elements together in a way that leads the viewer into the image.

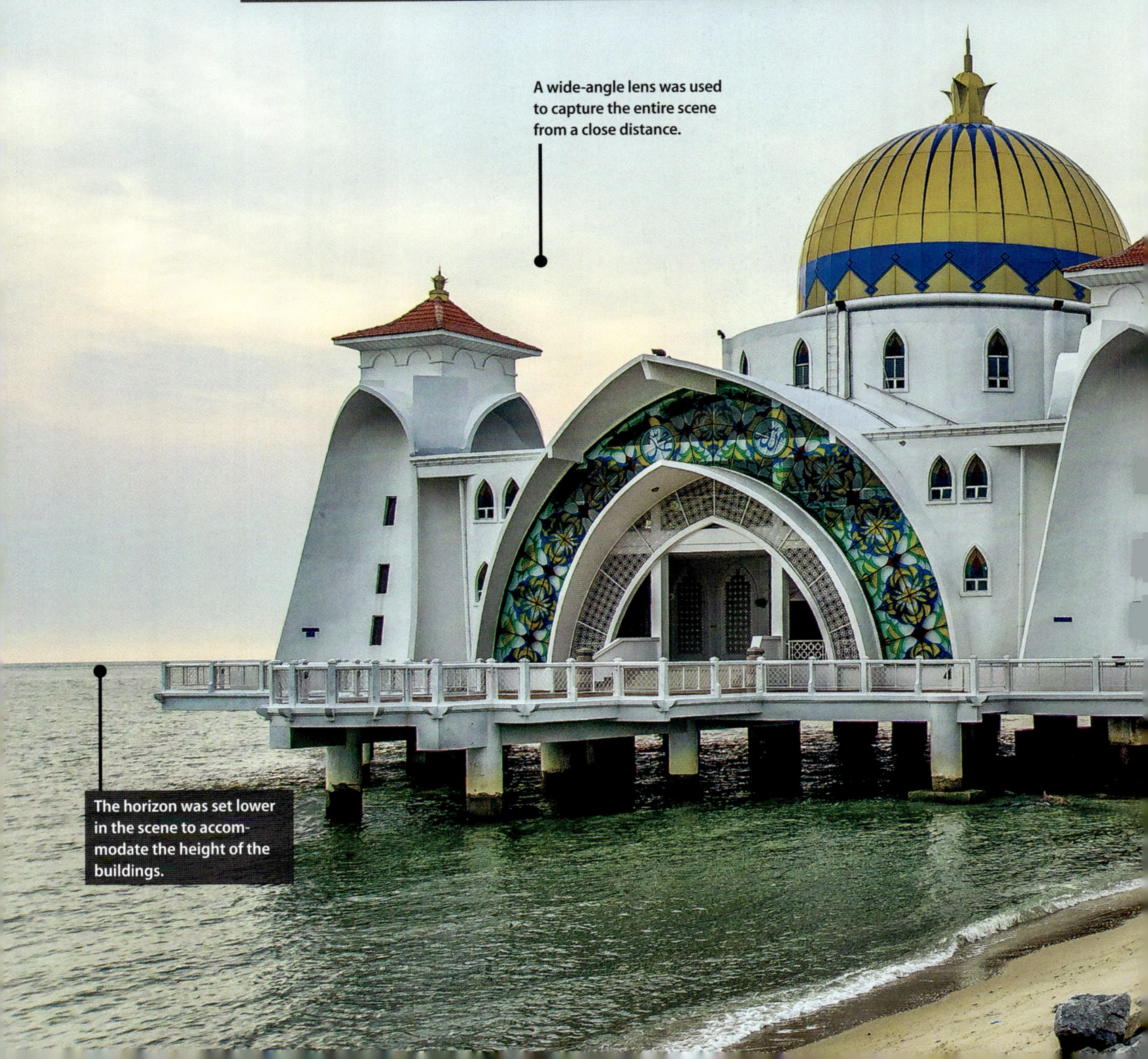

ISO 800 • 1/2000 sec. • f/5.6 • 24mm lens

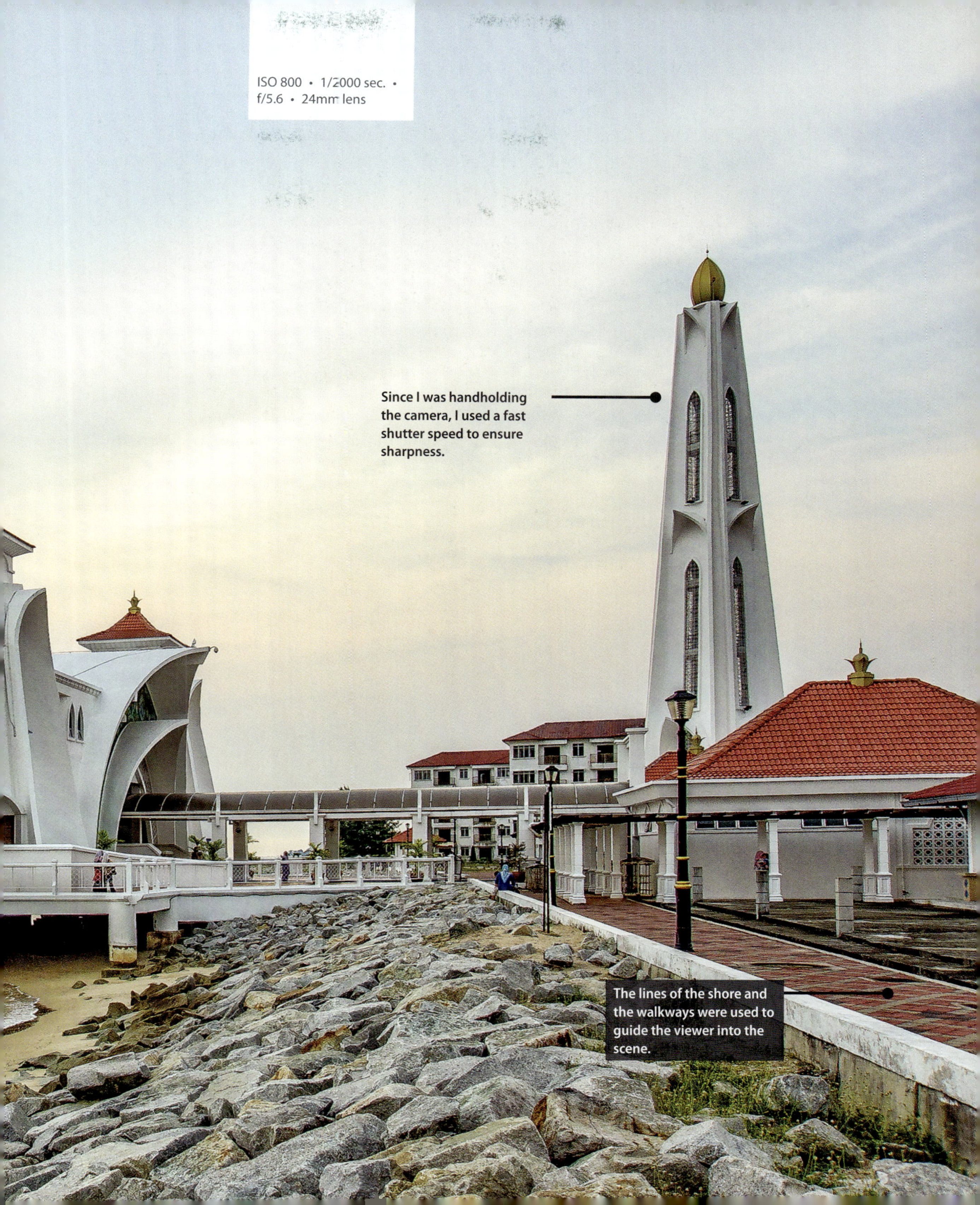

Since I was handholding the camera, I used a fast shutter speed to ensure sharpness.

The lines of the shore and the walkways were used to guide the viewer into the scene.

Depth of Field

Long focal lengths and large apertures allow you to isolate your subject from the chaos that surrounds it. I utilize the Av mode for the majority of my shooting. I also like to use a longer focal length lens to shrink the depth of field to a very narrow area (**Figure 8.1**).

The blurred background and foreground force the viewer's eye toward the sharper, in-focus areas, which gives greater emphasis to the subject.

Occasionally, a greater depth of field is required to maintain a sharp focus across a greater distance. This might be due to the sheer depth of your subject, where you have objects that are near the camera but sharpness is desired at a greater distance as well (**Figure 8.2**).

Or perhaps you are photographing a reflection in a puddle. With a narrow depth of field, you could only get the reflected object or the puddle in focus. By making the aperture smaller, you will be able to maintain acceptable sharpness in both areas (**Figure 8.3**).

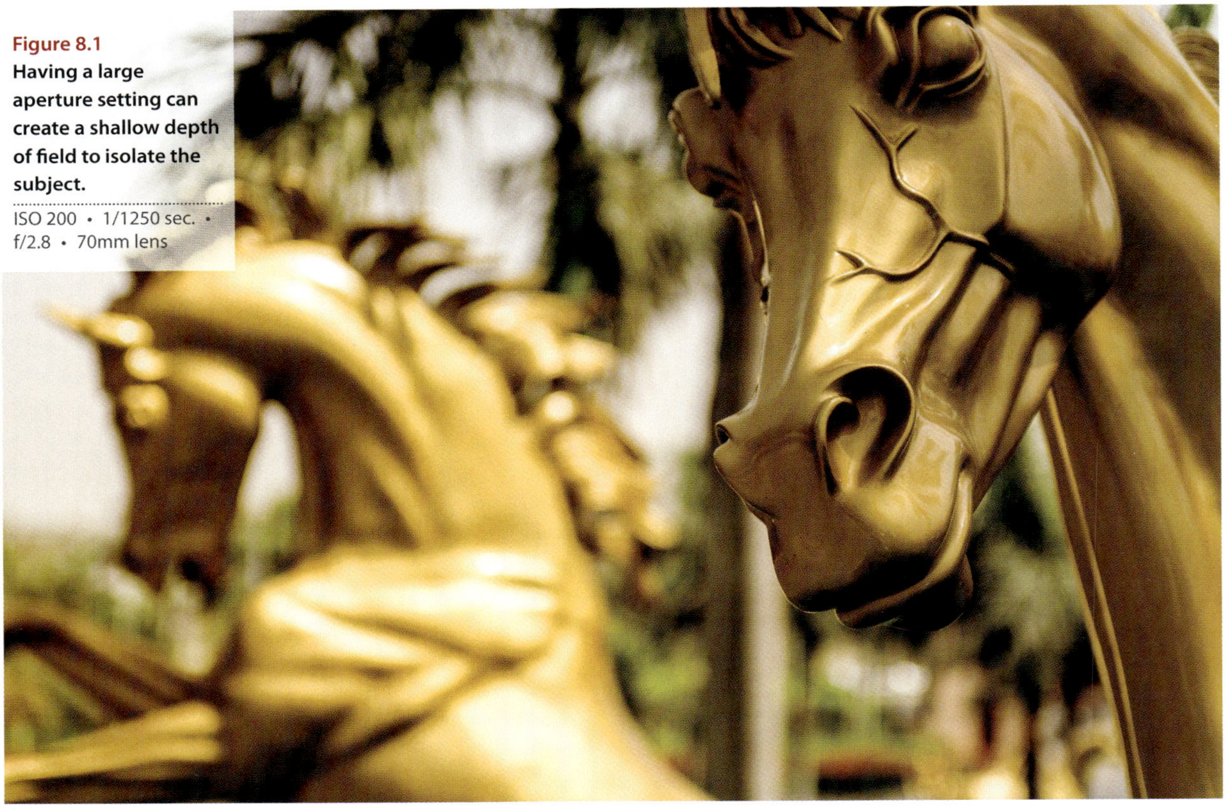

Figure 8.1
Having a large aperture setting can create a shallow depth of field to isolate the subject.

ISO 200 • 1/1250 sec. • f/2.8 • 70mm lens

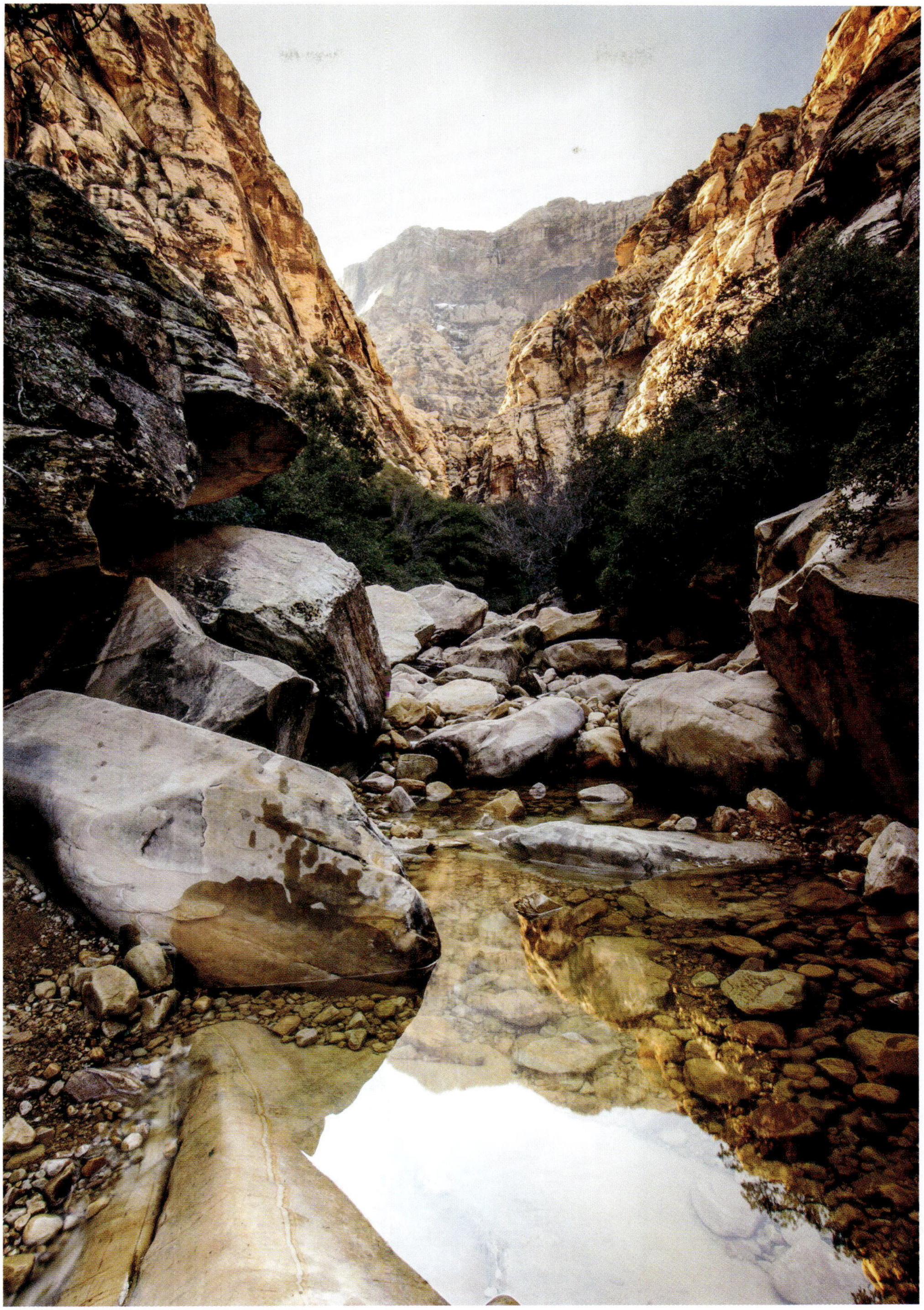

Figure 8.2
Getting sharp focus from near to far requires a small aperture setting. A wide-angle lens doesn't hurt either.

ISO 100 • 1.5 sec. • f/22 • 14mm lens

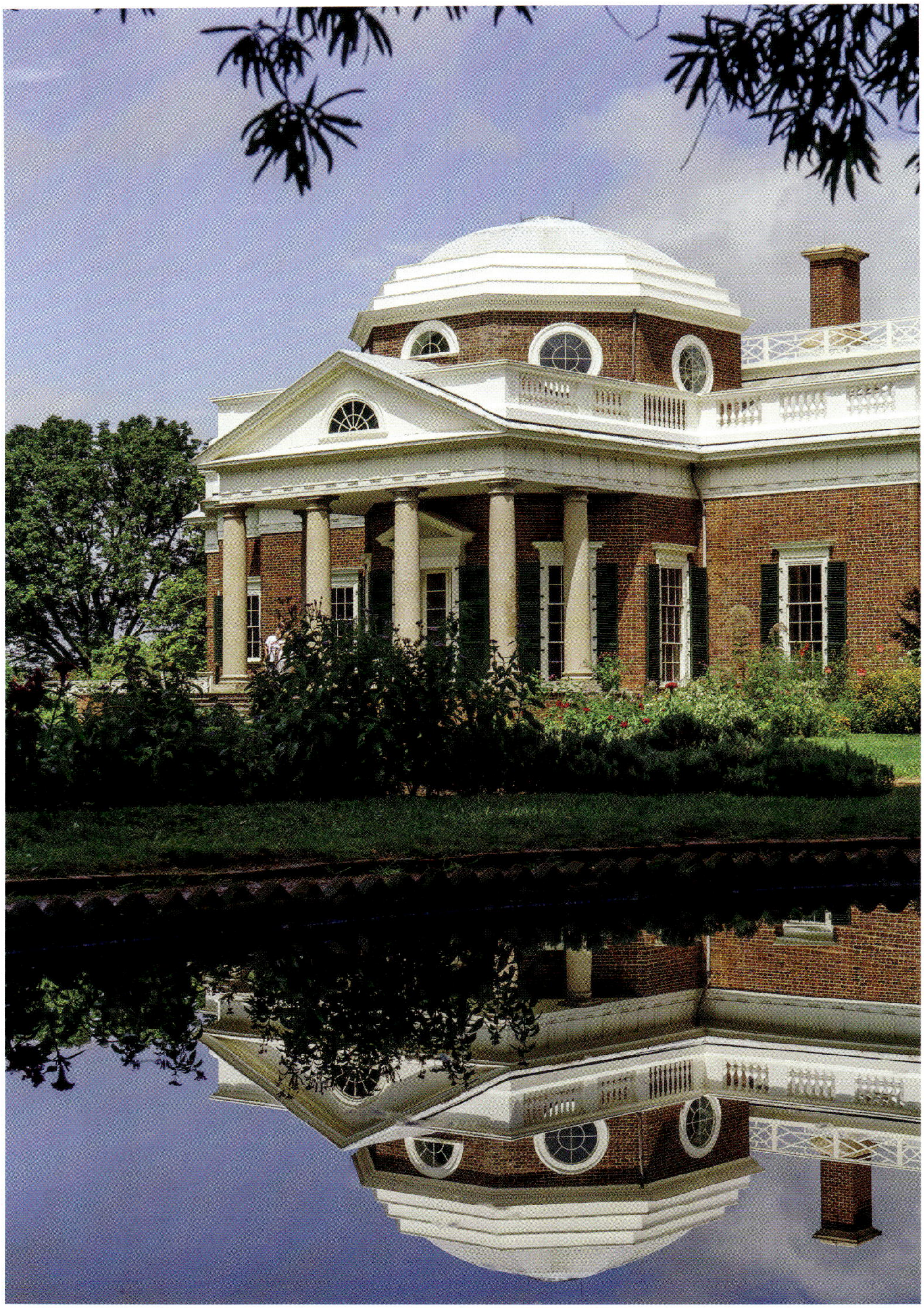

Figure 8.3
Getting a distant subject in focus in a reflection, along with the reflective surface, requires a small aperture.

ISO 400 • 1/125 sec. • f/11 • 55mm lens

Photographing reflections

A mirror is a two-dimensional surface, so why do I have to focus at a different distance for the image in the mirror? This was one of those questions that drove me crazy when I began to learn about photography. The answer is pretty simple, and it has to do with light. When you focus your lens, you are focusing the light being reflected off a surface onto your camera sensor. So if you wanted to focus on the mirror itself, it would be at one distance, but if you wanted to focus on the subject being reflected, you would have to take into account the distance that the object is from the mirror and then to you. Remember that the light from the subject has to travel all the way to the mirror and then to your lens. This is why a smaller aperture can be required when shooting reflected subjects. Sit in your car and take a few shots of objects in the side-view mirrors to see what I mean.

Angles

Having strong angular lines in your image can add to the composition, especially when they are juxtaposed to each other (**Figure 8.4**). This can create a tension that is different from the standard horizontal and vertical lines that we are so accustomed to seeing in photos.

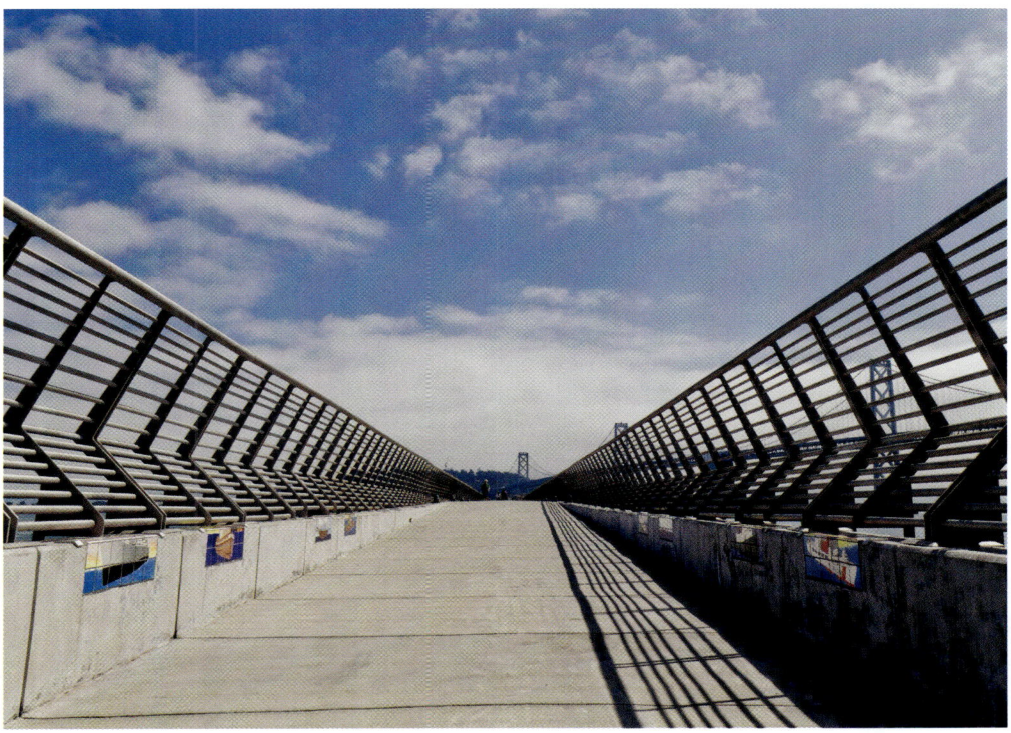

Figure 8.4
The strong angular lines of the railings and shadows create a dynamic composition.

ISO 100 • 1/250 sec. • f/11 • 18mm lens

Point of View

Sometimes the easiest way to influence your photographs is to simply change your perspective. Instead of always shooting from a standing position, try moving your camera to a place where you normally would not see your subject. Try getting down on your knees or even lying on the ground. This low angle can completely change how you view your subject and create a new interest in common subjects (**Figure 8.5**).

Patterns

Rhythm and balance can be added to your images by finding the patterns in everyday life and concentrating on the elements that rely on geometric influences. Try to find the balance and patterns that often go unnoticed (**Figure 8.6**).

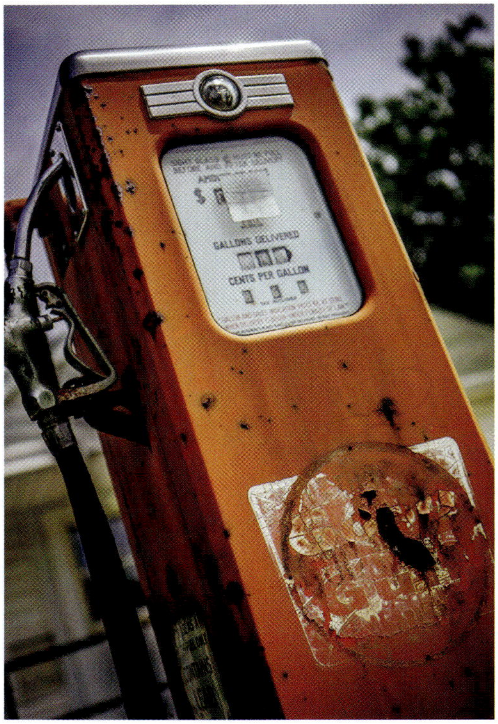

Figure 8.5

I chose to shoot this old gas pump from a low angle and gave it a tilt for visual tension.

ISO 100 • 1/800 sec. • f/2.8 • 50mm lens

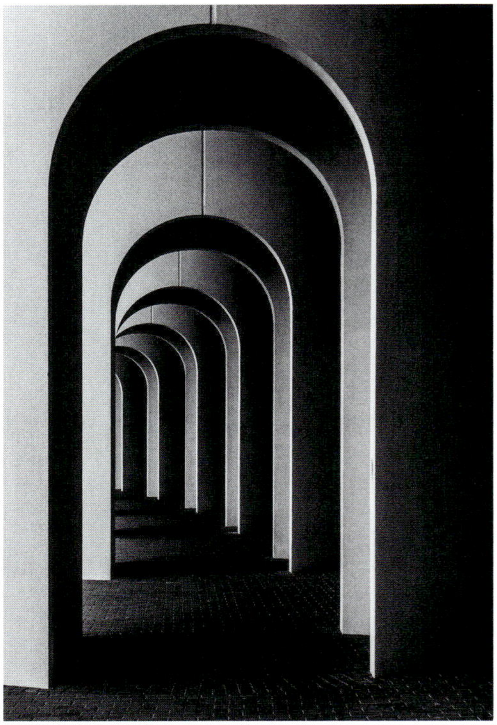

Figure 8.6

Arched pathways always make for classic compositions.

ISO 1250 • 1/1600 sec. • f/5.6 • 29mm lens

Color

Color works well as a tool for composition when you have very saturated colors to work with. Some of the best colors are those within the primary palette. Reds, greens, and blues, along with their complementary colors (cyan, magenta, and yellow), can all be used to create visual tension (**Figure 8.7**). This tension between bright colors will add visual excitement, drama, and complexity to your images when combined with other compositional elements.

You can also use a color as a theme for your photography. One of the shots that I am known for is something that I call "The Blue Sky Shot." If I am out shooting when the skies are blue, I can almost guarantee that I will try to use the sky as part of a background for some element of my image (**Figure 8.8**). The blue sky can act as a color contrast to my subject, giving a pleasing contrast, visual interest, and isolation to my subject.

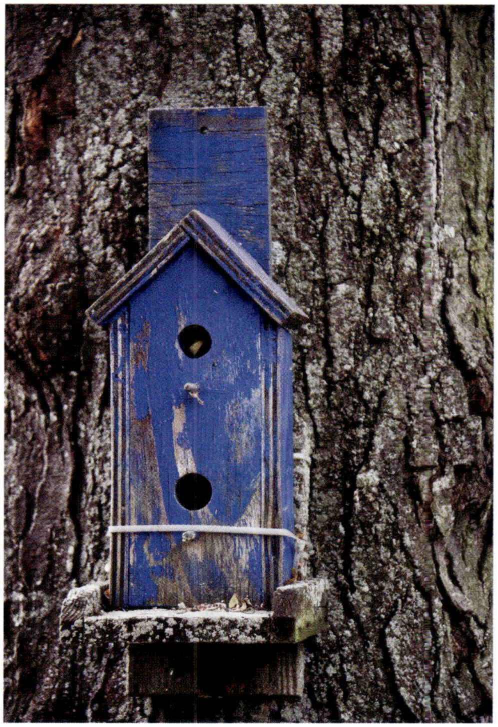

Figure 8.7

I loved how the vivid blue of the old birdhouse contrasted with the gray bark of the tree.

ISO 400 • 1/250 sec. • f/5.6 • 90mm lens

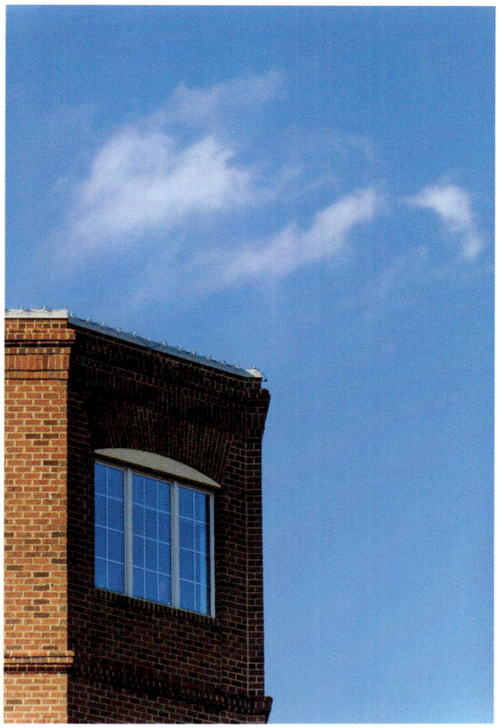

Figure 8.8

The predominance of the blue sky is used as a balance to the warm brick building below.

ISO 200 • 1/2500 sec. • f/2.8 • 200mm lens

Contrast

We just saw that you can use color as a strong compositional tool. One of the most effective uses of color is to combine two contrasting colors that make the eye move back and forth across the image (**Figure 8.9**). There is no exact combination that will work best, but consider using dark and light colors, like red and yellow, or blue and yellow, to provide the strongest contrasts.

You can also introduce contrast through different geometric shapes that battle (in a good way) for the attention of the viewer. You can combine circles and triangles, ovals and rectangles, curvy and straight, hard and soft, dark and light, and so many more contrasting elements (**Figure 8.10**). You aren't limited to just one contrasting element either. Combining more than one element of contrast will add even more interest. Look for these contrasting combinations whenever you are out shooting, and then use them to shake up your compositions.

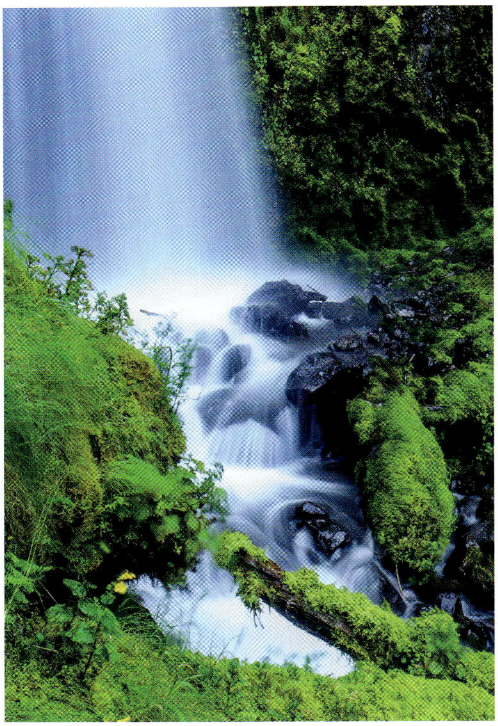

Figure 8.9
The bluish tones of the waterfall create a nice contrast to the vibrant moss of the landscape.

ISO 100 • 1.3 sec. • f/22 • 35mm lens

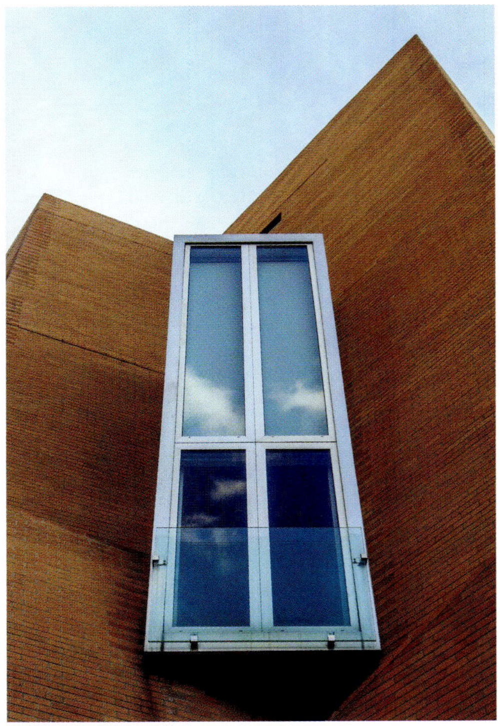

Figure 8.10
I loved the contrast of colors in this image combined with the geometric shapes of the window and walls.

ISO 400 • 1/30 sec. • f/22 • 48mm lens

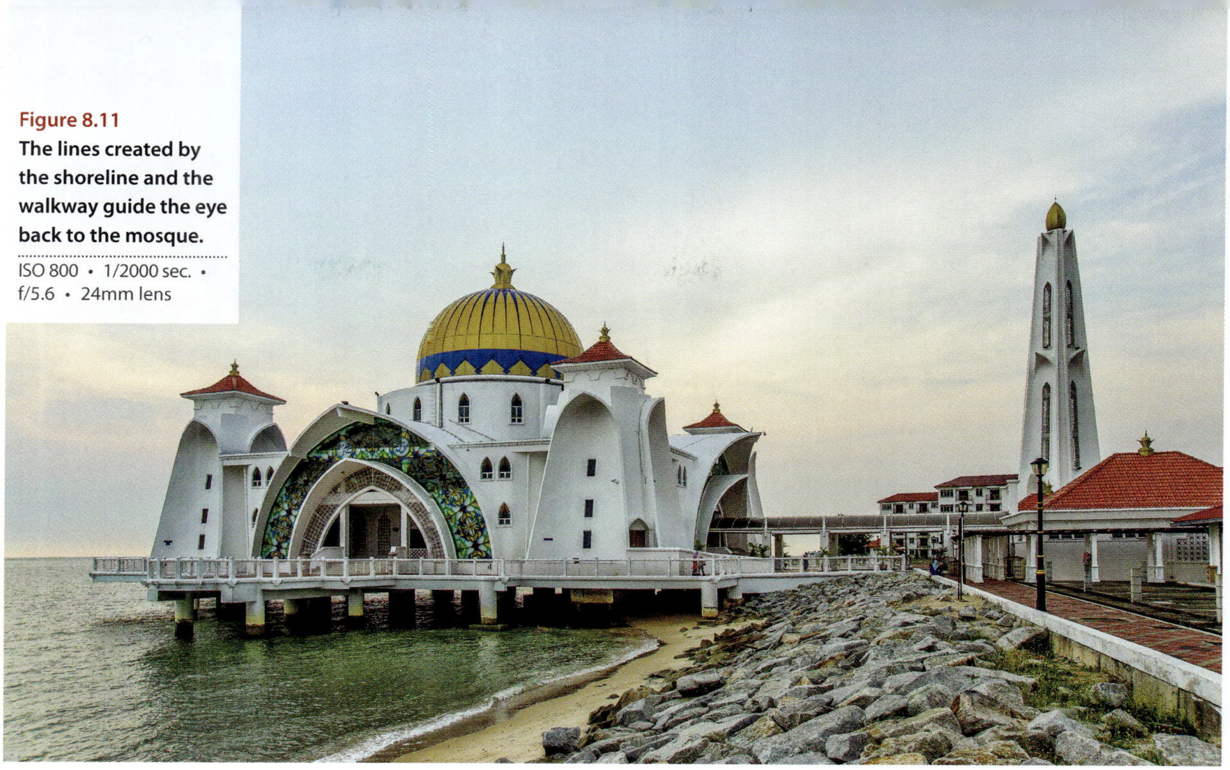

Figure 8.11
The lines created by the shoreline and the walkway guide the eye back to the mosque.
ISO 800 • 1/2000 sec. • f/5.6 • 24mm lens

Leading Lines

One way to pull a viewer into your image is to incorporate leading lines. These are elements that come from the edge of the frame and then lead into the image toward the main subject (**Figure 8.11**). This can be the result of vanishing perspective lines, an element such as a river, or some other feature used to move from the outer edge into the heart of the image.

Splitting the Frame

Generally speaking, splitting the frame right down the middle is not necessarily your best option. Although it may seem more balanced, it can be pretty boring. You should use the rule of thirds when deciding how to divide your frame (**Figure 8.12**).

With horizons, a low horizon will give a sense of stability to the image. Typically, this is done when the sky is more appealing than the landscape below (**Figure 8.13**). When the emphasis is to be placed on the landscape, the horizon line should be moved upward in the frame, leaving the bottom two-thirds to the subject below.

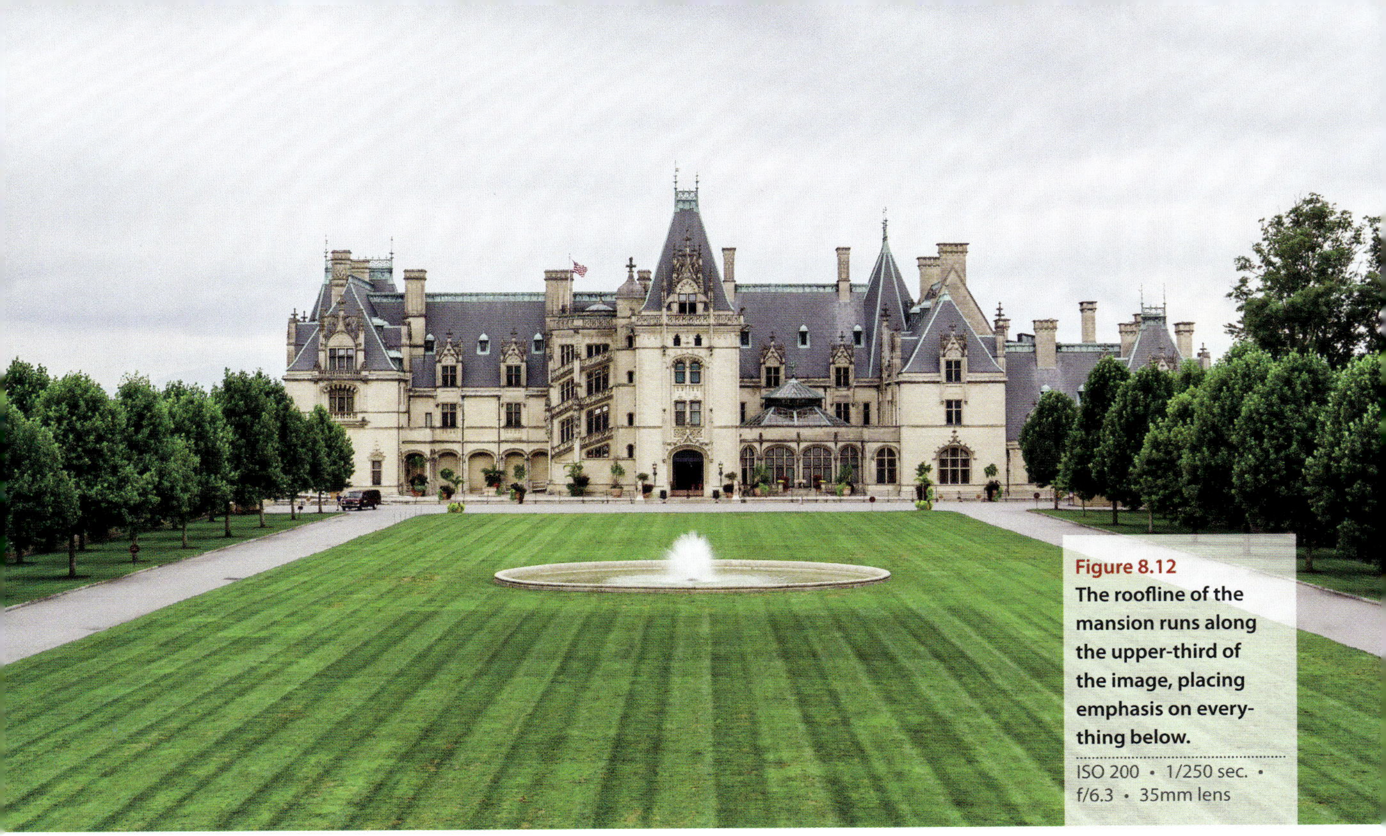

Figure 8.12
The roofline of the mansion runs along the upper-third of the image, placing emphasis on everything below.

ISO 200 • 1/250 sec. • f/6.3 • 35mm lens

Figure 8.13
The sky was much more interesting than the brush below the rock formation, so the horizon was placed low in the scene.

ISO 400 • 1/60 sec. • f/14 • 35mm lens

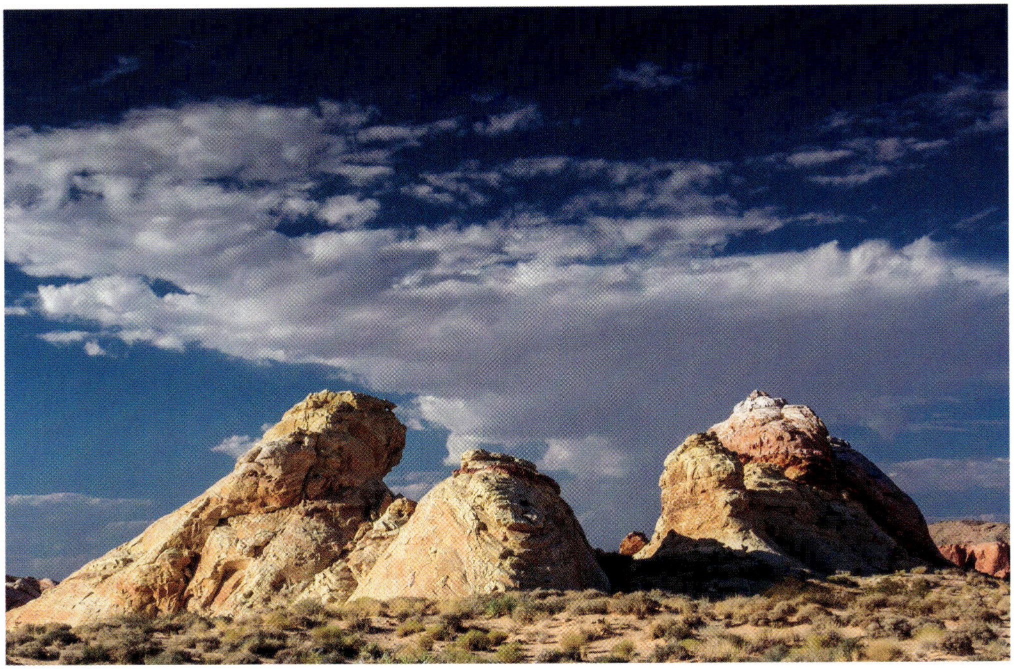

Chapter 8 Assignments

Apply the shooting techniques and tools that you have learned in the previous chapters to these assignments, and you'll improve your ability to incorporate good composition into your photos. Make sure you experiment with all the different elements of composition and see how you can combine them to add interest to your images.

Learning to see lines and patterns

Take your camera for a walk around your neighborhood and look for patterns and angles. Don't worry so much about getting great shots as much as developing an eye for details.

The ABCs of composition

Here's a great exercise that was given to me by my friend Vincent Versace: Shoot the alphabet. This will be a little more difficult, but with practice you will start to see beyond the obvious. Don't just find letters in street signs and the like. Instead, find objects that aren't really letters but have the shape of the letters.

Finding the square peg and the round hole

Circles, squares, and triangles. Spend a few sessions concentrating on shooting simple geometric shapes.

Using the aperture to focus attention

Depth of field plays an important role in defining your images and establishing depth and dimension. Practice shooting wide open, using your largest aperture for the narrowest depth of field. Then find a scene that would benefit from extended depth of field, using very small apertures to give sharpness throughout the scene.

Leading them into a frame

Look for scenes where you can use elements as leading lines, and then look for framing elements that you can use to isolate your subject and add both depth and dimension to your images.

Share your results with the book's Flickr group!
Join the group here: flickr.com/groups/7dmarkii_fromsnapshotstogreatshots

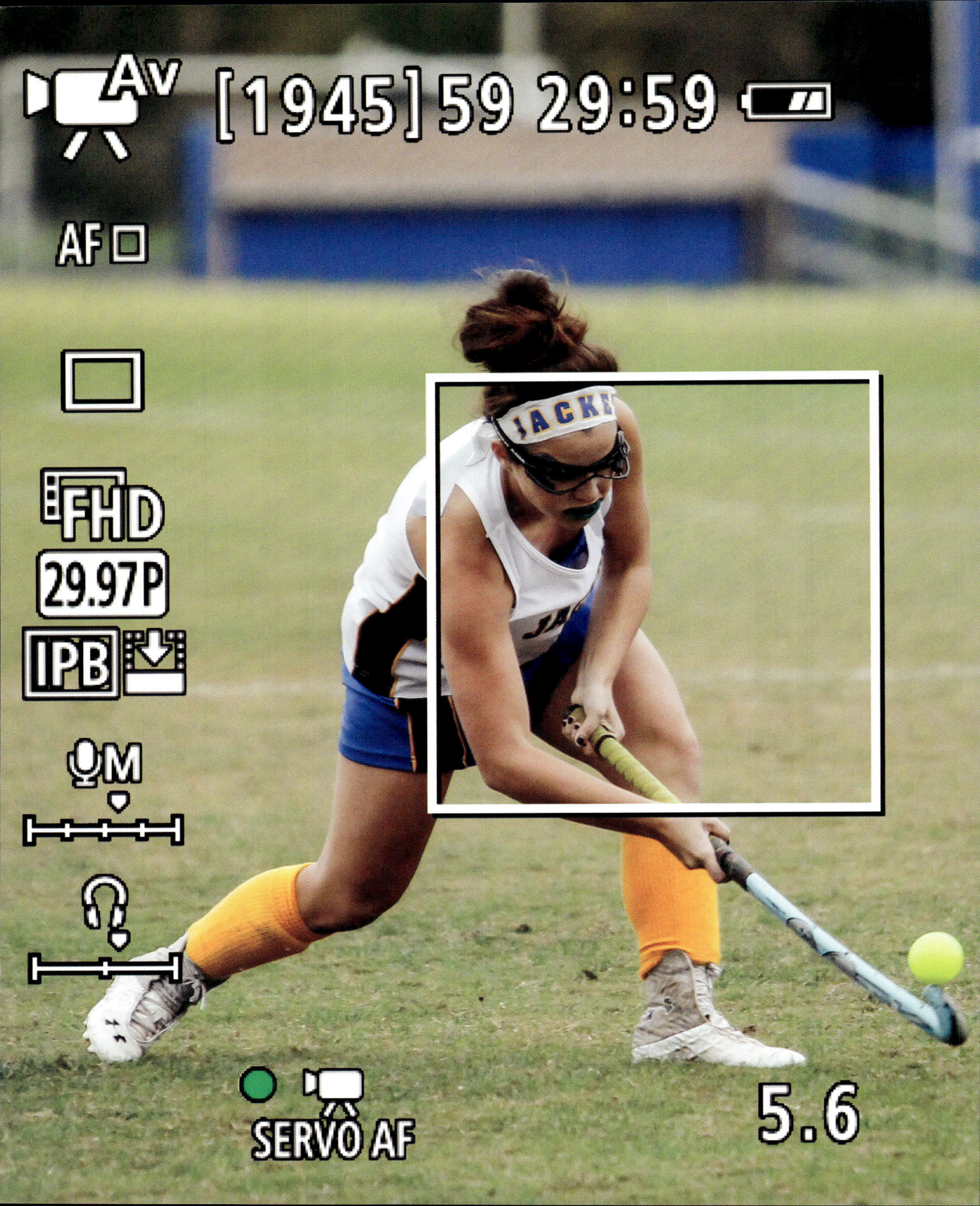

Av
[1945] 59 29:59
AF
FHD
29.97P
IPB
M
SERVO AF
5.6

9

Lights, Camera, Action!

Making Movies with the Canon 7D

Over the past few years there has been a technological revolution in play in the world of video creation. With the advent of video-capture technology in DSLR cameras, there is no longer any reason to carry around that handycam, and for good reason. The handycam, much like the point-and-shoot camera, was great at quick and easy capture, but it lacked the ability to capture professional-looking video. Now photographers have the ability to reinvent themselves by producing professional-quality video along with their still shots to create stunning multimedia productions. Now that you have the 7D Mark II, all of these creative possibilities are at your fingertips, just waiting for you to explore.

It's All About the Lenses

Video cameras have been around for a long time, so why is it such a big deal to create movies with your DSLR camera? The answer is simple: It's all about the lenses. If you have any experience using a video camcorder, you know that it always seems like everything is in focus. Although this isn't always a bad thing, it can also be pretty boring. Using the movie feature in the 7D Mark II allows you to use faster lenses (larger apertures), which can give you more shallow depth of field in your videos. This shallow depth of field can add a sense of dimension and depth that is normally lacking in most of your standard video cameras. The truth is that many videographers have turned their attention from video cameras costing many thousands of dollars to the much more affordable DSLR video camera to produce similar high-definition results with more cinematic qualities.

Using the 7D Mark II will not only allow you to capture video with a more shallow depth of field; you also have the flexibility of using different lenses for different effects. Although you may own only one lens right now, you have the ability to buy specialty lenses to enhance your video as well as your still capture. Any lens that you can use for still photography on your 7D Mark II can also be used for video, including ultra-wide lenses such as the EF 15mm Fisheye f/2.8 ED lens (**Figure 9.1**), the EF-S 18-200mm f/3.5-5.6 IS, or even the EF-S 60mm Micro f/2.8D for getting extreme close-up videos.

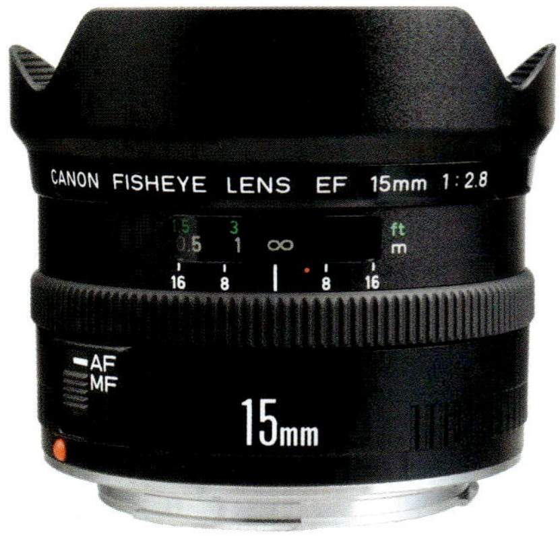

Figure 9.1
Using specialty lenses such as this 15mm fisheye will add a different perspective to your video.

Quick start to recording a movie

It's easy to get started recording movie files on your 7D Mark II. For quick and easy recording, start off by selecting either the Scene Intelligent Auto or Program mode. Turn the Live View/Movie switch to the Movie recording mode (**Figure 9.2**). When the picture appears on the rear LCD screen, compose your scene, and then press the start/stop button. Your video will now begin recording, and you will see a red dot appear onscreen to let you know that you are actively recording. The camera will automatically focus on the subject in the middle of the screen and continuously focus while you record. To end the recording, just press the start/stop button again. That's all there is to it. Of course that's just the simple way of recording a movie, but there are many more possibilities and options to help take you beyond basic movie recording. Let's start with the quality of the movie.

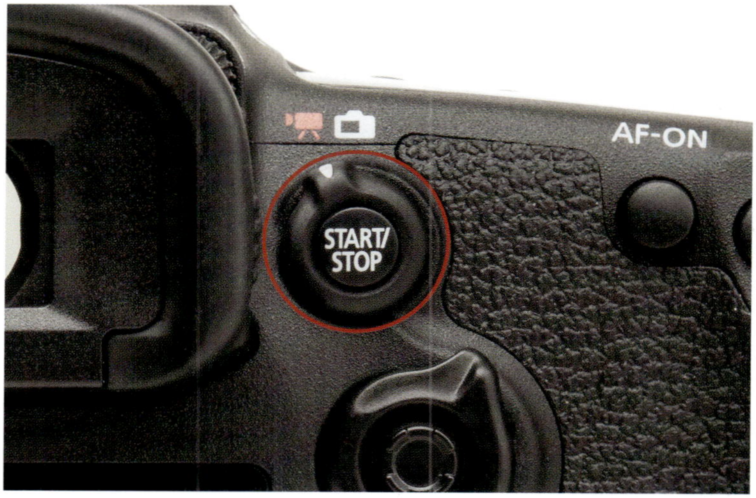

Figure 9.2
Turn the Live View/Movie switch to Movie mode, and press start to begin recording.

Video quality

One of the great features of the 7D Mark II is the ability to capture video in two different formats, much like JPEG and RAW in still shooting. The difference between the two movie formats, MOV and MP4, is based on the CODEC that is used to record the video and its compatibility with your playback system. It sounds complicated but really isn't. A CODEC is the coder/decoder software algorithm used by the capture format to convert the video into a usable format. MOV is often associated with Apple's QuickTime viewer, whereas MP4 is a little more widely acceptable by other video software. Your choice will be dictated by your own software/hardware needs, so be sure to look at the program you will use for playback or editing to see which format is right for you.

Both formats can capture video in three different sizes that are labeled FHD, HD, and VGA. These labels refer to the physical dimensions of the movies in pixels. Full High Definition (FHD) is the highest resolution, at 1920x1080 pixels. HD, or High Definition, is 1280x720 pixels. The lowest quality is VGA, which records at 640x480 pixels. There are also compression methods that are associated with the different quality settings.

The highest quality compression is called **ALL-I** and it treats every frame as a keyframe that is individually compressed, resulting in a very high-quality video file. It is also a very large file in comparison to the other compression choices and is best used when high-quality video editing will take place. Due to the increase in file size, it is best to use this format only when capturing short clips.

The **IPB** format performs more compression on the video. Generally speaking, it uses one keyframe every half second or so, and then throws out parts of the other frames and compresses it all to create smaller file sizes. IPB is best used for long video captures and for segments where detailed editing will not be required. Consider this as your everyday format for general movie recording. There is also an **IPB Light** option that is available only for the MP4 format. It creates the smallest file size of the three and is widely compatible with the widest array of playback devices. This would be my choice for any movie that I was making that was going to go straight to YouTube.

The other choice to be made when selecting a movie recording size is the capture rate. Movies are basically a bunch of still frames that are captured in a sequence to give the appearance of motion when played back. You can choose between three different capture rates or frames per second (fps): 59.94fps, 29.97fps, and 23.98fps. The frame rate you select should be dictated by your video needs. Motion picture films are generally shot in 24fps, so if you want your video to have a cinematic look, you should use the 23.98fps option. Broadcast video and generally most video that you would put online is captured at 29.97fps. The fastest frame rate, 59.94fps, is generally used when you are capturing motion that you might want to slow down in postproduction editing. Capturing at this rate gives you twice the frames as a normal video and lets you get a smoother-looking shot when slowed down. It also has a bit crisper, less fluid look when played at regular speed.

Selecting a recording format and size

1. Turn on Movie shooting by moving the Movie/Live View selector switch to the Movie mode.
2. Press the Menu button and navigate to the fourth shooting menu. (You must have the camera set to the Movie shooting mode or you will not see the correct menu options.)
3. Use the Quick Control dial to highlight Movie Rec Quality and press Set (**A**).
4. Highlight the MOV/MP4 option and press Set (**B**).

A

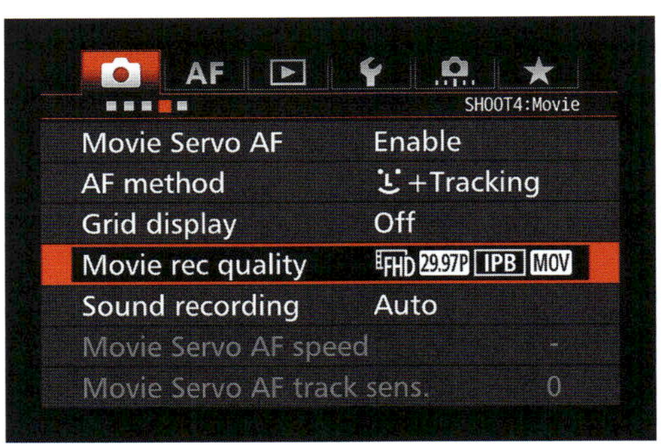

B

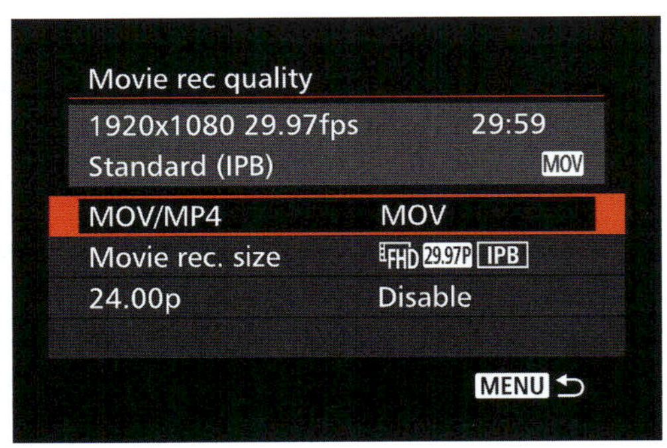

5. Select the format of choice and press the Set button to lock in the change and return to the previous menu (**C**).
6. Move down one option to Movie Rec. Size and press Set (**D**).

C

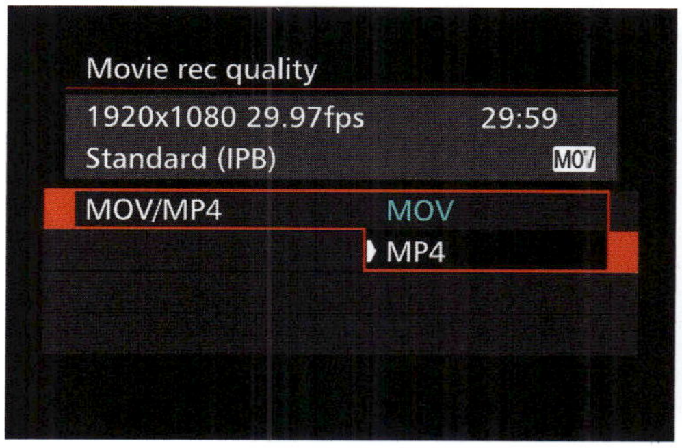

D

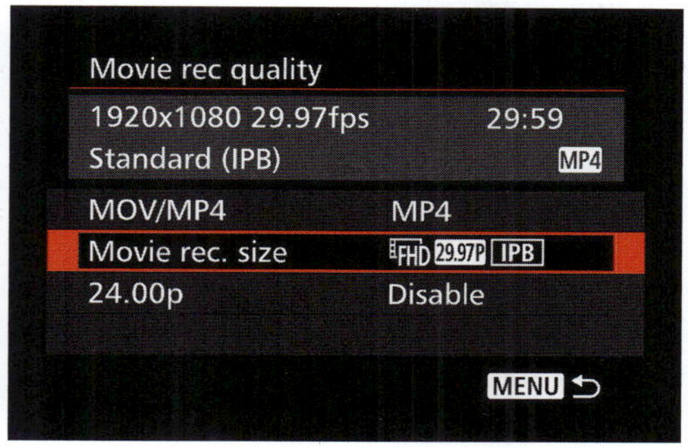

7. Select the recording size you need for your movie and press the Set button (**E**).
8. Press the Menu button twice to return to the live Movie mode.

E

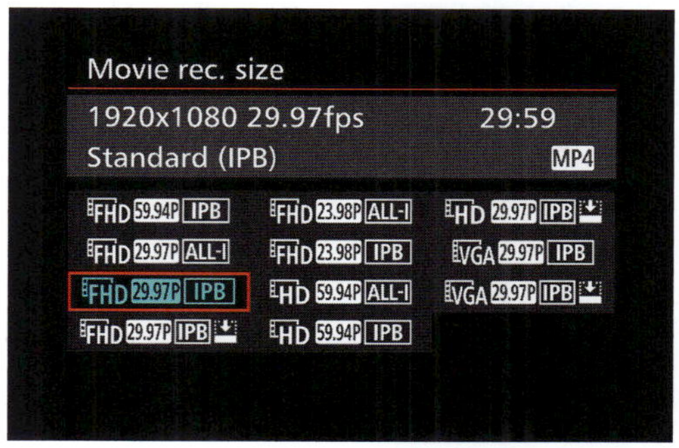

Compression, quality, and file sizes

When you record a movie, the actual size of the movie file will differ greatly depending on several factors. The first is the physical dimensions of the movie, e.g., 1920x1080 or 1280x720. The next factor is the frame rate. The more frames per second you have, the more information the file will contain. The final size determiner is the compression that you choose. You will get a smaller video file with an HD 29.97 IPB setting than you will with an FHD 29.97 ALL-I setting, even if you record for the same amount of time. To see a complete table of recording times and file sizes per minute, check out page 334 of your manual.

Progressive scan

You might have noticed a letter P next to the different frame rates when you were selecting a video-capture rate. That P stands for Progressive. When it comes to video, there are usually two terms associated with how video is captured and displayed on a monitor/screen: *progressive* and *interlaced*. The two terms describe how the video is drawn by line for each frame. Video frames are not displayed all at once like a photograph. In progressive video, the lines are drawn in sequence from top to bottom. Interlaced video draws all of the odd-numbered lines and then all of the even-numbered lines. This odd-even drawing can present itself as screen flicker, which is why the progressive video standard is most preferred, especially when viewing high-definition images.

Recording time

No matter which file format and size you select for your movies, there are some technical limitations to the files that you won't be able to overcome. The first is the maximum file size for recording. The camera limits the recording size for files to 4 GB. This doesn't mean that the camera will stop recording, but it will create a new file once you hit the 4 GB size limit. This means that you will not be able to play back the video continuously because it will be separated into more than one file. If you wish to watch them as one continuous video, you will need to combine the files together in an editing program. The second limitation is the actual continuous length of time that you can record. The camera has a recording limit of 29 minutes and 59 seconds. Once you hit that mark, the camera will stop recording and you will need to start the recording process again by pressing the start/stop button.

Sound

The 7D Mark II records audio to go along with your video, but there are a couple of things to keep in mind while recording. The first is to make sure you don't block the microphone on the front of the camera. If you look closely at the top of the camera body, you will notice some small holes just above the name badge on the front of the camera (**Figure 9.3**).

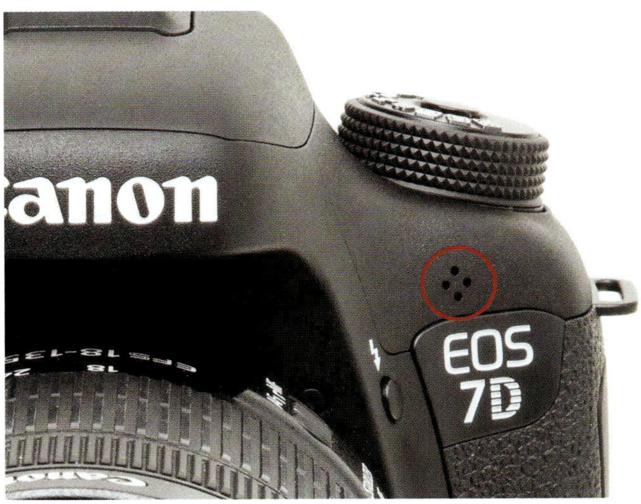

Figure 9.3
The 7D Mark II's built-in microphone.

The next thing you need to know about the sound is that, because the microphone is part of the camera, any noise that the camera makes, like focusing the lens, will be audible in your movies. If you find that the lens focus noise is distracting or you plan on using your own soundtrack to be added to the video at a later time, you can opt to turn the audio recording off.

Turning off the sound

1. Turn on Movie shooting by moving the Movie/Live View selector switch to the Movie mode.
2. Press the Menu button and navigate to the fourth shooting menu, highlight Sound Recording, and press Set (**A**).
3. Select the Sound Rec. option, and press Set (**B**).

A

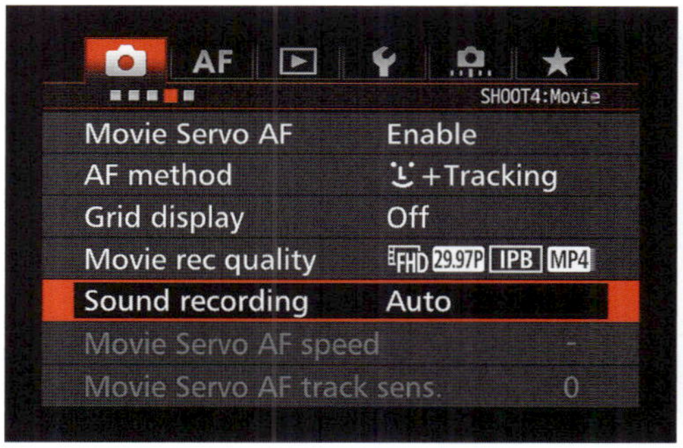

B

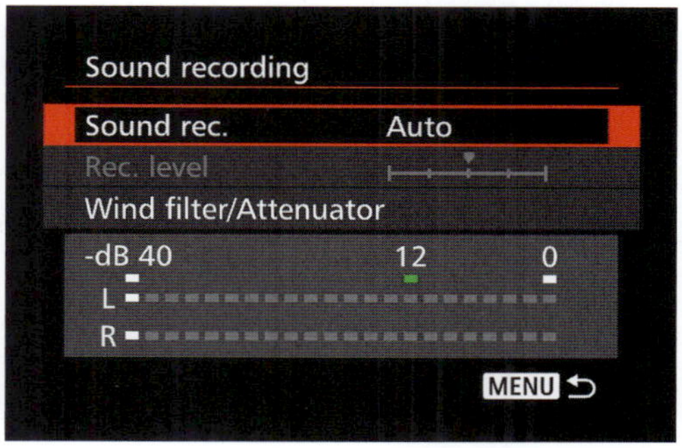

4. Select the Disable option, and press Set to lock in the changes (**C**).
5. Press the Menu button twice to return to recording mode.

C

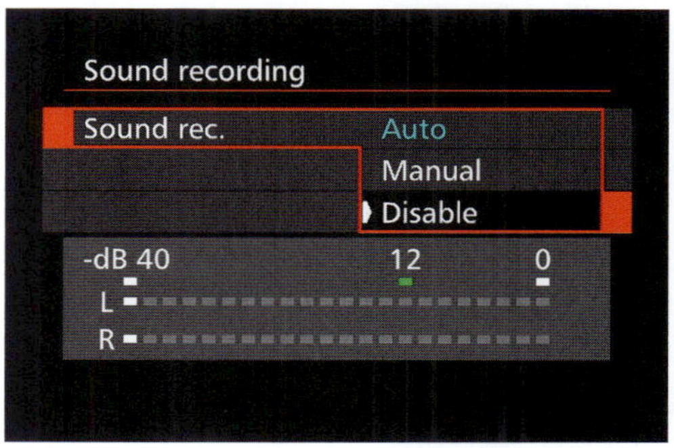

Better sound for your movies

If you want to record sound with your camera but eliminate the camera noise, consider using an external microphone. An external mic means that you can have much more control over the quality of the audio because you are using a device whose sole purpose is to record audio. Currently, there is a growing market of microphones for DSLR cameras, including mics with hot shoe adapters so you can mount the mic directly to the camera and record without having to worry about holding the external mic (**Figure 9.4**).

As previously stated, one of the benefits of using an external microphone is the elimination of camera noise in your videos. Another advantage is that you can use microphones that are designed to do a better job of recording directional audio, such as that coming from subjects in front of the camera. Most of these are long and slender and are referred to as shotgun mics, such as the Rode mic I use for my video work.

Another option to help reduce lens noise is to use one of the new STM Canon lenses (**Figure 9.5**). The current lineup of STM lenses is a little small, but Canon is introducing more options all the time. Currently, Canon offers STM lenses in 24mm, 40mm, 18-55mm, 18-135mm, 24-105mm, and 55-250mm. The STM stands for Stepper Motor and is a new autofocus method designed specifically for shooting video, while providing for a more quiet and smooth focus operation on Canon cameras. All of the STM lenses use the EF-S mount, which are made specifically for the 7D Mark II format. Using an STM lens doesn't require any special procedures; just mount it on the camera and start shooting.

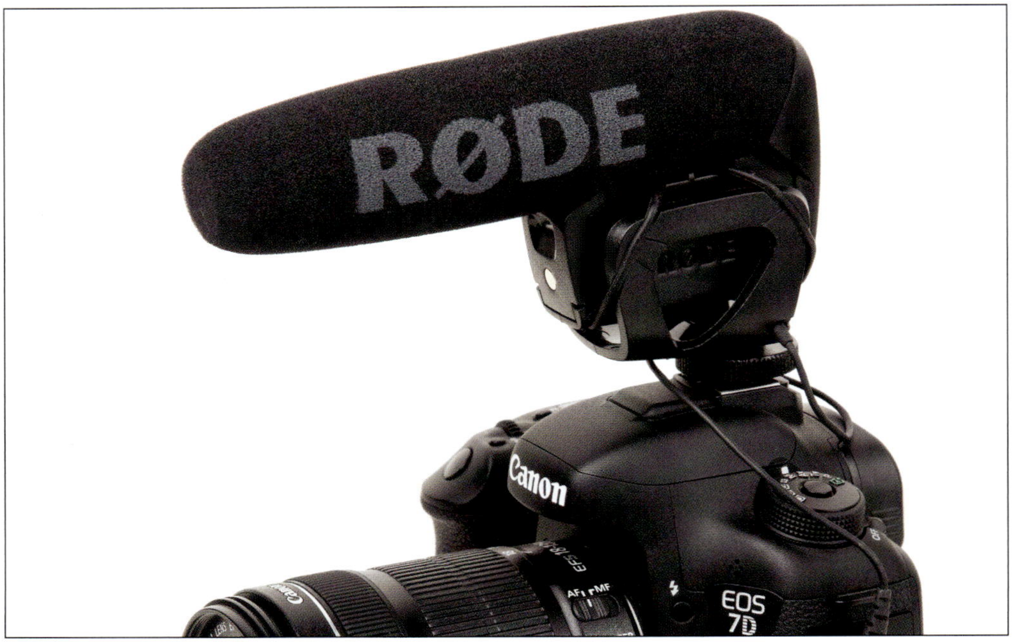

Figure 9.4
Using an external microphone like this model from Rode will help eliminate camera noise from your videos.

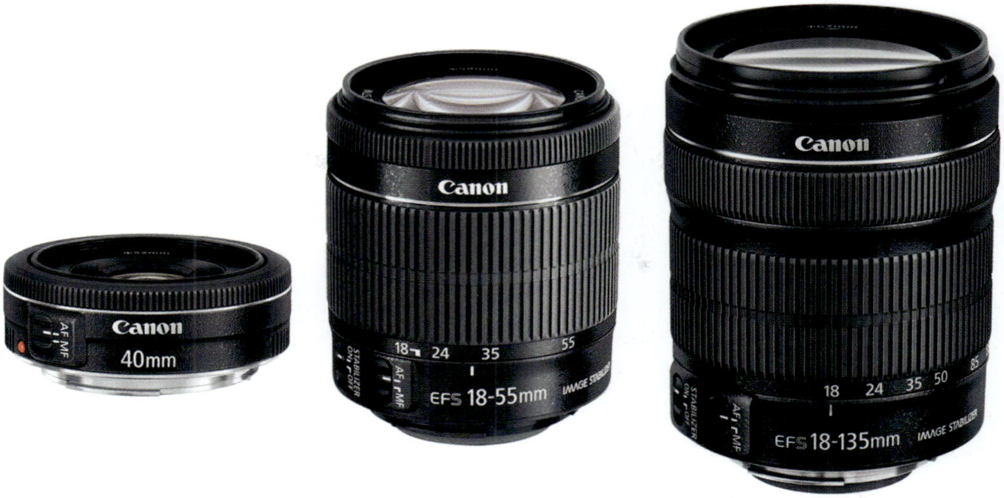

Figure 9.5 Using lenses with STM technology will provide quieter AF focus operations.

Controlling your audio

Typically, your camera's audio setting will be set to Auto, which means that the camera is controlling the recording level of the microphone. If you find that the audio is too loud or too soft for your movie, you can manually override the audio levels and set them up for your needs. The best way to know how your audio is sounding is to monitor it with headphones. You will find a standard 3.5mm stereo headphone jack on the side of the camera, just below the microphone jack. To make adjustments to the audio levels, you need to change the recording level to Manual mode.

Setting up Manual audio levels

1. Turn on Movie shooting by moving the Movie/Live View selector switch to the Movie mode.
2. Press the Menu button and navigate to the fourth shooting menu, highlight Sound Recording, and press Set (**A**).

A

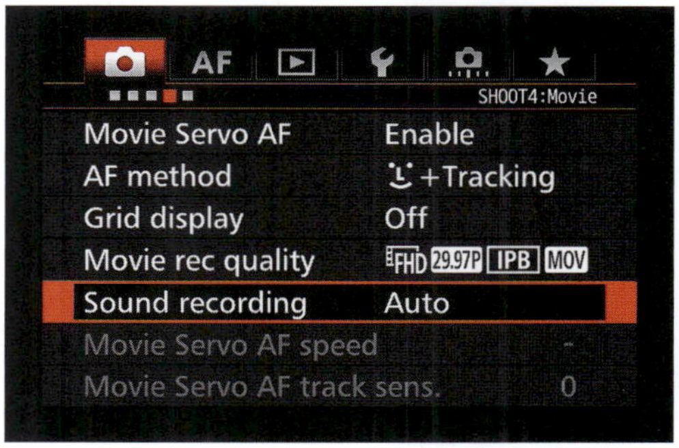

3. Select the Sound Rec. option, and press Set (**B**).
4. Select the Manual option, and press Set to lock in the changes (**C**).

B

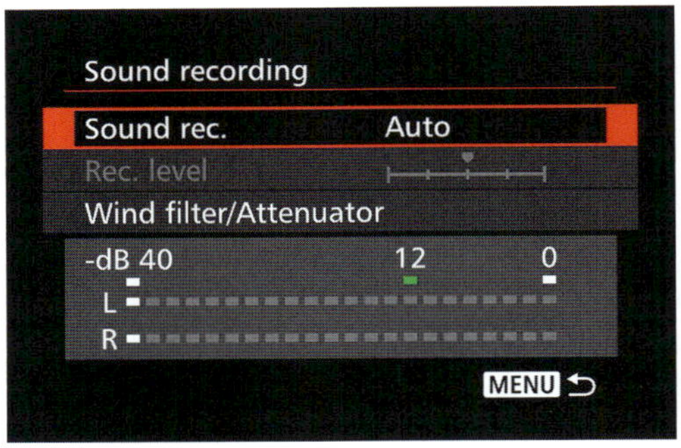

C

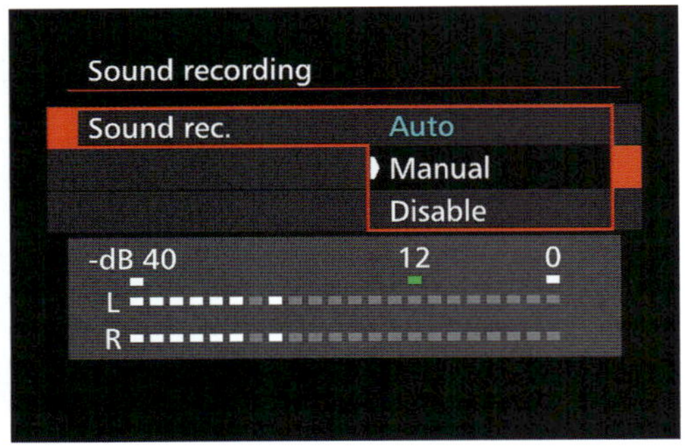

5. Move down one menu item to the Rec. Level option, press Set, and then use the Quick Control dial to change the recording level based on the live audio level meter displayed at the bottom of the screen (**D**).
6. Press the Menu button twice to return to shooting mode.

D

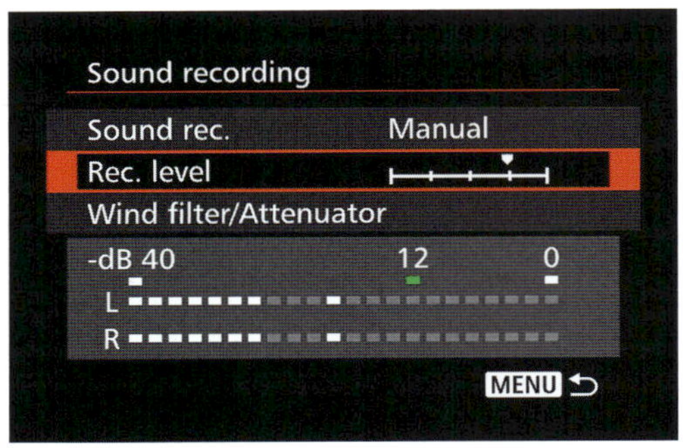

Once the Audio mode is set to Manual, you will notice that an audio level meter is now visible in the LCD screen while previewing and recording your movie. This will give you an indication of the current audio levels and help you make adjustments as necessary (**Figure 9.6**).

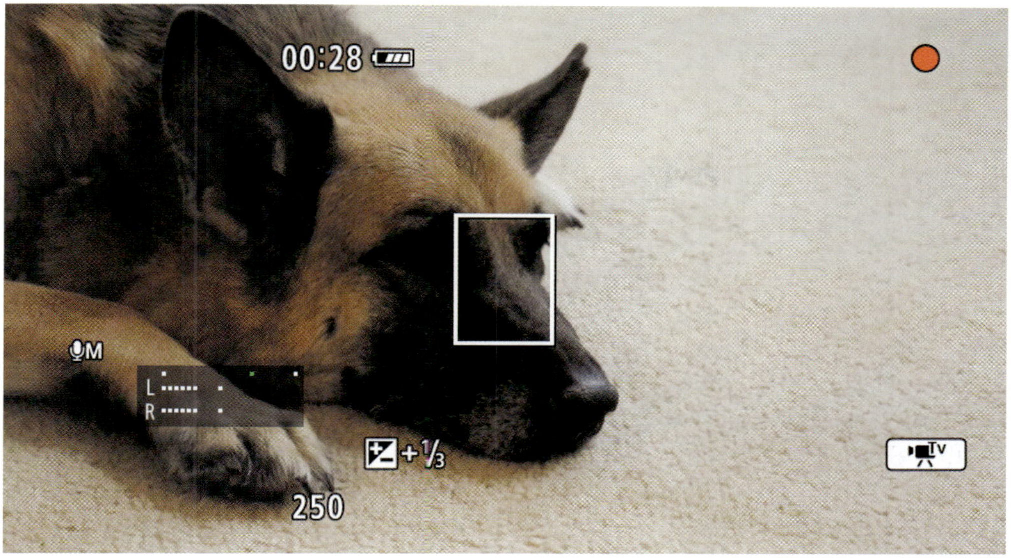

Figure 9.6
An audio level meter will be displayed when the audio recording level is set to Manual mode.

Focusing the camera

As mentioned in Chapter 6, "Say Cheese!," you have three different focusing methods to choose from when shooting movies, and they are the exact same ones used for Live View shooting. Depending on the method you choose, Face+Tracking, FlexiZone – Multi, or FlexiZone – Single, the camera will continuously try to focus on your subject. You can force focus by pressing the AF-On or shutter release button if you feel that the camera is not focused on the appropriate subject. You can also hold the focus by pressing either one of these buttons while recording. If you don't want the camera to continuously focus, you can turn off the Movie Servo mode and adjust the focus when you think it's appropriate.

Turning off Movie Servo

1. Turn on Movie shooting by moving the Movie/Live View selector switch to the Movie mode.
2. Press the Menu button and navigate to the fourth shooting menu, highlight Movie Servo AF, and press Set (**A**).

A

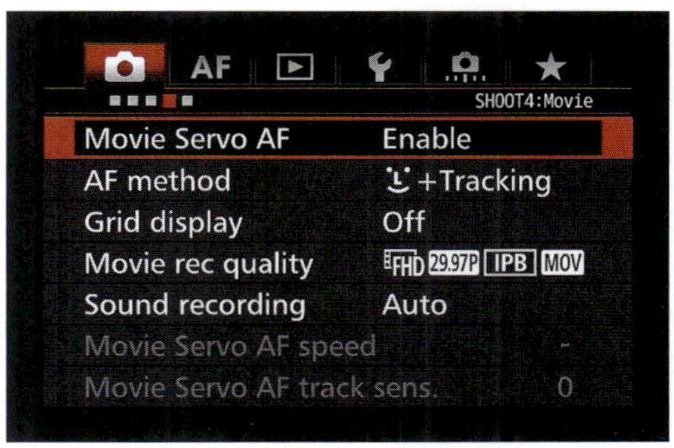

3. Set the option to Disable, and press Set to lock in the change (**B**).
4. Press the Menu button to return to Movie mode and use the shutter release or AF-On buttons to set the focus prior to or during shooting.

B

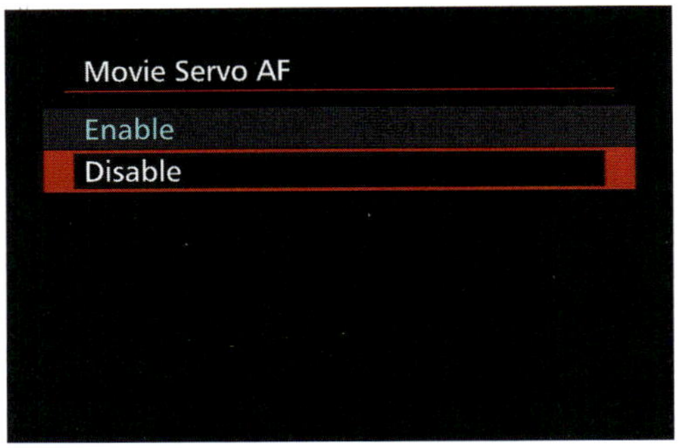

If you want to ensure that your focus is precise, you can press the magnify button to zoom in on your subject and set the exact focus prior to recording. You can use either the AF focus with the shutter release or AF-On button while zoomed in, or set your lens to Manual Focus mode and manually focus on your subject. This method is used quite a bit when you have a shallow depth of field set up, and you are using a focus rail to move the camera from an out-of-focus position and then slide it closer to the subject to have it slowly come into focus. This is big in advertising and product videos. It is also a handy focus method when your subjects won't be moving around.

Getting a shallow depth of field

As I said earlier, getting the look of a production cinema camera means working with shallow depth of fields. There are two ways of achieving this; the first is Aperture Priority mode (Av). When working in Av mode, you will be responsible for setting the aperture and the camera will then select the shutter speed and ISO automatically. You can control the brightness to some extent by using the Quick Control dial to change the exposure compensation.

> **Manual Callout**
>
> If you want to keep your aperture locked in to one particular setting, you might want to try using the Manual Exposure Shooting mode. Setup for this function can be found on page 320–321 of your manual. My suggestion is that you leave the camera's ISO set to Auto instead of selecting your own. This way the camera will keep the video exposure looking good while working in different light levels but still allow you to use the aperture of your choice.

If you want total control over your exposure, you might want to explore shooting in Manual mode. Unlike Av and Tv modes, Manual mode lets you control all of the exposure variables within limits. For example, you can set the shutter speed as high as 1/4000 of a second but no slower than 1/30 of a second. Using Manual mode is best for those circumstances where you want a certain look to your movie, like someone standing under a lamppost at night, and you need more control over the exposure controls. The downside is that any time there is a change in lighting, you will need to make manual adjustments, which can be a little time-consuming.

Giving a Different Look to Your Videos

Using Picture Styles

Something that a lot of people don't realize is that you can use the Picture Styles to give your video a completely different look. Sure, you can use the Standard style for everyday video, but why not add some punch by using a different Picture Style setting? You can set up your own user-defined style to add some color saturation and sharpness, or you can use one of the predefined styles. Maybe you want to shoot a landscape scene. Go ahead and set the Picture Style to the Landscape setting to improve the look of skies and vegetation. If you want to get creative, try using the Monochrome setting to shoot in black and white. The great thing about using the Picture Styles is that you will see the effect right on your LCD screen as you record, so you will know exactly what your video is going to look like. Want to take things up a notch? Try customizing the Picture Styles and do things like shoot sepia-colored video. Check out the "Classic Black-and-White Portraits" section of Chapter 6 to see how to customize the look of your Monochrome Picture Style.

White balance

Another great way to change the look of your video is to select a white balance that either matches your scene for accurate color rendition or, better yet, choose one that doesn't match to give a different feel to your video. You can completely change the mood of the video by selecting a white balance setting that is different from the actual light source that you are working in. Don't be afraid to be creative and try out different looks for your video.

Tips for Better Video

Shoot short clips

Even though your camera can record fairly long video sequences, you should probably limit your shooting time to short clips and then edit them together. Here's the deal: Most professional video shot today is made up of very short video sequences that are edited together. If you don't believe me, watch any TV show and see how long you see a continuous sequence onscreen. I am guessing that you won't see any clip that is longer than about 10 seconds. You can thank music videos for shortening our attention span, but the reality is that your video will look much more professional if you shoot in shorter clips and then edit them together, which brings me to the next tip.

Stage your shots

If you are trying to produce a good-looking video, take some time before you begin shooting to determine what you want to shoot and where you want to shoot it from. You can mark the floor with tape to give your "actors" a mark to hit. You can also use staging to figure out where your lens needs to be set for correct focus on these different scenes.

Manual focus

This will be difficult to do at first, but the fact is that if you want to change the point of focus in your video while you are recording, then you should learn to manually focus the lens. The autofocus system will work while you are recording, but it is not always the best option. For one thing, the focus motor can be a little loud during focus operations. This isn't a problem unless you are recording sound with your video, in which case you will hear the autofocus motor moving back and forth as your camera refocuses. Even if you aren't recording audio or you're using an external mic, the autofocus can be slow, and it has a tendency to move in and out of focus several times before settling on the right spot.

To change your focus, you need to set the camera lens to manual focus, and then use the focus ring on the front of the lens. This will be difficult at first, especially if you have never had to manually focus in the past, but with a little practice you can become fairly adept.

Using Movie Servo AF

If you aren't keen on manually focusing your camera, you can try out one of the automatic AF modes. The default mode is called Movie Servo AF, and although it does a pretty decent job of maintaining autofocus, it's good to understand the limitations. First, it's a little slow. You can speed the process along by halfway pressing the shutter release button, but this will make the AF motor work faster and impart extra noise. Second, it helps to have a defined subject for the AF to track on. When it does lock on, it will allow you to follow focus with your subjects as they move about the frame. If at any time you want to disable the AF, you can press the flash button on the front of the camera. This will temporarily turn off the Movie Servo AF and maintain the current point of focus. To turn the AF back on, just press the flash button once again.

Capturing a still frame

You may find that at some time during your movie recording you want to capture a high-resolution still frame. This is totally possible by using the shutter release button. While you are in record mode, press the shutter button fully to initiate a still frame capture. This is similar to taking a picture in Live View mode. Once the image has been saved, the camera will continue recording the video sequence. Your image will be saved as a separate file on your memory card.

Avoid the quick pan

Your camera uses something called a rolling shutter while recording video that, as the name implies, rolls from the top to the bottom of the frame. If you are panning quickly from one side to another, you will see your video start to jiggle like it is being shot through Jell-O. This is something that can't be overcome except by using a slower panning motion. If you are going to be shooting a fast subject, consider using a faster frame rate and smoother motion, such as the 59.94 frames per second option. The more frames you record, the smoother the video will look when played back.

Use a fast memory card

Your video will be recording at up to 60 frames per second, and as it is recording it's placing the video into a buffer, or temporary holding spot, while the camera writes the frames to your memory card. If you are using a slower, bargain memory card, it might not be able to keep up with the flow of video—and the result will be dropped frames. The camera will actually not record some frames, because the buffer will fill up before the images have time to be written. This will be seen as small skips in the video when you watch it later. You can prevent this from happening by using an SD card that has a speed rating of class 6 or higher (**Figure 9.7**). These cards have faster writing speeds and will keep the video moving smoothly from the camera to the card.

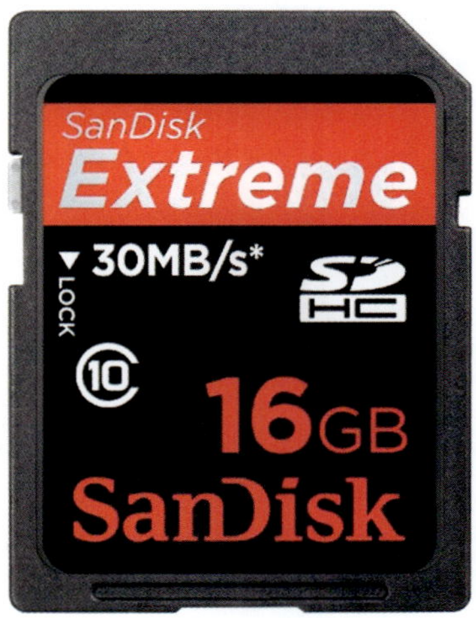

Figure 9.7
A fast card such as this SanDisk SDHC Class 10 card will help capture more of your video frames.

Class 10 for the Win

Although the manufacturer suggests class 6 or faster media, my recommendation is that you only use class 10 cards for video applications. I have found that some class 6 cards just can't meet the demands of video and have caused my camera to pause or stop while in the middle of a video shoot.

Get yourself a Mini-HDMI cable

When you're ready to play back your video, you can run the video directly from your camera to your TV. If you want to get the best-quality picture on your TV, you will want to use a TV capable of displaying high-definition video, which also means that you will want to use an HDMI cable to connect the camera to the TV. HDMI (High Definition Multimedia Interface) cables will carry your uncompressed video to your HDTV in all its glory. The only problem is that your camera didn't have an HDMI cable included in the box when you bought it. This means that you will have to purchase one to take advantage of the HD playback. If you are thinking that you already own an HDMI cable for connecting your other media components to your TV, you might want to take another look. Your camera utilizes a Mini-HDMI connection, so most standard cables designed for video components won't work. If you do decide to purchase one, make sure you get a Mini-HDMI-to-HDMI cable. You can find them at most electronics stores where HD cameras and TVs are sold. (Here's a little hint for purchasing a Mini-HDMI cable: Search the Internet for the best prices. Most electronics stores have huge markups on cables, and you can usually find a suitable one online for about a third of the price of those that you would find in your local store.)

Turn off the sound

In Chapter 2, "First Things First," I told you how to turn off the audio option while recording your video. If you don't have an external mic hooked up to your camera, your only audio option is to use the built-in microphone on the camera. The truth is that the microphone does not produce audio that is up to the quality of the video. To make your videos stand out, try turning it off and then add a music soundtrack. You will be amazed how the right music can enhance a video. Of course you will need to do this on your computer, which will require special video-editing software, which leads us to our next section.

Watching and Editing Your Video

Watching video

There are three ways for you to watch your videos:

- In your camera
- On your TV
- On your computer

To watch your video clips on your camera, simply press the Playback button and press the Set button to activate the play commands. Press Set again to start and stop the movie. Use the Quick Control dial to choose other playback commands. You can use the Main dial to control your volume. To exit the playback screen, press the Menu button and use the Quick Control dial to select the next movie file you want to play. Pretty simple.

To watch on your TV, you can use the Mini-HDMI cable discussed earlier and connect to your HDMI-compatible TV. You'll need to tune your TV to the channel used for HDMI input, and then play the video just as you would if you were watching it in-camera.

If you would like to watch your video on your computer, you will first need to download the files or access them using an SD card reader. For Apple owners, you can use Apple's QuickTime Player to watch the video. If it is too large for your screen, try pressing Command-0 to make the video half-size, or press Command-3 to fit the video to your screen. For Microsoft Windows users, try recording in the MP4 video format. If you prefer the MOV format, you can download the Apple QuickTime Player (www.apple.com/quicktime). The basic player is free and will allow you to view your MOV files.

Editing video

If you are a Mac owner, you can edit your HD video using the iMovie application. Windows XP users will have to purchase an editing program for editing HD video, since the Windows Movie Maker application doesn't do a good job of handling HD video resolutions. There are many different applications for Windows editing, such as Adobe's Premiere Elements 10 video-editing software. You can find more information and download a trial version at http://www.adobe.com/products/premiere-elements.html.

If you are using the Windows 7 or Windows 8 operating system, then you should check out the Windows Live Movie Maker program. It has a variety of editing features, handles HD video, and allows you to send your finished videos to places like YouTube and Facebook. If you don't already have Windows Live Movie Maker on your system, try this site for more information on how to download and install the free program: http://windows.microsoft.com/en-us/windows-live/movie-maker.

Expanding your knowledge

I have given you a couple of quick tips and suggestions in this chapter to get you started with your movie making, but if you really want to get serious, there is a lot more you need to know. Videography can be a complex endeavor, and there is much to learn and know if you want to move beyond the simple video capture of the kids in the backyard or the trip to the amusement park. If you want to explore all your camera has to offer in the way of video movie making, then I suggest you read *Creating DSLR Video: From Snapshots to Great Shots* (**Figure 9.8**). The author, Rich Harrington, is a true master at shooting and editing digital video and a top-notch instructor and author. I can tell you that his book is packed solid with everything you need to know about taking your DSLR video making to the next level and beyond.

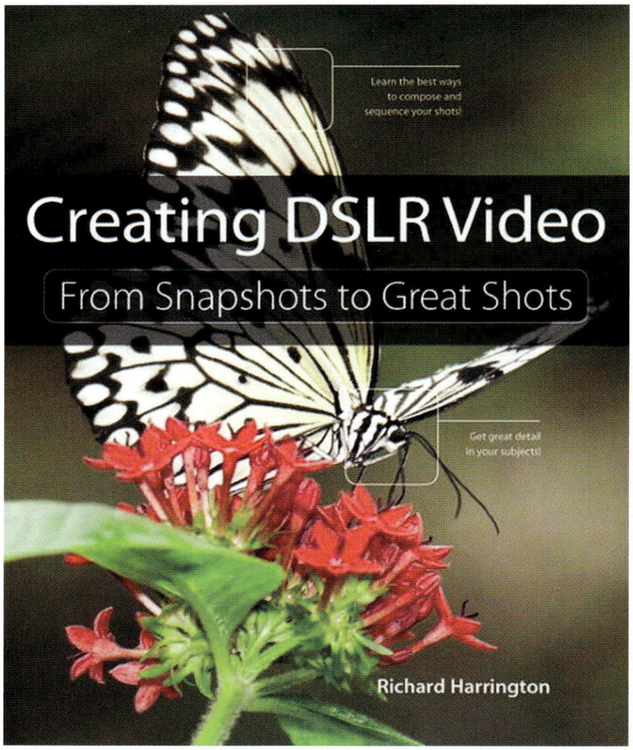

Figure 9.8
I highly recommend *Creating DSLR Video* for taking your movie making to the next level.

Chapter 9 Assignments

Now that we've covered most of the basics behind shooting video with your 7D, take some time to familiarize yourself with all of the features listed in this chapter. Here are a few exercises to get you started.

Movie recording sizes

Take some time to discover the different movie recording sizes on your 7D. Set the camera to one of the HD settings (1920×1080 or 1280×720), then change the setting to SD (480×640). Note the different aspect ratios (16:9 vs. 4:3) and areas that are covered with the semitransparent mask. Shoot a few short videos in each recording size, and then play them back on your computer.

White balance and picture styles

Set your camera on a tripod and set it to Movie shooting mode. Set the exposure so you can see your scene properly, then change the white balance, scrolling through all the different options, and watch the screen as you try each setting. Do the same with the picture styles and pay attention to the colors in your scene as you make the changes.

Set your focus

Familiarize yourself with the different autofocus modes by going into the menu and trying out each of them. Once you've got the hang of it, set the lens to MF (Manual Focus) and zoom in using the Magnify button on the back of your camera to focus on a specific area of your scene.

Understanding the built-in microphone's limitations

Make sure the Sound Recording feature is set to On and the Shooting mode is set to Manual, and then start to record a short video clip. During the recording process, change the shutter speed by turning the Main dial to the right or left. Then, while still recording, set the lens to MF and set your focus manually by turning the front part of the lens. Stop the recording, and then go into Playback mode. Pay attention to the noise made while you were making changes to the exposure and focus—it's a lot louder than it seemed, right?

Share your results with the book's Flickr group!
Join the group here: flickr.com/groups/7dmarkii_fromsnapshotstogreatshots

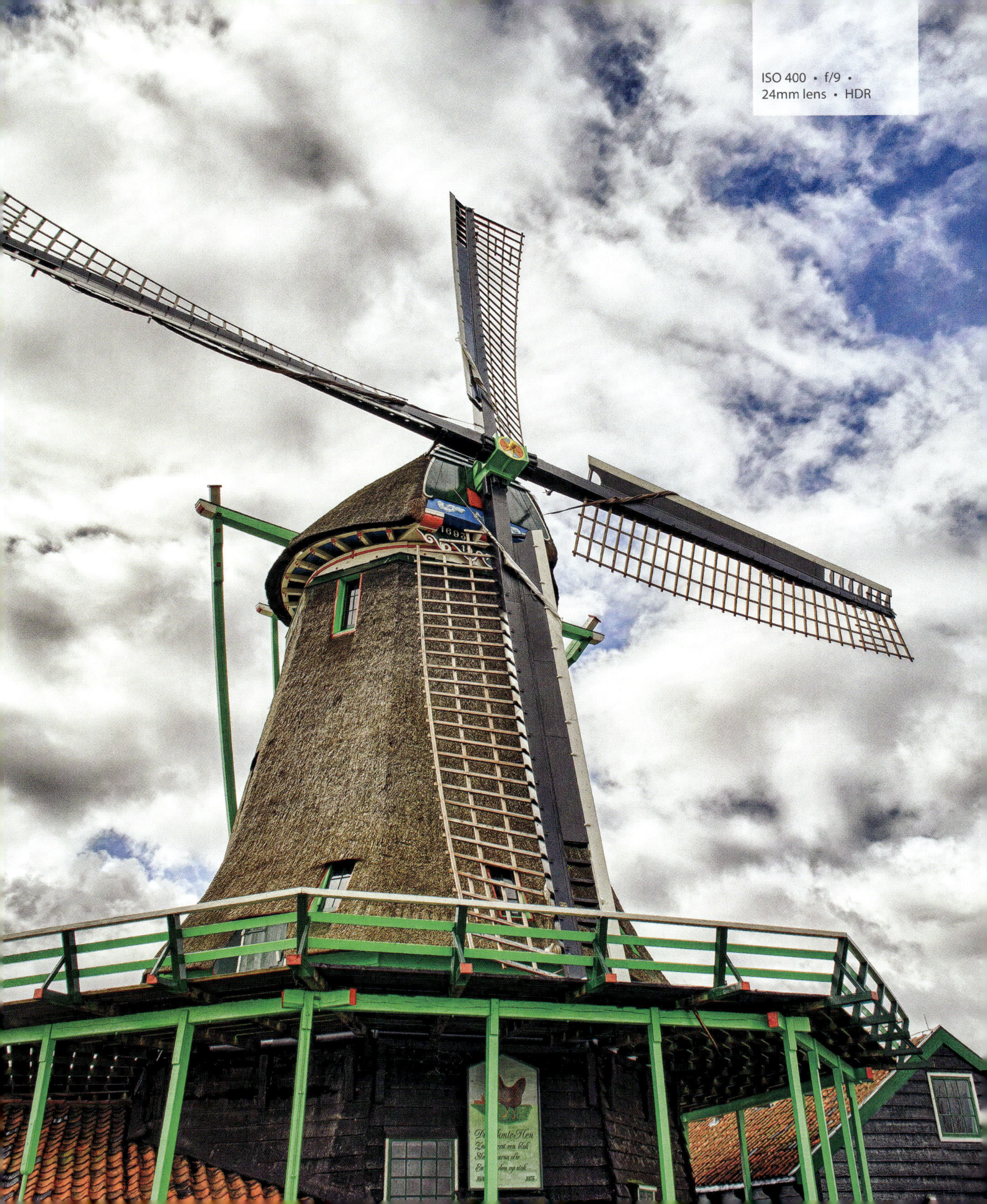

ISO 400 • f/9 • 24mm lens • HDR

10 Advanced Techniques

Impress Your Family and Friends

We've covered a lot of ground in the previous chapters, especially on the general photographic concepts that apply to most, if not all, shooting situations. There are, however, some specific tools and techniques that will give you an added advantage in obtaining a great shot. Additionally, we will look at how to customize certain controls on your camera to reflect your personal shooting preferences and always have them at the ready.

Poring Over the Picture

This image is just a portion of a panorama that I created using multiple overlapping photographs that were combined with a stitching program. The minute I stepped up on the hill overlooking this view in Death Valley, I instantly knew that it was too grand to be contained in just one photograph. Some scenes just cry out to be captured wide, and this was certainly one of them.

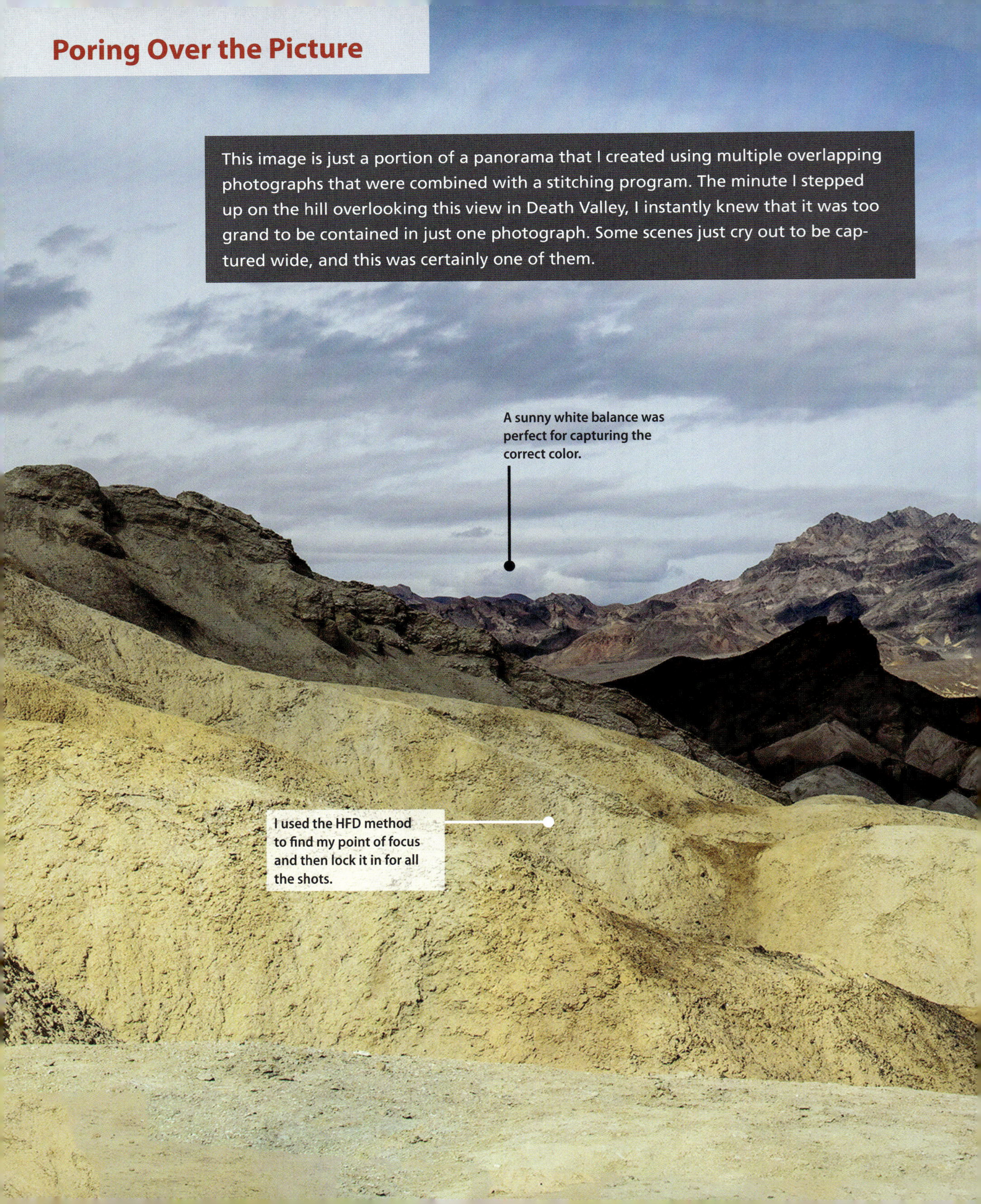

ISO 400 • 1/125 sec. • f/14 • 24mm lens

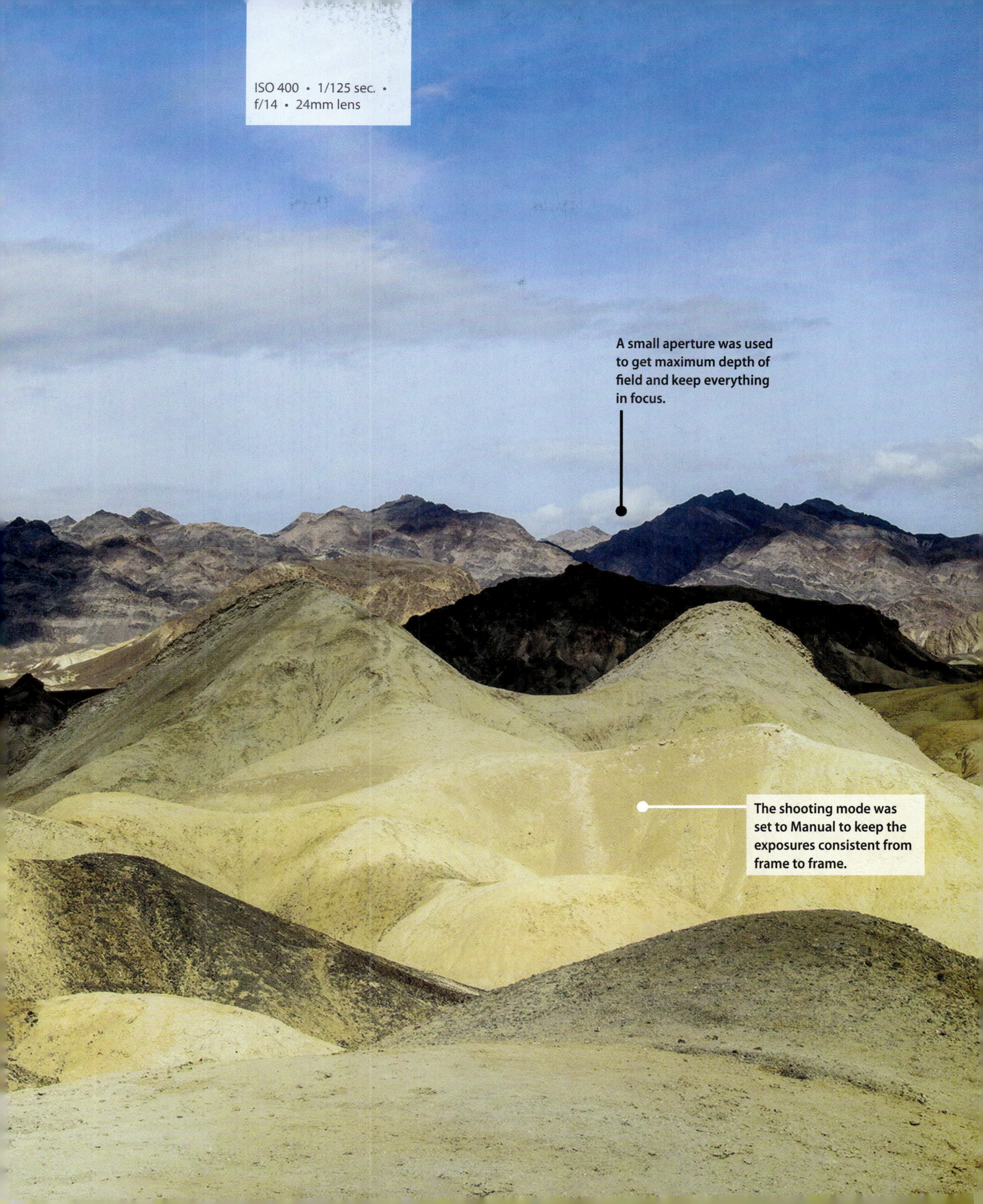

A small aperture was used to get maximum depth of field and keep everything in focus.

The shooting mode was set to Manual to keep the exposures consistent from frame to frame.

Advanced Techniques to Explore

This section comes with a warning attached. All of the techniques and topics up to this point have been centered on your camera. The following two sections, covering panoramas and high dynamic range (HDR) images, require you to use image-processing software to complete the photograph. They are, however, important enough that you should know how to correctly shoot for success, should you choose to explore these two popular techniques.

Shooting panoramas

If you have visited the Grand Canyon, you know just how large and wide open it truly is—so much so that it would be difficult to capture its splendor in just one frame. The same can be said for a mountain range, or a cityscape, or any extremely wide vista. There are two methods that you can use to capture the feeling of this type of scene.

The "fake" panorama

The first method is to shoot as wide as you can, and then crop out the top and bottom portions of the frame (**Figure 10.1** and **Figure 10.2**). Panoramic images are generally two or three times wider than a normal image.

Creating a fake panorama

1. To create the look of the panorama, find your widest lens focal length. If you're using the kit lens that came with the 7D Mark II, it would be the 18mm setting on the 18–55mm kit lens.
2. Compose and focus your scene and select the smallest aperture possible.
3. Shoot your image. That's all there is to it from a photography standpoint.
4. Then, open the image in your favorite image-processing software and crop the extraneous foreground and sky from the image, leaving you with a wide panorama of the scene.

As you can see, the image was shot with a lot of headroom, which includes a large portion of the clouds. It looked like a good crop at the time, but after opening the image in my post-processing software, I had second thoughts about it. I used the crop tool to take off the top two-thirds of the frame and a little bit of the water and came up with a panorama that is much more dynamic and visually interesting.

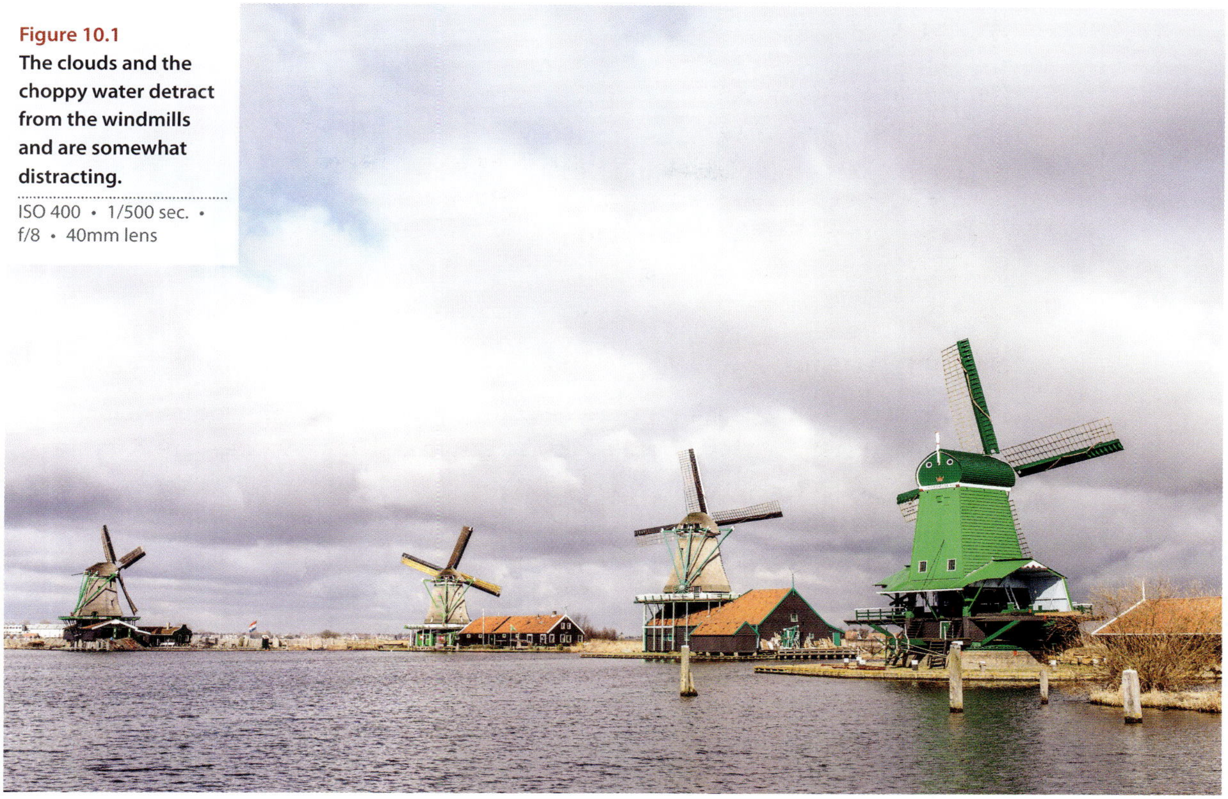

Figure 10.1
The clouds and the choppy water detract from the windmills and are somewhat distracting.

ISO 400 • 1/500 sec. • f/8 • 40mm lens

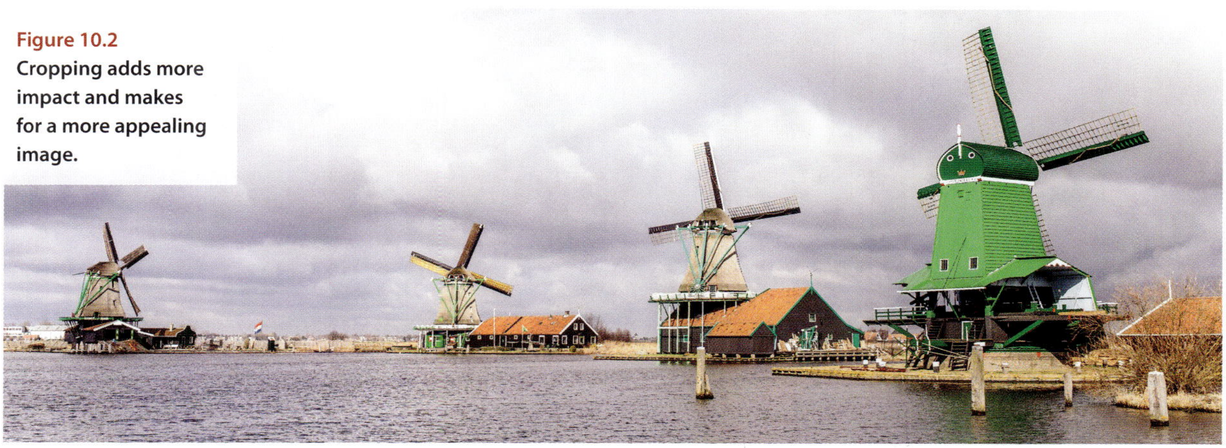

Figure 10.2
Cropping adds more impact and makes for a more appealing image.

The multiple-image panorama

The previous method is sometimes referred to as a "fake" panorama because it is made with a standard-size frame, and then cropped down to a narrow perspective. To shoot a true panorama, you need to use either a special panorama camera that shoots a very wide frame or the following method, which requires the combining of multiple frames.

The multiple-image pano has gained in popularity in the past few years; this is principally due to advances in image-processing software. Many software options are available now that will take multiple images, align them, and then "stitch" them into a single panoramic image. The key to shooting a multiple-image pano is to overlap your shots by about 30 percent from one frame to the next (**Figure 10.3** and **Figure 10.4**).

It is possible to handhold the camera while capturing your images, but the best method for capturing great panoramic images is to use a tripod.

Now that you have your series of overlapping images, you can import them into your image-processing software to stitch them together and create a single panoramic image.

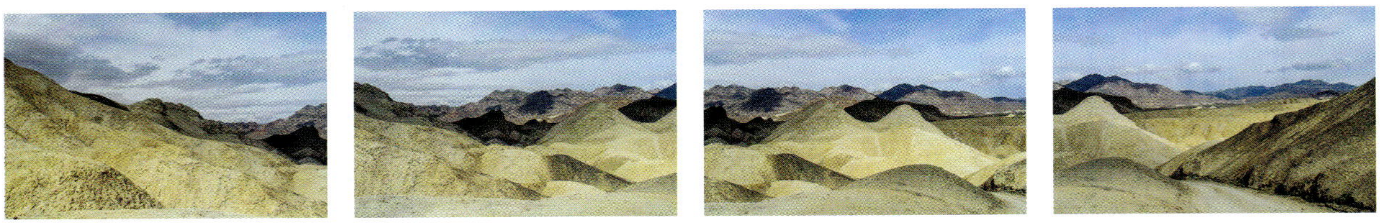

Figure 10.3
Here you see the makings of a panorama, with four shots overlapping by about 30 percent from frame to frame.

ISO 400 • 1/125 sec. • f/14 • 24mm lens

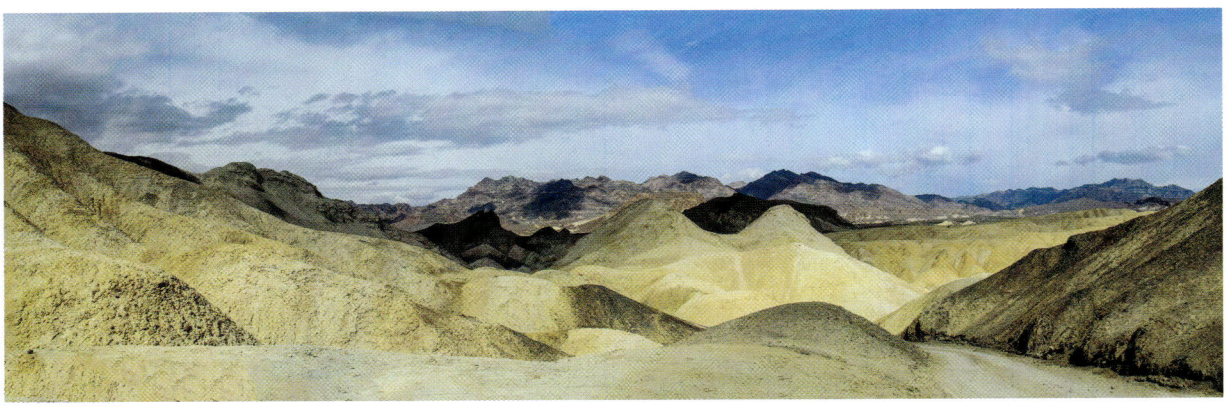

Figure 10.4
I used Adobe Photoshop to combine all of the exposures into one large panoramic image.

Shooting properly for a multiple-image panorama

1. Mount your camera on your tripod and make sure it is level.
2. Choose a focal length for your lens that is, ideally, somewhere between 35mm and 50mm. (I used an 18mm here, which worked well, but a wide-angle lens can distort the edges, making it harder to stitch together.)
3. In Av mode, use a very small aperture for the greatest depth of field. Take a meter reading of a bright part of the scene, and make note of it.
4. Change your camera to Manual mode (M), and dial in the aperture and shutter speed that you obtained in the previous step.
5. Set your lens to manual focus, and then focus your lens for the area of interest using the HFD method of finding a point one-third of the way into the scene. (If you use the autofocus, you risk getting different points of focus from image to image, which will make the image stitching more difficult for the software.) If you want to use the autofocus to set your initial point of focus, just remember to set the lens to Manual Focus (MF) before shooting your images.
6. While carefully panning your camera, shoot your images to cover the entire area of the scene from one end to the other, leaving a 30 percent overlap from one frame to the next.

Sorting your shots for the multi-image panorama

If you shoot more than one series of shots for your panoramas, it can sometimes be difficult to know when one series of images ends and the other begins. Here is a quick tip for separating your images.

Set up your camera using the steps listed here. Now, before you take your first good exposure in the series, hold up one finger in front of the camera and take a shot. Now move your hand away and begin taking your overlapping images. When you have taken your last shot, hold two fingers in front of the camera and take another shot.

When you go to review your images, use the series of shots that falls between the frames with one and two fingers in them. Then just repeat the process for your next panorama series.

Shooting high dynamic range (HDR) images

One of the more recent trends in photography is the use of high dynamic range (HDR) to capture the full range of tonal values in your final image. Typically, when you photograph a scene that has a wide range of tones from dark shadows to bright highlights, you have to decide which tonal values you are going to emphasize, and then adjust your exposure accordingly. This is because your camera has a limited dynamic range, at least as compared to the human eye. HDR photography allows you to capture multiple exposures for the highlights, shadows, and midtones, and then combine them into a single image (**Figures 10.5** through **10.8**). Not long ago you would have needed a software application to combine all of the images together and map the different tones into an acceptable range, but not with the 7D Mark II. This is the first camera produced by Canon that actually does all the work for you, along with providing some artistic choices for the final image.

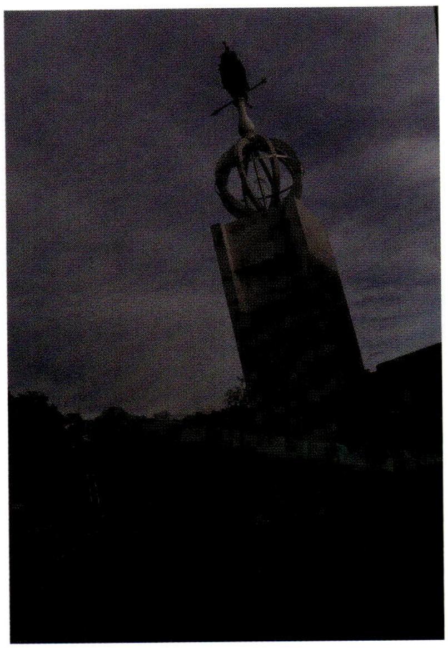

Figure 10.5
Underexposing two stops will render more detail in the highlight areas of the clouds and sky.

ISO 100 • 1/4000 sec. • f/5.6 • 18mm lens

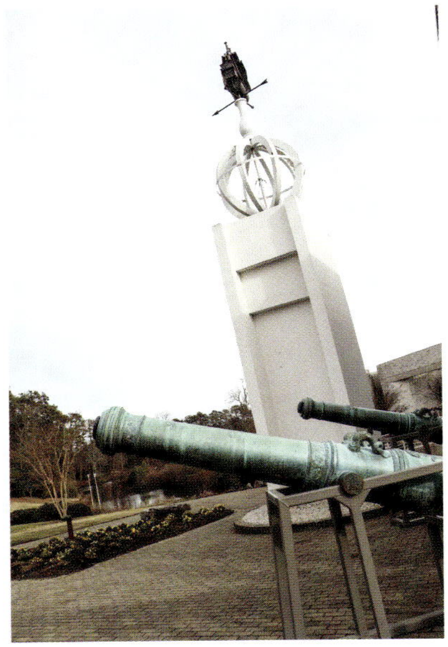

Figure 10.6
This is the normal exposure as dictated by the camera meter.

ISO 100 • 1/1000 sec. • f/5.6 • 18mm lens

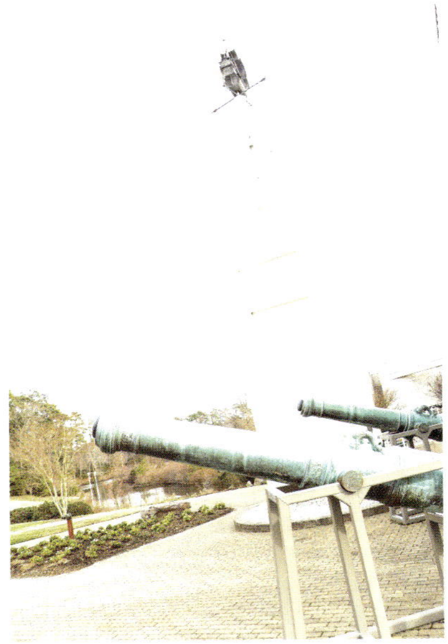

Figure 10.7
Overexposing by two stops ensures that the darker areas are exposed to get detail in the shadows.

ISO 100 • 1/250 sec. • f/5.6 • 18mm lens

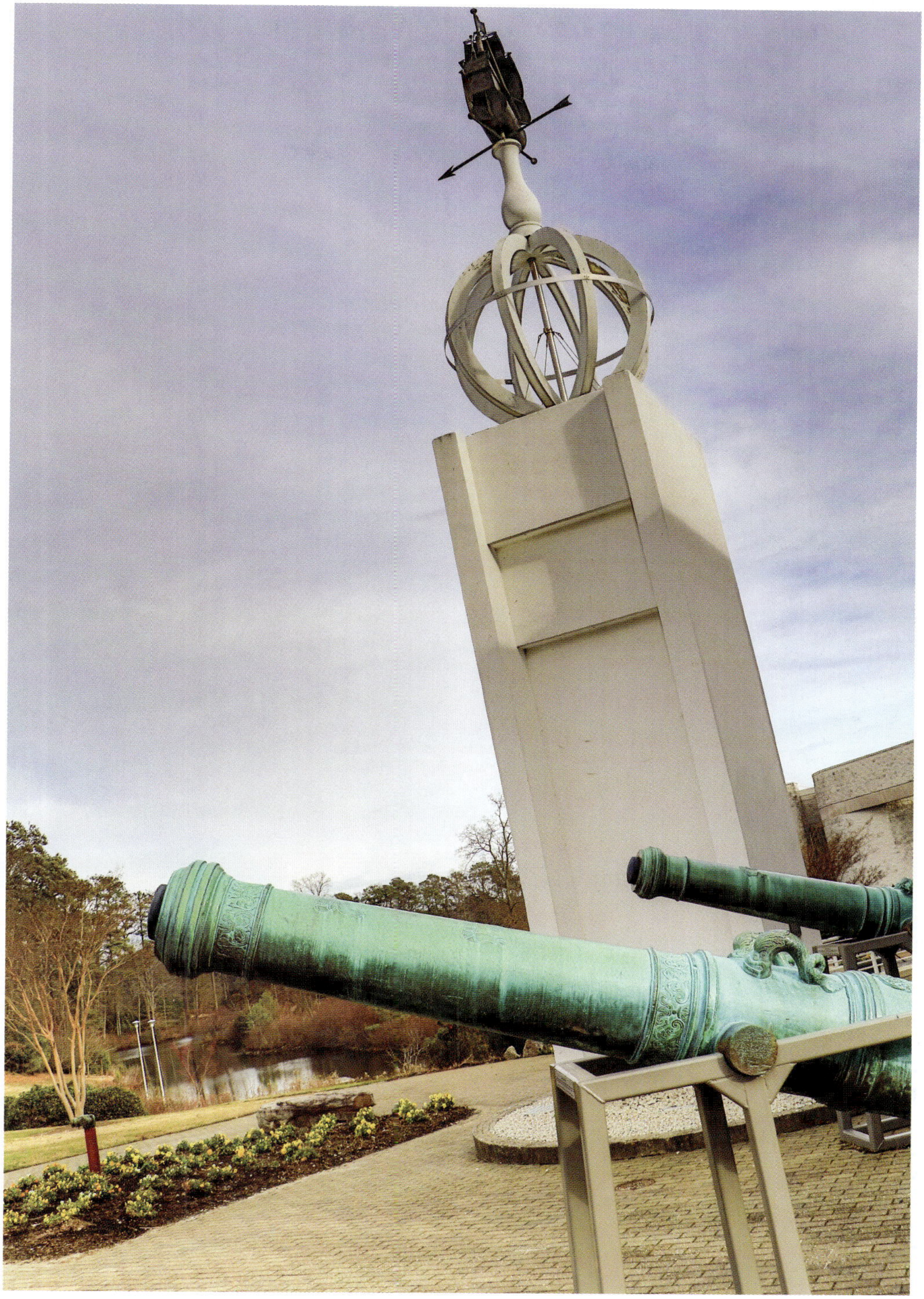

Figure 10.8
This is the final HDR image that was rendered from the three other exposures you see here.

Setting up for shooting an HDR image

1. Set your ISO to 100, if possible, to ensure clean, noise-free images.
2. Set your program mode to Av. During the shooting process, you will be taking three shots of the same scene, creating an overexposed image, an underexposed image, and a normal exposure. The camera is going to be adjusting the exposure by using the shutter speed, not the aperture, so that your depth of field is consistent. (Even if the camera is set to Tv mode, the camera will still make shutter speed adjustments when using the HDR option.)
3. Set your camera file format to JPEG or RAW+JPEG. The camera will produce a JPEG file as the completed HDR image, but you can choose to save the source files, so having the RAW files could come in handy.
4. Press the Creative Photo button on the back of the camera, and then use the Quick Control dial to navigate to the HDR option, and press Set (**A**).
5. Go to the Adjust Dyn Range option, and press Set (**B**).

A

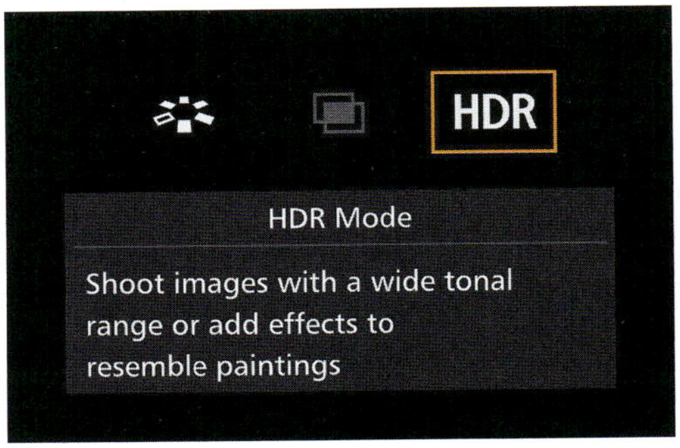

B

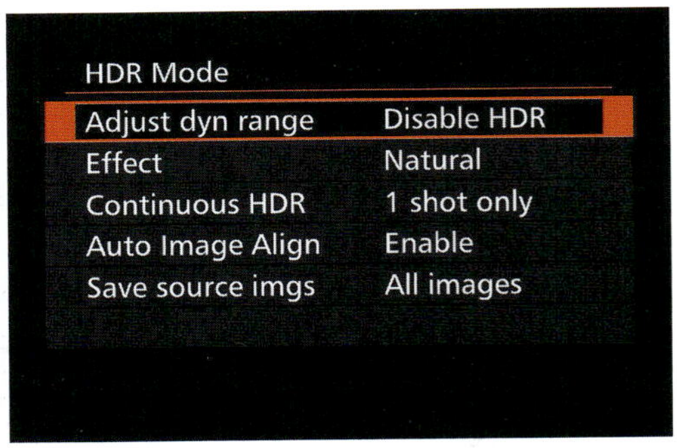

6. Select the amount of dynamic range you want to cover, from Auto to + and – 3 stops. I prefer to use the 2EV option, which provides 2 stops of over, 2 stops of under, as well as a normal exposure (**C**).

C

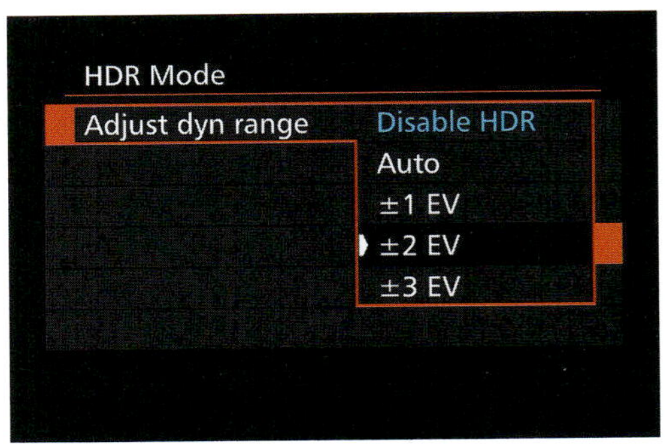

7. The next step is to select how much effect you want applied to your image. The default effect is Natural, but if you would like something a bit more artistic, highlight this option, and then press Set (**D**).

D

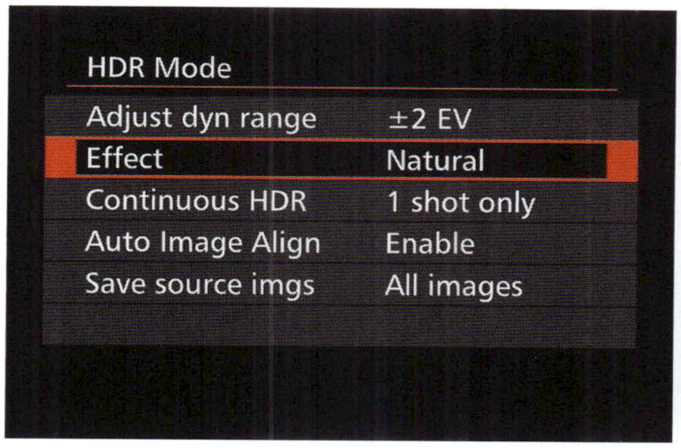

E

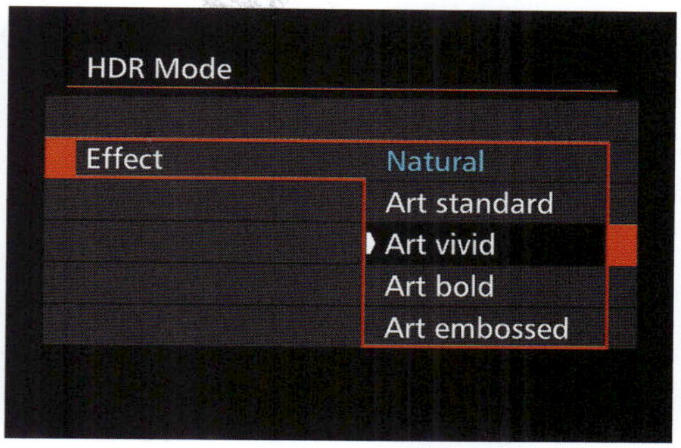

8. There are five different effects that you can apply to your final image, and I suggest that you give them all a try to see which one is best for your subject. My preference is the Art Vivid setting, which adds vibrancy and sharpness to the final image (**E**).

There are also options for Continuous HDR that let you choose between doing one HDR image or continuously shooting HDR images until you turn off the feature; an Auto Image Align feature that you can turn off if you have your camera on a tripod; and a Save Source Imgs option that lets you keep all the source images along with the final HDR or just the HDR image alone. These options can all be changed later as you decide how you would like your HDR workflow to operate.

Once you are happy with your choices, you can lightly press the shutter release button to return to shooting mode. You should see an HDR indication in the rear and top LCD screens. Now simply compose your shot and press the shutter release button. The camera will take three successive photographs, and then create the final HDR image based on your settings. It might take a little time before you see the final image on the rear screen.

Bracketing your exposures

In HDR, bracketing is the process of capturing a series of exposures at different stop intervals. You can bracket your exposures even if you aren't going to be using HDR. Sometimes this is helpful when you have a tricky lighting situation and you want to ensure that you have just the right exposure to capture the look you're after. You can bracket in increments as small as one-third of a stop. This means that you can capture several images with very subtle exposure variances, and then decide later which one is best.

To get the best HDR results, be sure that you are using an aperture that will let you handhold the camera steady for all three exposures. For the best results, you might want to consider using a tripod or putting your camera on a steady surface to get the best alignment for your images. If your final image is too light or dark, try using some Exposure Compensation.

Auto Lighting Optimizer

Did you know that your camera provides a function that can automatically make your pictures look better? It's called Auto Lighting Optimizer. It works this way: The camera evaluates the tones in your image, and then lightens any areas that it believes are too dark or lacking in contrast (**Figure 10.9** and **Figure 10.10**). This is different than the HDR, because it is only working on a single exposure and boosting the shadows while pulling the exposure down slightly to darken the highlights. This optimization is applied automatically in the Intelligent Auto shooting mode.

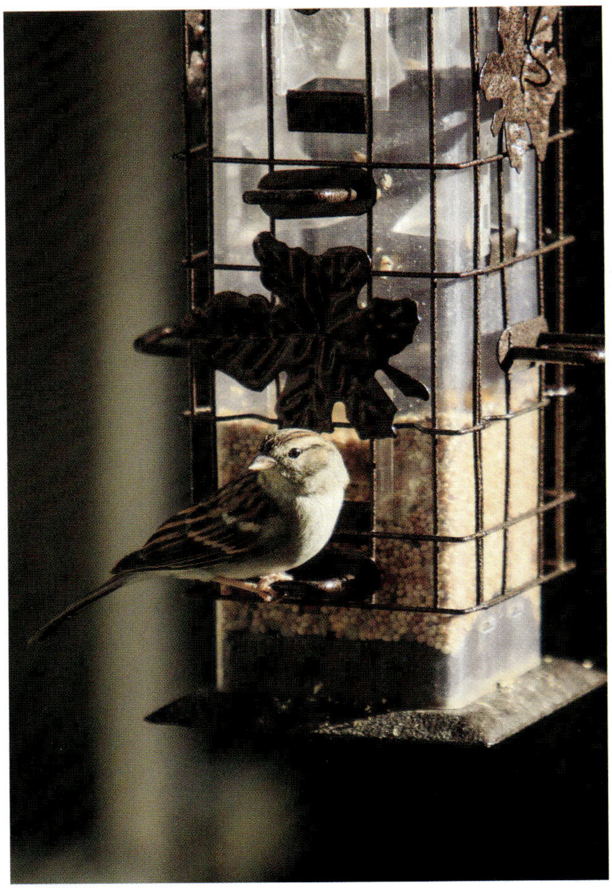

Figure 10.9
Without the Auto Lighting Optimizer, the shadows are dark and contrasty.

ISO 800 • 1/400 sec. • f/4 • 280mm lens

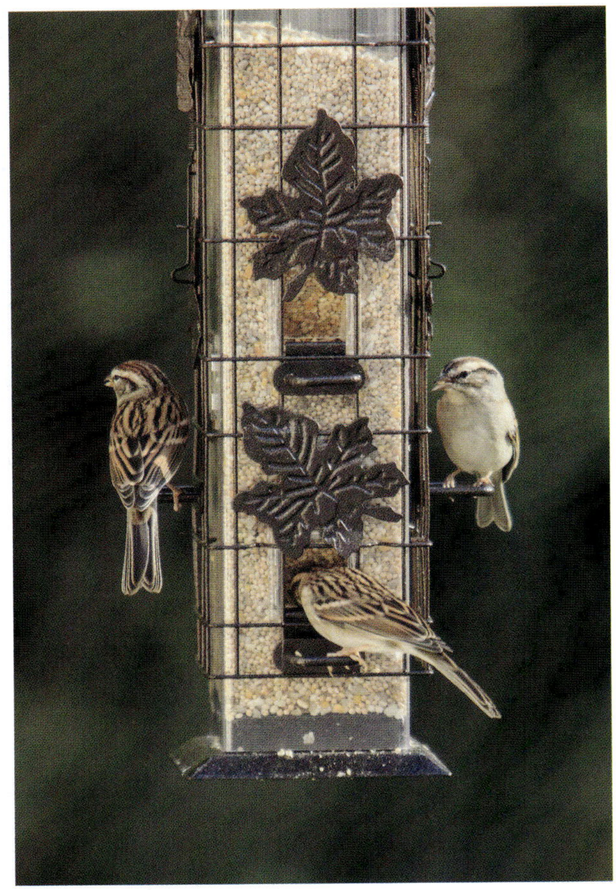

Figure 10.10
Although the exposure hasn't changed, the shadows are brighter after changing the Optimizer to the Strong setting.

ISO 800 • 1/400 sec. • f/4 • 280mm lens

You can choose from four levels: Disable, Low, Standard, and High. You will need to evaluate the strength of the effect on your images and change it accordingly. I typically leave it set to Standard so that I have brighter, more detailed shadow areas in my photographs. If you are using exposure compensation to darken your image, you might find that your image is too bright with this option turned on. Also, you should disable it if you are using Flash Exposure Compensation, since it will try to work against you when you alter the flash strength. As always, you need to keep in mind that this function only applies to JPEG images. If you are shooting RAW only, you might see the effect in your image review screen, but it won't be applied to the final RAW image.

Setting up the Auto Lighting Optimizer

1. Press the Menu button and use the Main dial to get to the second Shooting menu tab; then highlight Auto Lighting Optimizer and press the Set button (**A**).

A

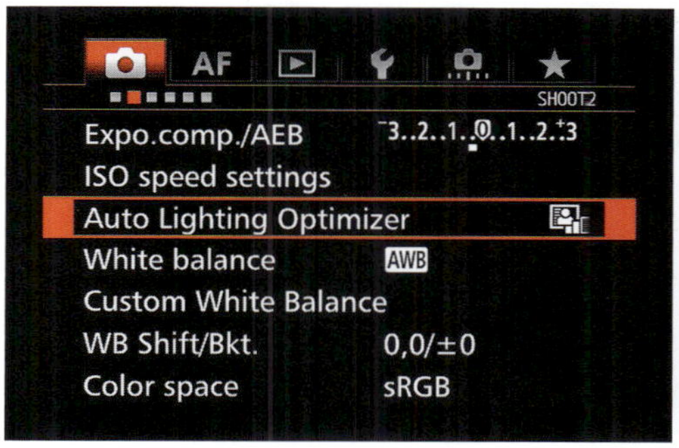

B

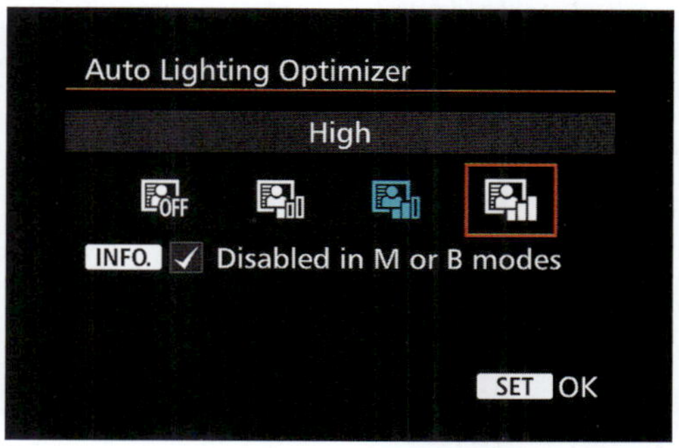

2. Use the Quick Control dial to select the level of optimization that you prefer, and press the Set button to lock in the change (**B**).

Friday Night Flicker

When I first started shooting high school football games I had to deal with a really annoying problem: light flicker. This is a problem that is not readily visible while shooting, or even when watching a game. But it quickly becomes apparent while reviewing images. The first time I came across it, I thought something was wrong with my camera. I tried everything I could think of, but I still had the same problem of random poor exposures (**Figure 10.11**). Then I found out that it wasn't the camera but the lights in the stadium. The problem is the way that most small stadium, and even indoor sports lighting, is wired. Not to get technical, but the lights tend to cycle at a certain frequency that can create poor exposures and color shifts. Your eyes don't see it, but when you start shooting rapid frame captures at very fast shutter speeds, it will most certainly mess with your images.

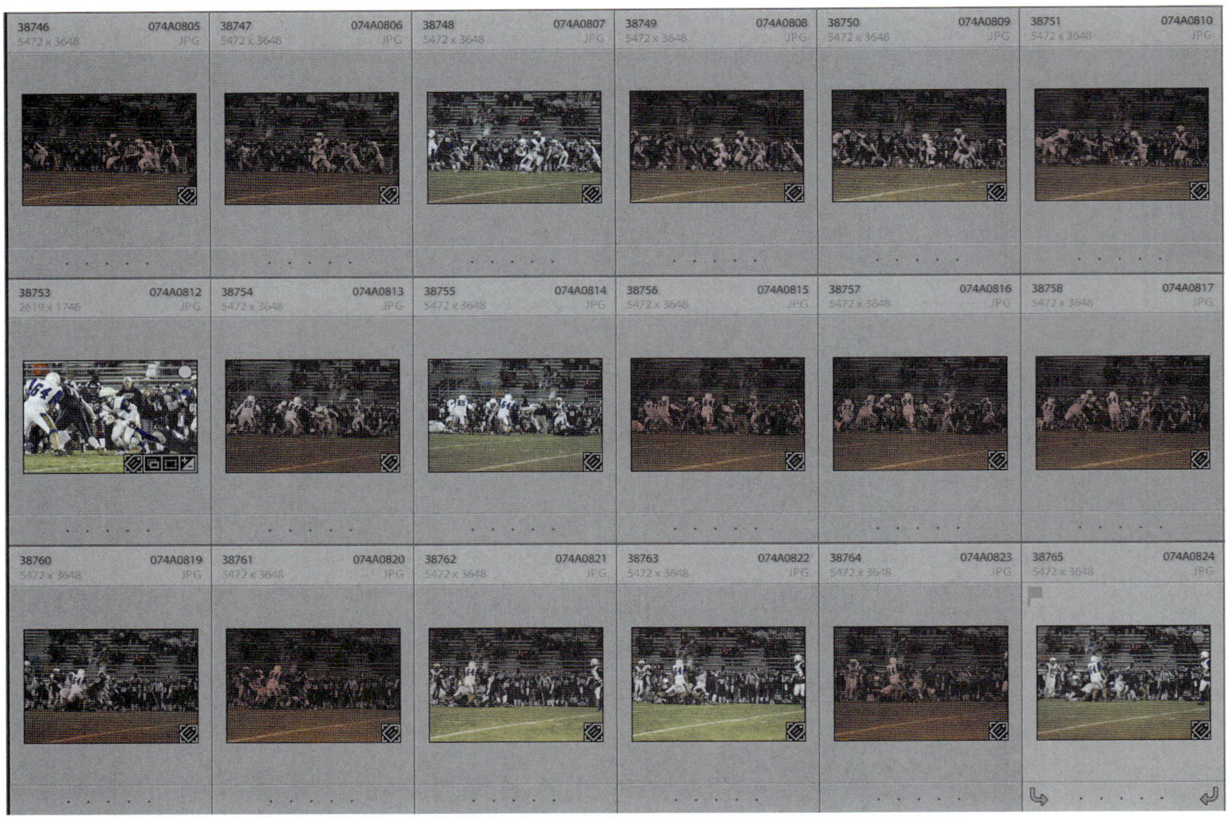

Figure 10.11
This is typical of the random exposure problems that occur from shooting under stadium lights.

ISO 8000 • 1/800 sec. • f/2.8 • 200mm lens

Typically, what you will see are a few good exposures and a bunch of poorly exposed images. The only way to combat this problem was to either shoot at about 1/60 of a second (not really an option for sports), or shoot a lot of images and hope that you were lucky enough to get a good exposure during a crucial moment of the sequence. That was the case until the 7D Mark II came along with its anti-flicker technology. This has not received a lot of mention in press releases, but if you shoot sports at night, it is one of the biggest innovations to come along in some time.

When you engage the Anti-flicker function, the camera will analyze the frequency of the light you are shooting in and then time the camera exposures at the moment when the lighting is optimal. Even though it is limiting the frame rate slightly, there is no perceptible change in speed when using it. The easiest way to know when you should turn it on is to just look through your viewfinder. If the camera sees lighting conditions that might interfere with your exposures, it will display the word Flicker in the viewfinder. This is your clue to turn on the Anti-flicker setting.

Turning on Anti-flicker

1. Press the Menu button and navigate to the fourth shooting menu.
2. Use the Quick Control dial to highlight the Anti-Flicker Shoot. menu option, and press Set (**A**).
3. Set the option to Enable, and press the Set button to lock it in (**B**).

A

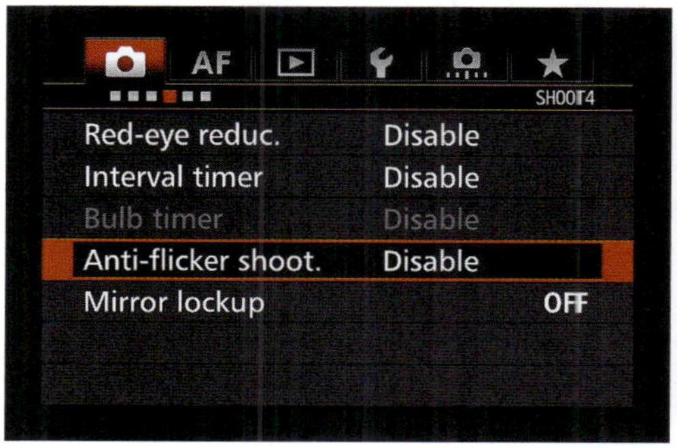

B

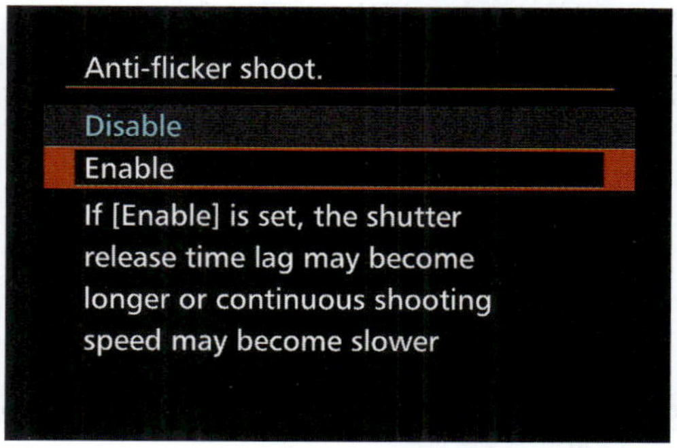

4. Press the Menu button or shutter release button to return to shooting mode.

For the best results, you should set your camera's shooting mode to Tv or M to keep a consistent shutter speed (**Figure 10.12**). Also, Anti-flicker will not work with Live View shooting or in movie mode, so plan on shooting with the viewfinder if you find yourself in need of some flicker reduction.

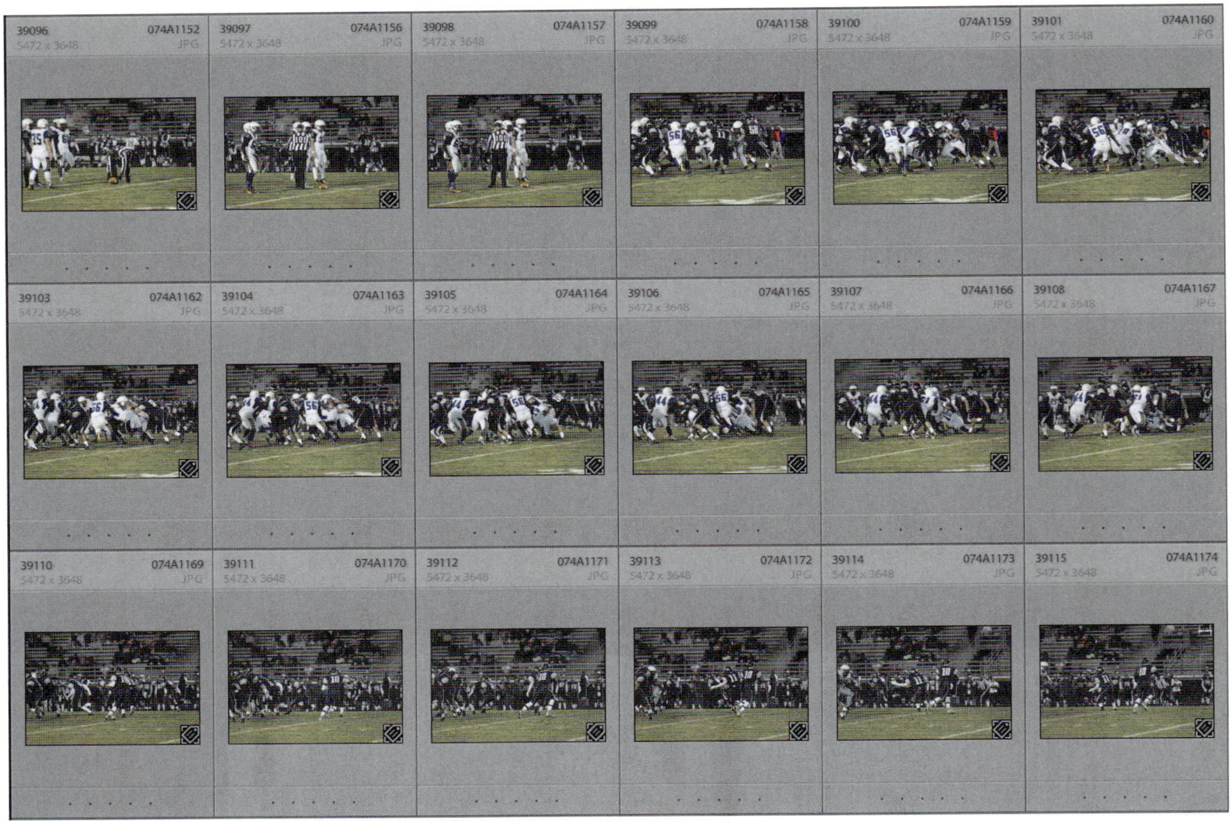

Figure 10.12

After you apply the Anti-flicker function, exposures and colors remain consistent from image to image.

ISO 8000 • 1/800 sec. • f/2.8 • 200mm lens

Customizing Your Camera Layout

Have you ever picked up a camera and thought, "Gee, I really wish this button was over there." Well, you are in luck because the 7D Mark II has the ability to reassign the functions of most of its buttons and dials. You can completely customize the layout of your camera to personalize it to your needs. The customization options also make it easier to get to some functions that are usually accessible only by going to the menu system. For example, I usually shoot with the RAW file format, but there are times when I would like to have a JPEG image as well. Using the customizations, I can reprogram the M-Fn button to change the camera to RAW+JPEG mode with a simple press of the button. Another modification I like to make is to the Set button. When taking a photo, I will often zoom in on the preview to check details and focus. Instead of having to find the zoom button on the left side of the camera, I assign the zoom function to the Set button, where I can quickly locate it and zoom in on my shot. Numerous customizations are available that are laid out in table format on pages 446–449 of your manual. I find that the best way to customize is to explore the settings in the customization menu system.

Setting customized controls

1. Press the Menu button and navigate to the third Custom Function menu.
2. Highlight the Custom Controls option, and press Set (**A**).
3. Use the Quick Control dial to highlight the button, switch, or dial you want to customize, and press Set (**B**).

A

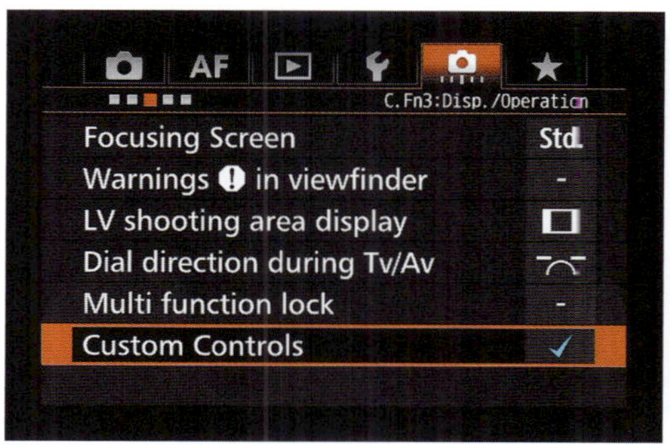

B

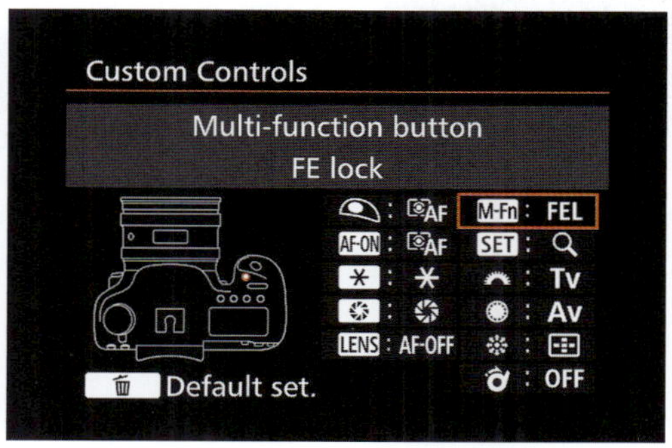

4. Pick the function that you want to assign to the control, and press the Set button to lock in the change (**C**).
5. Continue customizing the controls as desired, and then press the Menu button twice to exit the menus and return to shooting mode.

C

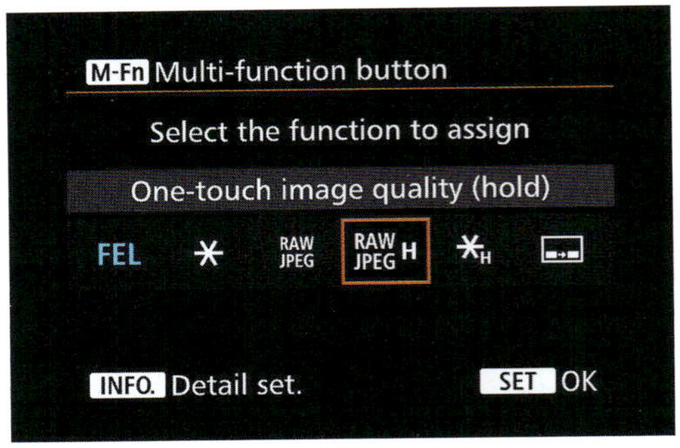

There are a couple of things that you should be aware of when creating customizations. The first is that each control has a limited number of customizations, so you won't be able to assign any function to any control. You need to look at the options available for each control. Also, the controls will not reset to default by using the Clear All Custom Func. option in the fifth Custom Functions menu. To reset all of the controls to their defaults, you need to go back into the Custom Controls menu and press the Erase button. It's the one with the trashcan icon on it.

Getting a custom view

The customization of your camera doesn't need to end with just the camera controls. You can also customize the information that you view through the viewfinder. This is a great feature that puts the information you need right in front of you so that you don't need to take your eye away from the viewfinder and possibly miss that all-important shot. You can also include a grid overlay and camera-level indicator if you need it. These can be handy tools for composing your shot. I like having my shooting functions displayed as a reminder of my settings. I also like having the Flicker alert turned on so I know when there are lighting conditions that might require me to turn on the Anti-flicker function.

Customizing the viewfinder

1. Press the Menu button and navigate to the second Setup menu screen, highlight Viewfinder Display, and press Set (**A**).
2. To turn on the level, highlight the Viewfinder Level option, press Set, and then choose Show and press Set.
3. To turn on the grid, highlight the VF Grid Display option, press Set, and then choose Enable and press Set.

A

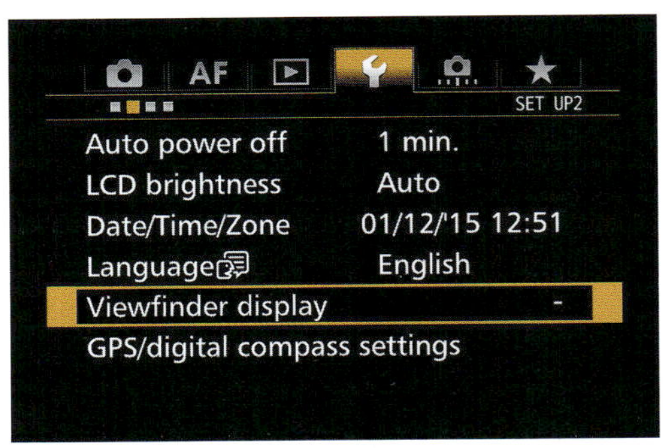

4. To turn on the shooting function options, highlight the Show/Hide In Viewfinder option and press Set (**B**).
5. Use the Quick Control dial to highlight an option, and press the Set button to add a checkmark to it. Keep repeating this process until you have all of the options marked that you wish to add to the viewfinder (**C**).

B

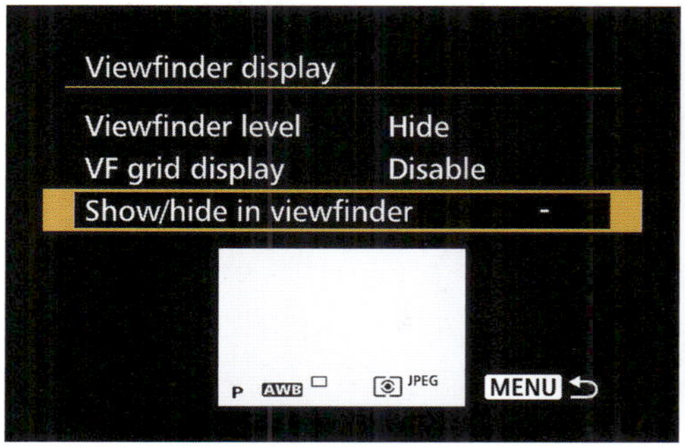

C

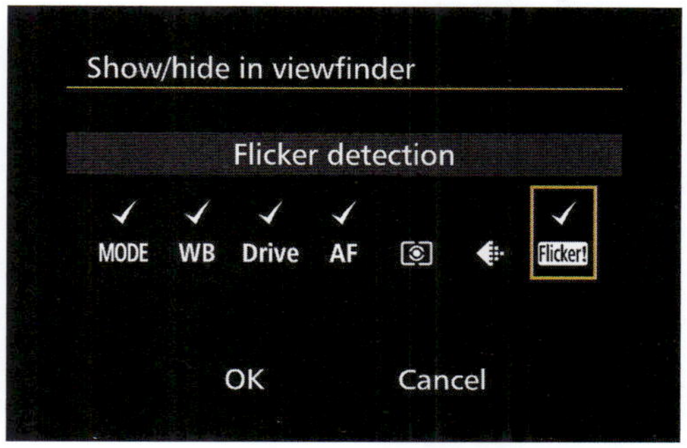

6. Highlight the OK option to set in your changes, and press the Set button.
7. Press the Menu button twice to return to shooting mode.
8. Now that you have the options enabled, all you need to do is look through your viewfinder and press the shutter button lightly to activate all of the screen information (**Figure 10.13**).

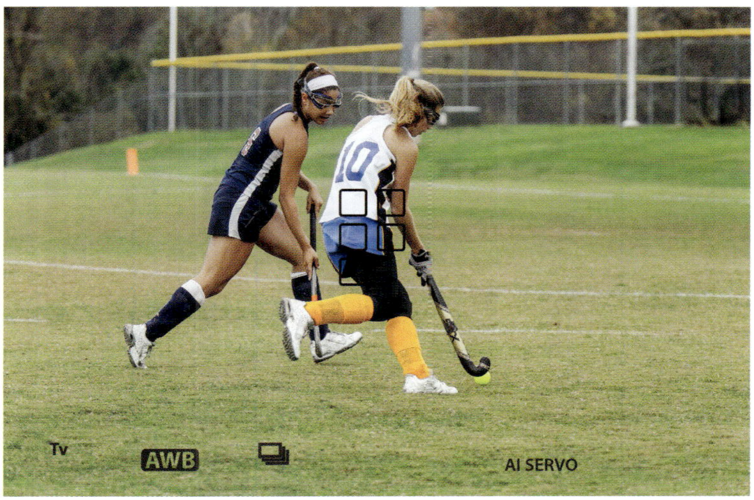

Figure 10.13
Customizing the viewfinder lets you keep up with your settings while you shoot.

The My Menu setting

If you don't like sorting through all the menus to get to the options that you use most frequently, the My Menu setting was made for you. It lets you choose the menu items that you want to quickly access and puts them all in one easy-to-find location. You can add six items to the menu, but if that isn't enough, you can create more menu tabs to add even more options. You even have the choice of naming each tab and hiding the normal menus in favor of your customized menu tabs. It really is the ultimate in customizations. Of course, I recommend that you use the camera for a while to discover what menu items you access the most, and then keep a list so that you can organize your menu options in the best order possible. You can see the menu I created for my personal use in **Figure 10.14**.

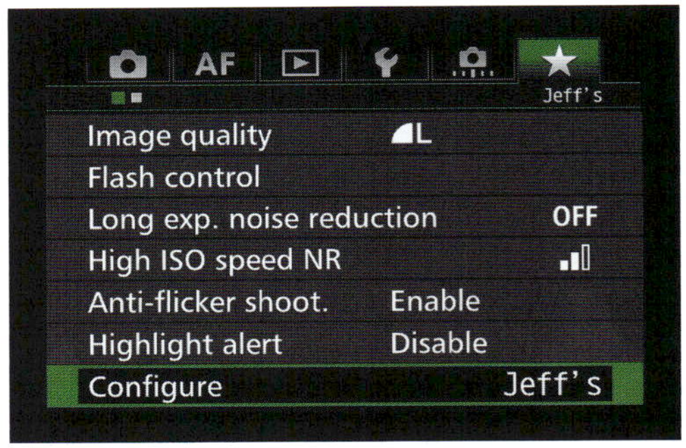

Figure 10.14
Here are the six functions I have stored in the My Menu function.

Creating menu tabs

1. Press the Menu button, and select the tab with the Star, using the Main dial.
2. Select Add My Menu Tab, and press Set (**A**).
3. Verify that you want to add the screen by highlighting OK and pressing Set.
4. At the next screen, Configure will be highlighted. Simply press the Set button to enter the configuration screen.
5. Here, you have many options, but the first thing to do is to register some menu items to the My Menu tab. Highlight the Select Items To Register option, and press Set (**B**).

A

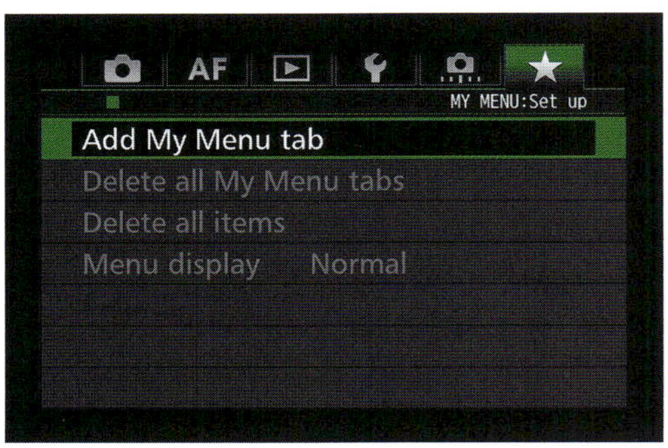

B

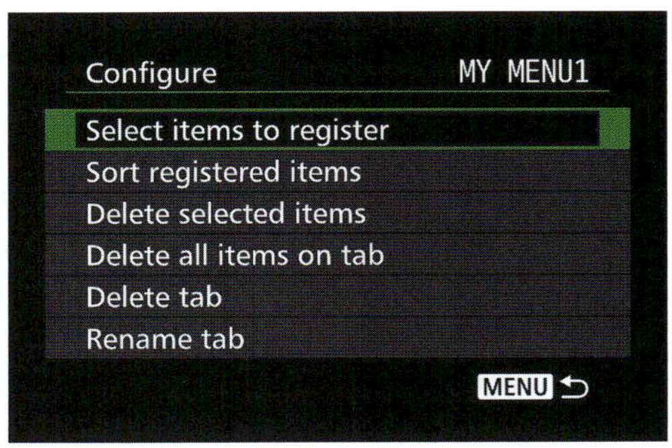

6. You will now see a list of just about every menu item in the camera. Use the Quick Control dial to highlight an item, and press Set to add it to your list (**C**).
7. You will get a verification screen after selecting an item. Just press OK to add it, and then go back to the list to select more items (**D**).

C

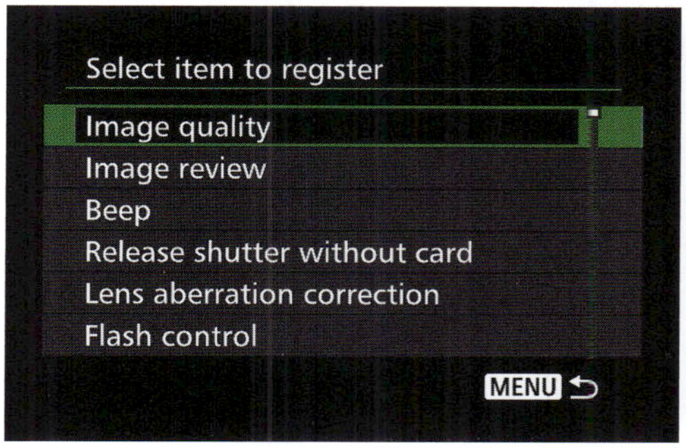

D

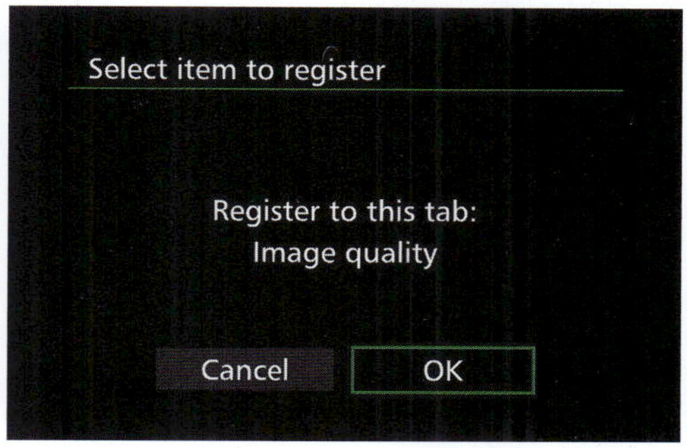

8. You can only add six items to each menu tab before having to create a new tab.

Once you are done, you have the option of sorting the items, deleting added items, adding new items, deleting all the items in the tab, or even deleting the tab itself. You can also rename the tab, which might be handy if you want to group items with n different tabs. You can also go back to the first My Menu setup menu screen, and then go to the Menu Display option to choose how your customized menu is seen. You can even choose to hide all of the regular menus, showing just the My Menu tabs that you created (**Figure 10.15**).

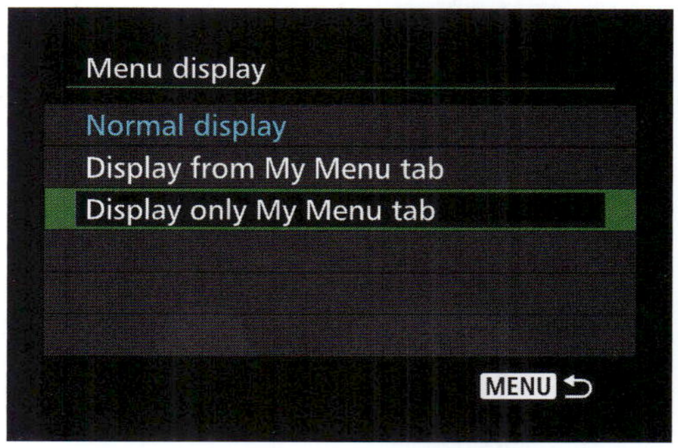

Figure 10.15
My Menu lets you hide the standard menus and display only your customized items.

Creating custom shooting modes

Some of the customization features that I use the most on the 7D Mark II are the custom shooting modes. They are found on the shooting mode dial, along with Tv, Av, P, etc. I like this custom mode so much because it allows me to instantly set up my camera to frequently used settings with a turn of the dial. For instance, I have a studio that I shoot in from time to time, and I often start with the same camera settings each time. That is to say that I have the Mode set to Manual, my shutter speed set to 1/200 of a second, my aperture at f/11, my white balance set to Flash, and my ISO set to 100. I may change those settings slightly, but they are usually the settings I use to begin my shooting session. With the custom mode, all I have to do is register all of those settings to one of the three custom modes, and presto, the next time I walk into my studio, all I have to do is turn the mode dial to that setting and I am ready to shoot. It is a tremendous timesaver, and I highly recommend you try it for any shooting scenario you frequently find yourself in, be it landscapes, night sports, HDR, or you name it. The best part is that it is incredibly easy to set up.

Setting up the custom mode

The most important step is to set up your camera for the shooting scenario that you want to repeat. That means adjusting all of the camera and menu settings just as you would use for that situation.

1. Once you have everything set, press the Menu button, navigate to the fourth Setup menu, highlight Custom Shooting Mode (C1-C3), and press Set (**A**).
2. On the next screen, choose Register Settings, and press Set (**B**).

A

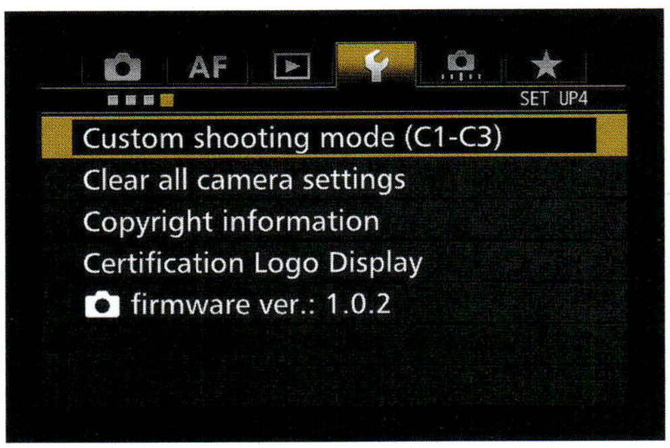

B

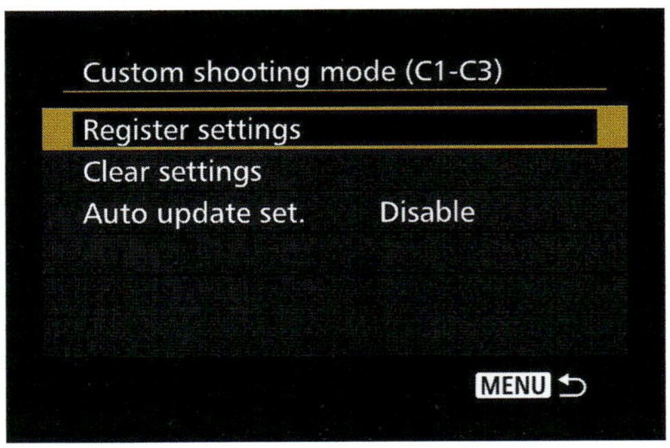

3. Choose the custom position on the dial where you would like to store your settings (C1, C2, or C3), highlight it, and press Set (**C**).

C

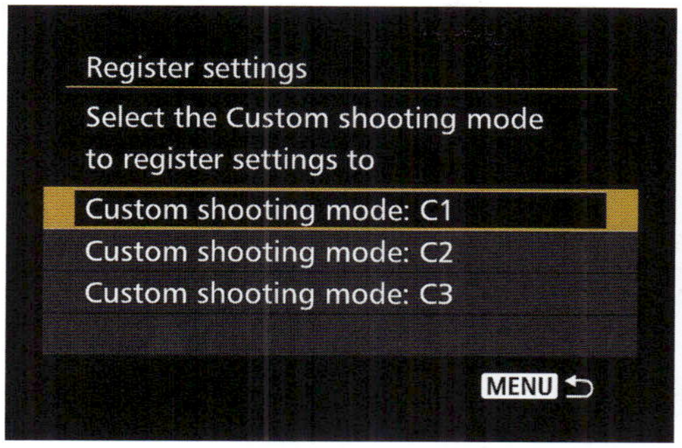

D

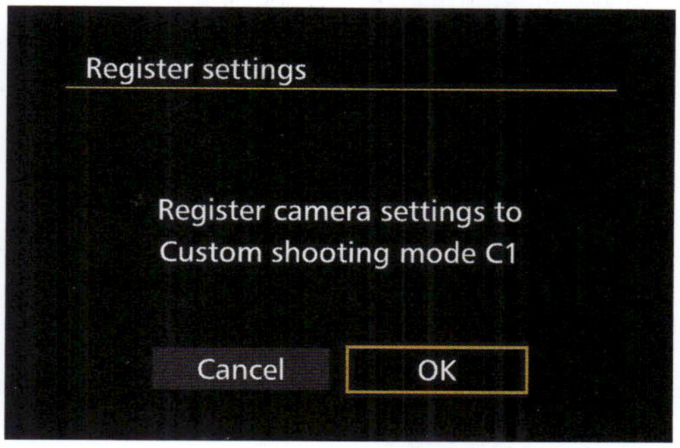

4. On the next screen, click OK to register your settings, and you are all set (**D**).

Customizing Your White Balance

Previous chapters have addressed the issue of setting your white balance, but what if you are in a situation that doesn't fall neatly into one of the existing categories like Daylight or Tungsten? You might want to consider creating a custom white balance. This is especially helpful if you are working in a mixed lighting scenario, where you have more than one kind of light source that is shining on your subject. A perfect example might be inside with fluorescent lighting fixtures overhead and daylight coming in through a window. To ensure that you are getting the best-possible results in a situation like this, you can perform a quick white balance customization by using the Custom White Balance option. Don't worry, though; it's easier than you might think. Typically, the only thing you will need is a piece of white paper.

Creating a Custom White Balance

1. Begin by having your subject hold a piece of white paper, and then take a picture of it. You can have the camera set on any white balance preset for this (**A**).
2. Press the Menu button and navigate to the second shooting menu, highlight Custom White Balance, and press the Set button (**B**).

A

B

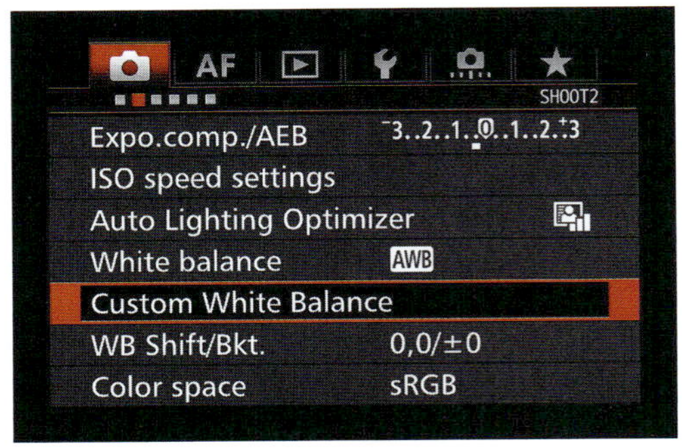

3. The camera should then display the photo that you took of the white paper. If it is the correct image, press the Set button. If not, use the Quick Control dial to locate the image (**C**).
4. Confirm that this is the image you want to use by highlighting the OK option and pressing Set (**D**).

C

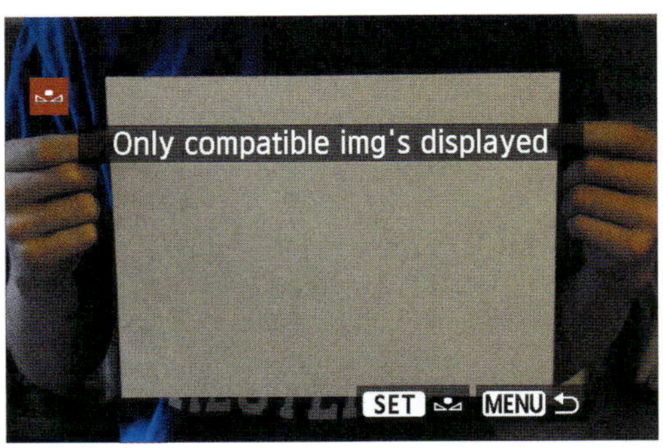

D

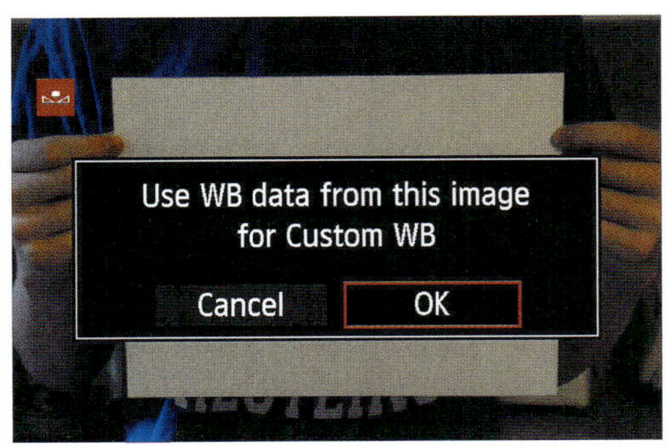

5. Click OK, and then change your camera to the Custom White Balance setting (**E**).

You are now ready to take images with much more accurate color for the environment where you are shooting.

E

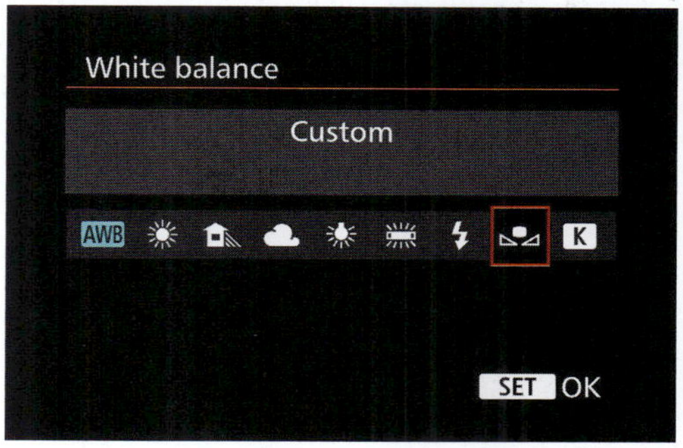

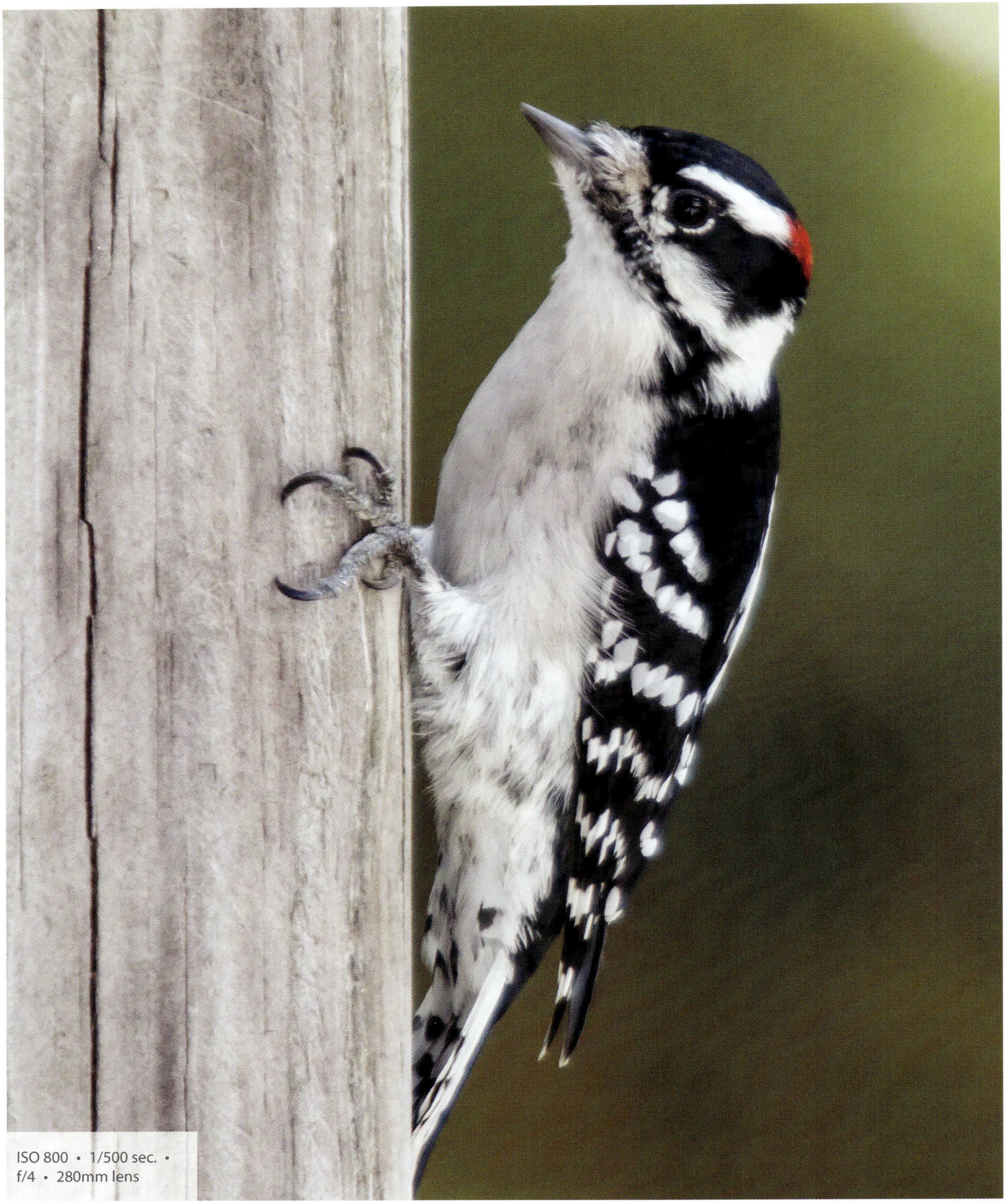

ISO 800 • 1/500 sec. • f/4 • 280mm lens

Chapter 10 Assignments

Many of the techniques covered in this chapter are specific to certain shooting situations that may not come about very often. This is even more reason to practice them, so that when the situation does present itself you will be ready.

Capture some highlights and shadows

One reason for not shooting in the middle of the day is the harsh lighting, which brings dark shadows and bright highlights that can be difficult to capture. Instead of putting the camera away, try shooting some HDR. Explore the different artistic options and see which settings work best for different subjects. Be warned, though—HDR shooting can be very addictive.

Customize your colors

Working in a mixed lighting environment can be very frustrating. Instead of settling for one of the predefined choices or Auto, why not try to create your own? All you need is a piece of white paper to take your colors from yuck to spot-on.

Capture a wide vista

Okay, this one requires some software magic, but it can give you some great results. The first method of creating a fake pano is really easy, and it can be completed with a crop tool in most any imaging software package. Just shoot really wide and with an eye for how you will crop it afterward. Adobe Photoshop CC, Photoshop Elements, and Windows Photo Gallery have panorama stitching programs. If you don't have access to one of those programs, Mac users can find a number of stitching programs by searching for panorama in the App Store. Once you have made a panorama, do yourself a favor and have it printed. It might just become your favorite form of photography.

Share your results with the book's Flickr group!
Join the group here: flickr.com/groups/7dmarkii_fromsnapshotstogreatshots

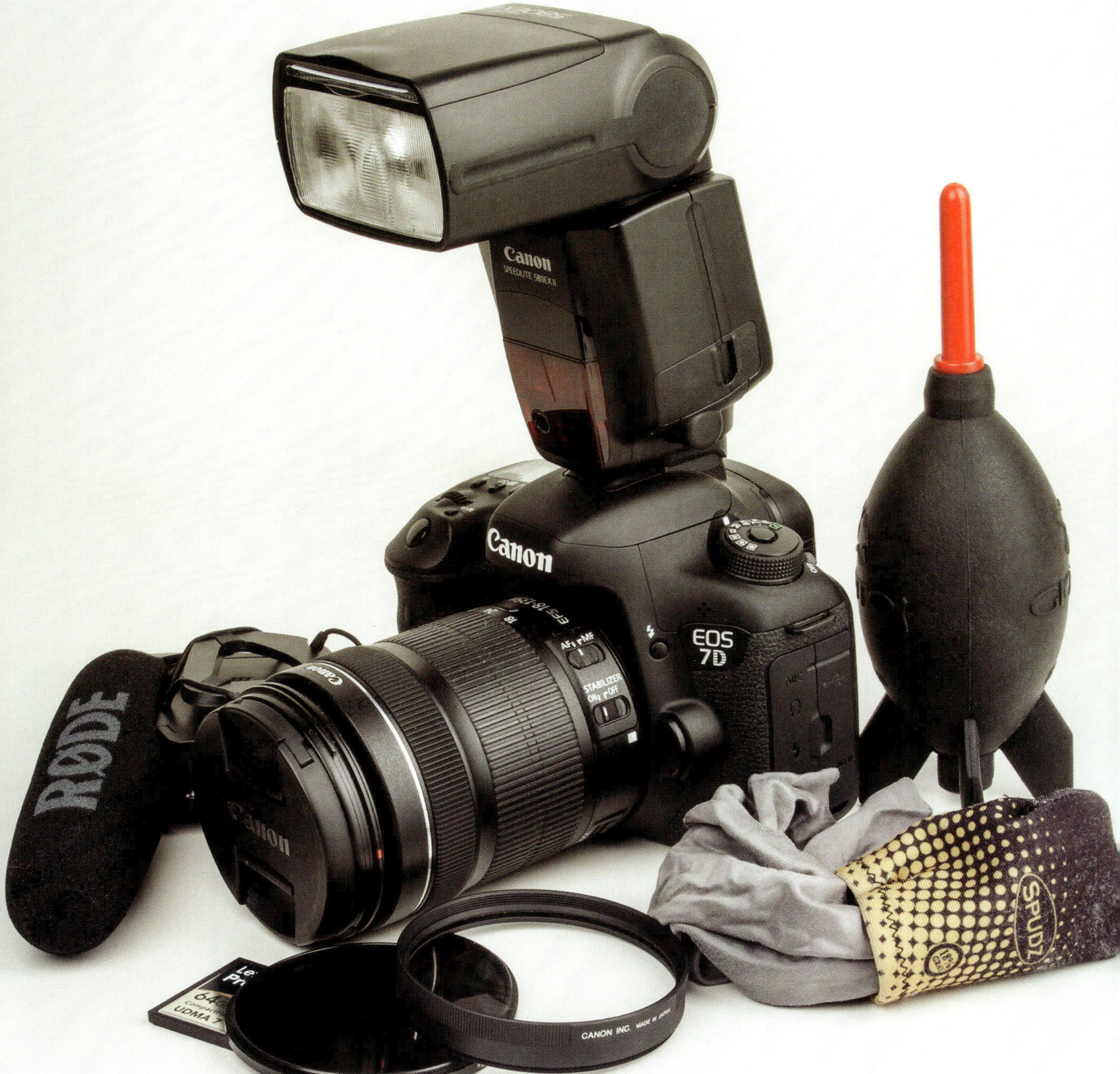

ISO 100 • 1/125 sec. •
f/16 • 32mm lens

11

Pimp My Ride

Upgrades and Accessories to Expand Your Camera's Creative Potential

If you bought your camera with a lens, you basically had everything you needed to begin shooting with your 7D Mark II. I took great care to ensure that almost all of the techniques covered in the book were not beyond your basic camera setup. That being said, some accessories are essential for certain types of photography. Other accessories aren't necessarily essential, but they will improve the look of your images.

Let's take a look at some items that I believe are must-have accessories for your photography.

Poring Over the Picture

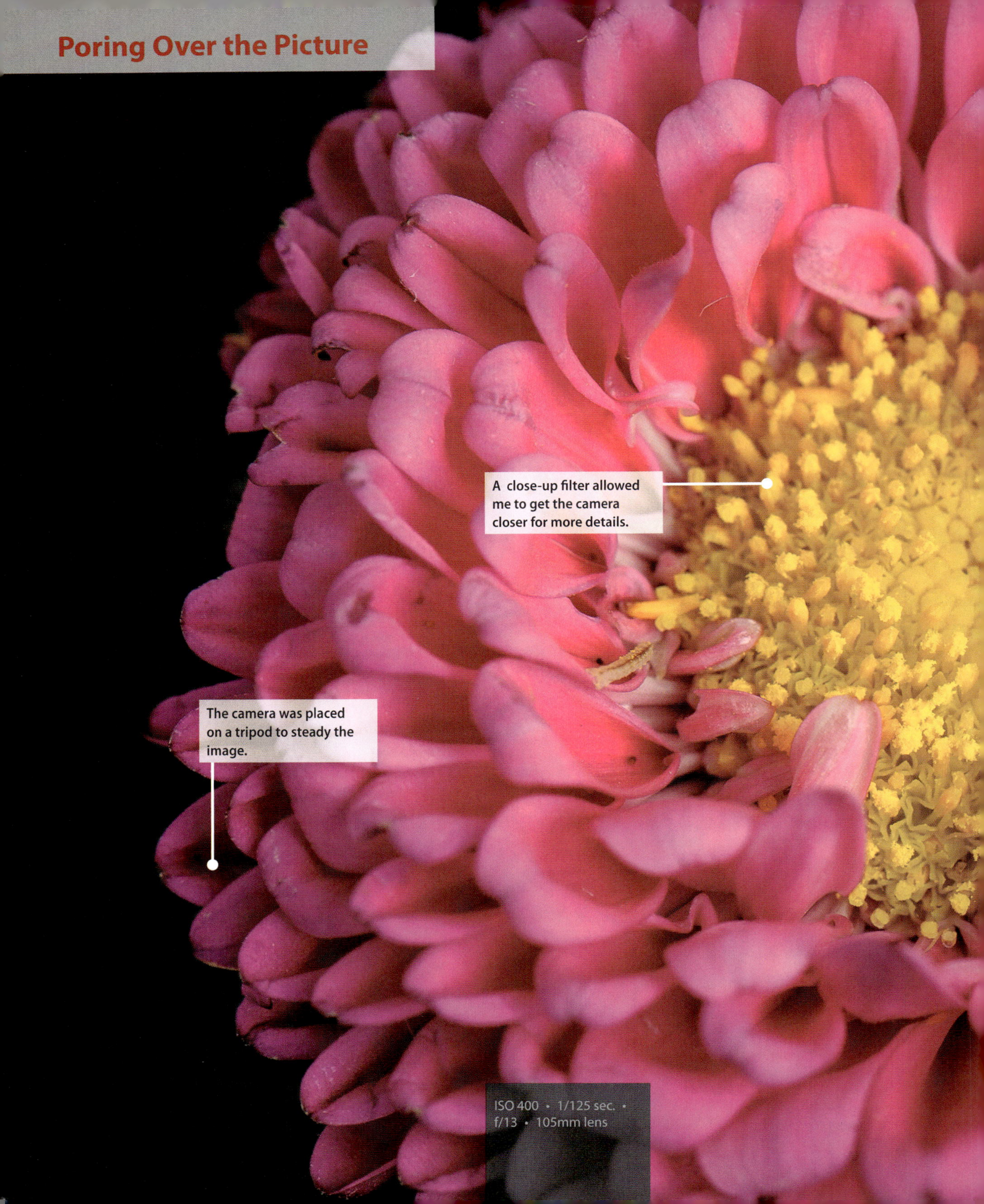

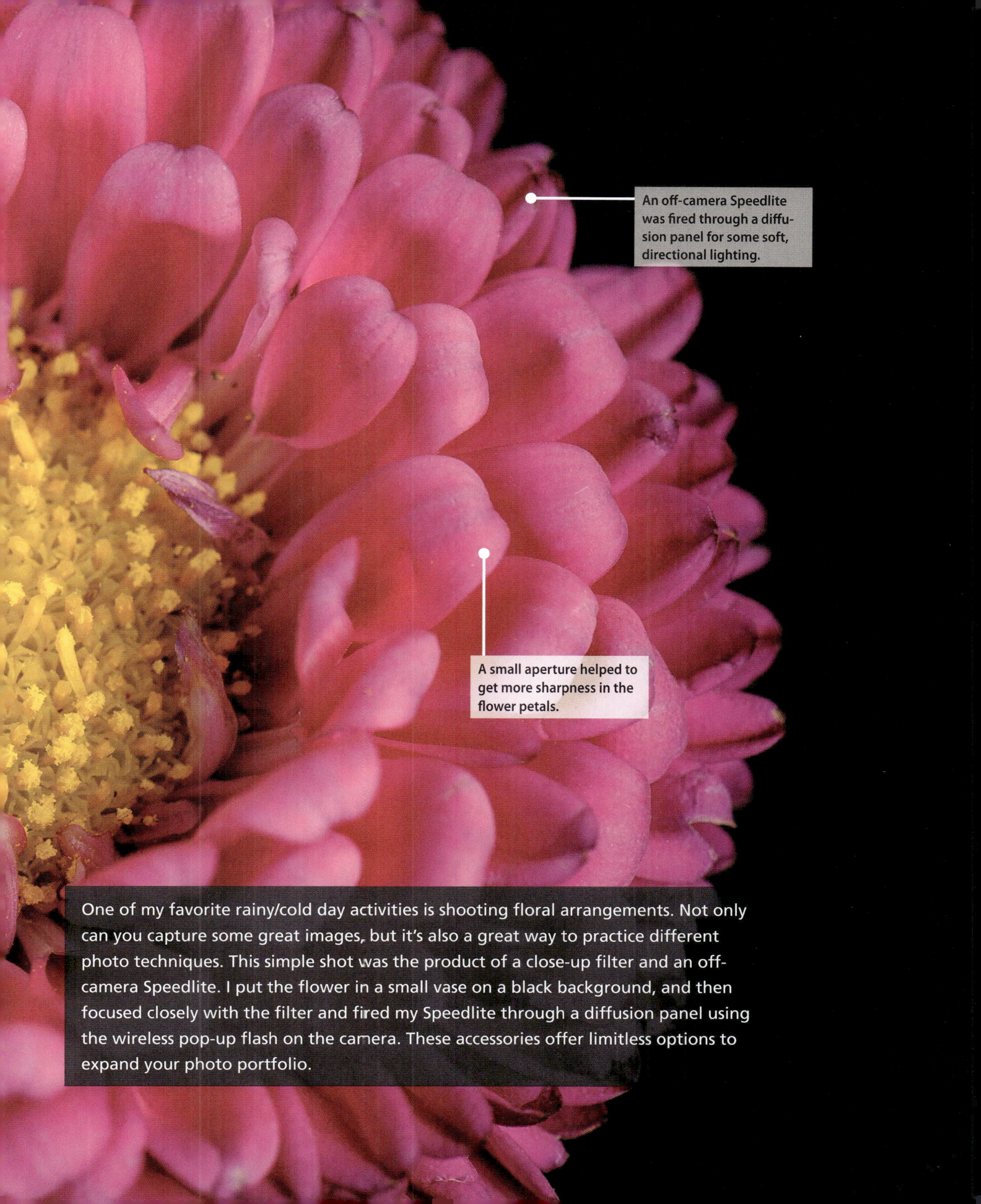

One of my favorite rainy/cold day activities is shooting floral arrangements. Not only can you capture some great images, but it's also a great way to practice different photo techniques. This simple shot was the product of a close-up filter and an off-camera Speedlite. I put the flower in a small vase on a black background, and then focused closely with the filter and fired my Speedlite through a diffusion panel using the wireless pop-up flash on the camera. These accessories offer limitless options to expand your photo portfolio.

Filters

You should have several filters in your camera bag. Each one serves a unique purpose. Some say that digital imaging programs such as Adobe Photoshop can duplicate the effects that the filters offer. This may be true, but I would rather screw on a filter than spend countless hours trying to replicate an effect on my computer. Here's another benefit to using a filter: lens protection.

Skylight

Probably the cheapest, yet best investment you can make for your camera is a skylight filter. This filter is used more for its protective effects than for any visual boost. At one point in time, the skylight/UV/haze filters were used to filter out UV light in order to add sharpness to distant subjects, correct a minute bluish color cast, or reduce the effects of haze in a film image. A digital camera offers the benefit of having filters that are built into the camera in front of the image sensor to eliminate the effects of haze, UV, and infrared light. Therefore, most of the visual benefits of using a skylight filter are not evident. So why, if there is no real visual difference, should you use a skylight filter? Because what it does offer is protection for your valuable lens for a relatively low price.

A Canon EF-S 18–135mm IS lens will cost you about $550. A 67mm HOYA Skylight 1B filter costs around $36. As someone who often either forgets or loses lens caps, it's reassuring to me that a $36 filter protects the precious glass on the front of my lens without degrading the quality of my image. If it does get scratched, I just unscrew it and buy another. That beats the heck out of $550 or thereabouts to replace or repair a scratched front lens element.

Polarizing

This one ranks right up there at the top of the list of must-own photography accessories. You won't find a self-respecting landscape photographer who doesn't have at least one polarizer in his or her camera bag (**Figure 11.1**).

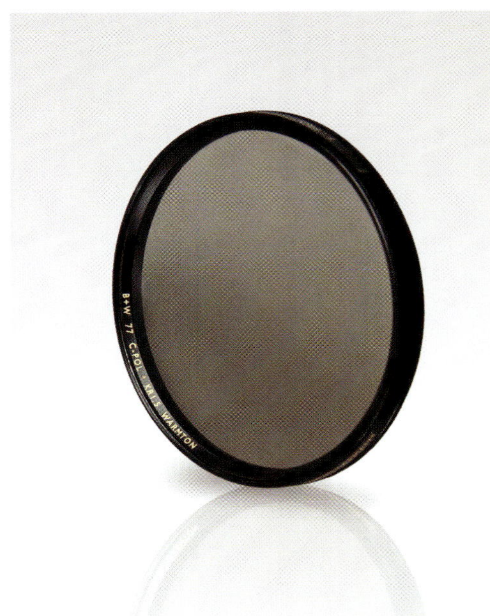

Figure 11.1
A B+W circular warming polarizing filter.

Light travels in straight lines, but the problem is that all those lines are moving in different directions. When they enter the camera lens, they are scattering about, creating color casts and other effects. The polarizer controls how light waves are allowed to enter the camera, only letting certain ones pass through. So what does that mean for you? Polarizing filters will make blue skies appear darker, vegetation color will be more accurate, colors will look more saturated, haze will be reduced, and images can look sharper (**Figure 11.2** and **Figure 11.3**). Not bad for a little piece of glass.

Most polarizers are circular and allow you to rotate the polarizing element to control the amount of polarization you need. As the filter is rotated, different light waves will be allowed to pass through, such as a reflection on a lake. Turn the filter a little and the light waves from the reflection are blocked, making the reflection disappear. Another benefit of the filter is that it is fairly dark, so when used in bright lighting conditions, it can act as a neutral density filter (you'll learn more in the next section), allowing you to use larger apertures or slower shutter speeds. The average polarizing filter requires an increase in exposure of about one-and-a-half stops. Figuring out your exposure change for the filter should not be an issue for you since you will be using the camera meter, which is already looking through the filter to calculate exposure settings. You should consider it, though, if your intention is to shoot with a fast shutter speed or use a small aperture for increased depth of field.

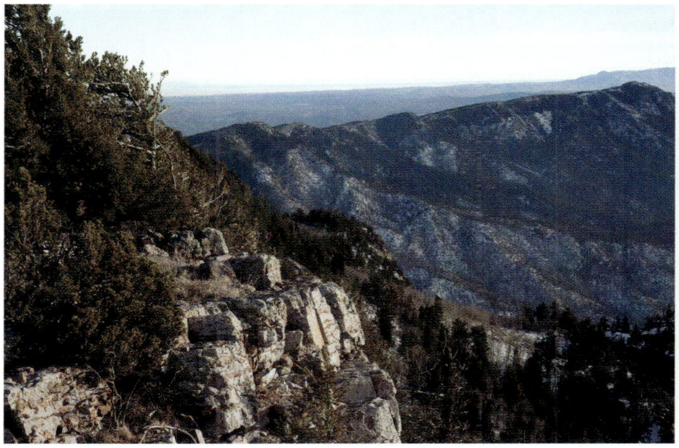

Figure 11.2
Without using the polarizing filter, the scene looks a little low on contrast and has a blue color cast from the sky.

ISO 800 • 1/125 sec. • f/11 • 120mm lens

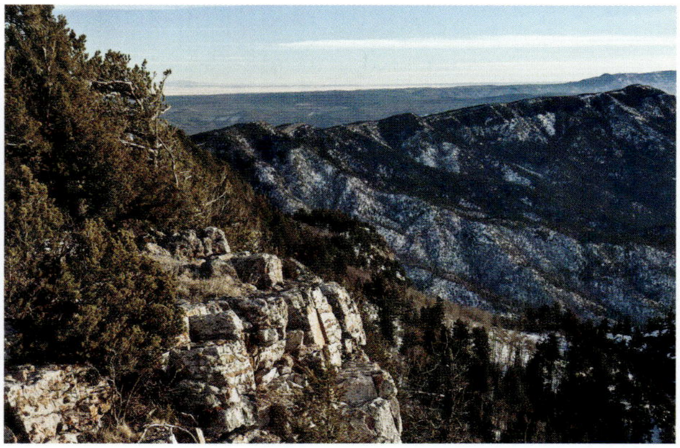

Figure 11.3
Once I add a polarizer, the colors are much more accurate and the color cast is now gone.

ISO 800 • 1/60 sec. • f/8 • 120mm lens

Neutral density (ND)

Sometimes there is just too much light falling on your scene to use the camera settings that you want. Most often, this is the case when you want to use a slow shutter speed but your lens is already stopped down to its smallest aperture, leaving you with a shutter speed that's faster than you want.

A classic example of this is shooting a waterfall in bright sunlight. To get the silky look to the water, you must set the shutter speed to about 1/15 of a second or slower. The problem is that a proper exposure for bright sunlight is f/16 at 1/100 of a second with the camera set to ISO 100 (this comes from the Sunny 16 rule). If your lens has a minimum aperture of f/22, the slowest shutter speed you would be able to use is 1/50.

The way around this problem is to use a neutral density (ND) filter to make the outside world appear to be a little darker. Think of it as sunglasses for your camera. ND filters come in different strengths, which are labeled as 0.3, 0.6, and 0.9, etc. They represent a one-stop difference in exposure per each 0.3 increment. If you need to turn daylight into dark, the 0.9 ND filter will give you an extra three stops of exposure (**Figure 11.4**). This means that, in my earlier example, you could get an exposure of f/16 at about 1/10 of a second. This would be an ideal exposure for getting a silky smooth waterfall (**Figure 11.5**).

My personal favorite filters come from B+W. If you would like to learn more about B+W filters, check out www.schneideroptics.com.

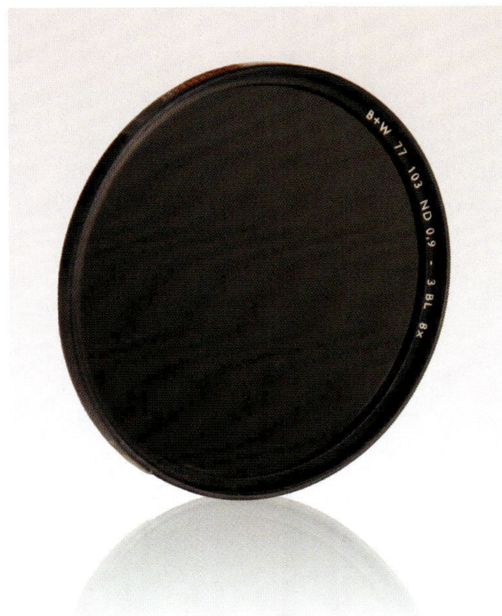

Figure 11.4
A B+W 77mm 0.9 ND filter.

Graduated ND

Another favorite of the landscape photographer, the graduated ND has the benefit of the standard ND filter but graduates to a clear portion (**Figure 11.6**). This allows you to darken just the upper or lower portion of your scene while leaving the other part unaffected. This filter is most commonly used to darken skies that are too bright without

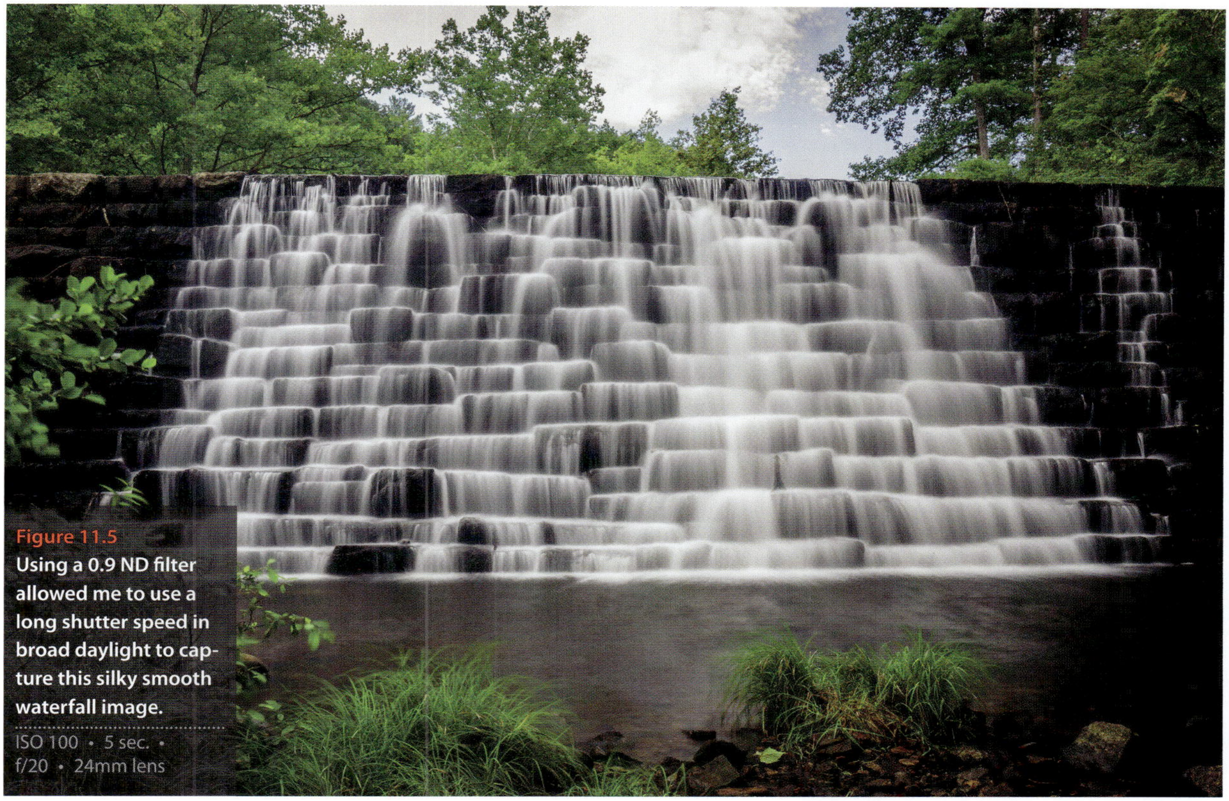

Figure 11.5
Using a 0.9 ND filter allowed me to use a long shutter speed in broad daylight to capture this silky smooth waterfall image.
ISO 100 • 5 sec. • f/20 • 24mm lens

affecting the ground area. If a regular ND is used, the entire area will get darker, so there is no visual change in the image as far as the brightness ratio between the sky and the ground is concerned.

You can purchase the graduated ND as a screw-on filter, but most photographers prefer to use the larger 4x6-inch version, which allows them to control exactly where the filter transitions from dark to transparent in the scene. There are many different options when looking for graduated ND filters, such as the density factor (number of stops), as well as how gradual the transition is from dark to clear. A hard grad filter has a very distinct line where the filter goes from dark to clear. This is usually a good choice when you have a flat horizon line to work with, like where the sky meets the ocean. A soft grad filter has a more gradual change from dark to clear, with the darkest area being at the top and then a gradual change to the clear area of the filter. This is a better choice if you have uneven horizon lines like you might find when photographing a mountain range.

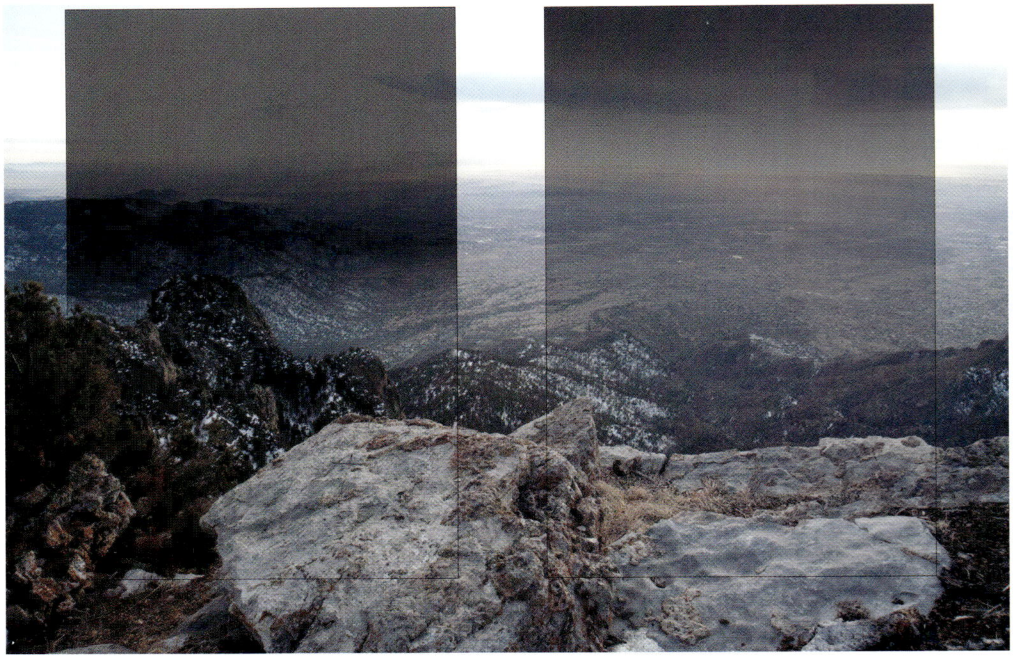

Figure 11.6 **Graduated filters come in different strengths and transitions, from soft to hard.**

Tripods

If you only buy one accessory for your photography, do yourself a favor and make it a tripod (**Figure 11.7** and **Figure 11.8**). In general, any tripod is going to be better than no tripod at all. A tripod helps you take sharper photos and lets you shoot in any lighting condition. There are more choices in tripods than there are in DSLRs. So how do you go about choosing the right one for you? The main considerations are weight, height, head, and of course, cost.

The weight of your tripod will probably determine whether you will carry it along with you farther than the parking lot. Many different types of materials are used in tripods today. The lightest is carbon fiber, which is probably the most expensive as well. More than likely, you should consider an aluminum tripod that is sturdy and has a weight rating that is suitable for your camera as well as your lenses.

Make sure that the tripod extends to a height that is tall enough to allow you to shoot from a comfortable standing position. Nothing ruins a good shoot like a sore back. Taller tripods need to be sturdier to maintain a rigid base for your camera. You will also want to consider how low the tripod can go. If you want to do macro work of low-level subjects such as flowers, you will need to lower the tripod fairly close to the ground. Many new tripods have leg supports that allow you to spread the legs very wide and get the camera low to the ground.

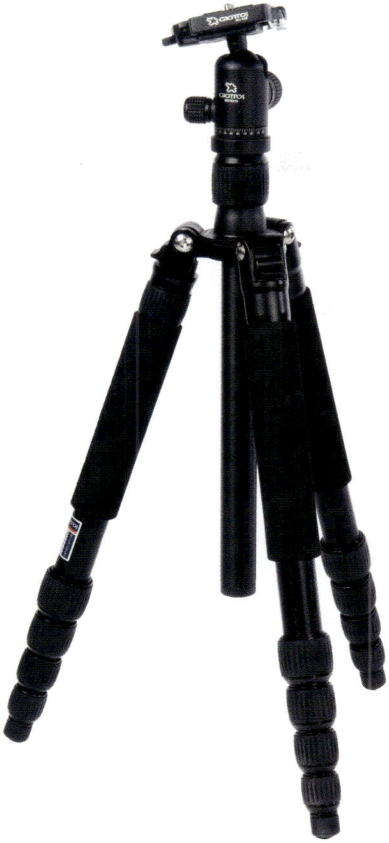

Figure 11.7
The Giottos Vitruvian 9255 tripod.

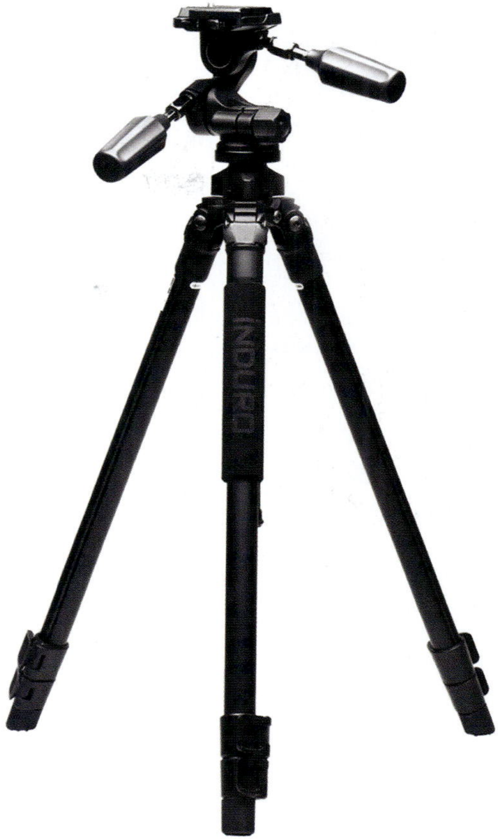

Figure 11.8
The Induro Adventure AKP1 tripod.

The other determining factor when purchasing a tripod will be the type of head that it employs to secure the camera to the legs. There are two basic types of tripod heads: ball and pan. Ball heads use a simple ball joint that allows you to freely position the camera in any upright position and then clamp it down securely (**Figure 11.9**). This type of head is flexible and quick to use, but it can sometimes be difficult to switch between portrait and landscape orientations. They also tend to be slightly more expensive as well.

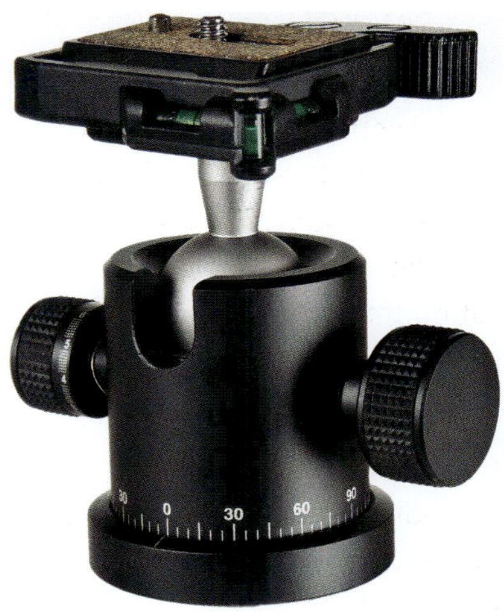

Figure 11.9
The Giottos MH 1001-652 ball head.

Pan heads employ a swivel and usually two hinged joints that allow the camera to pan left and right, move up and down, and adjust the position along the horizontal axis (**Figure 11.10**). Handles are typically employed to allow movement of the camera and lock down the position. The pan head is by and large the most popular tripod head style on the market. If you plan on shooting a lot of video with your 7D Mark II, you might want to consider the pan head style since it will deliver more functionality for your videography, specifically panning from side to side.

If you want to make your tripod shooting move faster, consider buying a tripod that uses a quick-release head (**Figure 11.11**). There are many styles of quick-release brackets; most use a small plate that screws into the bottom of the camera and then quickly locks into and releases from the tripod head. This allows you to go from handheld shooting to the tripod in just a matter of seconds.

The other thing to consider when purchasing a tripod is the leg locking system. Whether it is a lever-lock, locking rings, or some other system, make sure that you test it thoroughly to see how easy it is to lock and unlock the leg positions. Also check to see how smoothly the legs retract and extend. Avoid legs that stick because they will probably only get stickier over time.

You can find more information on Giottos tripods and accessories at www.giottos.com. Manfrotto tripod products can be found at www.manfrotto.com.

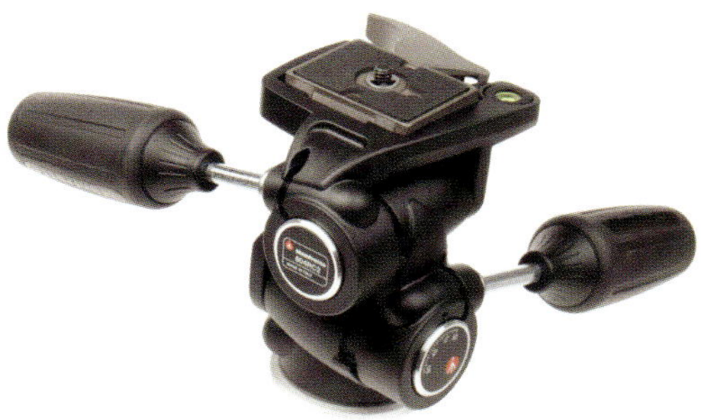

Figure 11.10
The Manfrotto 804RC2 pan/tilt tripod head.

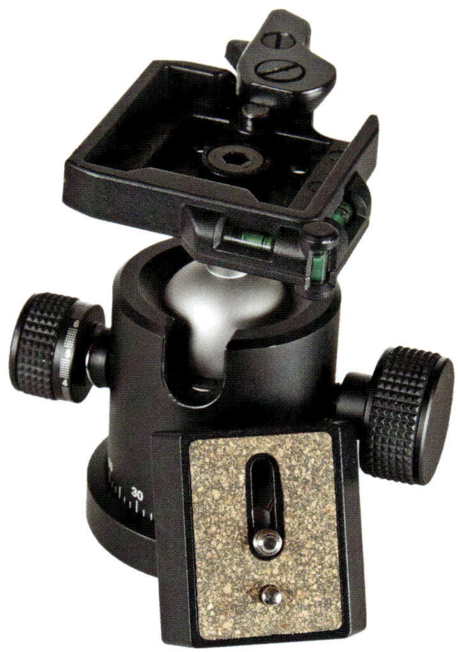

Figure 11.11
The quick-release plate used on the Giottos ball head.

Cable Release

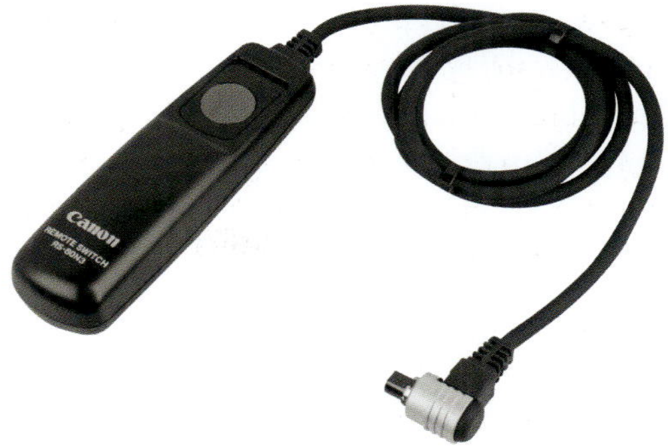

Figure 11.12
The Canon RS80-N3 remote cord lets you activate the shutter without touching the camera.

When shooting long exposures, you can use the self-timer to activate the camera or you can get yourself a cable release. The cable release, which is an electronic release, attaches to the camera via the remote port and lets you trip the shutter. It is also the preferred tool of choice when shooting with the camera set to Bulb (see Chapter 10, "Advanced Techniques"). The idea of the release is that it allows shutter activation without having to place your hands on the camera. This is the best way to ensure that your images will not be influenced by self-induced camera shake. The RS80-N3 remote cord will handle most, if not all, of your cable release needs (**Figure 11.12**). It sells for around $40 and will not only work with the 7D Mark II but with several other Canon DSLR models on the market.

Macro Photography Accessories

Extension tubes

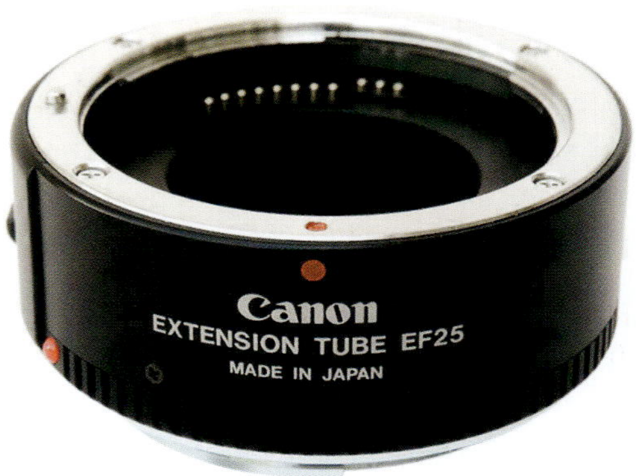

Figure 11.13
The Canon EF-25 extension tube for Canon lenses.

Extension tubes are like spacers between your lens and your camera. The tubes are typically hollow, and their sole purpose is to move the rear of the lens farther away from the camera body (**Figure 11.13**).

A lens can only get so close to a subject and still be able to achieve a sharp focus. This is because as the subject gets closer, the focal point for the lens moves back to a point where it is actually behind the image sensor. Using an extension tube lets you move that focal point forward by placing the rear of the lens a little farther away from the camera sensor, thus letting you get the lens closer to the subject and enlarging it in your picture.

The tubes come in varying sizes, which are typically measured in millimeters. The more common sizes are 12mm, 20mm, 25mm, and 36mm. The longer the tube is, the greater the magnification factor (up to 1:1). The tubes are best used with lenses that are 35mm in focal length and longer. A wide-angle lens will have such a short focusing distance that you will be right on top of your subject. Canon manufactures several extension tubes, or you can buy them from third-party manufacturers. Prices vary, but you will pay more for tubes that use optics in their design. You can also purchase sets of tubes with varying lengths that can be used individually or stacked together for greater magnification.

Close-up filters

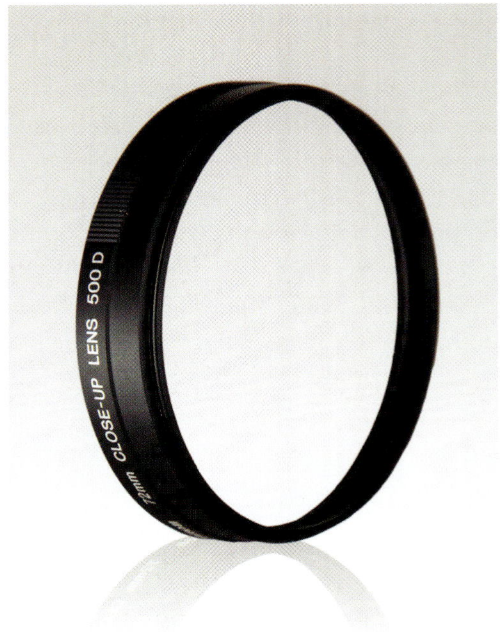

Figure 11.14
The Canon 500D close-up filter.

Another great way to jump into macro work is by purchasing a close-up filter (**Figure 11.14** and **Figure 11.15**). Close-up filters also come in varying magnifications but tend to be a little more expensive than extension tubes. This is because they are usually made of high-quality glass that works in concert with the lens. The filters and lenses can have some advantages over tubes, too. Because they screw onto the front of your lens, they don't interfere with any of the communication functions between the lens and camera body. They also result in less loss of light, so exposures can be slightly shorter than when you're using extension tubes. They do, however, work similarly to tubes in that they allow you to shorten the minimum focus distance of your lens so that you can move closer to your subject, thereby increasing the size of the subject on your sensor. Close-up lenses usually come in magnification factors like +1, +2, +3, +4, and +5. They can also be stacked, strongest to weakest, to increase the magnification factor.

The other difference is that they are usually screw-threaded onto your lens, which means that you have to purchase a specific thread diameter. So if your favorite lens has a 68mm filter thread, this is the size you would use for the close-up filter. The big downside to using this type of macro device is that if you want to use different lenses that have different thread sizes, you will have to buy multiple filters. This is why I prefer to work with a zoom lens so that I can have a range of focal lengths to use with just one filter. Also, just as with most glass filters, the larger the diameter, the higher the price.

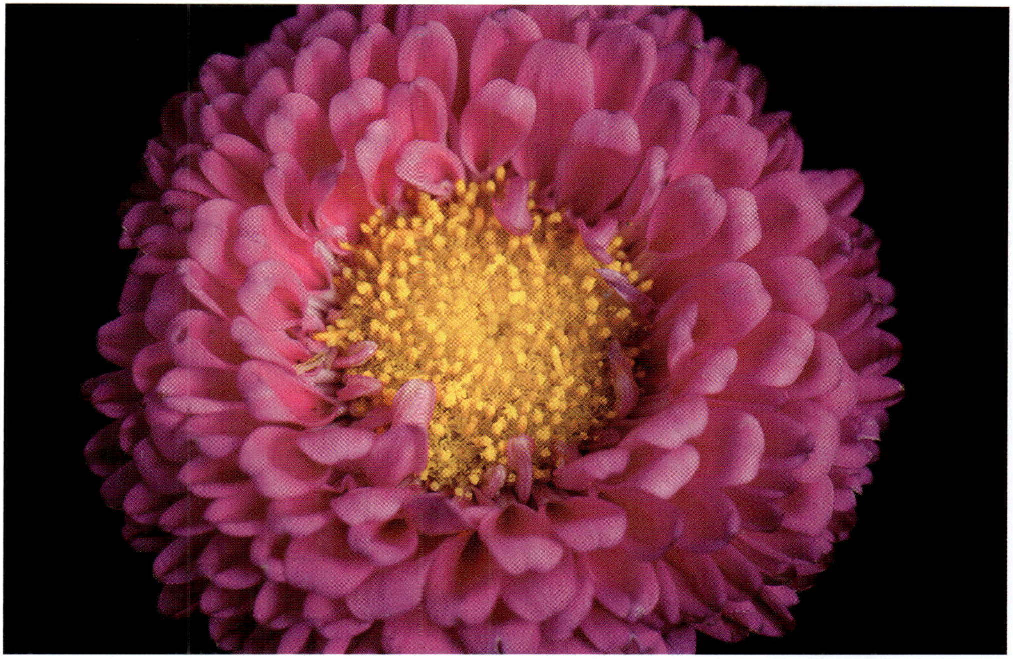

Figure 11.15
I used a close-up filter to help capture this flower image.
ISO 400 • 1/125 sec. • f/13 • 105mm lens

Hot-Shoe Flashes

In Chapter 7, "Mood Lighting," I covered the built-in flash and what you can accomplish with it. Now that we have covered that topic, let me say that you really, really need to get yourself a hot-shoe mounted flash if you want to take better flash images (**Figure 11.16**). For one thing, the external flash is going to be much more powerful than the pop-up version. Also, much more flexibility is built into the Speedlite system of flashes than you could ever hope to get from the built-in version.

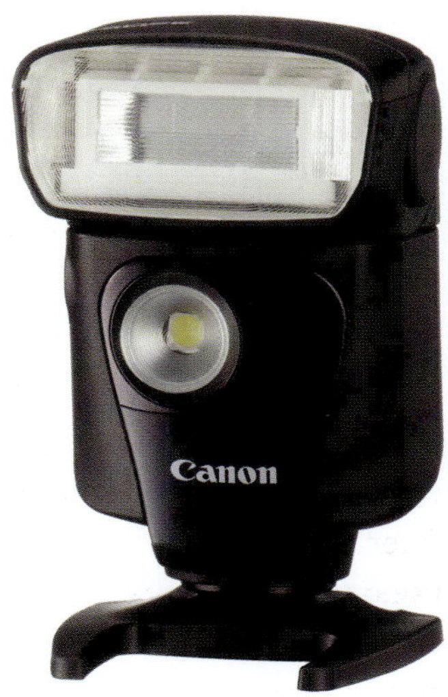

Figure 11.16
The Canon Speedlite 320EX will add power and flexibility to your flash photography.

Canon currently has several Speedlite flashes for sale, but my recommendation is that you purchase the 320EX or, better still, the 430EX II Speedlite. They will run somewhere in the neighborhood of $199 for the 320EX to $299 for the 430 EX II, which can be a pretty hard pill to swallow at first. The pill will go down much easier once you have used one of these powerful and flexible flashes. Not only will your on-camera flash photography be much better, but you also gain the option of moving to a wireless configuration for even better flash results.

Getting a Grip

If you do a lot of shooting over extended periods of time and find that your camera runs low on juice before your shooting day is done, you might want to consider using the BG-E8 battery grip (**Figure 11.17**). The grip has three advantages. First, it lets you shoot with two batteries in the camera so that you can extend your shooting sessions. Second, it has a duplicate set of dials and a shutter release that make vertical shooting much more comfortable. And third, if you have large hands like me, you will find that the grip gives you a lot more camera body to hold, which also makes shooting a more comfortable experience. You can secure the BG-E16 from any decent camera shop for around $215, and don't forget to buy a second LP-E6N battery.

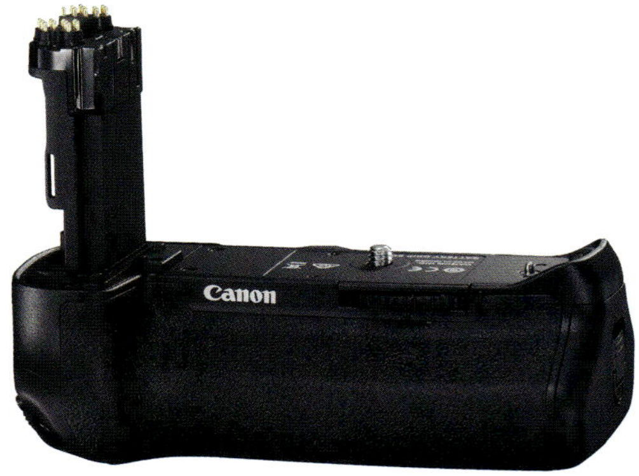

Figure 11.17
The Canon BG-E16 battery grip gives you extra power and a better grip for your camera.

Diffusers

While I am covering flashes, let's discuss a tool that lets you improve the light you are using in your portrait photography. A diffusion panel is a piece of semitransparent material, usually white, that you place between your light source and your subject (**Figure 11.18**). The fabric does as the name implies: it diffuses the light, spreading it out into a soft, low-contrast light source that makes any subject look better. You could make your own or buy one of the many commercially available versions. I prefer the 5-in-1 Reflector Kit made by Westcott. It not

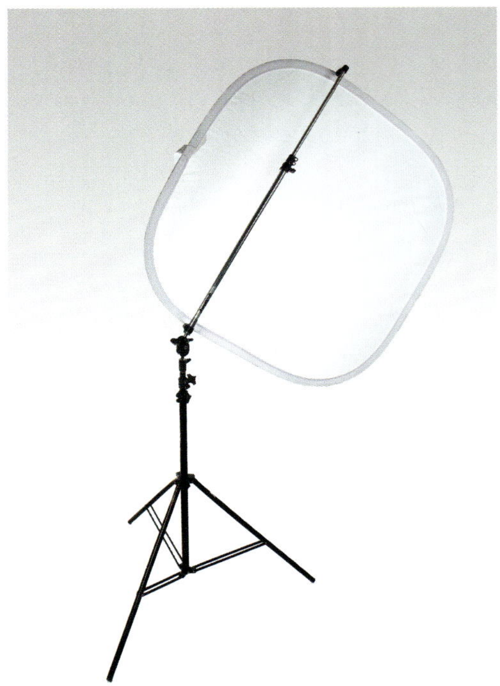

Figure 11.18
A diffusion panel can reflect or soften light to add soft shadows or a nice fill light.

only has a very nice diffusion panel, but also has reflective covers that slip over the diffusion panel so that you can bounce some fill light into your scene. Best of all, the entire system is collapsible, so it fits into a pretty small package for traveling.

You'll find more information on Westcott diffusion panels at www.fjwestcott.com.

Camera Bags

This topic is tricky because I have yet to find the perfect bag for my own gear. All I can do here is tell you what I like to use and let you base your opinions on that.

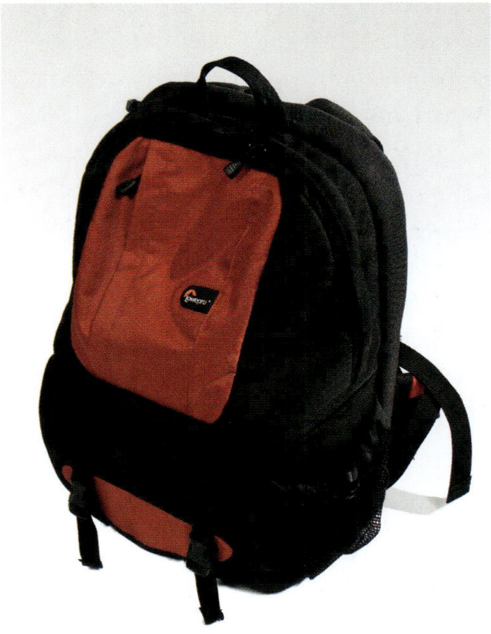

Figure 11.19
The Fastpack 250 from Lowepro.

First of all, I like to travel with my photo gear. Typically, my travel involves flying. This means that all of my camera equipment will be traveling in the cabin with me, not in the luggage compartment. I can't emphasize this enough: *Do not pack your camera in your checked luggage!* Thousands of cameras, lenses, and accessories are lost and/or stolen from checked luggage each year. The best way to ensure this doesn't happen is to take your gear on board and place it in the overhead storage. I like to bring my laptop as well, so I have found a couple of backpack camera storage systems that allow me to fit a camera body, several lenses, some accessories, my laptop, and even some snacks into one backpack-style bag that still fits under the seat in front of me. I also prefer a backpack because I like the freedom of slinging the bag over my shoulder, leaving my hands free for other luggage. I have been using a Lowepro Fastpack 250 for most of my travel needs for the past few years (**Figure 11.19**). The thing that I like about this bag is that it doesn't look like a camera bag, so it doesn't automatically scream "Steal me, I'm worth thousands!"

The other bag that you should look into is a more traditional, shoulder-style bag. These bags are made to handle all sorts of camera bodies, lenses, and accessories, and they're usually completely configurable, with movable padded partitions so that you can completely customize the bag to your own needs. My current bag of choice is the Lowepro Magnum 200 AW, which sells for about $150 (**Figure 11.20**). This small-looking bag just swallows up my gear and never quite seems full.

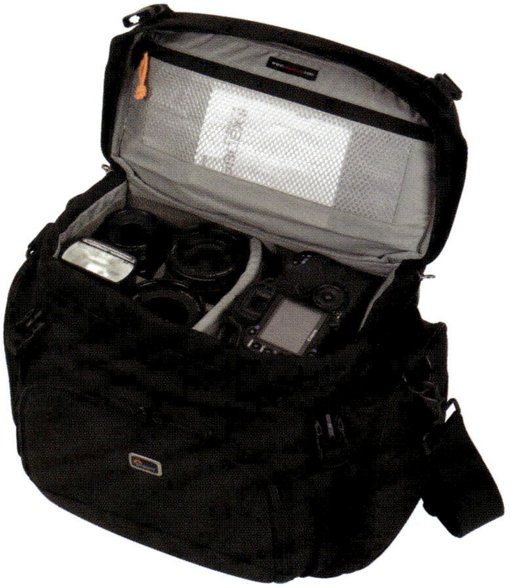

Figure 11.20
The Magnum 200 AW from Lowepro.

These two bags are the ones that I am using currently, but finding the perfect camera bag is truly the Holy Grail for photographers. The fact is that you can go through a lot of them searching for one that perfectly fits your every need and never find it. I know; I have about six bags presently taking up residence in my closet.

You can check out the full line of Lowepro camera gear at www.lowepro.com.

Bits and Pieces

Since I just covered camera bags, let me share with you a couple of items that always travel in my bag.

The battle against dust is always a losing one, but that doesn't mean that you can't have your small victories. To help in the war against the dust speck, I carry three weapons of cleanliness.

The lens cloth

A good microfiber lens cleaning cloth always comes in handy for getting rid of those little smudges and dust bunnies that seem to gravitate toward the front of my lens. I use one called a Spudz, which folds into its own pouch and has the added benefit of being gray (**Figure 11.21**). This means that I can use it as a gray card to get meter readings in Spot metering mode, or as a way to correct the white balance in my images down the road when I bring them into my imaging software.

More information on Spudz cleaning cloths can be found at www.alpineproducts.com.

The LensPen

For stubborn smudges on my lens, I pull out my trusty LensPen (**Figure 11.22**). This nifty little device has a soft, retractable dust removal brush on one end and an amazing cleaning element on the other that uses carbon to clean and polish the lens element.

More information on LensPen products can be found at www.lenspen.com.

Air blowers

Some folks prefer to use canned, compressed air to blow away dust, but these cans may release fluid when they are tilted. For this reason, I always use my Rocket-Air Blower from Giottos (**Figure 11.23**). This funny-looking device is great for getting rid of tough dust, and it uses a clean air path so that the dust that you are blowing away doesn't get sucked into the ball and redeposited on your equipment the next time you use it.

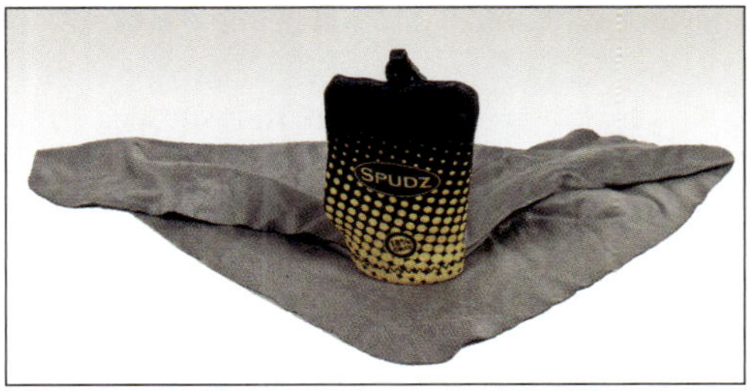

Figure 11.21
The Spudz microfiber cleaning cloth.

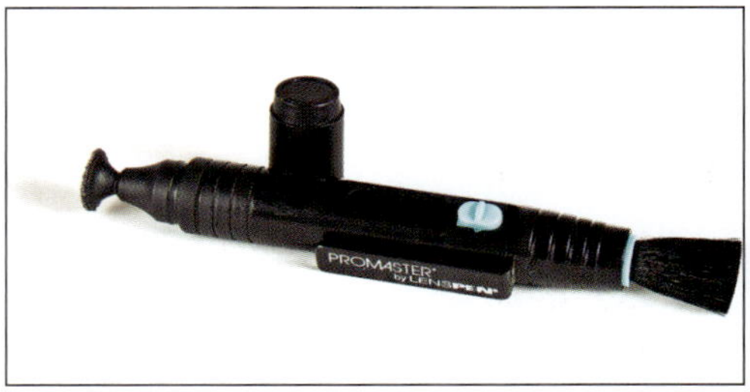

Figure 11.22
The LensPen lens cleaning tool.

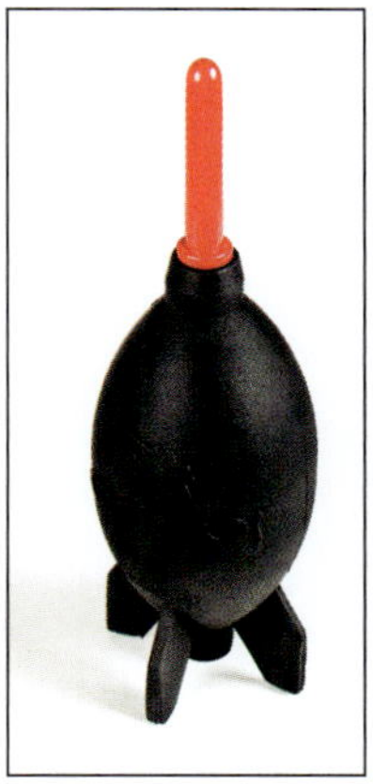

Figure 11.23
The Giottos Rocket-Air dust blower.

Better LCD vision

Having a large LCD screen is an amazing thing. The only problem is that it can be hard to see in bright daylight conditions. I overcome this by using a Hoodman Loupe (**Figure 11.24**). The loupe doesn't magnify your screen; it just provides a light-tight little tent for you to get a better look at your rear LCD. It has a handy little lanyard so you can let it hang around your neck and keep it within easy reach for checking out those great shots you just took. If you are going to work out in the bright sun, you will definitely want to get one of these for your camera bag.

To check out all of the Hoodman accessories, head to www.hoodmanusa.com.

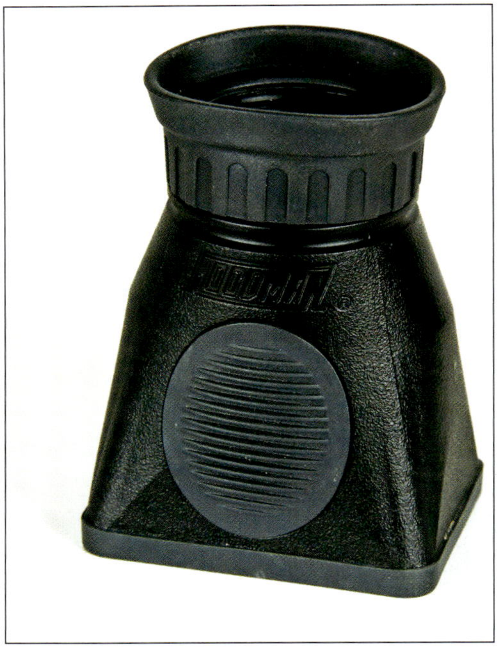

Figure 11.24
The Hoodman Loupe lets you see your LCD screen even in bright sunlight.

Conclusion

You can spend a lot of time worrying about having the right gadget, filter, or accessory to make your photography better. It can become an obsession to always have the latest thing out there. But here's the deal. You already have almost everything you need to take great pictures: an awesome camera and the knowledge necessary to use it. Everything else is just icing on the cake. So, while I have introduced a few items in this chapter that I do think will make your photographic life easier and even improve your images, don't get caught up in the technology and gadgetry.

Use your knowledge of basic photographic principles to investigate everything your camera has to offer. Explore the limits of your camera. Don't be afraid to take bad pictures. Don't be too quick to delete them from your memory card, either. Take some time to look at them and see where things went wrong. Look at your camera settings and see if perhaps there was a change you could have made to improve the shot. Be your toughest critic and learn from your mistakes. With practice and reflection, you will soon find your photography getting better and better. Not only that, but your instincts will enhance to the point that you will come upon a scene and know exactly how you want to shoot it before you even get your camera out of the bag.

Index

D

E

F

N

O

P

Q

R

S